# CRICKETING LIVES

## A CHARACTERFUL HISTORY
## FROM PITCH TO PAGE

RICHARD H. THOMAS

FOREWORD BY
DANIEL NORCROSS

REAKTION BOOKS

Published by Reaktion Books Ltd
Unit 32, Waterside
44–48 Wharf Road
London N1 7UX, UK
www.reaktionbooks.co.uk

First published 2021
First published in paperback 2022
Copyright © Richard H. Thomas 2021
Foreword © Daniel Norcross 2021

All rights reserved

No part of this publication may be reproduced, stored in a retrieval
system, or transmitted, in any form or by any means, electronic,
mechanical, photocopying, recording or otherwise, without the
prior permission of the publishers

Printed and bound in Great Britain by
CPI Group (UK) Ltd, Croydon CRO 4YY

A catalogue record for this book is available from the British Library

ISBN 978 1 78914 647 9

RICHARD H. THOMAS is Associate Professor in Journalism at Swansea University. He has written about cricket for *All Out Cricket*, *Wisden Cricket Monthly*, *The Conversation* and *The Nightwatchman*.

'What an enthralling voyage this book affords, with its vivid style and sequences of fascinating detail.' – David Frith, founding editor of *Wisden Cricket Monthly*

'A wonderful read. Exhaustive and comprehensive as a reference tome, but also infused with a passion for the game and its players that distinguishes a mere cricketing aficionado from a true cricket lover.' – Phil Steele, BBC Sport

'In the unlikely event that you won't find any cricket to watch over the summer, this joyous book should fill a gap. Thomas, a journalism lecturer, concentrates on the game's rich tapestry of people and anecdotes ... this book is a chance to feast not just on the heroics of Stokes and "Beefy" Botham, but the early days of cricket – Oliver Cromwell who liked it initially but later tried to ban it, Frederick, Prince of Wales, who died in 1751 after being hit by a ball ... the playboys and profligates, boozers and buccaneers between the wars, the brutality of Bodyline ... you name it, it's all here. Terrific.' – *Daily Mail*

'So colourful and well told is this book, heavy on research but light in touch, that it should interest even those who find the game dull.' – Patrick Kidd, *The Critic*

'Richard Thomas has found a hugely entertaining way to present the enduring story of how our splendid game got to where it is today. He even manages, and fair play to him for this, to end on an upbeat note ... The key to Thomas's success is in part the ability to tell a story well ... but that ability is much enhanced by the depth of his knowledge.' – CricketWeb.net

# CONTENTS

# GLOSSARY

**Action** – As in 'bowling action'. The individual, often idiosyncratic way a bowler delivers the ball.

**All out** – The end of an innings, when all wickets (usually ten) have been taken, leaving one batsman 'not out'.

**All-rounder** – A player adept at batting and bowling, or, sometimes, batting and wicketkeeping.

**Amateur** – One who plays without pay. Very old-fashioned.

**Ashes** – Small urn of dust contested by England and Australia.

**Asterisk** – * Next to a batsman's score means 'not out'.

**Average** – Measure of quality. The higher the better for batsmen, the lower the better for bowlers.

**Bails** – Small pieces of wood on top of the stumps.

**Beamer** – Head-high delivery that doesn't bounce. Frowned upon.

**Big Bash** – Twenty20 competition in Australia.

**Blazer** – Formal cricket gear, often worn by captains at the toss.

**Blue** – Awarded to those representing some universities at senior level.

**Bodyline** – Ashes series in 1932/3 when England's short-pitched bowling proved controversial.

**Bouncer** – A delivery that rises towards the batsman's upper half.

**Boundary** – The outer marking of the field of play, and also a hit for four.

**Box** – Essential piece of protective equipment for men. You know why.

**Bye** – A run that doesn't come off the bat.

**Centurion** – One who makes a century. Not a Roman.

**Century** – 100 runs.

**Chucking** – An illegal delivery by the bowler owing to a crooked arm. Also called 'throwing'. No greater crime.

**Close fielder** – Fielder positioned close to the batsman. Perilous and slightly mad.

**County Championship** – The competition for long-form cricket between English counties (and Glamorgan).

**Cover drive** – An often-handsome off-side stroke made by a batsman.

**Crease** – The line on the pitch over which a bowler may not land when delivering the ball.

**Cut** – Off-side stroke generally made square or behind square of the wicket.

**Declaration** – When a captain strategically ends his team's innings.

**Deep** – The outer extremes of the wider field of play.

**Delivery** – The bowler sending the ball to the batsman.

**Dismissed** – Out.

**Double** – Old-fashioned mark of all-round quality, involving 100 wickets and 1,000 runs in a season.

**Drive** – A batsman's classic shot, to the leg side or off side.

**Duck** – What a batsman gets when dismissed without scoring. Out first ball gets the 'golden' version.

**Edge** – The outer extreme of the bat.

**Fast bowler** – A bowler whose main weapon is speed.

**First-class** – 'Official' level of cricket.

**Flannels** – Old-fashioned term describing on-field apparel. Now 'cottons', 'nylons' and 'lycras'.

**Flight** – The trajectory of the ball when delivered by a slow/spin bowler.

**Follow on** – Having finished short of the opponents' first innings total by a specified margin, a team can be asked by the opposing captain to bat again straight away, out of the usual sequence.

**Gentlemen** – Well-to-do cricketers from yesteryear who played as amateurs.

**Googly** – Leg spinner's delivery expected to spin from leg to off to a right-handed batsman, but then actually spins the opposite way.

**Groundsman** – Responsible for preparing the playing surface. Called a 'curator' in Australia.

**Gulley** – A fielding position near the slips.

**Half-volley** – A delivery that makes simultaneous contact with bat and ground, enabling a particularly powerful stroke. Loved by batsmen.

**Hard wicket** – A firm playing surface where the ball moves quicker off the wicket.

**Hat-trick** – Three wickets in successive balls. Rare, and enthusiastically celebrated.

**Hook** – Dramatic stroke involving a wide arc of the bat to the leg side. Exhilarating or embarrassing.

**ICC** – The International Cricket Council – in charge of world cricket.

**Innings** – When a batsman or team is at the wicket, or 'in'.

**IPL** – Indian Premier League: the glitziest, most lucrative Twenty20 competition in the world.

**Knock** – Slang for 'innings'.

**Kolpak** – Named after a Slovakian handball player. Eligibility technicality enabling international cricketers to appear in county cricket without being categorized as overseas players.

**Laws** – Cricket's on-field rules. But don't call them that, for goodness sake.

**Leg before wicket (LBW)** – A mode of dismissal for batsmen. Essentially, when the ball hits the pad but would otherwise have hit the wicket. Best to leave the batsman alone for a bit after this one.

**Leg side** – The wider playing area nearest the batsman's legs when in their usual stance. Will be different for right- and left-handers. Also called the 'on side'.

**Leg spinner** – Bowler who imparts spin via their wrist action. The usual delivery spins from leg to off for right-handed batsmen, and the other way around for left-handers.

**Leg theory** – Persistent, short-pitched bowling at the batsman's body and head. See 'Bodyline'.

**Length** – Position on the pitch where the bowler lands the ball.

**Maiden** – A completed over yielding no runs off the bat. A measure of penurious bowling.

MCC – Marylebone Cricket Club. Apply to join, then wait.

**Medium pace** – Neither fast nor slow bowling, usually with some additional added value such as accuracy, swing or movement off the pitch. Without any such accoutrements, can be rather insipid.

**Middle** – General term to describe being on, or near, the wicket.

**Mid-off** – Fielding position on the off side, just wide of the wicket.

**Mid-on** – Same, on the other side.

**Mid-wicket** – Leg-side fielding position, roughly midway between the two sets of stumps.

**Nets** – Practice area surrounded by netting.

**New ball** – Replacement ball provided by the umpire at the start of the match or at some predetermined time within it. For bowlers getting thrashed, a source of hope.

**Nightwatchman** – A reasonably reliable batsman with lesser scoring ability sent in towards the end of a day's play instead of risking a more capable player. Occasionally outplays everyone else.

ODI – One Day International.

**Off side** – The part of the wider playing area nearest the batsman's bat when in their usual stance. Will be different for right- and left-handers.

**Off spinner** – Bowler who imparts spin to the ball by using their fingers. The usual delivery spins from off to leg for right-handed batsmen, and the other way around for left-handers. Also called a 'finger spinner'.

**Off the mark** – A batsman's first run.

**Overthrow** – When the ball is thrown back to the middle (often inaccurately) by a fielder and then eludes those trying to collect it to the extent that the batsmen are able to take more runs.

**Owzat** – With added exclamation mark, the traditional way to appeal to the umpire.

**Pads** – Leg protection for batsmen and wicketkeepers.

**Pair** – Two ducks in the same match. Humiliating.

**Partnership** – The combined efforts and output of a pair of batsmen.

**Pavilion** – A building often housing changing rooms, dining room and spectator seating areas. Can be grand or ramshackle.

**Pitch** – The playing surface, 22 yards long. Not metres.

**Players** – Generic name for on-field participants, and an old-fashioned way to describe professional cricketers.

**Reverse sweep** – Where the batsman changes their grip on the bat and plays a sweep in the opposite direction to a normal sweep.

**Reverse swing** – The phenomenon, usually achieved with an older ball, where the ball swerves in the air the opposite way to that expected. All to do with aerodynamics and physics. Good luck with that.

**Series** – A number of successive Test matches between the same teams.

**Short leg** – A leg-side fielding position close to the batsman. Occupied by the brave and dispensable.

**Shot** – The particular way a batsman hits the ball. Also called a 'stroke'.

**Single** – One run, where the batsmen cross only once.

**Sledge** – A generally derisory on-field comment to an opponent. Often explicit.

**Slip** – A fielding position alongside the wicketkeeper. There might be more than one.

**Spin** – The ball's deviation off the pitch.

**Square leg** – A fielding position level with the wicket on the leg side.

**Stance** – The batsman's position as they wait for the ball.

**Sticky dog** – Australian for a wet wicket.

**Stumped** – When the batsman is out of their crease and the wicketkeeper dismisses them by removing the bails.

**Stumps** – Slender pieces of shaped wood. Three of them make up the wicket. Now often coloured, sponsored and capable of flashing.

**Sweep** – Shot usually played against slower bowlers involving the batsman hitting across the line of the ball to send it towards the leg side.

**Test match** – Long-form international cricket. For traditionalists, the ultimate.

**Timeless Test** – Test match without a time limit, the intention being to play until there's a positive result.

**Ton** – A century.

**Toss** – The formal spinning of a coin to decide who bats first.

**Umpires** – On-field officials operating in pairs. Also found in TV production vehicles.

**Uncovered wickets** – Wickets left to the vagaries of the weather without protection.

**Victims** – Bloodthirsty description of batsmen removed by bowlers, wicketkeepers or fielders.

**Walking** – A batsman effectively giving themselves out without waiting for the umpire's decision.

**Wicket** – Polysemous word meaning the three stumps, the playing surface and the end of a batsman's innings.

**Wisden** – Chronicles almost everything that happens on a cricket field anywhere in the world. Often called the cricketer's 'bible'.

**Yorker** – A delivery aimed at the base of the bat, or the batsman's feet. Steel toe caps advised.

# FOREWORD

## DANIEL NORCROSS

There must have been a time in my life when I wasn't in love with cricket, when I didn't instinctively stop and stare whenever I saw two or more people playing with a bat and ball, either on the television or at my local common in Tooting, or, perhaps most joyously, in a lamplit square in Syracuse at 2 a.m. There must have been a time, but I don't remember it.

I was six years old, sat in a gloomy living room with my father, the curtains closed to shield the television from the sunshine. England were getting bruised, battered and beaten by the exotically moustachioed Dennis Lillee and the fearsome Jeff Thomson. All the Australians wore their shirts unbuttoned to their navels, revealing their imposingly hairy chests, pawing at the ground like bison and generally getting the better of the team I was supposed to be supporting.

Despite the prevailing narrative of disappointment, there was a man in my team who never backed down, who ensured that, whatever the final result, England always emerged with dignity intact. Dubbed 'the bank clerk who went to war', David Steele was a curious hero for a six year old. His hair was entirely grey, he wore glasses and he lacked any obvious charisma, though he did chew gum. (Every cricketer chewed gum in the 1970s.) While Steele was batting, I could dare to dream. And since cricket is such a long game (as its unenlightened detractors never fail to point out), there was plenty of time in which to do this.

It is in this liminal space between the present and the desired future that romance blossoms. This is true to a degree of all sports, but cricket offers so many more fantastical possibilities. It is a team sport, but it is played as a series of one-on-one contests, one ball at a time. The game is never lost or won until the last wicket is taken. If your football team is 5–0 down with five minutes to go, there is no way back. But as Ian Botham and Bob Willis proved at Headingley in 1981, no matter how grave the situation gets in cricket, there is always a chance. Accordingly, every virtue is rewarded: the wiliness of spinners, the artistry of the swing bowler, the brute strength of the out-and-out quick bowler. Batters too come in many shapes and sizes.

The cunning, the generous, the carefree, the solemn, the loyal, the aggressive, the charming . . . even the outright cheat (if I may describe W. G. Grace on occasion as such) has their place in cricket. It is perhaps this that makes it, for me, more than just a game. In its players we recognize the virtues and vices of our own character. And it is this celebration of character – the honourable and devious, heroic and ruthless personalities who have shaped our game – that marks out Richard H. Thomas's book as such an entertaining and rewarding companion.

Through a love of cricket we might learn not only to dream of the magical possibilities that life has to offer, but to appreciate that it is not simply the conventional qualities that matter. Our limitations, foibles and flaws are just as valuable.

# INTRODUCTION

Australian journalist Keith Dunstan suggested that unless taught at birth, cricket, 'like living in igloos, skateboarding and eating tripe', remains as incomprehensible as nuclear physics.[1] For many it is utterly baffling, as anyone who watched former England all-rounder Andrew Flintoff trying to explain the game to singer Jennifer Lopez on BBC's *Graham Norton Show* in 2013 will surely agree. In 2008 the *Daily Telegraph* quoted research rating the laws of cricket as one of the world's fifty most confusing things. Coming in at number eight, the game's governing principles are apparently more bewildering than the theories of Stephen Hawking and Spaghetti Junction.[2]

Non-believers have offered plenty of serviceable definitions for cricket. It has been called 'organised loafing' and 'grown men wearing white vests knitted by their mums, standing on a field for three days trying not to look bored'.[3] Bill Bryson concludes that cricket has no problems that golf carts wouldn't fix. Not wishing to insult something enjoyed by so many, he offers cricket as the only sport incorporating meal breaks, and where 'spectators burn as many calories as players'. The main participants, he continues, 'wear riding hats, heavy gloves of the sort used to handle radioactive isotopes, and a mattress strapped to each leg'. By the time the games finish, he concludes, 'all your library books are overdue'.[4] Player-turned-commentator Peter Roebuck, who had a testy relationship with the sport and the people in it, offered an even pithier assessment. It is 'a dry game', he suggested, 'in a wet land'.[5]

But others are less cynical. In his 2011 'Spirit of Cricket' lecture, Sri Lankan Kumar Sangakkara claimed that cricket was so powerful it transcended war and politics.[6] Mathematician and cricket fan G. H. Hardy summarized the feelings of many hopeless addicts by suggesting that even if he knew he was going to die later in the day, he'd still like to know the cricket scores.[7] Concluding his own 'Spirit of Cricket' lecture in 2016, former New Zealand captain Brendon McCullum spoke for thousands when he advocated that our 'wonderful' game should be treasured and revered.[8]

Perhaps the greatest definition emanates from the unlikeliest source. In 1932/3, and in pursuit of the Ashes, Douglas Jardine polarized opinion through his controversial 'Bodyline' bowling tactics where the ball was directed at the batsman's body. Speaking in New Zealand after the Australian leg of the tour had concluded, Jardine captured cricket in one splendid sentence: 'That beautiful, beautiful game', he said, 'that is battle and service and sport and art.'[9] Elitist and from a bygone age, but there can be no better description.

This book aims to be true to Jardine's definition. Cricket is enjoyed through sublime practitioners; the heat of the battle is felt through the game's conflicts and contests; service is appreciated through journeymen who have had their moments in the sun and set the stage for others. Sport is captured by the joy and love of the game, and art is apparent within the elegance of its aesthetes. Here we follow a loose chronology, but not slavishly. It is a book of personal choices, and your favourites may not feature. Indeed, a parallel book about equally influential figures might not mention those you will read about here. It celebrates the notion that cricket means something different to everyone. It venerates those involved in the game and delights in the beautiful words used to describe them. It might help an ephemeral cricket fan to develop a longer commitment. Those who follow the game more assiduously might find some new stories herein. Cosy up with a chapter a night and you might dream about batting with Victor Trumper or winning the Ashes. Best of all, you'll be reminded that it really is a beautiful, beautiful game.

# 1

# LUMPY, MYNN AND SILVER BILLY

*Until the Mid-nineteenth Century*

Who first decided to hurl a ball at three wooden sticks? Homer – an unlikely cricket fan – mentions that Princess Nausikaa once threw the ball at, or to, a nearby handmaiden only for it to be lost. It was 'wild return, overthrow, faulty backing up and lost ball' all at once.[1] If there is no evidence that this was anything to do with cricket, there are traces of the game – or at least its name – in Finnish and Viking history. It seems that it began after the Roman Empire, before the Norman invasion and 'almost certainly somewhere in Northern Europe'.[2]

But the notion that cricket might be an Anglo-Saxon creation is contentious.[3] The French, for example, have compelling evidence that someone called Estiavannet arrived at the village of Liettres in 1478 and found people playing boules near a post called a 'criquet'. It wasn't for the faint-hearted; there was an inflammatory comment, and someone was killed.[4] In 2015 the village arranged some Twenty20 games involving teams from Whitstable and Ghent to celebrate its claims as cricket's birthplace. Since they were played on a cow pasture, the bounce would have been variable, but at least nobody died.

However, there seems to be more written about the game's origins in England than anywhere else. The Normans, it is claimed, played something like it as far back as 1066, and Joseph of Exeter mentions it in a poem at the end of the twelfth century. Chaucer describes the game in his *Canterbury Tales*, and references to 'creag' involving King Edward 1 in the thirteenth century may be the earliest trace of royal involvement with leather and willow.[5] Thereafter the mist clears a little, and there is evidence, to take one example, of the game being played in Surrey and Kent between the last few years of the sixteenth century and the middle years of the seventeenth.

Oliver Cromwell liked the game initially, but eventually tried banning 'krickett' altogether. Under Cromwell, suggests Simon Hughes, England was ruled by religious extremists who snuffed out anything looking like fun and for a while, 'God suspended cricket.'[6] The game's first big challenge was dealing with the Lord Protector. But Cromwell, like uncovered wickets, did not last, and the game might actually owe him something; his revolution forced the aristocracy to their country estates, where they found their tenants playing a 'rough-and-ready but lively and intriguing game'.[7] Their interests in gambling had been stirred and when royal order was restored, the wealthy returned to town and the game became popular in high society.[8]

By the early eighteenth century, cricket had spread from the Home Counties outwards to the (mainly English) countryside. The first set of laws were developed in 1744 and cynics might conclude that the game thereafter signed itself over to administrators. By this time Frederick, Prince of Wales, had become interested in it, and with royal patronage, cricket thrived. He awarded a cup to a winning side in 1733 in cricket's first recorded example of a trophy being conferred rather than cash. This happy progress was halted in its tracks when the prince died in 1751. The mode of death is significant, albeit contested. It was probably an embolism, but some claim the prince's death was the result of a blow from a cricket ball. If so, it was a unique case of 'play stopping reign'.[9]

Seemingly, 1751 was a notable year, as the gambling associated with cricket became more serious. The Earl of Sandwich organized a match between Old Etonians and All England that promised £1,500 for the winning team. The total bets amounted to £20,000, but in reality 'All England' meant 'eleven chaps who had not gone to Eton'.[10] In 1751 surely nobody imagined that in the future, cricket would more than once be brought to its knees by betting.

Cricket's epicentre was situated just north of Portsmouth. Former England batsman David Gower suggested that the Hambledon team of the late eighteenth century raised cricket 'from a sport to an art'.[11] At this time, work opportunities for professional cricketers increased and Hambledon exemplified the game's new financial order.[12] If you've recently clicked your tongue and shouted at the television that cricket is all about money, you're 250 years too late. But Hambledon did something for the evolution of less serious cricket, too; in making the Bat and Ball hostelry the hub for club meetings and post-match reflection, it inextricably linked cricket to the pub. Three centuries later, which village club could do without the local boozer?

Village cricket begins and ends in the pub. It's where teams are picked, where Dutch courage is taken and sorrows drowned. Whatever the nature of on-field conflict, notes Michael Simkins, it's all forgotten 'once a couple of pints of Tetleys or Greene King are down your neck'.[13] Other brands are also available.

The Bat and Ball is peerless among cricketing pubs. Opposite the ground at Broadhalfpenny Down, in the eighteenth century it was run by Richard Nyren, who himself played for a Hampshire XI between 1772 and 1786. Under his guidance, cricket started to look like cricket. With an annual subscription to the club of three guineas, it was not for the financially challenged; however, in its pomp there were '157 members, including eighteen with titles and six MPs'. Drinking was prominent.[14] Indeed, Roger Protz claims that it was a visit to the Bat and Ball in 2005 that inspired him to write *The Beer Lover's Guide to Cricket*, having gone there to assess how the old inn had 'recovered from the trauma' of being turned 'briefly and unsuccessfully' into a restaurant.[15]

But Hambledon's position as cricket's command post is not exclusive. Indeed, there is a compelling case for Guildford, since almost nowhere else can claim such 'a cluster of fundamental landmarks' in cricket's evolution.[16] As a cricketing hub, Guildford was at least as influential as Hambledon and there is evidence that the game was played there as early as 1550. It also claims to have hosted the first women's game in 1745.[17]

In fact, perhaps Hambledon became more famous than Guildford only because it was fortunate to have its history recorded by John Nyren.[18] The son of Bat and Ball landlord Richard, John played the game but was even more famous for his writing; his 1833 book *The Young Cricketer's Tutor* is considered cricket's first great tome.[19] So cricket started nowhere and everywhere. Wherever there were stones to idly throw and handy-sized sticks lying about, someone put one and one together and made a game out of two.

Hambledon Cricket Club is still going, its thriving junior membership indicating that its fortunes in 2018 were rather healthier than they were in 1796, when nobody attended the AGM.[20] At another such meeting, John Nyren noted that while only three members turned up, they managed to imbibe nine bottles of wine. Toasts were made to 'The Queen's Mother, The King, Hambledon Club, Cricket, To the Immortal Memory of Madge and The President'.[21] Knowing who – or what – 'Madge' is will in no way enhance your appreciation of cricket or the things players talk about when they've had a drink.

By the end of the eighteenth century, Hambledon was all but finished as a cricketing powerhouse as people migrated towards the major towns.[22] But the little village did something important for cricket. Under the stewardship of the famous club, cricket's refinements began to develop.[23] Inevitably, as cricketers recognized that skill could distinguish genius from journeyman and could be translated into hard cash, the game began to attract what it has never been without since – star players. One of the first of these big names came from Send, a dozen or so miles from Guildford. His name was Edward 'Lumpy' Stevens.

There are three theories as to why he was known as 'Lumpy'. The first two were his rotundity and the voraciousness of his appetite, but perhaps the most credible was connected to the fact that winning the toss in those days meant that, within reason and an agreed geographical radius, you could choose where the match was played.[24] In this case if Lumpy had anything to do with the decision-making, wickets were pitched on the most uneven ground possible, the rationale being that this would help him much more than the opposing batsmen. Clear the sheep away and start playing; if cricket is a batsman's game now, back then it was dominated by bowlers.

Whatever the inspiration for his nickname, Lumpy was a solid citizen. Capable of bowling quickly yet accurately – all underarm in those days – he was famed for flighting the ball rather than rolling it along the ground, which is what everyone else did. It made him a daunting contemporary combination of 'Glenn McGrath and Malcolm Marshall'.[25] Landing the ball on the 'lumps' with unerring accuracy made him quite a handful. Self-identifying as 'a bit of a smuggler', he had been minding his own business working as the Earl of Tankerville's gardener until His Lordship discovered that this portly horticulturist could control a cricket ball as if it were on a string.[26] The relationship dynamic between master and servant changed when Lumpy's cricket ability was discovered and even though the earl was famously bad-tempered, in cricketing matters, Lumpy was in charge. His

Lordship always acquiesced, clearly realizing that Lumpy provided a vital source of income. Betting ruled, patrons engaged
professionals to win and make them wealthy, and Lumpy certainly
did the business for the earl.[27] He played into his fifties and retired
to tend His Lordship's roses at Walton-on-Thames. When he died
in 1819 – well into his eighties – the earl commissioned a tomb-
stone for Lumpy's grave.[28] The old bowler had probably paid for
it himself, indirectly.

Who knows how many terrified batsmen Lumpy blasted out,
but what seems beyond doubt is that he was without peer in terms
of skill and statistics. His cricketing influence, though, extends further. In 1775 John Nyren wrote that during a game in London, in a
single-wicket tournament between five players from Hambledon
Club and five from All England,[29] Hambledon needed fourteen
runs to win when last man, John Small, arrived at the wicket. He
duly knocked off the runs, but not without incident. Three times
Lumpy beat the bat, only to see the ball pass between the two
stumps without dislodging the bail. Thereafter, a third stump and
a second bail became the new norm.

Hot on the heels of the game's first superstar bowler came its
first superstar batsman. Pictures of William Beldham – later
known as 'Silver Billy' because of his long and resplendent locks
– hang prominently in the pavilions at both Lord's and The Oval.
In 1997 John Woodcock named Beldham as number 39 in his list
of the one hundred greatest cricketers. Beldham's first-class record
over 34 seasons was hardly startling but he was all about style. John
Nyren described Silver Billy on the attack with bat in hand as 'one
of the most beautiful sights'.[30] When he batted, 'men's hearts
throbbed, and their cheeks turned pale and red' – Michelangelo,
indeed, 'should have painted him'.[31]

However, betting was still the boss. Beldham reported that
matches were bought and sold and significant sums were won

and lost.[32] In one match both batsman and bowler had been nobbled: one refused to bowl straight and the other refused to take advantage. Everyone was suspicious or under suspicion, as no one knew what was legitimate on-field play and what wasn't.[33] 'Despite his celestial hair', Silver Billy was 'no angel', but the old boy claimed only to have been bought once.[34] That seems to have been as saintly as you could get back then.

After a career with Hambledon, then Surrey, Hampshire and sometimes the newly established Marylebone Cricket Club (MCC), Silver Billy gave up playing cricket but not his interest in it. Indeed, in 1852, aged 87, he walked seven miles to watch a match.[35] When former England batsman Graham Thorpe presided over the ceremony recognizing the permanent memorial to Silver Billy in the Surrey village of Wrecclesham, he reflected on how his own life had some similarities to Beldham's. Both lived in Wrecclesham

Billy Beldham,
mid-1850s.

and both played for England, although, as Thorpe acknowledged in the presence of his two daughters, this was where the similarity ended.[36] Silver Billy, it has been claimed, fathered 36 children, making him as prolific off the field as on it. He is remembered these days for the famous photograph taken towards the end of his life sometime in the mid-1850s. In a top hat and smock, he looks into the lens, grimly bewildered. Not everyone's idea of a master batsman, he might be most people's idea of an old man who would keep your ball if it landed in his garden.

Lumpy and Silver Billy were cricket's first batting and bowling luminaries, but the eminent all-rounder of that period was Alfred Mynn. In cricketing terms, he dominated the first half of the nineteenth century in the same way that W. G. Grace dominated the second.[37] His superiority is evident from his nickname – 'the Lion of Kent'. He played mainly for that county, as well as Sussex and MCC. According to John Woodcock's 1997 list, only Garry Sobers was a better all-rounder, and it is said that one of the greatest sights in cricket was watching Mynn running in to bowl.[38] His was a gentle approach to the wicket – perhaps only four or five paces. He had a round arm action at a time when such a style was causing general consternation. He was cricket's 'Falstaffian Frontiersman', who believed that preparation for a match involved 'beef and beer'.[39] Little wonder that estimates of his weight vary between 18 and 24 stones (115–50 kg), and that he was diabetic. But statistics do not tell the whole story. For example, while his bowling captured 1,036 wickets at the startlingly good average of around ten, his batting was modest in that he made only one century and averaged 13.42 across his career.

A former Dean of Rochester – Samuel Reynolds Hole – recalls watching Mynn smite the ball during practice at Trent Bridge, Nottingham. With 'tall figure and handsome face', wrote Hole, Mynn hit the ball 'over the booths, over the Bingham Road and some distance into a field of potatoes on the opposite side thereof'.[40] It was a stroke seemingly big enough to send the ball from Nottinghamshire to Derbyshire. Like the giant all-rounders that would follow him, Mynn captured the public's imagination and they loved him 'unconditionally'.[41]

But cricket almost claimed his life. In 1836 he played for the South versus the North and during what passed as the warm-up, the ball struck Mynn on the ankle. Despite serious injury, he managed to bat and bowl. By day three, though, the South held on to a slender lead, and Mynn's leg was badly swollen. While anyone else would simply have given up, the Lion of Kent limped out to bat and, 'in constant agony, hit the bowling all over the field'.[42] He made 125 not out, which was his only first-class century and the first ever to be made with a runner – another batsman doing everything but hitting the ball – assisting all the way through. By now, however, Mynn's leg was in a shocking condition. He needed medical attention, but because of his immobility, his general bulk and the unsuitability of the stagecoach summoned to take him, he was lashed to the roof for the hundred-mile trip to London. After being examined at the Angel Tavern in St Martin's Lane, it was decided to amputate the leg at the hip. Only Mynn's request for time to pray before the operation meant that the attending surgeons reconsidered, and he was left intact. Within two years Mynn was fully restored, but the whole episode did no end of good to those who manufactured batting pads.

Master cricketer, though, does not mean ace financial manager. Money, or the lack of it, was a recurring issue. Permanently embarrassed, Mynn spent time in a debtors' prison. An easy mark for bookmakers, once he was 'hissed at in Maidstone market after Kent lost a game after they had scored 278 in their first innings'.[43] Ostensibly an amateur, Mynn found multifarious ways to make money out of the game and fixing matches was one of

Alfred Mynn,
*c.* 1850s.

them. However, such blemishes were 'meticulously overlooked' by *Wisden* when paying tribute to him.[44] Cricket has a fluid interpretation of heroism and is largely forgiving of Alfred Mynn. Indeed, as the cricketing colossus of the time, Mynn predominates with his outstanding skills and his 'debts, his pranks, his religious credulity and intolerable suppers . . . [his] loyalty, his clumsy courtesy, his courage'.[45]

Was the cradle of cricket in Hampshire or Surrey? It settled in a pub, the Lord Protector tried to destroy it and a future king tried to promote it, but it might have killed him. Lumpy and Silver Billy played it, the Lion of Kent excelled at it and the bookmakers controlled it. From now on, expect the unexpected.

W. G. Grace, early 1900s.

# 2

# THE 'GOLDEN AGE', GRACE AND TRUMPER

*The Turn of the Twentieth Century*

W. G. Grace is indexical of cricket, of England, of the Victorian age and of a Corinthian approach to sport. Nobody, wrote Ronald Mason, competes with the 'comprehensiveness' of his contribution to cricket and the nation's social history.[1] He was the greatest cricketer but also 'one of the greatest men of his age'.[2] He is everywhere, with 'busts ... statues ... pictures' and 'avatars of him the world over'.[3] Indeed, here we all are, still writing about him, well over a hundred years since he died.[4]

However, the game Grace inherited from Alfred Mynn was different from the one Lumpy and Silver Billy handed to the Lion of Kent. It was starting to look something like it does now, with recognizable fixtures becoming established and overarm bowling commonplace. The first overseas tour had taken place (to Canada and the USA) and Test cricket between England and Australia was imminent. Crowds, kit, pitches and reporting had all matured, and with advances in photography, much of it was there to see. But the fame that W. G. acquired was wholly unprecedented. The Victorians worshipped such 'masculine authority and success' and celebrated 'a father figure of Olympian adoration'.[5] Photographs of the young William Gilbert reveal an almost apologetic figure, somehow uncomfortable in his own skin. But soon came the familiar paunch, the chin became covered by tight curls and his dominance emerged.

His first cricketing achievement of note was in 1864 aged only sixteen, when he scored 170 and 56 not out in a club match at Brighton. He failed to score on his first-class debut, but this was merely a blip. The following year, Grace was 'accepted without incongruity' as one of England's leading amateurs, emphasizing the point with a maiden first-class century that was actually a double – an unbeaten 224 for an England XI versus Surrey at The Oval.[6] Thereafter, until his retirement forty years or so later, he established statistics that seemed 'forever unmatchable'.[7] Grace's batting reached its peak in the 1870s, and there was no better platform to showcase his majesty than the first ever Test match.

Except that Grace wasn't playing. When the England team came up short in the inaugural Test against Australia in Melbourne in 1877, W. G. was back in Gloucestershire, finally attending to the medical studies that had already taken considerably longer than they should have. So began a period of eleven years when Grace was simultaneously a medical student and one of the most famous men in Victorian England. He was a pupil of Mr Robert Tibbitts, known to students as 'Slasher'.[8] Presumably it wasn't a cricketing nickname.

When Grace made his international debut at The Oval in 1880, the home side were led in their first ever home Test by Lord Harris, described as 'the single most influential man to have been involved in cricket' and, by inference, a serious challenger to W. G.'s dominance.[9] But the good doctor was an infinitely more accomplished player than His Lordship, a point confirmed by an imperious century on Test debut. Even with his famously unswerving ability to look after himself first, W. G. must have been proud to share his first England appearance with brothers E. M. and G. F.

E. M. was the oldest of the three, an inventive batsman but a 'sublimely unorthodox human being' who had four wives and eighteen children.[10] Perhaps cricket's first 'sledger', as a teammate and opponent he was combative and unyielding, and apparently no player more regularly took on players, umpires and spectators.[11] Playing club cricket well into his sixties, he took 212 wickets in one season but claimed 208 chances were missed off his bowling. Guilty teammates were often sent a 'card of reminder' on each anniversary of their desperate mistake.[12]

The third Grace debutant was G. F., known as 'Fred'. Apparently more handsome than his brothers, neither was he as 'gruff'.[13] Usually a dasher with the bat, he had a disastrous debut, making a four-ball pair. In fact, neither E. M. nor G. F. appeared in Test cricket again. E. M. continued his long career with Gloucestershire, but poor Fred was dead – aged just 29 – within two weeks of his Test debut. After allegedly catching a chill from a damp mattress, he had a cold by the time the match finished, which developed into pneumonia. Even his family of doctors couldn't save him.

Once W. G. qualified, he attended to the needs of his patients in the winter and the county club paid for a locum so that he could play cricket for them in the summer. Accordingly, for two decades, he maintained the pretence of amateurism while being more handsomely remunerated than any of the professionals around him. If 'shamateurism' was already well established, W. G. took it to a new level.[14] While journeymen professionals were modestly remunerated, he demanded thousands to play and to tour, cherry-picking opportunities that suited him and passing on those that didn't. For an Australian tour in 1891–2, for example, Grace charged £3,000, plus expenses for himself, his wife and two children, and added the cost of the locum engaged to run his practice. His fees amounted to 20 per cent of the entire cost of the tour, leaving each professional with less than 10 per cent of Grace's bounty.[15]

For such reasons, W. G. divides opinion. Some, like cricket writer and historian David Frith, are tangibly annoyed at his antics. Grace's gamesmanship and bullying thrived, Frith notes, 'facilitated by timid umpires and opponents and sycophants who, overwhelmed by his force of character, allowed him to prevail'.[16] Examples are numerous and include unsuspecting batsmen being invited to look directly into the sun to admire a 'flock of birds' that often wasn't even there.[17] W. G. the bowler had all the tricks, but so did W. G. the batsman. There are many tales of him refusing to leave the crease after being dismissed. He once coerced a scorer into making his individual 399 into 400.[18] All such stunts were pulled on the basis that the crowd had come to see him play and should be given their money's worth. Grace's name on the team sheet meant that ticket prices were higher, but not all his teammates enjoyed his dominance and eye for a commercial opportunity; after one tour Surrey and England's champion bowler George Lohmann announced that he would never tour with Grace again, 'not for a thousand a week'.[19]

Others saw a more benevolent side. Denzil Batchelor claims that Grace was once kind enough to forensically scrutinize the scorebook so that an opposing batsman could be elevated from 99 to 100.[20] Donald Trelford notes that W. G.'s granddaughter recalls a genial old man whose beard she used to plait.[21] He once saved the life of a teammate who gashed his neck on some railings, and another time, he stitched the eye of an opposing wicketkeeper who paid him back by stumping him.[22] Once, appalled by the domestic violence suffered by a female patient, Grace punched the guilty husband on the nose.[23] He was a sensitive man and 'too upset by the First World War to discuss it in level terms'.[24] He was also, understandably, grief-stricken when two of his children predeceased him, and almost lost his appetite for cricket altogether when his twenty-year-old daughter died of typhoid.

So Grace was either a self-serving bully or a sporting titan who enriched everything around him. What seems beyond doubt is the magnitude of his contribution to cricket. Quite simply, 54,896 runs and 2,876 wickets represent around five stellar modern careers. In those days, too, without refined equipment and flat wickets, 'a run truly was a run'.[25] W. G. not only transformed cricket from a casual recreation to the national game, but by elevating the art and skills of batting, he transformed it into a proper contest between bat and ball, overthrowing the dominant fast bowlers who usually only needed rough wickets to confirm their

W. G. Grace and the future king, Edward VIII, 1911.

supremacy. Not one man or one team, for a while Grace was prac-tically the whole of English cricket. 'A billboard. A cheat. A batsman. A bastard,' reflects Jarrod Kimber, 'but what a bastard.'[26]

Grace's last Test match at Nottingham in 1899 was the first for Australian batsman Victor Trumper, who made an ignominious first-innings duck and only eleven in the second. Soon enough, though, he made his impact. *Wisden* proclaimed that within the pantheon of great Australian batsmen, Trumper was considered 'the best and most brilliant'.[27] This was before the freak of nature that was Donald Bradman, but in terms of style rather than sta-tistics, Trumper might still be number one. Few batsmen 'dazzled the eye and entranced the beholder' quite like the young fellow from Sydney.[28] Indeed, although his scores across the 1899 series were unremarkable, in the Lord's Test – his second for Australia – he made 135 not out. It was an innings of such quality that W. G. Grace presented him with a bat, noting that 'the present cham-pion' was hereby passing on the baton to 'the future champion'.[29]

Cruelly, Trumper never reached middle age, but his legend permeates cricket culture, national culture and beyond. Oscar-winning lyricist Sir Tim Rice, for example, tried his hand as a singer in 1974, performing under the pseudonym Victor Trumper.[30] The player sparks nostalgic fondness like no player before or since. It's all too easy, notes David Frith, to admire someone from long ago who can't besmirch his own memory, but the worst part of Trumper 'was his name'.[31] That his life was cut short at the age of 37 by Bright's disease has amplified the legend, as 'there is a love – and usually a sadness – at the heart of a cult.'[32] Indeed, someone left a note under the bronze bust created by Melbourne sculptor Louis Laumen just before it was auctioned, more than eighty years after Trumper's death. 'To one we have read about, but never saw in action,' said the note, 'he remains an immortal to all lovers of the game.'[33]

Victor Trumper, *c.* 1905.

To say we have never seen him in action is not quite true. There are various ancient film clips of him engaged in some gentle practice, and a few seconds of film of him batting against South Africa at Sydney in 1910/11. Generally, it was a wonderful series for him – not that you'd know it from the footage. He dashes for a single but falls over and drops his bat. When he climbs to his feet, the umpire gives him out and he walks off briskly, but this was well over a century ago and so everything on film happened briskly. For Trumper devotees, it's like discovering that in some of the only existing film of Van Gogh in action the artist is varnishing the garden shed.

Notwithstanding this brief footage, we know of Trumper through descriptions characterized by an elegance and panache not evident in writings about Donald Bradman, for example. Trumper was only a shooting star, but the brightest in a sky of comets. While Bradman is assigned machine-like functionality, Trumper attracts purple prose. As kids, Australians were 'mightily proud' of Bradman, but they all wanted to be Trumper; while Bradman was the aeroplane, Trumper was the 'soaring eagle'.[34] Denzil Batchelor suggests that while other players remain in the shadows, Trumper 'thunders in our ears like a roll of drums and still shines forth like an army with banners'.[35]

Gideon Haigh recognized the mystic nature of his subject when researching his book *Stroke of Genius: Victor Trumper and the Shot that Changed Cricket*. Documentary material was elusive, writes Haigh, and with no contemporaries left, mythology and legend were 'thick indeed'. Getting to grips with Victor Trumper was like 'entering a hall of mirrors' where 'everyone is quoting everyone else' and 'stories and their origins have long since parted ways'. In his own time, though, Trumper was admired and loved, and those talking of him do so with an unparalleled 'emotional incandescence'.[36] All of this is despite the fact that Trumper's overall record is unexceptional by modern standards. His Test average of 39.04 is just below the threshold of 40, supposedly signalling world class, but it wasn't what he did but the way in which he did it.[37] As Neville Cardus suggested, the full genius of Mozart was not revealed by simply counting the notes within his compositions.[38]

In 1902, three years after his Test debut and on his second tour of England, Trumper made an eye-watering 2,570 runs. In all, 24 centuries were scored on the tour, and Trumper was responsible for eleven of them. One stands out. In the fourth Test at Old Trafford on a wet wicket, he put England to the sword from the off. Ably supported by fellow opener Reggie Duff, who had a face 'like a good-looking brown trout', Trumper made an error-free 103 not out before lunch, his batting representing 'a marvel of ease and certainty'.[39] It was the first instance of a batsman making a century before lunch on the first day of a Test. The most quixotic marker of attacking batsmanship, this feat has been managed by only five others in the 120 years or so since. Given that he was the ultimate dasher, those he put in the shade often seemed unperturbed. England skipper Archie MacLaren, for example, conceded that the comparison between himself and Trumper was like placing a cab-horse next to a Derby winner.[40] Trumper's batting was not greedy; it was just brilliant, with no 'vainglory'.[41] But if he was a fine batsman, perhaps he was an even finer man. There is

Australian Test team, 1911: Victor Trumper (middle row, fourth from left), Warwick Armstrong (middle row, extreme left), Warren Bardsley (sitting on floor, extreme right).

none of the unsavouriness that lurked around the edges of W. G. Grace. Trumper, for example, would give gate money to the 'hopeless rabble' outside the match, and often a young lad visiting his sports shop would have his savings refused and a new bat presented to him anyway.[42]

But cricket – and life – is cruel. Like his Old Trafford opening partner Reggie Duff, who succumbed to alcoholism aged only 33, Trumper didn't make it to forty. The majesty of his talent was not matched by the strength of his constitution. The delight of Trumper is not found within statistics. Never has a cricketer had such wonderful things written about him, and while 'Victor Trumper' never made it as a pop star, in cricketing terms his memory remains fond and enduring.

# 3

# MORE GOLDEN AGE CHAMPIONS

*Victorians and Edwardians*

Grace and Trumper both died in 1915. Grace had always looked like Methuselah, but Trumper had plenty more bowlers to savage. The two were only part of this purple patch for cricket, and though W. G. was gargantuan, he did not hold a monopoly on cricketing charisma or achievement.

Only A. N. Hornby and Andrew Stoddart have captained England at both rugby and cricket, and surely nobody will do so again. Stoddart organized the British Lions' inaugural tour of Australia and New Zealand in 1888, finishing the trip as captain after the original skipper drowned. Stoddart appeared ten times in England's three-quarter line between 1885 and 1893, captaining the team four times as an exciting, fast and elusive wing three-quarter.[1] As a cricketer, Stoddart made sixteen Test appearances between 1888 and 1898. His record at the highest level was good despite the fact that he had only started playing cricket relatively late at the age of 22, taking to it 'like a master'.[2]

It was after 4 August 1886 that the world really noticed him as a cricketer. Opening the batting for Hampstead against Stoics, 'Drewy' Stoddart immediately set about the bowling. At lunch, his team were 370 for 3. Stoddart, on 230 not out, undoubtedly dined well. Refreshed, but his appetite for runs unsatisfied, he continued relentlessly until he miscued and was caught with his personal score at 485. Declarations were prohibited back then, and so Hampstead batted until they were all out for 813. Besides the physical effort of his six-hour innings, Stoddart's social activities either side of it were astonishing. David Frith reports that Drewy spent the evening before the match dancing, then playing poker, when a run of luck kept him at the tables 'until dawn'.[3] He freshened up with a quick dip at the local swimming baths before a leisurely breakfast. Then he began his frenzied assault on the Stoics bowlers.

Afterwards he played tennis, went to the theatre, ate supper and took to his bed some time before three, proving his magnificence as both a batsman and a socialite.[4] Within ten days of his quadruple century, he made 207 for Hampstead, and 98 and 116 for Middlesex. His star continued to rise with a Test century at Adelaide in 1891/2 and another at Melbourne in 1894/5, where his 173 not out was described as 'the definitive captain's innings'.[5] In 1900 Stoddart thrilled a Whit Monday bank holiday crowd by making 221 in as many minutes.

But his story does not end well. His health broke as he grieved the deaths of various close friends and associates. Nothing had prepared him for life after cricket, or away from the public gaze. Miserable, bereft and rudderless, it was only 'a short step to the drawer where he kept his revolver'.[6] The *Pall Mall Gazette* wondered how Drewy Stoddart had been reduced to take his own life and asked: if his admirers had known how serious his struggles were, 'would they not gladly have ended them?'[7] The tragedy was incomplete: his Coventry grave was damaged by bombing in the Second World War and then in the 1970s, vandalism prompted the Church authority to remove all the headstones, including his.

Victorian England was a fertile ground for the unusual, quirky and eccentric, and Charles Aubrey Smith ticks all those boxes. Educated at Charterhouse and then Cambridge, he turned out for Sussex at various times. As a player, he was not in the class of Grace, Trumper or Stoddart; his place in the game's history is notable for his life outside it. He did, though, play one Test match for England, captaining the team in the first Test against South Africa in 1888/9 at Port Elizabeth. He bowled a brisk medium pace incorporating 'a curious, curved approach to the wicket' that started from 'deep mid-off'.[8] However unusual it was, it was too good for the South African batsmen. Smith took five wickets in the first innings and two in the second. He was taken ill for the second Test, and his place was taken by 23-year-old Montague Parker Bowden, known to all as 'Monty'.

Neither Bowden nor Smith played for England again, and their lives diverged. Initially they stayed in South Africa to establish a stockbroking business together, and Bowden played some cricket for Transvaal. Soon, though, the market crashed, the partnership ended and Bowden joined Cecil Rhodes's expedition to Mashonaland in the hope of a change of luck. By the end of 1891 he had settled near the town of Umtali, living in a mud hut he called 'the Hilton', reflecting his aspirations to establish a hotel and staging post.[9] He played what would turn out to be his final game of cricket in 1892 and within a week had expired from a fever, his body guarded by a man with a loaded gun to keep the wildlife away. He died without knowing he had played in a Test match, let alone been the captain; while it is now accepted as South Africa's first Test, at the time it was thought to be just another tour match.[10]

While Bowden was laid to rest in a coffin made from whisky cases, his old partner Smith fared rather differently. After his ignominious adventures within the financial markets, he returned to England and became an actor, specializing in roles requiring a 'professional Englishman', or taking 'the Jane Austen approach' to playing 'monarchs or crusty martinets'.[11] Eventually one of Hollywood's most prolific actors, he appeared in *Tarzan the Ape Man*, *Bulldog Drummond Strikes Back*, *Clive of India*, *The Lives of a Bengal Lancer*, *Little Lord Fauntleroy*, *The Four Feathers* and *The Adventures of Mark Twain*.

His cricket career, however, continued. He created the Hollywood Cricket Club, recruiting, among others, David Niven, P. G. Wodehouse, Boris Karloff, Basil Rathbone, Ronald Colman, Errol Flynn and Laurence Olivier to play in front of 'some occasionally bemused locals'.[12] Imagine Ted Dexter running a social team featuring Russell Crowe, Colin Firth and Andrew Strauss, with Kate Winslet doing the sandwiches, suggests Martin Williamson, and 'you wouldn't be too far off the mark'.[13] The club was simultaneously 'rigidly British' and 'gaudily American', functioning as 'a rich blend of country-house civility, New World chutzpah and a discreet trysting place for the rich and famous'.[14] The main problem was finding eleven people to form a team to play against, the only requirements being having a detectable pulse and a willingness to spend an afternoon with some eccentric showbiz types.

'Pompous and not over-endowed with humour', Smith raised the Union Jack above his home each day.[15] He was never seen in public without his white flannels, striped blazer and boater, and this was exactly how he turned up at Lord's one day. Middlesex bowler Jack Young recalls that Smith was accompanied by two young cricketers, undoubtedly on a handsome retainer to bowl at the old thespian – perhaps 'five bob each'.[16] Young recalls Smith struggling against some very gentle net bowling until he was struck by a quicker one. Dropping the bat, reports Young, Smith 'roared that he had not travelled ten thousand miles to see how well they bowled' and 'didn't they know what a half-volley was?'[17] Even if his batting did not wow the critics (career average 13.63), Smith was knighted for his contribution to Anglo-American relations and safely remains the only England captain to have co-starred alongside Elizabeth Taylor.[18] Bowden and Smith; surely the fortunes of two teammates never turned out more differently.

W. G. Grace was the sun of Victorian cricket, but other bright planets orbited him. There was a changing of the guard in June

1899, when he led England for the final time in the Test match against Australia at Trent Bridge. He was only weeks short of his 51st birthday, feeling his age and mourning the death of his daughter. Plenty of people wondered whether he should retire with his dignity intact, since he now struggled to make an on-field impact, and some of his teammates expressed frustration with his incommodiousness. He knew his time was up.

Alongside Grace in his final Test were some of cricket's new powerhouse personalities who would lead the game into what was later called its 'Golden Age'. One of these was Kumar Shri Ranjitsinhji, known then and since as 'Ranji'. Part of the Indian nobility, he had travelled to England in 1888 as a sixteen-year-old and attended Trinity College, Cambridge. Soon, he became the first Indian to gain a blue. Then on to Sussex, and in 1896 he became the first non-white player to represent England at cricket, the first to score 3,000 runs in a first-class season and the first to score 100 runs before lunch in a Test match – on his England debut at that – although this wasn't on the first day, à la Trumper.[19] While his 24,692 first-class runs including 72 centuries at an eye-catching average of 56.37 mark him as one of the best batsmen of any era, there was more to Ranji than numbers. To begin with, he was a pure stylist who revolutionized batting by 'opening up the leg side'.[20] Like Trumper, Ranji attracted rich prose. Contemporary social scientists would undoubtedly frown at many of the early descriptions of Ranji and his cricket, with their allusions to the mystery of his princely life, his deft skills and his stylish silk shirts. Even so, the underlying sentiment seems to have been simple adoration and an appreciation of the exquisiteness of his batting.[21]

But Ranji's point of racial difference meant his passage to cricket's top table was problematic. Getting into the Cambridge team was his first struggle until it became impossible for reluctant selectors to continue ignoring him. By 1896 the sheer weight of his runs for Sussex and the way that he 'captivated' the public meant that when he was named in the team to face Australia, most agreed that he should be included.[22] MCC President Lord Harris, however, felt that Ranji's relationship with England was too transient and should prevent his selection. The day before this judgement, Ranji had become the first amateur to pass 1,000 runs for the season.[23] The Lancashire committee ignored the implicit 'whites only' approach to team selection, and picked Ranji, not least because he was such a financial draw.[24] A ponderous 62 in the first innings was followed by a majestic 154 not out in the second, and the only ones still unhappy were those blinded by prejudice. Though not a 'flagbearer' for his race, Ranji pioneered the notion that cricket 'need not be a white man's game'.[25]

When he became the Maharaja Jam Saheb of Nawanagar in 1907, he was generally a 'popular and benevolent ruler', and his service to the Chamber of Princes and the League of Nations was distinguished.[26] But despite such lofty living, the Indian superstar was almost permanently strapped for cash. Simon Wilde's excellent *Ranji: The Strange Genius of Ranjitsinhji* unravels the grim financial truths of debt and desperate fundraising. His public image was a facade: Scyld Berry has suggested with some justification that Ranji was 'not everything he claimed to be' and managed a lavish lifestyle only by leaving bills unpaid and spending money he didn't have.[27] It is generally understood that he fathered an illegitimate son while at Cambridge and that the child was given up for adoption, never to be acknowledged or provided for by his father. There was also talk of some skulduggery enabling Ranji to take his throne, but since he died suddenly in 1933, memories of him have most often been fond.

Charles Burgess Fry was another of the big personalities of that era. Apart from being perhaps the most accomplished all-round

K. S. Ranjitsinhji,
*c.* 1897.

sportsman in history, C. B. Fry, astonishingly, was also probably the most intellectually able. All this, as well as being one of the most famous people to come from Croydon. (Other contenders such as Malcolm Muggeridge and Peter Cushing are simply swept aside.) Fry was school captain at cricket and football and excelled at languages. At Oxford, he was awarded blues for football, cricket and athletics, and only missed one for rugby because of injury. He was, however, good enough to appear three times for the Barbarians. He held the British long jump record and, for a while, the world record.

He won the long jump and 100-yard sprint at what is claimed to have been the first world's athletic championships in London in 1894. He was an expert at the hammer, discus and javelin, and at skiing, angling, rowing, tennis and ice skating. He only missed the 1896 Olympics 'because he didn't know they were taking place'.[28] He played a football international for England and appeared in the 1902 FA Cup final for Southampton.

Fry's sporting prowess was endless. When he was pushing seventy, apparently the Southampton professional teaching him golf became so fed up at being outplayed at every hole that he resigned. At the same age, Fry took up clay pigeon shooting and 'broke the heart of his local county champion'.[29] Way beyond his three score years and ten, his party piece was to jump backwards from floor to mantelpiece from a standing start. In sum, he represented England 'at pretty much everything bar taekwondo'.[30]

But the man's brain was as brilliant as the rest of him. As a journalist, he gave sports writing 'a new dignity'.[31] *The Times* published his Latin verses. He was 'a bit of a dab at Astronomy and a bobby-dazzler at Higher Mathematics'.[32] He was offered the throne of Albania, although this was actually less impressive than it sounded, since long before adopting Norman Wisdom as their national hero, the Albanians primarily wanted a fine Englishman who could fund himself to the tune of £10,000 per annum.[33] Ranji, of course, could have put his hand on the cash (even though it might not have been his), but thought better of it, not wishing to subject his friend to life in a lonely castle and perhaps 'a bullet in the ribs'.[34] It has been claimed that a speech given by Ranji but written by Fry was in some way responsible for getting rid of Mussolini from Corfu. Fry's vocation for public service was satisfied by the stewardship of the naval training ship *Mercury*, preparing boys from all social classes to command 'merchant liners or His Majesty's men-of-war'.[35]

The notion that Fry was a manufactured cricketer rather than a naturally gifted one enhances the legend. He made over 30,000 first-class runs at an average of over 50, including 94 centuries. In 1901 he hit six centuries in successive innings. His record across 26 Test matches is, in truth, unspectacular, but as England's captain in the 1912 Triangular series, he remained unbeaten. After a quiet 1913 he reappeared in 1914, and his return to cricket featured more prominently in the *Daily Telegraph* than reports of the Mediterranean fleet or Lloyd George's budget.

Yet he was still human. Percy Chapman – England captain in the 1920s – remembered seeing Fry at a festival match, carrying a tea tray for a group of adoring ladies. The great champion hurdled a picket fence but didn't quite make it. More seriously, and

C. B. Fry, *c.* 1896.

despite a lifetime of remarkable achievement, Fry's personal life was unhappy. Periods of poor mental health were not helped by his wife, 'a dominatrix ten years his senior who openly flaunted her relationship with another man'.[36] Almost thirty years after his father's death, Fry's son empathically concluded that his mother had ruined his father's life.[37]

Fry's 1939 autobiography, *Life Worth Living*, was warmly received despite reports that it was 'full of inaccuracy and exaggeration, all in Fry's favour', and while he does not mention his own mental frailties he is 'horribly unsympathetic' about similar afflictions in others.[38] A flirtation with Hollywood was fondly remembered, but so too was a meeting with Hitler in the early 1930s.[39] Fry seems to have been impressed by the Führer and appears to have accepted Hitler's claims that the Jews were working with the Bolshevists to assert control.[40] But for this catastrophic misjudgement, it seems sure that Fry would have been knighted. Today, suggests Simon Barnes, within a society that chews up its heroes, he would be despised as 'a dilettante, a waster, a show-off; a man who never settled to any one thing'.[41]

Cricket history, though, remembers him as a hero, and so does popular culture. Indeed, he was the subject of the fifth ever episode of the TV show *This Is Your Life*. In December 1955, almost sixty years since his England debut, Fry was surprised to be called on stage at BBC Television Theatre at Shepherd's Bush, London, by Eamonn Andrews. Members of the 1912 England side were reunited with their skipper. Jack Hobbs, Sydney Barnes, Jack Hearne, Tiger Smith and Wilfred Rhodes all showed up and the 'reminiscing went on deep into the night'.[42] Less than a year later, the champion was no more, and the adoration was repeated in sadder circumstances. John Arlott provides a balanced summary of Fry's life and times. Besides being 'magnanimous, extravagant, generous, elegant, brilliant and fun', Fry could be 'autocratic, angry and self-willed', but was 'the most variously gifted Englishman of any age'.[43] It is hard to imagine anyone getting close to becoming his equal.

Another soon to be legend made his England debut in Grace's last Test match in 1899. If there was ever a player whose life charted cricket's twentieth-century evolution, it was Yorkshire's Wilfred Rhodes. He played cricket for England while Victoria was Queen, and died 74 years later, weeks before Garry Sobers played his last Test in England. At the beginning of his career, batting pads were made from cane strips and cricket flannels were held up with striped ties. At the end of it, cricket was sponsored by razor manufacturers and was broadcast worldwide.

In 1899, though, Rhodes was a rookie. He'd performed well for Yorkshire, but there was little sign of him becoming one of the most statistically dominant cricketers of all time. By themselves, 39,969 first-class runs are staggering enough – that's Sachin Tendulkar's career plus another 50 per cent. In that match in 1899, Rhodes batted at 10 for England but within a dozen years, he had opened the innings against Australia in Melbourne and put on 323 with Jack Hobbs. Neville Cardus concluded that Rhodes had made himself into a batsman by 'practice and hard thinking'.[44] Denzil Batchelor noted that Rhodes was naturally suspicious of every ball bowled at him, 'like a conscientious judge making sure that he has extracted the essential evidence from a hostile witness'.[45]

While he was doing that, he was taking 4,204 first-class wickets. Nobody else ever got – or will ever get – within 10 per cent of his tally. If his batting was a little utilitarian, his bowling was characterized by strategy and laying traps so precise he'd have made a magnificent poacher. One observer noted that when Rhodes got you out, it meant he knew how to get you out every time he ever bowled at you. Harold Larwood recalled Rhodes placing a fielder close to the wicket to snare the prized wicket of Australian Bill Ponsford. Traditionally, the most junior players field closest to the bat. Perhaps it's because they have the sharpest reflexes, but cynics would say they are the most dispensable. On this occasion, Larwood felt in danger. Rhodes ran in but stopped, staring at the youngster who had shuffled backwards, out of position. Almost straight after putting the rookie back from where he had strayed, Rhodes got one to spit off the surface, and Ponsford lobbed a gentle catch for Larwood, who didn't need to move. 'You can move back a bit now, sonny,' muttered Rhodes acerbically.[46] He had a reputation for dourness. Once he castigated a young Yorkshire colleague who was 'having fun' thrashing the ball and running furiously between the wickets with an incredulous 'We don't play cricket for fun.'[47] Meticulousness meets mental fortitude; in a game of patience there was only ever one winner. If batsmen hit him for a boundary, they were simply adding to a tab they'd have to settle – with interest – some time later.

Skill, strategy and determination; add longevity and the mix becomes unsurpassable. As a Test selector, he was as frustrated as everyone else at four draws when England hosted Australia in the 1926 Ashes series. In an impassioned plea, chairman of selectors Pelham Warner asserted that 49-year-old Rhodes was still the premier left-armed slow bowler in the country and best placed to break the deadlock.[48] He played, and his four second-innings wickets delivered a 289-run victory and the Ashes. Every England selector since 'has always taken their boots to a match, just in case'.[49]

At the time, England rarely sent full-strength squads anywhere other than Australia and in 1929/30, very much in his dotage, Rhodes toured the West Indies. Well into his 53rd year, he hardly stood out within an England team with an average age of 37. At twenty, Nottinghamshire bowler Bill Voce was the team fledgling; Rhodes had played 25 Tests before he was born. In four Tests after his 1926 recall, Rhodes bowled 301 penurious overs for

Wilfred Rhodes, 1928.

sixteen wickets, 116 of them going for no runs. When he turned out in the fourth Test at Kingston in April 1930, he became, at 52 years and 165 days, England's oldest ever international player. Surrey's Andrew Sandham took the match plaudits with the first ever Test match triple century, but within a high-scoring draw, Rhodes bowled one ball short of 45 overs, took two wickets and conceded 39 runs, each one probably cussed at by the old bowler.

On his return from the Caribbean he announced his retirement from cricket. The news was apparently greeted with surprise, but quite what other big announcement would be anticipated from a 53-year-old sportsman is not clear. The significance of the moment, however, was obvious to all present. Rhodes had played 1,110 first-class games across 32 years. He'd watched ten prime ministers, three monarchs and 25 England captains come and go; had won games for England batting at 11 and at 1; and had bowled on wickets that were wet, dry and all variations in between. It was the end, and Rhodes recalled that it was uncompromising professional Wilf Barber who managed some words when others were too emotional. They simply encapsulated the grittiness of the time: 'I'll give you ten bob for your pads.'[50]

Those stewarding cricket into its Golden Age were characterized by pathos, adventure and matchless achievement, but these great characters were fortunate to be around at a time when cricket was developing and maturing in a highly receptive environment.[51] Players were 'confident, vigorous and competitive', fortified by the relative prosperity and positivity of the period, enhanced by England's military strength.[52] 'Leisured pace and stylized method' were central to the Edwardian lifestyle.[53] In sum, the Golden Age was a 'temporal utopia' and 'a pristine point of contrast to the inter-war practice of cricket and by implication, to the politics, industrial processes and aesthetics of the contemporary national culture'.[54]

# 4

## GENTLEMEN, PLAYERS, VARSITY AND ROSES

### *Background Developments*

C ricket was a big deal by the beginning of the twentieth century. Some key contests had become established and these transcend our loose chronology, which is hereby temporarily interrupted. Some notable, institutional and traditional team clashes reflect British life, forever tiered according to class. In the eleventh century, for example, the multi-layered social landscape embraced freeholders, serfs and slaves. In the twenty-first century, the seven social classes are the 'precariat', 'emergent service workers', 'traditional working class', 'new affluent workers', 'technical middle class', 'established middle class' and 'elite'.[1] For a long time, though, cricket was simply divided into 'Gentlemen' and 'Players'. Amateur 'Gentlemen' usually had more initials and private means. Professional 'Players' earned a meagre living from cricket and endured colder showers, smaller dressing rooms and constant condescension. Those playing cricket for money were implied to be inferior and matches between them and the 'toffs' were understandably testy.[2]

The Gentlemen versus Players contest began in 1806, and for fifty years or so, it wasn't much of a contest at all as the public showed only passing interest in what was always a win for the Players. The Gentlemen had to put their own money up to keep the fixture going. Only the arrival of the Grace family breathed some life into the contest as they bolstered the Gentlemen's prospects. By the time the two sides met at Lord's in mid-July 1914, the fixture represented the best domestic cricket could offer and a win for the Gentlemen by 134 runs represented a 'watershed at the end of the Golden Age'.[3]

But amateurism had a shelf life. By the late 1950s many who called themselves 'amateurs' were stretching the concept as they secured lucrative jobs within the game that annoyed the Players. England spinner Jim Laker was particularly vocal on the issue, suggesting – with tongue only partly in cheek – that he might have made more money from cricket if he was an amateur. His former Essex colleague Trevor Bailey was an 'amateur' but presumably earned a decent whack as the secretary of the county side. But the difference in terms and conditions extended beyond financial reward. The inequalities between the two sides were variously manifested. First, Players were referred to by their surnames; the courtesy of initials was afforded only to the Gentlemen. Players were also often given basic changing facilities and had to enter the field through a different gate. While the Gentlemen were put up in style, the Players had to lump it.

Surrey poet Albert Craig famously asserted that 'all the Gentlemen should be players and all the players should be Gentlemen' but there was comedy potential to underpin the tension.[4] 'Before you came in, I knew you were no Gentleman,' said the Players' wicketkeeper once, adding, 'Now that I've seen you batting, I realize you aren't a player either.'[5] By 1962 the concept was obsolete, and the decision was made to call everyone 'cricketers'. The final game was played at Scarborough in July, although nobody knew it was the last one at the time. The teams epitomized the historical contrasts that had characterized the contest from inception. The Players were led by Fred Trueman and comprised a collection of uncompromising competitors including Brian Close and Tony Lock; they defeated an Oxbridge-dominated Gentlemen team led by A. C. Smith and featuring A. R. Lewis,

Gentlemen team versus Players, 1899: W. G. Grace (middle row, second from right), Archie MacLaren (back row, centre), K. S. Ranjitsinhji (middle row, second from left) and C. B. Fry (sitting on floor, centre).

R. M. Prideaux and R. A. Hutton. Trueman expressed relief that the whole thing was over and, unusually, everyone seemed to agree with him.

While Gentlemen versus Players so obviously pitted the upper against the working class, the most famous varsity contest might be considered as the privileged classes playing among themselves. Accordingly, the class system was hardly evident when the University of Oxford played their Cambridge counterparts in what is recognized as the oldest regular first-class fixture. First held in 1827, it has been played every year since 1838, apart from during wartime. Up until the Second World War and for a while afterwards, the fixture was a major draw, both as a social occasion and because of the quality of players involved.[6] Even into the 1970s, both universities regularly supplied cricketers destined for the highest level. Cricketing alumni and captains of Oxford, for example, include C. B. Fry, R. E. Foster (the only man to captain

England at both cricket and football), Colin Cowdrey, the Nawab of Pataudi (later Mansur Ali Khan), Imran Khan and a host of others. Cambridge boasts a similar list, including nineteenth-century England captain the Hon. Ivo Bligh, Sammy Woods (who played Tests for both England and Australia and captained England at rugby union), F. S. Jackson, England cricketer and Welsh rugby international Maurice Turnbull, and England batsman and future Bishop of Liverpool David Sheppard. More recently, those wearing the light blue of Cambridge included future England captains Ted Dexter, Tony Lewis, Mike Brearley, Michael Atherton and Pakistani Test captain Majid Khan.

All that, though, is in the past, and the fixture has been diminished by 'counter-attractions' as well as, perhaps more importantly, 'increased academic standards and unsympathetic admissions tutors'.[7] Gone, it seems, are the days when Bertie Wooster types could wangle a Politics, Philosophy and Economics degree on the basis of a swanky cover drive. Nowadays, university output is measured by graduation ceremonies and research funding, not batting averages and beating your Varsity competitors. The modern manifestation of the competition embraces what many might consider a contemporary abomination – Twenty20. Culturally, mortar boards and gowns have been replaced by a 'tracksuited director of cricket'.[8]

University matches against the first-class counties have become, in the main, early season warm-ups for the counties. As a gently enjoyable way to start the season, every April various journalists arrive at the Parks (Oxford's ground) or Fenners (the Cambridge equivalent) and, pint in hand, snooze contentedly 'while one of the counties tormented the students'.[9] As the 'slaughter of the innocents', it's a bizarre version of rag week where other people have more fun than the students.

But these matches can still be excellent learning opportunities. In 2012, 20 per cent of England-qualified cricketers came through the university cricket system, now embracing Durham, Leeds/ Bradford, Cardiff and Loughborough.[10] Michael Henderson suggests that university cricket should be preserved, since traditionally student players have dominated cricket and alumni 'ran it'. 'It is a poor game that does not honour the ones who shaped it,' he reflects.[11] While university cricket, for some, might evoke the game's 'toffee-nosed heritage', once in a while there is some macabre enjoyment when a county side is humbled by students.[12]

The last of these enduring, chronology-transcending cricketing fixtures is not characterized by any contrasts between amateur and professional, upper class and working class, fancy living and student budgeting. Instead it's about geographical proximity and neighbourly discomfort. Yorkshire versus Lancashire – the Roses match – is competitive and uncompromising in equal measure. In days past, it was the biggest show in town and a 'sporting re-enactment of a centuries-old rivalry'.[13] In 1926, for example, 78,617 engaged and partisan observers watched the teams play at Old Trafford.

There is some competitive needle for sure. Three cheers for Lancashire hotpot, crumbly cheese, Joy Division, the Bee Gees and Eccles cakes, writes Jeanette Winterson in *Country Life*.[14] In combative response, Nigel Farndale acerbically suggests that Lancashire's biggest problem is that 'It's not Yorkshire.'[15] It has been thus since they first squared up using bows, arrows and vats of oil. There are other county rivalries but none like this. Cricketwise, hostilities began in 1867 when Yorkshire won at Whalley, near Blackburn. Roy Kilner, a Yorkshire all-rounder of the 1920s, defined the ideal Roses match as having 'no umpires and fair cheating all round'.[16] It is still an emotional affair – in 2014 Yorkshire's Andrew Gale was censured for referring to Lancashire's South African Ashwell Prince as 'a Kolpak'.[17] Calling out anyone as a nomadic, cricketing gun-for-hire is especially pertinent within a fixture that is all about belonging. Summarizing 150 years of spikiness, former Yorkshire player turned director of cricket Martyn Moxon reflected that nobody goes looking for trouble, and that it's 'more of an unfortunate case of stuff happening'.[18]

But fixtures between the two weren't always exciting. Unsurprisingly echoing some of the personalities participating, Roses matches have acquired a reputation for dourness. Allegedly an unwritten law suggests that there should be no boundaries before lunch, since that would offend an otherwise solemn ritual with some unwanted frippery. Michael Parkinson reports that among his father's sage cricketing advice was the adage that any prospective wife should be able to sit through a Roses match without yawning.[19] But anyone might have stifled their drowsiness in 1946, when Lancashire's Winston Place and Phil King took four hours over their centuries. Roses cricket is no place for lily-livered neutrals. Neville Cardus recalled a Yorkshire clergyman admonishing the England selectors for damaging the wider interests of the game by picking Lancashire and Yorkshire players, thus drawing them away from their 'main and primary duties'.[20]

Only when one considers the respective roles of honour does Yorkshire develop some bragging rights. Lancashire's trophy cabinet is smaller, but they have been traditionally stronger in the shorter formats. Overseas talent like West Indian Clive Lloyd and Indian wicketkeeper Farokh Engineer complemented local lads such as David Lloyd, David Hughes, Harry Pilling and 'Flat Jack' Simmons. While, in the 1970s and '80s, a final at Lord's became a regular excursion for Lancashire, Yorkshire cricket killed itself slowly with a thousand bitter cuts, the internal strife waged between those who supported and those who opposed captain and leading player Geoffrey Boycott. The club was left 'demoralised, impoverished and moribund'.[21] More of Boycott later.

Until 1991 Yorkshire accepted only home-grown cricketers. It was a 'proud tradition', with many instances of ambulances driving pregnant mothers-to-be along the motorway so their sons wouldn't be born in Nottinghamshire, Derbyshire or – God forbid – Lancashire.[22] The affinity those from Yorkshire had with the club, reflected Boycott, provided an extra spur to compete.[23] In 1992, though, the introspection ended, and Yorkshire's cricket committee did the unthinkable. It abandoned the Yorkshire-born policy that looked increasingly out of step with modern Britain and modern cricket. The first overseas signing to arrive was a young Indian called Sachin Tendulkar. Posing in a flat cap with a pint of local ale, he became a 'most incongruous Tetley Bitterman'.[24] When Tendulkar later became the world's best batsman, old men in Bingley and Huddersfield undoubtedly reminded anyone listening that it was all down to his formative years in Yorkshire.

More recently, Bradford-born Adil Rashid is a high-profile representative of Yorkshire's thriving cricket-loving Asian community. Many would justifiably argue that he shouldn't be a novelty, and that there should be many more like him. But naming part of some element of the county's new cricket centre at Bradford after him might help redress the racial imbalance.[25]

Despite the more liberal recruitment policies, defections across the Pennines are rarer than hen's teeth. When David Byas joined Lancashire in 2002, there was widespread surprise, not least from Byas, when in his first innings for his new county he was despatched LBW first ball by umpire Barrie Leadbeater – a Yorkshireman.

The move is indicative that this is another contest possibly lacking some of its original combative tension. The increasingly hybrid nature of cricket means that the bitterest old scores remain in the past. Indeed, perhaps it hasn't been the same since the war, suggested Fred Trueman, since after serving alongside each other, the old rivalry was 'difficult to recreate'.[26] Perhaps peace really has broken out when an Old Trafford crowd dispenses with 'parochialism' to boo Australian David Warner for challenging Joe Root – a Yorkshireman – to some late-night fisticuffs.[27]

The splitting of the county championship into two divisions in 2000 means that the two are no longer guaranteed to face each other. The biggest show in town is now sometimes played in front of the proverbial one man and his dog, except when the dog might have 'a prior engagement'.[28] It is still capable of raising temperatures, but these days Yorkshire and Lancashire are like two curmudgeonly old men who shake their sticks at each other, then nurse half a pint apiece while fixing the world's problems.

5

# THE GREATEST RIVALRY
*Even Bigger Background Developments*

Cricket's fairly slack chronology will not resume just yet, since the establishment of the highest-profile and most enduring of contests requires some explanation. Hereby we cover England's early engagements with Australia, straddling the last quarter of the nineteenth century and the first few pre-war years of the twentieth.

If Gentlemen versus Players, Oxford versus Cambridge and Lancashire versus Yorkshire had all got the mercury rising, they are only starters when compared to the entrée. The first ever Test match between England and Australia was played at Melbourne in 1877 and was dominated by Australian Charles Bannerman, who was apparently far superior to 'the rustic thumpers' around him.[1] In the first innings, he made 165 – the first ever Test century – against an England bowling attack still apparently queasy after the long sea voyage. Hampered by a hand injury, seasick opponents or not, this represented something of a professional comeback for Bannerman, who had been fired from the Sydney mint aged nineteen for 'insolence' and 'general insubordination'.[2]

Even then, there were off-field shenanigans. The 1876/7 trip was shambolic, and few England players made any money. In the first ever Test they didn't even have a reserve player. When he should have been keeping wicket for England, Surrey's Ted Pooley was in jail in New Zealand after a betting disagreement turned ugly. In the words of fellow tourist Alfred Shaw, Pooley's tour came to 'an unpleasant end'.[3] But Australia were also without a key player. Fast bowler Fred 'the Demon' Spofforth declined to play when Jack Blackham was chosen as wicketkeeper ahead of his friend Billy Murdoch.[4] With his imposing 'black moustache', 'steely brown eyes' and an 'unmistakable aura of hostility', for once the Demon was not missed by his team.[5]

One Aussie who did play was eighteen-year-old Tom Garrett. After Bannerman's century, Garrett was the second-highest scorer with 18 not out. Almost 132 years to the day after Tom Garrett's first Test match appearance at Melbourne, his musician-turned-politician great-grandson Peter Garrett performed there with his band *Midnight Oil* to support those affected by Victorian bushfires. That first two-match series finished with one win apiece, and Australia won the only Test the following year in 1878/9. England got their own back in the only Test of 1880 at The Oval, when W. G. Grace made a century on his debut. The 1881/2 series in Australia was claimed 2–0 by the hosts. And so to The Oval, for the only Test of 1882. Up to that point, players had been playing for bragging rights, but events following the denouement of the match introduced something more iconic.

Australian sporting supremacy was established almost before they even set foot on dry land after a two-month voyage. Responding to an on-board wager, all-rounder George Bonnor won £100 by throwing a cricket ball almost 120 yards. By the time of the first Test, the team had won 24 out of 28 matches.[6] The match was low scoring and short on quality but brimming with excitement. On a sodden wicket, Australia capitulated to England bowlers Barlow and Peate, and 63 looked no score at all. England's 101 wasn't much better, Spofforth's 7 for 46 being characteristically fierce, and spurred on by some 'derogatory remarks' overheard in the pavilion.[7] The temperature rose further when in Australia's second innings, Sammy Jones was controversially run out. Having made it home for a single, Jones left his crease to tap the pitch. W. G. removed the bails and appealed, and Jones was duly dispatched. Australia were all out for 122, and England needed only 85 to win.

With England within seven of their target, the tension was so great that one spectator died of heart failure. Another bit through the handle of his umbrella. But Spofforth's wrathful revenge was irresistible. He took another seven wickets to complete match figures of fourteen wickets for 90 runs. They were to be the best match figures produced by an Australian for ninety years. England were humiliated, their embarrassment enhanced by a spoof obituary in the *Sporting Times* that read, 'The body will be cremated and the Ashes taken to Australia.'[8] It was the first mention of 'the Ashes', and now there was something tangible to play for. The gauntlet had been thrown down, and the most 'nationalistic and jingoistic contest' in cricket had begun.[9]

Irrespective of who wins, the Ashes themselves do not move. At the Lord's Museum, the Ashes urn grabs the most attention. Behind toughened glass, no one can touch it and like the Holy Grail, it is always 'tantalisingly out of reach'.[10] With the exception of 1891/2, England dominated the Ashes between 1882/3 and 1897. But from the start of 1898, Australia won ten of the next fourteen Tests, most by comfortable margins, and so they had every reason to feel bullish when landing in England in 1902. Led by Joe Darling, the party included Sammy Carter (who combined wicketkeeping with a career as a funeral director) and future captains Clem Hill, Monty Noble, Warwick Armstrong and Hugh Trumble, who'd been in charge previously. As if that wasn't enough, Victor Trumper was in the form of his life.

England – also strong – were led by Lancastrian Archie MacLaren, an imposing figure with a certain 'grandeur'.[11] In a Test career lasting fifteen years, he made five hundreds against

Australia, and chalked up the first ever quadruple century in first-class cricket with 424 against Somerset in 1895. *The Observer* noted that the Somerset team on the day comprised 'nine amateurs, including one parson and two doctors', and that MacLaren strenuously challenged the first-class status of the match in which Australian Bill Ponsford eclipsed him with 429 in 1922/3. When the Australian's new record appeared in *Wisden*, an incensed MacLaren threatened to make representation to MCC.[12]

MacLaren was often referred to as 'the noblest Roman of them all', but Gideon Haigh suggests such notions are largely down to the hagiographic worship of 'youthful acolyte' Neville Cardus.[13] Certainly, MacLaren wasn't an especially successful England captain, leading them in four Ashes series without winning the urn. Indeed, while he conducted his career as though mounting a 'cavalry charge against the forces of darkness', in reality he did little more than 'tilt against windmills'.[14] Off the field he pursued careers, with varying degrees of failure, as a banker, teacher, secretary to Ranji, magazine editor, stud farmer and hotelier. As a limousine salesman, by all accounts what he tried to sell to his customers rarely coincided with what they wanted or needed. A quest for Hollywood stardom foundered, and a cameo appearance alongside Aubrey Smith in *The Four Feathers* was consigned to the cutting-room floor.

Haigh asserts that MacLaren was 'frankly unpleasant', and such traits were evident in the dressing room, where he emphatically suggested to one team that he wouldn't have picked any of them himself.[15] Some felt that while MacLaren made his opponents feel inadequate, he made his own players feel the same way.[16]

Nonetheless, MacLaren's England team of 1902 started well enough. If contemporary cricket incorporates kaleidoscopic kit, sunglasses and multicoloured bat stickers, the England team photo before the first Test at Edgbaston suggests it was not always so glitzy. Everyone wears a cap, but otherwise it is reminiscent of a church hall jumble sale. Nothing matches, and the chunky knits worn by Fry and Ranji were perhaps the work of overzealous relatives. Another, worn by J. T. Tyldesley, is perhaps three sizes too large and the trouser turn-ups sported by MacLaren and Jessop are big enough to merit their own postcodes. Sartorial uncertainty notwithstanding, England posted a formidable 376 for 9 declared, thanks to a masterly hand from Lancastrian Tyldesley, who, despite his enormous sweater, made 138. There was rain, but not enough to account for Australia's pitiful response of 36 all out. The damage was done by Rhodes, who took 7 for 17, although his Yorkshire colleague George Hirst had terrorized the Australian batsmen to the extent that they relaxed when facing the friendlier-looking spinner. Following on, Australia's second innings was curtailed by rain, and the match was drawn. The bragging rights, momentum and just about everything else were England's.

Tests were played over three days, and one decent deluge could wipe a match out. The second match at Lord's was abandoned and the series moved to Sheffield's Bramall Lane, Yorkshire's cricketing home at the time. Responding to Australia's 194, England could only manage 145, their innings played out in fog generated by the nearby factory chimneys.[17] By virtue of their second innings of 289 and another substandard England reply, the visitors drew first blood in the series with a 143-run victory. England's players – especially C. B. Fry – were unhappy that they had been scuppered by the choice of venue and its facilities, while Yorkshire were disappointed that it was not the pay day they'd hoped for.

Australia took their lead to Manchester. After Trumper's famous onslaught had helped Australia to a first innings of 299, England almost matched them, with their 262 including a fine century by Stanley Jackson. At Harrow School, Jackson's fag had been Winston Churchill. The Yorkshire batsman would later become

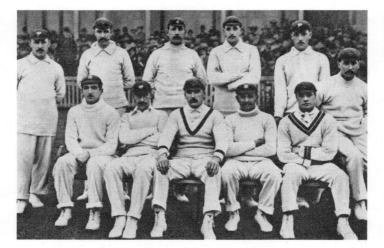

England Test team 1902: Back row, left to right are George Hirst, Dick Lilley, Bill Lockwood, Len Braund, Wilfred Rhodes and J. T. Tyldesley. Front row, left to right are C. B. Fry, F. S. Jackson, Archie MacLaren, K. S. Ranjitsinhji and Gilbert Jessop.

Lieutenant-Colonel of a West Yorkshire Regiment battalion, an MP, Financial Secretary to the War Office, Chairman of the Unionist Party and the survivor of an assassination attempt when serving as Governor of Bengal. On this day, though, it was his fortitude in the face of the Australian bowling that kept England in the hunt. Australia were skittled for 86, chiefly due to England bowler Bill Lockwood, whose 5 for 28 followed his 6 for 48 in the first innings.

It was something of a miracle that Lockwood was playing at all. During the England tour of Australia in 1894/5, he had almost drowned in Sydney Harbour. Another time, when team-mate Bobby Peel's pop bottle exploded, Lockwood was left with a glass splinter in his finger.[18] When he carelessly fired his gun during a shooting party, another teammate described him as 'a most uncomfortable chap to be out with on this sort of expedition'.[19]

After his wife and child died a short time later, he found consolation in alcohol. His performance at Manchester, therefore, was all the more astonishing. In the 1902 match Australia might not have even made it as far as 86, since top scorer Joe Darling was dropped by England debutant Fred Tate from Sussex. Tate had already made a bad start; as 'a last-minute selection', he arrived so late he had to sleep 'in someone's attic'.[20]

Few doubted England would make the 124 needed to win the Test and level the series. When Trumble and Saunders dismissed the home side three runs short, poor Tate was blamed for the failings of a whole team. He'd dropped a critical catch and was bowled when victory was within grasp. The unfortunate label 'Tate's match' overlooks the magnificence of Trumper, Jackson, Lockwood and some sensational fielding.[21] While this is perhaps the 'saddest' of all 'one-cap wonder' stories, the kindly Raymond Robertson-Glasgow excuses it by noting that deep square leg and Old Trafford in general were 'both extremely difficult places'.[22]

His England colleagues refused to look at the inconsolable Tate as he hid in the corner of the dressing room. Mustering up some hope, he muttered something about 'a little lad' at home who would somehow make good. How proud he must have been when his son Maurice made his home Ashes debut 24 years later, eventually becoming one of England's best medium pacers. Maurice received a telegram from his father before the game, beseeching him 'to redeem my mistake'.[23] It rained and England drew, but in the Test against Australia at Sydney in 1924/5, Maurice took 11 for 228. Fred was revenged, and a 'touching paternal tale' was concluded.[24]

If Old Trafford was 'Tate's match' for disheartening reasons, then the final Test at The Oval was 'Jessop's match' for wholly positive ones, unless you were Australian. Tate had been discarded, along with Ranji, another indifferent performer at Old Trafford.

In their places came Gilbert Jessop and George Hirst. Nobody knew it at the time, but they were probably the most inspired selections in history.

Australia posted an imposing 324, despite Hirst's 5 for 77. His 43 was also pivotal in England's below-par reply of 183. Quite astonishingly, like his great friend Wilfred Rhodes, Hirst was an all-rounder from Kirkheaton, near Huddersfield. The answer to 'who is the best all-rounder in the world?' would have been an each-way wager on 'he bats right, bowls left and was born in Kirkheaton'. It doesn't seem an obvious incubator of cricketing brilliance, but it was, and as an English cricketing Klondike, this corner of Yorkshire will not be eclipsed. Its first claim to fame was that it was the birthplace of Allen Hill, who in that first ever Test match at Melbourne in 1877 took the first wicket and, shortly afterwards, the first catch. Six months or so later, Rhodes was born, although the event was most likely lost on six-year-old George Herbert Hirst, whose family kept the local pub, the Brown Cow Inn. They would become among the best cricketers in England, the world and of all time, their cricketing reign lasting from Hirst's county trial until Rhodes retired from the first-class game 41 years later. As a boy, says A. A. Thomson, by way of explaining his book about the pair and his wider literary style, 'I worshipped Hirst and Rhodes as I worshipped Dickens'; the three were 'the most wonderful things that happened in my life'.[25]

Hirst left school at ten. This was Huddersfield, after all, not Hollywood. If his education was practically non-existent, his cricket stats were incredible – 36,356 runs at an average of 34, and 2,742 wickets at less than 19. If you bat *and* bowl, he argued, you're twice as happy and you enjoy yourself twice as much.[26] In addition to his punishing batting and fast swerve bowling, he was a masterful fielder at mid-off. Accordingly, Lord Hawke called Hirst 'the greatest county cricketer of all time'.[27] The contrast between the rumbustious Hirst and the more complex Rhodes was evident in their respective batting. While heart fashioned Hirst's cricket, for Rhodes the game was played in his head. It would be absurd, though, says Thomson, to imagine that 'Rhodes has no heart as that Hirst had no head'.[28]

They were different, but together they became bigger than the sum of their considerable individual parts. At The Oval in 1902, though, someone had to set it all up first. England needed 263 to win and even with a team studded with superstars, they had passed that score only once in four preceding Tests. It was an unlikely prospect and at 48 for 5, it looked like a lost cause. Ben Stokes, after all, was 117 years in the future. It needed the greatest performance of someone else's career, and that someone was Gilbert Jessop.

Jessop was called 'The Croucher' on account of his hunched batting stance, and not for any crablike or ponderous qualities. Quite the opposite. His debut first-class innings began with a hat-trick ball which he hit for four, followed by another later in the over. During the 179 times he passed 50 in his career, Jessop scored 79 runs an hour, which increased to 83 runs an hour during his 53 centuries.[29] That was faster than just about anyone. Two out of the seven fastest centuries of all time by minutes, and two out of the top five fastest double centuries were made by Jessop. He made a hundred within an hour a dozen times – even in contemporary cricket, such a feat would be accompanied by headlines filling the biggest back page. Moreover, so dominant were his centuries, he contributed 72 per cent of the runs made while he was at the wicket. He made the top score in 25 per cent of all his innings. Everything about Gilbert Jessop's batting seems extraordinary, but the best was reserved for The Oval in 1902.

With England in dire straits, he began treating the Australian bowling like 'village green stuff'.[30] He brought up his fifty in 38 balls, and in a partnership of 109 for the sixth wicket, F. S. Jackson – no slouch himself – contributed only eighteen. In only 77 minutes, Jessop made 104, including seventeen fours and a five. It was *the* innings to epitomize cricket's Golden Age.[31] It stands out, well over a century later. C. B. Fry noted that if ever an innings should have been filmed, it was that one.[32] Jessop played in eighteen Tests and never scored another century, but his immortality was secured with 77 minutes of cricketing carnage.

But no sooner had he reached his hundred than Jessop was out. 'The Croucher' had propelled England to the brink of victory, but they were still agonizingly short. Lockwood and Lilley came and went, and with nine wickets down, the barrel-chested Hirst, batting at number 8, was joined by Wilfred Rhodes. Within a decade, Rhodes would be opening the batting for England, but in 1902, he was the last man, with fifteen runs still needed. It is claimed that he was met by Hirst's reassurance that 'we'll get them in singles'. Some say that Rhodes took exception at being cast as the grandmother who didn't know how to suck eggs. 'Rhodes knew what he was doing,' wrote A. A. Thomson, and Hirst 'knew that he knew'.[33] Along they plodded until they made the fifteen. Hirst's innings of 58 not out was in its own way 'almost as remarkable as Jessop's'.[34] Denzil Batchelor added something to the legend when he explained that years later, a friend asked Aussie captain Joe Darling whether he'd have preferred Hirst and Rhodes or England's openers MacLaren and Palairet to face those last overs. Darling, reports Batchelor, 'chewed his heavy black moustache' and 'disdained to reply'.[35]

All very good, except that 'we'll get them in singles' was probably never mentioned at all. Remembering The Oval escape of 1902, Frank Keating suggested that Neville Cardus was occasionally prone to 'inventing quotations to colour his descriptions'.[36] In this instance, both Hirst and Rhodes denied ever uttering 'such tripe'.[37] Regardless, Hirst the bowler took 5 for 77 and 1 for 7, and then scored 43 and 58 not out. Without the Yorkshireman's contributions, Jessop's brilliance wouldn't have mattered.

The next two Ashes series were dominated by some familiar characters. In the 1903/4 series in Australia, Trumper made two centuries and three fifties, and Rhodes took 28 wickets. In the first Test at Sydney, and on his England debut, R. E. 'Tip' Foster made 287. For many years this stood as the highest ever individual Test score. When it was bettered by Bradman and then by Len Hutton, Denzil Batchelor claimed that those who saw Foster's marathon would agree it was the best of them.[38] Foster was the third of seven brothers, all of whom were educated at Malvern College and played first-class cricket for Worcestershire. Talk about a dynasty. When Tip stepped out as England captain against South Africa in July 1907, he became the only man to have captained England at both football and cricket. His was a life studded with brilliant and pioneering achievements, but medical science could not keep pace, and a matter of weeks before the start of the First World War, he succumbed to diabetes.

England won the 1902/3 Test series and retained the Ashes. One player emerging during the series who had an immediate impact on the 1905 series in England was Bernard Bosanquet. At Lord's in 1900 a newly invented delivery that looked like a leg spinner but behaved like an off spinner claimed its first victim. Leicestershire's Samuel Coe was stumped off a delivery that bounced four times. It was clearly a work in progress but encouraging enough to merit some further work. The googly was born. Bosanquet's 6 for 51 facilitated England's win at Sydney in 1903/4 and at Trent Bridge in 1905, his 8 for 107 enabled another emphatic win. General inaccuracy and outside interests meant that it was his last great day in the cricketing sun. He gained Oxford half-blues for hammer-throwing and billiards, fathered colourful 1970s newsreader Reggie and was the first player to score two centuries and take ten wickets in a match.

England's trip to Australia in 1907/8 never recovered from the early loss of captain Arthur Jones, who missed the first three Tests through illness. His whole cricket career was similarly blighted. *Wisden* effused about his off-side play and added that 'a better all-round fieldsman has never been seen.'[39] He also enjoyed bright moments in rugby union as both a player and referee, but, suffering from consumption (tuberculosis), he found himself in a sanatorium. He was given up as 'incurable', explains *Wisden*, and 'the end came as a release from his sufferings.'[40] Two England captains were gone within seven months in 1914, neither death anything to do with war.

In addition to Trumper, England's Jack Hobbs and Australia's Warwick Armstrong, there was another standout contributor in the 1907 series convincingly won by Australia. Surrey's George Gunn was a witty larrikin but brilliant with a bat, and cunning too. Not originally selected to tour, he just happened to be in Australia 'for his health' and was picked ahead of Jack Hobbs for the first Test. It was a 'monstrous decision', concluded Batchelor, since no batsman in the world should have been picked before Hobbs at the time.[41] Gunn repaid the selectors with a hundred in two and a half hours and a 'faultless' batting display.[42] He followed 74 in the second innings with another century in the final Test.

It was all carried off with a nonchalance others wished they had, but only Gunn did. In a thirty-year career, the crease was merely Gunn's stage for mischief and contrariness. He was an 'audacious batting genius' and a 'quizzically humorous' but 'moody character'.[43] He patted back bad balls and smashed good ones just because he could. Once he lectured Neville Cardus about how spectators needed to be entertained, then took four hours over 48, hugely enjoying his own joke. He played his last match in England colours in his 51st year and made 85. In his seventies he used a walking stick in the nets to show the youngsters how to bat, maintaining that they paid 'too much attention to the wicket – and the bowling'.[44]

By the time of the The Oval Test in 1909, England had lost the Ashes, but could still salvage a 2–2 series draw. Then as now, The Oval wicket was hard and flat. The sun was out, but England's pre-match preparation was anything but plain sailing. Having selected thirteen players, two had to be discarded, but that was about as much as anyone agreed on. With a fast wicket and a win required, it was time for clear plans to match clear skies, but that was wishful thinking.

The first discard was Kent spinner Colin Blythe. He had taken eleven wickets in the first Test – England's sole victory of the summer. Omitting him was eccentric enough, but another selection decision raised even more eyebrows. According to *Wisden*, Claude Buckenham was among the 'deadliest' pace bowlers available to England.[45] But Buckenham was sent back to Essex – so big a mistake, reported *Wisden*, 'that it is difficult to find words' to describe it.[46] Upon realizing that England had no fast bowler, there was general astonishment,[47] which was multiplied when skipper Archie MacLaren inexplicably gave the new ball to Douglas Carr, a 37-year-old googly bowler with a few weeks' first-class experience at Kent. Jaws had never dropped lower. The ragtag and bobtail attack relied on Sydney Barnes and Wilfred Rhodes, who could at least boast 157 Test wickets between them. The other five bowlers used by England in the match collectively boasted only two.

If Archie MacLaren thought the furore over Carr's selection was the entirety of his nightmare, he was wrong. For the fifth time in succession, he lost the toss. Then he juggled his bowlers with a strategy that appeared to come from the bottom of an empty teacup. Carr, for example, was flogged so hard that his seven wickets in the match cost 282. Worse still, the skipper himself dropped Australian Warren Bardsley en route to a first-innings century and was then leg before for fifteen to a full toss. Left-hander Bardsley's innings showed his prowess with shots to all parts of the ground, and he followed it with a second innings of 130. A 'solemn, non-smoking, teetotal vegetarian' dedicated to refining his technique, Bardsley went about his business without histrionics.[48] He enjoyed making runs against the old enemy, with five of his six Test centuries made in England. At the time *Wisden* called him 'the most dangerous batsman in the world'.[49]

It was the first time that the tall Frank Woolley was seen in England colours, but his debut was undistinguished in that he made eight in his only innings. That he made any runs at all is a credit to him. At the time bowlers were permitted to send down 'trial' balls without limit, and the protocol was that these were kept to a minimum.[50] But, exploiting this loophole, Warwick Armstrong stretched the notion to its elastic limit, reportedly keeping the nervous debutant waiting for nineteen minutes.[51]

England were batted out of the match soberly and sensibly by Bardsley, and Australia retained the Ashes. This was despite a gritty century by Lancashire all-rounder Jack Sharp, who exemplified the dual coders of the Golden Age, when simultaneous careers in football and cricket were perfectly conceivable. Few, though, played at the highest level like Sharp; he was capped twice by England as a rapid right-winger and thrice as a robust cricketing all-rounder in the 1909 series. He had already made 61 in the Leeds Test, though he didn't stand out at Manchester. At The Oval, he bowled 28 perfectly respectable overs for 101 and took three wickets, then hit his marvellous hundred in less than three hours. In later life he ran a successful sporting goods shop and served as director for many years at Everton. That he was

Australian Test team, 1909/10: Warren Bardsley (sitting on floor, extreme left) and Warwick Armstrong (middle row, centre).

discarded by England after scoring a fine hundred indicates a plethora of available talent, some fickle selectors, or perhaps both.

Often the venue for the final Test of the series, The Oval is the traditional stage for ends, goodbyes and denouements. In the concluding Test of 1909, Australians Bert Hopkins, Frank Laver and Monty Noble may not have known that this was their last hurrah. For England, it was time up for Carr, Sharp, Hutchings, Dick Lilley and the hapless MacLaren, who was not naturally sanguine at the best of times. It was the last Test in England for Victor Trumper, his powers now on the wane despite a classy first innings of 73. More widely, in England it was almost the end of Edwardian cricket. While there were dilettantes and show ponies with straw boaters and a more rakish approach to cricket and life in general, there was also grit and willpower. These were qualities that cricketers, and everyone else, soon needed.

# 6

# GOOD FOR NOTHING
# AND NOBODY
*The First World War*

As the last puff of Edwardian cricket was exhaled, South Africa joined England and Australia as a cricketing super-nation. First-class cricket started there around the time that Monty Bowden, Aubrey Smith and their colleagues made the trip in 1888/9 and was maturing by the time England toured in 1909/10. Two eminent players emerged during the series, one from each country. Reigning supreme for the hosts was George Aubrey Faulkner. From Port Elizabeth, he didn't fail in any of the five Tests, and 545 runs at an average of 60 and 29 wickets at an average 21 amounted to the 'greatest all-round contribution to a Test rubber'.[1]

If the mark of a great all-round cricketer is that they might be selected as either batsman or bowler, then most certainly Faulkner was one. A year after securing the series win against England, he did much the same thing in Australia, plundering 1,534 runs at an average of 59, and capturing 49 wickets at 25.59 across the tour. Almost a century later, this aggregate of runs – in just fourteen first-class matches – had been bettered only twice by players visiting Australia.[2] No wonder Aussie grandee Clem Hill judged Faulkner to be the most effective batsman to ever visit the country.[3] Ian Peebles, an England spinner of the late 1920s, concluded that Faulkner was one of the 'six greatest all-rounders the game has yet seen'.[4] It seems that the South African had everything.[5]

In his wonderful *Spinner's Yarn*, Peebles reserves a whole chapter to reminisce about his old coach and describes the cricket school Faulkner had set up in west London. There was no natural illumination, and the overhead lighting was very murky. Since the fuse box was directly above the bowler, lofted straight drives would regularly hit it, plunging everything into darkness. The changing rooms and office were plain and confined, but ingenuity triumphed, and many benefited from the South African's shrewd coaching and advice.[6] Not that it brought him much good fortune or happiness. The school wasn't lucrative and a miserable first marriage compounded Faulkner's off-field problems.

Peebles was employed by Faulkner as a secretary. They fell out but were reunited when one day Peebles urged his driver to stop after he noticed his old coach in a bus queue. It seems unlikely that others standing with them realized that the rather down-beat figure was at one time the best all-rounder in world cricket. As the 1930 season drew to an autumnal close, the melancholy that had plagued Faulkner got the better of him. He wrote a note explaining, 'I'm off to another world, via the bat room,' and gassed himself. When Peebles visited the coach's young widow, she told him that despite having lost interest in just about everything else, each morning Faulkner had looked in the newspaper to see how many wickets Peebles had taken the day before. 'I was keenly aware of what I owed him,' reflected Peebles poignantly.[7]

The other great cricketer emerging from those Tests in South Africa was Jack Hobbs. In the 1909/10 series, his aggregate was only six runs fewer than Faulkner's, but this is only one of a number of astonishing statistics attributed to the Surrey man. In an era of gargantuan run-makers, he made the most. Wilfred Rhodes – who never wasted a compliment – attested that where and when Hobbs batted seemed irrelevant: 'he got 'em on good 'uns, he got 'em on bad 'uns . . . he got 'em all over t'world.'[8] Nobody makes 61,760 runs at an average of over 50, including 199 centuries, without the full range of strokes, and the prospect of facing Hobbs at The Oval was like 'bowling to God on con-crete'.[9] He was not only the greatest batsman of his time, but the greatest influence, as most tried to copy his correctness and ability to entertain.[10] When the ball came off anything than the middle of Hobbs's bat, it was, wrote Neville Cardus, a 'distur-bance of cosmic orderliness'.[11]

Denzil Batchelor suggests that before the First World War, Hobbs could annihilate bowlers through 'sheer youthful exuber-ance'.[12] Post-war, more cautiously acquiring perfection, he scored almost a hundred centuries after the age of forty, playing as if 'there had never been a Kaiser'.[13] Hobbs's biographer, civil-servant-cum-cricket-biographer Ronald Mason, once described his own batting to Hobbs and reflected with embarrassment that it was like telling Shakespeare 'about the one-act playlet I had just writ-ten for the tennis club social'.[14] To John Arlott, Hobbs was 'the Master'. 'He batted perfectly because he was the perfect batsman,' but he was also 'happy, wise, modest, kind' and 'the best loved of all cricketers'.[15]

Of the several great batting partnerships throughout Hobbs's career, his affiliation with Yorkshire's Herbert Sutcliffe was the show-stopper. Between them, they produced over 111,000 runs and exactly 350 first-class centuries. Not a misprint: 350. Separately they were remorseless, unflinching and as safe as the Bank of England. Together, they were more difficult to remove than Japanese knotweed. They shared 31 Test centuries and fifteen century stands in 38 Test innings and their average partnership was 87.81. Future Aussie Prime Minister Sir Robert Menzies took his wife to the Lord's Test in 1926. When she left at tea, the pair had been batting all day and eventually put on 182 for the first wicket. She remarked that she was familiar with their work, as the only other time she'd watched a Test match in Melbourne the year before, they'd put on 283.[16] Arlott started 'the Master's

Club', which began meeting in 1953 as near to Hobbs's birthday (16 December) as possible. There were no speeches and only one toast, to Hobbs himself.

If Hobbs was a brilliant batsman but a gentle soul, Sydney Barnes was a brilliant bowler and undoubtedly one of the grumpiest men ever to play cricket. Giving him some latitude, perhaps it was less about grumpiness and more about self-confidence. He had, however, plenty to be confident about since the smart money says that he was – and is – the most devastating bowler of all time. The statistics bear it out: when England bowler James Anderson became only the seventh England bowler and the first England player in 38 years to pass 900 points in the ICC Test Player Rankings in August 2018, it was pointed out that sitting at the top of the list with 932 points was Sydney Barnes.[17] Evidently, nobody will shift him any time soon. Of the five men who have a better Test bowling average than his 16.43, none is within 77 of his 189 Test wickets and none played within six of his 27 Tests. His armoury consisted of a fast ball, a well-disguised slower one

Jack Hobbs (left) and Herbert Sutcliffe, mid-1920s.

and a yorker.[18] He was able to move the ball both ways in the air, and could bowl off spinners, leg spinners and googlies.[19] He was not just one bowler, but a whole attack.

Yet his preference was to play league and minor counties cricket. Indeed, he remains the only major player selected by England based on achievements largely outside first-class cricket. Barnes played in the leagues between 1895 and 1938, and John Arlott concluded that as a consequence he was the least visible great cricketer.[20] In all types of cricket, estimates Arlott, Barnes took over 6,300 wickets at around nine runs each. Staggering, and still not accounting for all the times, 'even against the greatest batsmen and on good wickets', that he beat both bat and stumps.[21]

He was peerless in Tests between 1910 and 1914. The weather claimed an underwhelming experimental triangular tournament involving Australia, South Africa and England in 1912, but Barnes's 39 wickets meant that some of the 'contests' were anything but. In his last ten Test matches for England, he took 88 wickets for 940 runs, and one of those was ruined by rain, meaning that he didn't bowl at all. Essentially, in every match not truncated by rain, he took ten wickets. In 1952 Denzil Batchelor mused whether we will ever see such bowling again.[22] Perhaps the answer is 'Not yet.'

Barnes, though, was as grouchy as he was brilliant, emitting 'a chill wind of antagonism' even on sunny days.[23] Described by C.L.R. James as looking like a man 'who has seen as much of the world as he wants to', one imagines that Barnes didn't think much of the bit of it he saw.[24] He was continually at odds with cricket's administrators, who didn't like him but knew he was a box-office draw. For Barnes, compromise was 'poison' and 'obedience' equalled 'submission'.[25] His career was characterized by pay disputes and tussles with the establishment, who eventually came to view him as 'an impossible bugger' who ultimately wasn't worth the trouble.[26] After taking 49 wickets in the first four Tests against South

Africa in 1913/14, the commercially aware bowler refused to turn out for the final Test because MCC had reneged on a promise to pay his wife's hotel bill. 'He downed tools to see how they managed without him,' and when England won anyway, Barnes was deemed to have gone too far.[27] He was discarded at international level despite still being the best available bowler by a country mile.

David Frith famously found Barnes anything but a soft touch, even as a nonagenarian. This was no old-timer pleased to spin yarns and drink tea, and Frith concluded that his visit had greatly inconvenienced the old boy's schedule. He was, after all, still working, producing immaculate council documents in copperplate handwriting. He refused to sign a book with Frith's ballpoint pen, concluding, 'I'm not going into the office for you just to get my pen.'[28] The curmudgeon finally thawed a little, but the experience was 'a vivid taste of what it must have been like to be an opposing batsman'.[29]

While some in the post-Edwardian era had sunlight shining on them constantly, others had only a fleeting relationship with it. Like Ted Alletson, for example. The word 'journeyman' might have been invented for him. Eight unspectacular years for Nottinghamshire before the First World War yielded only 3,217 runs and 33 wickets. Perhaps 'journeyman' might even be gilding the lily. However, the name of this usually vigilant lower-order blocker is as indelible in cricket's history as Fry, Ranji, Barnes or Hobbs. While their legends were built over years and decades, his was based on the events of a single afternoon at Hove in May 1911. Completely confounding his reputation to that point, and long before the batting savagery of Twenty20, Alletson played what might still be the most destructive innings in cricket history.

Notts held a second innings lead of just nine runs with seven wickets down and defeat was almost inevitable. Pre-lunch, having gone in at number 9, Alletson made a brisk 47; during the break,

Sydney Barnes, *c.* 1965.

he asked skipper Arthur Jones for guidance. The response was a rather non-committal: 'I don't think it matters what you do now, Ted.' Deciding to be as nihilistic as his captain had been fatalistic, Alletson clearly fancied his chances against slow bowler E. H. Killick, and in cricketing terms went absolutely berserk, making 142 runs in forty minutes.[30] Goodness knows what he had for lunch. He hit 34 in one over off Killick, which remained a world record for 57 years. Five balls sailed out of the ground never to be seen again, another broke a pavilion clock, and yet another became embedded in a wooden stand. He scored 189 in ninety minutes with 23 fours and eight sixes. In one spell of five overs (three from the hapless Killick), he plundered 97 of the 100 runs scored. The innings might have been even shorter had time not been spent replacing the five lost balls.[31]

On the basis of one afternoon of mayhem, Alletson appeared in the Test Trial a week or two later. He did nothing of note and was never invited to appear in one again.[32] Indeed, he never made another century. The sun went behind a cloud soon after it appeared and Alletson followed his war service with a life down the pit. His 2 lb 3 oz (1 kg) bat – a feather in today's terms – fetched £15,000 at auction in 2003. In the greatest of all ironies, when The Innings public house commemorating Alletson's afternoon was officially opened in Worksop in 1975, the ceremony was officiated by Geoffrey Boycott, who once took six hours in a Test match over 106 not out.[33] If Alletson had been able to keep it going for that long, he'd have made 756.

Like many others, Alletson's cricket career was ended by war. When Archduke Franz Ferdinand was assassinated in Sarajevo in June 1914, the repercussions were swift. On the eve of the conflict – literally – there was the usual stuff happening at The Oval, where Hobbs made 226. The Roses match was interrupted at Old Trafford as the skippers of both sides – A. N. 'Monkey' Hornby of Lancashire and Sir Archibald White of Yorkshire – were told that they were required for an international conflict that put their local cricketing skirmish into perspective. When war was declared, The Oval was requisitioned by the Army, and as players from all counties joined up to serve, crowds unsurprisingly lost enthusiasm for something as seemingly petty as sport. Indeed, a letter in *The Sportsman* from an ailing W. G. Grace emphasized the inappropriateness of 'able-bodied men' playing cricket while others fought.[34] The season was abandoned, and Surrey were declared champions despite their final two county matches being cancelled.

Among those never to return from war was Yorkshire's combative all-rounder Major Booth. A man with such a name was inevitably set for military service, and although he made Second Lieutenant, he was never promoted to the level of his quirky forename. Having been named one of *Wisden*'s Cricketers of the Year in 1914, he had broken into the England team and was reaching his peak when everything stopped for war. *Wisden* described him as handsome and popular both on the field and off it.[35] He, and many local peers, joined up for military service as part of a regionalized recruitment drive, meaning that those you worked, drank and played cricket with would serve alongside you at the front. Booth and his friends were part of the 15th Battalion (1st Leeds), the Prince of Wales's Own (West Yorkshire Regiment), known as the 'Leeds Pals'.

Cricket was not the only realm stratified by class. On the eve of the Battle of the Somme, Booth cast aside the protocol that officers should not consort with the lower ranks and met up with Yorkshire teammates Arthur Dolphin and Roy Kilner.[36] In the advance on 1 July 1916 Booth was soon mortally wounded. Finding shelter in a shell crater, he was found by Private Abe Waddington, who was himself to become a Yorkshire cricketer of note representing England on two occasions. Waddington nursed Booth until he died, 'as tenderly', writes Mike Atherton, 'as the horrific conditions would allow'.[37] His body was only identified, nine months later, by his MCC cigarette case.[38] One of the first great cricketers from the town of Pudsey, he was followed by Herbert Sutcliffe, Sir Leonard Hutton, Raymond Illingworth and Matthew Hoggard.

Another to perish in 1916 was Kent's batting stylist Kenneth Hutchings. A. A. Thomson admitted to being something of a grim Northerner, but said that if he would have ever been forced to choose a 'last fragment of cricket' he would have opted for 'a glimpse of K. L. Hutchings cover-driving under a summer heaven'.[39] Kent's grief was amplified just over a year later when left-arm spinner Colin 'Charlie' Blythe was killed near Passchendaele. Deptford-born Blythe had started his career with a wicket with his first ball in 1899. He was slight, pale and too 'simple-looking' for his opponents to imagine that he could possess any 'guile'.[40] His 'mincing run' looked as if he had 'miscalculated the distance to the bowling crease and [was] afraid of over-stepping it'.[41] Indeed, it seemed as though Blythe was 'too timid' to bowl at all.[42] But 2,503 wickets in a fifteen-year career say different, and the full measure of his skill lies in their cost. Sri Lankan legend Muttiah Muralitharan bagged his wickets at just under twenty while Shane Warne's cost over 26 apiece. Blythe took exactly one hundred wickets for England in only nineteen Tests at less than seventeen each. If Wilfred Rhodes had a masculine artfulness, Blythe was 'all nervous sensibility' and comparatively effete.[43] A talented violinist and an epileptic, he was well-loved, his 'happy-go-lucky attitude and dialect' helping him to remain magnanimous, even to batsmen. 'Oh Mr Spooner, I'd give all my bowling to bat like that,' he once remarked to the Lancastrian batsman as the ball sailed away for six.[44]

Blythe is immortalized in *Kent v Lancashire at Canterbury*, which depicts a scene from a county match played in 1906. The painting celebrates Kent's championship title with the Canterbury pavilion in the background. Surrounded by an intensely packed and expectant close field, Blythe is captured just before delivering the ball to Johnny Tyldesley. Ironically for Blythe, 1906 was comparatively unsuccessful for Kent, despite 111 wickets at 19.90, but it was decided that in recognition of his career contribution, he should be the central figure in the commissioned work.[45] The painting was purchased for £680,000 by the Andrew Brownsword Art Foundation almost exactly a hundred years after its completion and then promptly loaned to Lord's, where it is still enjoyed as 'possibly the most evocative vignette of cricket's Golden Age'.[46]

Blythe knew his business on a cricket field. Against Northampton in 1907, he took 17 for 48. Only Jim Laker has bettered that since the start of the twentieth century, but not even he managed to match Blythe by taking them all in a single day. A sergeant with the King's Own Yorkshire Light Infantry, and having just finished a game in London, Blythe was visualized by Robert Winder 'hoisting his pack high on his shoulders' and waiting on the platform at Victoria, 'the smell of Lord's turf still in his nostrils'.[47] Weeks later, he was dead, hit by part of a shell that Neville Cardus described as having been made by somebody 'that had never known cricket' and directed by eyes 'that had never seen a Kent field'.[48] A metal splinter pierced Blythe's heart, passing through the wallet in his breast pocket and perfectly erasing his wife's face in the snapshot he kept within it. The 'excruciating relic' was duly consigned to Canterbury's pavilion museum.[49]

*Wisden*'s 1917 list of lost cricketers ran to 107 pages; 'name after name, man after man, agony after agony'.[50] Other countries lost stars besides England: South Africa lost Gordon White and Reggie Schwartz, half of the famous quartet of famous googly bowlers. A Deputy Assistant Quartermaster General, Schwartz was wounded twice during the conflict and was awarded the Military Cross. In a twist of irony too cruel to imagine, he died of influenza one week after fighting ceased. And not even the hardest heart could fail to be moved by the story of New South Welshman Norman Callaway. After an impressive start in grade cricket, he was selected to play against Queensland at the Sydney Cricket Ground (SCG) in February 1915. Arriving at the crease with his team precariously positioned at 17 for 3 in reply to Queensland's 137, he set about the bowling like a child toying with a cat. At the close of day one, he had made 125 not out, and the next, despite being dropped four times, he was finally dismissed for 207. The *Sydney Morning Herald* predicted great things, 'all going well with him'.[51] But in May 1917 he was killed in action in France, a career stalled for perpetuity on one match, one innings, 207 runs, average 207.00.

In Palestine the same year, Australian fast bowler Albert 'Tibby' Cotter (89 wickets in 21 Tests) also perished. Cotter bowled so quickly that he once hit W. G. Grace in the chest and the old boy demanded he be removed from the attack. In a break during the conflict, Cotter tossed away a ball of mud, with the words 'That's my last bowl . . . something's going to happen.'[52] He was shot dead shortly afterwards. There were suggestions that the details were suppressed because he had been killed by 'a surrendered Turk who had not been checked for weapons'.[53]

Of the generation of cricketers who fell in the Great War, many were more distinguished than Percy Jeeves. By the time he was killed in France in 1916, however, he had shown some promising form in a couple of seasons for Warwickshire and was good enough for seasoned observers such as Plum Warner to predict international honours at some future stage. Though his career was short, his name lives on in perpetuity: P. G. Wodehouse's spirited factotum is named after the gallant all-rounder. But while the real Jeeves 'may never have attempted to dissuade friends from wearing lilac spats or played hide-and-seek with a silver cow creamer', he was just as 'inimitable as the literary creation for which he served as unknowing muse'.[54]

War ended the most heroic and romantic of cricketing ages. When cricket returned in 1919 it had lost some innocent charm. The Kaiser had that to answer for, too.

7

# GOVERNANCE, GROUNDS, GRANDEES, BOOKS AND BENEFACTORS

*Three Hundred Years of Organization and Altruism*

Beyond the waste of war, but before the charting of cricket's recovery, there is another narrative diversion to consider – the wider history of administrative matters. It can only be more entertaining than it sounds. There are the laws to consider, the organization that administers them, the people who have served and the home they inhabit. The cricketing versions of the Ten Commandments, Mecca and Parliament, their influence remains undeniable.

Articles of Agreement for a particular match in 1727 were discovered comparatively recently at Goodwood House in West Sussex.[1] Such was gambling's grip on cricket, and with duelling still de rigueur, without some formal terms of reference, arguments might easily have been settled by gunshot. A more generally applicable set of rules seemed a better idea, and in 1744 a group associated with London's Artillery Ground drew them up. They were revised a dozen or so years later by several clubs, notably the Star and Garter in Pall Mall, which helped further revise them in 1774.[2] Note that cricket does not have 'rules', but 'laws', meaning that the game retains a 'formal gentlemanly Victorian nature'.[3] Cricket – most specifically keeping score – appealed to those who recognized the importance of accountancy and auditing, and the laws further enhanced notions of unification and comparison.

Laws must have a custodian to keep them current. This function is performed by Marylebone Cricket Club, a private members'

7

club formed in 1787 and based at Lord's in London. It seems strange that such a club should administer the laws of cricket across the world, especially since the game's 'centre of gravity' has long since relocated.[4] But if the International Cricket Council (ICC) runs the game internationally, and the England and Wales Cricket Board (ECB) locally, MCC maintains a notional place at cricket's top table. Its power has waned, however: although it is by far the 'most active cricket club in the world', and still administers the laws and turns out representative sides worldwide.[5] But 'that's about it.'[6]

One of MCC's key functions in the early part of the twenty-first century is to safeguard cricket's 'spirit' (however that's interpreted) and to promote its growth. Notwithstanding such aims, the overarching narratives about MCC are dominated by the exclusive nature of its membership, particularly the thirty-year waiting list.[7] Some members elected in 2018 first expressed an interest in joining before England's World Cup-winning captain Eoin Morgan started school. Anyone applying for membership could serve a sentence for murder and establish a sparkling new career before being admitted. Not that the club would want them, and unsavoury incidents, including the ejection of a member for verbal abuse, are unlikely to see its discerning standards relaxed.[8] In 2020 a man who used a fake membership was fined £10,000 and given a suspended prison sentence.[9] The odd queue-jump is occasionally sanctioned, but to be fair, Theresa May was prime minister when she was fast-tracked.[10]

Given that it has around 18,000 full members and 5,000 associate members with reduced rights, MCC assumes and hopes that all of them will not arrive together. It strictly enforces a dress code and while the famous red-and-yellow tie is not obligatory, for men proper trousers, a decent jacket and some other tie certainly are. Bare flesh, sports clothing and denim would undoubtedly horrify elderly members who are 'magnificently wizened old gents with wispy whiskers, egg-and-bacon ties and trousers straight out of the Boer War surplus catalogue'.[11]

With its rules occasionally appearing at odds with the twenty-first century, sometimes and often unfairly, MCC is a soft target for modernizers. Other times they might have reasonable points and sensible improvements to suggest, but many might be the result of growing weary of languishing on a waiting list. Try to find a member who will not defend MCC to the hilt. Against a contemporary cricket landscape of change, its anchoring to the past is a comforting reminder that some things don't require fixing. In any case, members would argue, the club is updating itself and these things often take a little time.

While cricket power resides in Dubai with the ICC, for many, London NW8 will always be the spiritual epicentre. Aside from its commercial importance, its emotional and cultural value is totemic. It certainly got the juices flowing for R. C. Robertson-Glasgow. Lord's in its pomp, he suggested, was all about 'top-hats, barouches, hampers, blazers in hue, ladies in the mode, chicken in aspic, strawberries in cream, and banners in the air'.[12]

The club's own explanation for establishing such a magnificent edifice is that as London grew, so did the 'nobility's impatience' with crowds.[13] Pursuing 'exclusivity', they approached a local cricketer – Thomas Lord – and asked him to establish a proper home for the game.[14] The current ground at St John's Wood was acquired in 1814 and when the first groundsman was appointed in 1864, pitch preparation was professionalized, the previous method of grass-cutting having involved a flock of sheep.[15]

After what sounds like a lively Extraordinary General Meeting in 1876, Middlesex County Cricket Club adopted Lord's as its home, and enjoyed their first few years rent-free. Shortly after they began to pay, the pavilion was demolished. Thomas Verity was engaged to design a new one on the basis of his work developing the Royal Albert Hall and Piccadilly Circus. Initially, Verity had planned a stone structure but was hampered by the availability of qualified masons. The compromise, opened in 1890, was the now familiar and universally loved 'brick and terracotta edifice'.[16] For a while, the new structure was known as 'the Gin Palace' since its construction was enabled by financial support from William Nicholson, a sometime cricketer, politician, distiller and father of fourteen.[17] Nicholson's support has long-lasting recognition: his company colours were red and yellow, or, at a push, 'bacon and egg'.

The first Lord's Test match was played in 1884, when England beat Australia by an innings and five runs. Besides now being home to Middlesex, MCC and the spirit of cricket, in 2013 it hosted a steak sandwich costing £20. When the ultimate feat of master batsmanship is a century before lunch, it is little wonder that those with ephemeral relationships with cricket might claim that it seems entirely arranged around eating. But at Lord's the game's relationship with food can be observed on more than one level.

MCC, for example, loves a good supper. All elements of the game are celebrated by pie and mash, curry and other more formal dinners. For Lord's spectators, the Nursery End food village offers variety, but at a price. On the day celebrity chef Jamie Oliver first introduced his £20 sandwich, only eleven punters were tempted, and former England captain Michael Vaughan suggested that he probably wouldn't have much luck at Headingley either, since Northerners preferred pies and peas.[18]

For many years, though, food at Lord's centred around Nancy Doyle. As a girl, she learned cookery from the nuns in Mullingar, fifty miles west of Dublin. Described in her *Wisden* obituary as 'small yet volcanic', she began her Lord's career in 1961 as a waitress, but eventually became catering manager.[19] Once, so concerned

was Middlesex captain Mike Brearley that his team were being
blunted by the sumptuousness of their feasting that he had a quiet
word with Nancy, hoping to rein things in. The most cerebral
captain of his generation was sent packing with the suggestion
that 'You worry about the \*\*\*\*\*\*\* cricket Michael, and I'll worry
about the \*\*\*\*\*\*\* food.'[20]

If contemporary cricket lunches undoubtedly involve players
removing the skin from their chicken, when Nancy Doyle was in
charge, there was no such calorific restraint.[21] The typical spread
was steak and kidney pie, chips and vegetables, apple pie, ice
cream and cheese. Carb loading continued at tea with doorstep
sandwiches and cake. The players absolutely loved her and she
them. The only mistake she ever made was 'when she dropped hot
apple pie and custard over Wilf Slack's lap during a Middlesex
Championship match'.[22] The genial Slack told her not to worry,
changed his trousers and made a double century. Curries, she
confessed, were not her strong point, and when England hosted
India, Pakistan or Sri Lanka she called in her daughter to help.
Awarded an honorary MBE in 1994, over thirty years she didn't
pick up anything more than cricket's absolute basics.[23]

Besides enjoying lunch, visitors to Lord's often visit the
museum. Apart from the Ashes urn, other priceless relics include
Donald Bradman's boots, demonstrating that his impossibly big
average was achieved with incredibly tiny feet. W. G.'s bat is
also there, wooden confirmation that equipment technology has
evolved considerably. Among the more offbeat artefacts is a dead
sparrow mounted on the ball that killed it. The fatal blow was
struck when Jahangir Khan was bowling during a match between
MCC and Cambridge University in 1936. In death the hapless bird
has acquired fame impossible in life. However, in terms of sheer
stomach-churning fascination, Denis Compton's kneecap takes
the biscuit. At the time it was giving him the most trouble, the

'daily media concern about Compton's knee far outstripped the attention being given to the Korean war'.[24]

There are those, however, who are not always in full accordance with the rules, traditions and ceremonial aspects associated with cricket's home. In 1987, for example, the great (and, to be fair, rather distinctive) Indian batsman Sunil Gavaskar clashed with stewards when they wouldn't let him re-enter the ground. Having nipped out to the team coach to fetch his blazer midway through MCC's match against the Rest of the World, quite reasonably he had expected to be readmitted. He felt sufficiently slighted to reject an honorary MCC membership three years later. If Lord's was to be considered the home of cricket, he fumed, 'then they should have people at the gate who can at least recognise the current Test players and the ones playing in the match'.[25] Ouch. Others have become preoccupied by members' seating: in 2016 member John Fingleton described the old benches as 'ergonomically, a disaster'.[26] Another member suggested that those deciding on bench specifications should be forced to sit on these 'instruments of torture' to enlighten the decision-making.[27]

Such gripes, however, are nothing compared to the strife caused by plans to redevelop the ground. To maintain Lord's position as a virtually automatic venue for Tests, finals and major matches, MCC has been faced with a choice. On one side of the argument are those who feel that the ground can be redeveloped using funds raised by selling off land. On the other side are those wanting to retain the whole estate and pay for new stands and facilities through membership revenue and autonomous funding. In 2017, members voted to redevelop the ground without selling anything off, and the result was that, since nobody else resides within it, MCC remains in sole charge.[28] During the wider debate on the issue, one even more radical idea was suggested – that the club should build a new stadium after 'demolishing the most famous cricket ground in the world'.[29] The suggestion was made by an Australian – the governor of Victoria. The likelihood of members agreeing was said to be zero, but perhaps even that seems a touch high.[30]

But what of those who have guided the club since inception? Of course, many of those running the game do it just for love, but even when acting in the best interests of the game, administrators have been formidable and uncompromising. One such titan was the 4th Baron Harris. With the notable exception of W. G. Grace, writes Bill Frindall, His Lordship was 'the most influential and devoted figure in the universal development of cricket'.[31] Less charitably, he was a great 'tartar' who ruled Kent and MCC with 'a rod of iron'.[32] Born in Trinidad, where his father was governor, Harris followed the classic route from Eton to Oxford and played for Kent for forty years. On the field, in four Tests as England captain, one fifty in six innings wasn't up to much, but you wouldn't have wanted to say it to his face. All that, however, is lost under the weight of his wide-ranging influence.

But controversy was never far away. In Sydney in 1878/9, as England captain, he engaged an umpire to travel with the team as they toured Australia, but the hapless official made some howlers in the match against New South Wales.[33] When home skipper Dave Gregory insisted that Harris dismiss the umpire after one mistake too many, the captains argued and thousands of spectators ran towards the middle of the field. For thirty minutes Harris was surrounded by a 'howling mob' before eventually being saved by a teammate.[34] 'They are capital winners out here,' remarked Lord Harris, but 'I cannot apply the same adjective to them as losers.'[35] How the Aussies must have loved him. After cricket, His Lordship held a range of top political positions, including a stint as governor of Bombay. In post, he was castigated for neglecting the city and was thought to be more interested in playing and promoting cricket than doing his day job.[36]

England Test team, 1884: Lord Harris (middle row, second from left),
next to W. G. Grace.

As an administrator he waged a dogmatic campaign against throwing, once insisting on the cancellation of a Kent fixture against Lancashire when his northern opponents picked a bowler with a dubious action. While some saw controversy in his pugnacious approach, others only saw 'sound judgement' and 'unimpeachable fairness', and while his views were strong, 'he never tried to impose them upon a meeting.'[37] Opinions of Harris appeared to vary, but his mark on the game is indelible. The Harris Garden at Lord's commemorates him, as does, more bizarrely, one of the gargoyles decorating the pavilion.

The next great cricketing grandee was Sir Pelham 'Plum' Warner. Known as 'the grand old man of cricket', his *Wisden* obituary notes that he was born in the Caribbean to an older father, the Attorney General of Trinidad. His dad was born just before the Battle of Trafalgar, meaning that between them, father and son 'saw warships develop from the three deckers of Nelson's time to the present-day atomic submarine'.[38] Cricket writer John Woodcock turned 93 in 2019 and could make a similar boast, his grandfather having been born before the Battle of Waterloo.[39]

Warner had a perfectly reasonable first-class career, but despite a Test century on debut for England, his record at the highest level was modest. *Wisden* notes that ill health often held him back, although he had a happy life and 'received virtually every honour the game has to offer, on and off the field'.[40] In 1911/12 he was the official captain of England's tour to Australia, which started badly and got worse. He was robbed of his travel documentation on his way to Tilbury Docks, then fell ill in Australia and was indisposed for the whole tour.

Warner's 'boyishly radiant nature' was tested to its limit when, as MCC tour manager, he presided over the Bodyline controversy.[41] Though he tried to manage the furore, he was unsuccessful. Nonetheless, the debacle did not damage him unduly. He was editor of *The Cricketer* from its inception in 1921 and was knighted in 1937. When he died in 1963 he had given 59 years of service to MCC as a member and an official.

After Warner, the ceremonial chalice passed to another Middlesex patrician, George Oswald Browning 'Gubby' Allen. Ironically for one who spent so much time in cricketing combat with England's traditional enemy, he was born in New South Wales and only left Australia at the age of six. Indeed, his Uncle Reggie played in a Test match against England in 1886/7. A fast bowler, he was also a sound, orthodox batsman and a very good close fielder. As John Arlott notes, he remained rather prone to injury, in later life needing six hip operations – 'three on each side'.[42]

Gubby Allen was a principled opponent of Jardine's leg theory strategy during the Bodyline tour in Australia in 1932/3 and was good enough to take 21 series wickets without it. That was near the start of his Test career, and perhaps he wouldn't have imagined that he might be skippering his country aged 45. 'Thoughtful but hard-pressed' as a captain, he struggled with the middle-aged

Pelham Warner,
*c.* 1895.

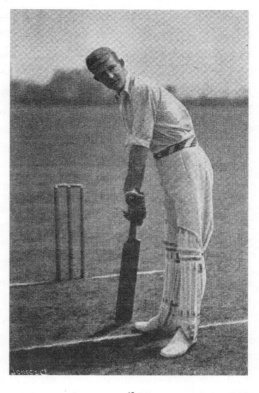

aches and pains that anyone might expect.[43] He was a reasonable
leader on the field, reflected Denzil Batchelor, but 'a grand cricketer'[44] who later become a hard-working and effective chairman
of selectors. Like Warner, he had his own nadir. As part of the
MCC establishment he was forced to handle the D'Oliveira affair
in 1968, but more of that later. Like others around him, he did
not emerge with his reputation unscathed.

Like Warner, Allen served in various roles for over fifty years.
He had his own chair in the committee room and, for much of
his life, lived in a house 'a wall's thickness' from Lord's with its
own private gate to the ground. Wielding power and influence,
he could be irascible. Perfectionists, noted Jim Swanton, are not

always easy to live with and Allen liked things done properly, 'whether in the committee room at Lord's or on the golf course, rewriting the MCC Coaching Manual, tending to his car or his roses, ordering his dinner, or even describing in close anatomical detail his latest strain, or his last hip operation'.[45] Middlesex bowler Simon Hughes remembers fielding near the boundary and noticing a Bentley nearby. The driver's window slid down and a disembodied but unmistakable voice barked, 'Hughes! Too many no-balls!'[46] Once Allen was apparently horrified to see an advertising board alongside the boundary. Pointed an accusing finger, he turned to those around him, asking, 'What on earth is that?'[47] The Indian Premier League would probably have killed him, poor chap.

Warner and Allen resided within cricket's innermost circle. They practically lived the same life; both were born overseas as colonial sons and both were educated at public school and Oxbridge. Both captained England, and both had unhappy first-hand experiences of Bodyline (Warner as co-manager and Allen as player). Both were administrators with sometimes difficult reigns; both were lifelong servants of MCC and cricketing knights with Lord's stands named after them. It was almost like a family lineage. Indeed, it was even rumoured that Allen was Warner's illegitimate son, but that was never proved.[48]

Not all administrators have lived quite so harmoniously. Victorian Peter McAlister, for example, made few friends when, as Australian chairman of selectors, he picked himself to tour England in 1909, compounding the outrage by making himself vice-captain. His primary motive was to monitor the players, who were increasingly disillusioned by his autocracy. Years of simmering tension between McAlister and Aussie Captain Clem Hill erupted in an almighty physical altercation when the selector called his skipper 'the worst captain in living memory'.[49] 'You've been asking for a punch all night,' noted Hill, giving plenty of warning ahead of what he did next.[50] The ensuing brawl lasted almost twenty minutes, which was commitment to the cause rarely witnessed outside of organized boxing.[51] Hill was stopped from sending his opponent headfirst through a third-storey window, which might have compromised his liberty, his captaincy and his place in the team. As it was, he kept all three, and in the process delighted those who believed that while administrators do the background stuff, the game, ultimately, is for the on-field talent. Try telling that to your groundsman the first weekend in April. Don't forget to duck.

But what good is all this history and detail if it is not recorded? Parliament has Hansard, cricket has *Wisden*. The famous almanack has served as the game's central repository of information since 1864, its first manifestation a 'plain, paper-bound booklet'.[52] With its 112 pages covered with a 'bland buff wrapper', it might just as easily have been 'a railway timetable or a stock prize gazette'.[53] And yet, the almanack is cricket's everlasting publication and functions as its 'bible, Mahabharata and superhero multiverse rolled into one'.[54]

In 1888 *Wisden* broke away from its single-minded statistical obsession, meaning that the almanack changed from a 'dry-as-dust' record of names and numbers and began to carry a 'literary cloak and cane'.[55] Its yellow cover is even recognized by people who think cricket is a noisy insect, and, the size of a house brick, it punches well above its weight. What it doesn't include in its 1,500 or so pages is not important. Besides a comprehensive record of scores embracing school and league cricket, it covers the game in the Vatican, Sierra Leone and anywhere a bat is waved with intent. Former England footballer Gary Lineker picked it as his book on *Desert Island Discs*, to sit on his sandy bookshelf alongside the works of Shakespeare and the Bible.

Alongside its reviews, records and retrospectives, *Wisden* obituaries are the definitive cricketing tributes and were developed by the great Victorian editor Sydney Pardon. When it was his turn for an obituary, the almanack wrote that while cricket was the big element within his life, he was also a student of 'drama', 'a devoted supporter of good music, and a keen follower of racing'.[56] Definitely a man you'd want sitting next to you in a pub quiz.

Quirks are explained, questions answered and quotes recorded. In the 2015 edition, on the very last of its 1,520 pages, it directs readers to examples of 'Batsman helped by bee', 'county batsman caught by banana' and 'seagull stops six'. The back story associated with 'manhunt stops play' is that a miscreant was caught after legging it from a dressing room with a stash of mobile phones.[57] Each year it selects five Cricketers of the Year. Picked by the editor, the choices are generally based on performances from the previous season. If it weren't so heavy, it might live in your top pocket.

Every year, it sells 50,000 copies, 'a figure most sports magazines can only dream of'.[58] It might even have some value on the black market – in 2017 a spokesman at the London Review Bookshop reported that its most-stolen authors were, in order, 'Baudrillard, Freud, Nietzsche, Graham Greene, Lacan, Camus, and whoever puts together the Wisden Almanack'.[59]

Like many who play the game it so painstakingly chronicles, it is forthright in its views and not slow to express them. In the 2014 edition, for example, the shift of cricket's administrative power was unequivocally savaged. A game in which India, England and Australia have all the power, it suggests, is 'catastrophic', and only cricket can contrive to 'move back in time while hailing a revolution'.[60] In an age when most of us 'cannot be bothered to scroll too far back up a WhatsApp chat', it nevertheless reflects the most timely opinions and current thinking.[61] Its publication each year signals the beginning of the cricketing year in an era when the game's calendar is stacked 'as haphazardly as the central aisle at Lidl'.[62]

It is also, when appropriate, a robust defender of tradition, living up to its reputation as the game's 'custodian and conscience'.[63] In the 2016 edition, for example, less than 10 per cent of the section about Australia addressed the Big Bash, at the time the fastest growing short-form competition on the planet.[64] While cricket's principled inner voice and central statistical archive has remained steadfast, yellow and traditional, its ownership has been controversial and contentious. In the 1980s 'it was being tossed about in choppy commercial waters like a cork on a stormy sea'.[65] It found its way into various different hands, most notably the capacious and welcoming ones of Robert Maxwell. Larger than life in every sense, Maxwell was the publishing tycoon who bailed out his empire by plundering his employees' pension fund. Among the revelations after his mysterious death at sea were that he used to hold board meetings without telling the board and used 'standard minutes' prepared before the meeting.[66] It was all to maintain his lifestyle; with a personality like 'an articulated lorry', his enjoyment of luxury was equalled only by 'Roman emperors'.[67]

In 1983, as the man who owned the company that owned the company that owned *Wisden*'s publisher, he appeared at the annual dinner to celebrate the famous yellow tome. With customary few words, Maxwell apparently 'started promising, off the cuff, to modernise this clearly out-of-date little number, making it bigger, more legible and altogether spiffier'.[68] One can imagine Gubby Allen, sitting next him, choking on his prawn cocktail. Cricketing elders ground their cutlery with stupefaction. If anything so dramatic should ever happen to *Wisden*, John Woodcock concluded that it would be like 'losing India', albeit India might wryly conclude that it had long since wriggled free by itself.[69] Had Maxwell actually carried out his heinous, revolutionary act, his own picture might have appeared on the cover of the 2003 edition, when the almanack broke tradition and abandoned its text-only cover to feature a photograph of Michael Vaughan.[70] Editor Tim de Lisle, though, still doffed his hat to the traditionalists, and the plain dust jacket was made available for free to those who couldn't quite embrace the change.[71]

In 1993 the almanack again found itself looking for a new owner. This time it was acquired by someone altogether quieter, more understanding and, fortunately, even wealthier than Robert Maxwell. One day at Lord's, as two former *Wisden* editors mused its uncertain future, John Woodcock suggested to Graeme Wright that the answer might be sitting nearby. John Paul Getty Jr, heir to a huge oil fortune, was a cricket nut and a major philanthropist. On that happily fateful day at Lord's, Getty was sitting in a stand that he had practically paid for single-handedly. Believing as he did that in cricket as in art, 'the best things should be in the safest hands', the American duly became *Wisden*'s new owner.[72]

Getty, though, was not the first to seriously bankroll the game he loved. Julien Cahn – later Sir Julien – first became keen on cricket at Trent Bridge at the beginning of the twentieth century. After inheriting – and enhancing – his father's furniture business, Cahn was able to indulge his personal whims, and established a private ground at Stanford Hall, near Loughborough, turning it into a Shangri-La. The huge mansion included a cricket ground, underground passages, a private cinema, a nine-hole golf course, a bowling green, a fully stocked trout lake, performing sea lions and 'an art-deco theatre with a Wurlitzer organ' where Sir Julien would perform magic tricks.[73]

While his philanthropy was spread among causes as diverse as hill farming and childbirth practice, his real passion was for cricket. Besides financing various parts of Trent Bridge, he had his own all-star team that toured the world. In all matches between

1923 and 1941 it lost only nineteen out of over six hundred games. This says something about both the international strength of the Cahn XI and the opposing batsmen, who, tempted by his legendary hospitality, were happy to get out in order to get stuck in. Not surprisingly, he became part of the cricketing establishment; it was Cahn, for example, who asked Harold Larwood to apologize to MCC after Bodyline, although he could not persuade the bowler to do such a thing.

Cahn was no passive patron. Not letting a brittle-bone condition stand in his way, and ever the innovator, his batting was facilitated by some equipment not found in any contemporary kit catalogues – inflatable pads. So bulky were the pneumatic inventions that Cahn was ferried to the wicket in a bath chair by a servant. His batsmanship was undistinguished, but the leg byes shot off his pads like pinballs and represented his main on-field contribution. One of Cahn's associates concluded that despite the largesse, he could be 'a martinet'. Once after arriving at the wicket, his pads began emitting a 'loud hissing noise', at which point he stormed off, 'sacked his chauffeur on the spot' in a rage and 'declared the innings'.[74] Innings closed owing to a slow puncture above the knee roll. It doesn't happen very often.

Unlike Cahn, John Paul Getty Jr was happy to watch the game without becoming a comical part of its history. For him, cricket was less of an indulgence and more of a salvation. His beginnings did not suggest that he would end up either a cricket fan or a philanthropist. His father John Paul Sr has been described as 'the stingiest billionaire in history'.[75] It is an unsurprising title given the oil tycoon's dispassionate response when his teenage grandson Paul – son of John Paul Jr – was kidnapped in 1973. The ransom demand was eventually reduced from $17 million to $3.2 million – less than a single day's profits for his company during the 1973 oil crisis – and yet old man Getty remained unmoved, even when delivered the poor boy's severed ear, on the basis that 'If I pay one penny now, then I'll have fourteen kidnapped grandchildren.'[76] Finally, his grandson was saved when someone reminded Getty that he could deduct $2.2 million of the ransom from his tax bill. The most jaw-dropping element of all was the deal he cut with the boy's father – his own son – to loan him the final $1 million at 4 per cent interest per annum.[77]

Before his cricketing epiphany, the life of John Paul Getty Jr was typical within a dynasty characterized by 'affairs, divorces, addictions and untimely deaths'.[78] With his first wife Talitha, he lived a bohemian lifestyle and seriously indulged in hard drugs. But Talitha died from an overdose in 1971, and two years later, the intensive coverage of the family's kidnap drama revealed their dysfunction for all to see. Getty retreated to his London townhouse, reclusively pondering how it had all come to this and what the way ahead might be, presuming, of course, that there was one.

During his retrospection and withdrawal, Getty set about finally kicking his heroin habit with the support and encouragement of a regular visitor. This was his neighbour and Rolling Stones frontman Mick Jagger, who insisted on watching cricket on Getty's television during these pastoral visits. Sir Paul, as most people knew him, had no choice but to watch too, reports Graeme Wright, and few would have 'explained the game's pleasures and subtleties better' than Jagger.[79] Ball by ball, over by over, the game claimed its wealthiest fanatic. While Jagger started the process, Getty's cricketing education was further finessed by Sir Gubby Allen, and unlike Robert Maxwell, Getty was motivated by tradition rather than revolution. His contribution to cricket was astonishing: besides buying *Wisden* to secure its future, he contributed millions towards building the Mound Stand at Lord's. When the future of the BBC's *Test Match Special* was threatened, he offered to buy an alternative radio station to house it. No wonder that on David Lloyd's watch as England coach, Getty was presented with an England cap and blazer.

Getty's homage to cricket continued when he created a cricketing paradise within the grounds of Wormsley, his 3,000-acre estate in Buckinghamshire. Despite initially thinking that building a cricket ground simply involved mowing the grass regularly and finding some flat ground, Getty built Wormsley to the highest quality, with every detail attended to. Anyone who has ever visited will testify that it is the dreamiest ground imaginable. It became a venue for Getty's own team and spectators would routinely include Baroness Thatcher, Spike Milligan, Jerry Hall and Keith Miller. But cricket for Getty was not confined to terra firma. His cricket manager Colin Ingleby-Mackenzie reported impromptu matches umpired by Getty himself on the deck of his yacht *Tabitha G*. 'Very few people have a yacht large enough to play cricket on,' mused Ingleby-Mackenzie, seemingly suggesting he'd tried it on several vessels previously.[80]

Getty was a private man who kept his enormous philanthropy low-key. From his deckchair, his contribution to on-field affairs amounted to occasional and light-hearted advice about when to declare. Whether organizing ice creams for the children at Wormsley or helping striking miners make ends meet, his philanthropy was estimated at £140 million. He loved the game and those within it, reflects Graeme Wright, in part because he understood its importance to national culture, but also because cricket 'had drawn him out of the reclusive world in which he sheltered for many years'.[81]

'Private' and 'low-key' are not the obvious descriptions one might apply to Allen Stanford, another one of cricket's wealthy bankrollers. The urbane Texan waltzed in from nowhere, arriving like some cricketing Willy Wonka and promising the world, and for a while looking as if he could deliver it. In June 2008 a helicopter landed at Lord's and out of it he got with a transparent box full of money. The ECB embraced him like a Messiah, albeit in one infamous match in Antigua, England were hammered by the modestly named 'Stanford Superstars' who carried off a cool million dollars apiece.

Nobody knew at the time, but Stanford was a fraudster on a gargantuan scale. The money in the suitcase belonged to someone else. Weeks later, his house of cards fell, and he was carted off in an orange boiler suit. 'I am and will always be at peace with the way I conducted myself in business,' he told the judge, who promptly gave him 110 years to think about it more deeply.[82] Plenty had been taken in by the smooth-talking conman. Getting involved with him in the first place was, concluded Stephen Brenkley, 'a grave error'.[83] Thereafter everyone in English cricket has been trying to forget him; in the ECB's 2008 report Stanford was not mentioned.[84] When you sleep with the Devil, you wake up in hell.

Cricketing benefactors such as Cahn and Getty will be remembered much more fondly and it's good to know, reflected Simon Hughes, 'that not all multi-millionaires find their utopia in football'.[85] Alongside those who see cricket as a chance to make money, there have been others, like Getty, who have funded some elements of the game for no other reason than that history needed to be preserved rather than stopping dead in its tracks.

# 8

# BOXING, SOUND THRASHINGS
# AND THE BIG SHIP
## *The 1920s*

In 1914 a tangibly chipper *Athletic News* suggested that cricket could 'bowl out the Germans', since the enemy had begun striking before their opponents 'could take their places in the field'.[1] By the end of the war, there was little to feel sanguine about.[2] Of the 370 men who played county cricket in 1914, almost 10 per cent were wiped out by conflict, the pool of Gentlemen amateurs being particularly affected.[3] While nobody was forgetting that bright lights such as Blythe, Hutchings, Booth, Cotter and Callaway might have gone out, the only way to reignite the past was to start playing again.

Test matches resumed in 1920/21 when Australia hosted England. The visitors had few fast bowlers or batsmen that could cope with the strength of the hosts and were emphatically thrashed in all five Tests.[4] Overseeing the wretchedness was England skipper Johnny Douglas, an experienced leader in Australia who had taken over in 1911/12 when Plum Warner fell ill. Douglas stepped in, captained England on his Test debut and eventually led his men to a 4–1 series victory. While he was England's hero then, in 1920/21 'nobody was asking for his autograph'.[5]

It was a difficult tour from the start. After docking at Fremantle, the ship was quarantined while the Australian authorities convinced themselves that the passenger who had died of typhus during the voyage had not infected anyone else. If that wasn't bad enough, there was some offshore sledging from former

Aussie fast bowler Ernie Jones, now a customs officer. From his rowing boat, he regularly told the tourists they wouldn't win a Test match. How right he was, but at that stage, Douglas was undoubtedly still bullish.

John William Henry Tyler Douglas had an impressive physique but was not a naturally talented cricketer. He batted 'as if losing a competitive stroll with a tortoise' and his inertia drove people potty, especially the Australians.[6] When he took three hours to make 33 against Victoria, the crowds dubbed him 'Johnny Won't Hit Today' to match his initials. His captaincy was also criticized for a lack of imagination because he couldn't accept that others might not have his own strength or resolve. His 'brusque military manner', though, concealed a 'kind nature'.[7] As a bowler he was above reproach, his supreme fitness enabling a brisk pace and long, accurate spells.

Such fitness was easily explained by his other sporting career. Douglas met Australian middleweight 'Snowy' Baker in the final at the 1908 London Olympics, a chaotic and breathless competition that all happened in one day. Douglas fought twice and Baker three times before the final, and after a virtuoso exhibition of powerful and artful boxing, the Englishman took gold. Baker's claim that Douglas won because his father refereed the contest has been subsequently disproved. Douglas Sr was there as President of the Amateur Boxing Association but was not officiating in the bout. Olympic victory certainly helped his son's self-confidence, and upon arriving in Australia in 1911/12, his greeting at an official function was: 'Mr Mayor and gentlemen, I can't make a speech beyond saying thank you but I'm ready to box any man in the room three rounds.'[8] Such a suggestion would have modern on-duty press officers choking on their canapés.

The family timber business enabled Douglas to remain an amateur. Just before Christmas in 1930, he and his father were returning from a business trip to Finland aboard the *Oberon* when it collided with another vessel off the Danish coast. It is alleged that the two captains were brothers attempting to exchange Christmas greetings. The *Oberon* sank in minutes. Denzil Batchelor wrote that when Douglas knocked Baker down in London in 1908, the champion had been 'unruffled' and had undoubtedly been the same as he went to his death trying to save his father.[9] In the end, 'the two did not quite beat the count.'[10] It was notable that Douglas Jr and Sr perished together, and that son would not leave his father. Throughout the ill-fated 1920/21 tour to Australia, Douglas was criticized for neglecting his team to spend time with his parents, who had also made the trip. When the skipper was actually with his team, it was scorer Bill Ferguson who kept them entertained.[11]

Ferguson's place in cricket was as significant as any of those whose runs or wickets he recorded. Dozens of touring team photographs from the first half of the twentieth century feature the same bashful figure at the end of a row. Those in white were the headline-makers, but the man in the suit outlasted most of them. A veritable Forrest Gump of international cricket, from 1905 to 1957, Bill Ferguson – 'Fergie' – saw W. G. play at the start of his career and Garry Sobers at the end. He was a one-man support system for international cricket teams from Australia, England, South Africa, New Zealand and the West Indies. Modern cricket teams travel with huge teams of various backroom staff, but Fergie did it all by himself as a general factotum on 43 international tours straddling two world wars. No wonder they called him 'Mr Cricket'.

His lifetime of fetching and carrying is a lesson in focus and determination. At the turn of the last century in Sydney, Ferguson was a government clerk engaged in what he himself called the 'most monotonous task known to man' – recording all the addresses in the city and the people who lived in them.[12] It was no life for a young fellow craving adventure. He wanted to explore 'Calcutta and Cardiff' and from 'Barbados to Brazil'.[13] Yes, Cardiff.

Ferguson saw his chance when Australia advertised for a scorer for their tour to England in 1905. With little or no experience, he proceeded with a high-risk, high-reward strategy with no obvious relevance to his job application: he signed up with the local dentist for treatment he didn't need. There was method in his madness, since the dentist was Australia's Test captain, Monty Noble. It must have been hard to bend the skipper's ear while his rear molars were being inspected, but a positive impression was made, and although the letter arrived after the team itself had sailed, Fergie was engaged. He found England dominated by 'manners, etiquette and breeding' and was regularly held accountable for his scoring by Clem Hill's wife, who had travelled with the team and kept her own parallel record of on-field events.[14]

Fergie's duties included runs, scores, averages, the care and carriage of everyone's luggage and the soothing of aching muscles. He was also a messenger, occasionally running back to summon relaxing teams from the hotel after unforeseen batting collapses. On the 1912 tour to England, he added something else to his repertoire. When Surrey hosted the tourists at The Oval, Jack Hobbs made a second-innings 81 and Fergie experimented outside the usual conventions of scoring. Using 'an ancient dipped nib' with 'meticulous, loving care', Fergie produced the immaculate first example of that staple of modern cricket coverage, the 'wagon wheel' scoring chart.[15]

It says much for the game of cricket that someone who only contributed outside of the boundary ropes could still become a legend. Other countries recognized his popularity with players and his uncanny ability to quietly attend to everything everyone else forgot about, all the while losing 'neither a single bag nor a single bye'.[16] He was tempted out of retirement for the West Indies tour of England in 1957, and *Wisden* reports that a fall at a hotel prevented him from finishing the tour. He died shortly after a spell in hospital.[17] What a life he had, and if, along the way, he'd found out this about him, and that about her, or even something else about him and her together, he wasn't telling.

Besides Hobbs, Kent all-rounder Frank Woolley and, occasionally, Douglas himself, England barely struck a blow in anger throughout the whole 1920/21 series. Arguably the biggest thrashing was administered at Melbourne, where the great Australian bowler Jack Gregory followed up a first-innings century by routing England with 7 for 69. The visitors lost by an innings and 91 runs, but if England had a wretched time, so did Australian debutant Roy Park. A doctor, he had abandoned a stellar Aussie Rules football career when he felt he'd been wrongly accused of sticking an opposition player. The war interrupted everything, and on his return from distinguished service, he put his efforts into cricket. By 1920/21, as a solid opening batsman, he was picked for the Melbourne Test, but was not any part of the reason his team won. He was bowled by the only ball he faced in the first innings, didn't get a second innings and was never picked again. Even if the selectors had finished with him, the cricket gods had not – Park's wife had been distracted and missed Henry Howell knocking over her husband's stumps. It was the only case in history where someone missed the entirety of a loved one's Test career because she bent down to pick up her knitting. What was perhaps even more astonishing at the game in Melbourne was that Australian leg spinner Arthur Mailey didn't bowl a single over in the match despite taking six wickets in the previous Test. With a Test batting average of around eleven, he certainly hadn't been picked for that. It was all rather odd, since across the four Tests he did bowl in, he took 36 English wickets.

Mailey was a cartoonist, writer, raconteur and, when the fancy took him, a lethal leg spinner. He was, according Neville Cardus, 'the most fascinating cricketer I have known'.[18] Anti-establishment and self-deprecating, there was something of Huckleberry Finn about him, since he had 'drifted' into cricket, attracted by being able to stand around doing nothing and not be 'blamed for it'.[19] He wasn't in a rush and anyone else's sense of urgency wasn't important. Perhaps this sprang from his modest Sydney childhood; of Irish stock, his parents were so poor that they greeted each new offspring by further subdividing their meagre living space with a hessian sheet.[20]

Mailey spun the ball prodigiously but was noted more for experimentation than parsimonious accuracy. Early in his Test career he was removed from the attack by skipper Warwick Armstrong after three successive maidens with the clear message that his job was to remove the batsmen and not simply to stifle them. Thereafter, he attacked. Fellow Australian leg spinners

New South Wales team, 1927: Donald Bradman (back row, third from right), Archie Jackson (back row, second from right), Bert Oldfield (back row, extreme right), Arthur Mailey (front row, extreme right).

Clarrie Grimmett and Bill O'Reilly conceded runs as unwillingly as if they were $20 notes, but if they were misers, Mailey was a 'millionaire'.[21] No maiden he ever bowled, he said famously, was on purpose. Even when he was hit for six, Mailey felt that he had still achieved something, whether that was understanding the batsman a little better or, more likely, simply entertaining the crowd. When Victoria scored 1,107 all out in 1926/7, Mailey was the only bowler still having fun, chuckling that his four wickets cost 362 runs. He complained with mock bitterness about dropped catches (in the stands), and that he had just found his length as Victoria passed 1,000.

Mainly, his bowling was deadly serious. Besides flummoxing England on hard Australian wickets in 1920/21, he also demonstrated he could perform on spongy ones. His 1921 and 1926 tours to England yielded 287 wickets at an average less than twenty. He wasn't into sledging, but his sardonic wit eventually undid him as a player. He wrote too honestly for those picking the Test team and they promptly banned him. In enforced retirement he developed fanciful rules for recreational cricket where nobody made a duck and the other side won, his wit disarming any toxicity.[22] He was happy to talk spin bowling to anyone who asked, and when he shared some guileful secrets with England's Ian Peebles, he responded to the official castigation that followed by protesting that slow bowling is an art, and art is 'international'.[23]

But Mailey had a full life without cricket. By the time of his first tour to England in 1921, his sketches and cartoons had so impressed a London magazine that they offered him a job at a handsome £20 a week.[24] As a journalist, he detested pressbox stuffiness and sang hymns to lighten the mood. Jack Pollard reports finding Mailey in London in 1956 when he should have been in Leeds reporting on a Test match. He hadn't enjoyed the attritional cricket, so had returned to London to buy Pollard 'a champagne lunch'.[25] Mailey's writing had humour and poignancy, and both are prominent within his description of one match between his club Redfern and another Sydney club, Paddington. It was a dream fixture: Paddington was Victor Trumper's club. In anticipation, Mailey imagines whether he'd actually get to bowl against his hero. He ponders on what Trumper might be doing at that moment – did he iron his own flannels or send them to the laundry? Should he dig the garden to kill time or take a nap? 'Wonder if he knows if I'm playing against him?' he muses, before concluding that Trumper would never even have heard of him.[26]

At last, he finally gets to bowl to Trumper and gets him out, stumped. Typically, the great champion is generous in defeat. 'It was too good for me,' he says to Mailey as he walks off. But the bowler could find no happiness, lamenting that he felt like a boy who had 'killed a dove'.[27] Mailey's book *10 for 66 and All That* is one of cricket's greatest – the title is a wry acknowledgement of his second-innings analysis against Gloucestershire in 1921. In semi-retirement he adorned his new butcher's shop with a sign proclaiming that he had bowled tripe, then written it, and now he was selling it.

While it was primarily Mailey's bowling that did the job against England in 1920/21, Warwick Armstrong's batting was no less important. In the five-match series, he made 464 runs and averaged over 77, flaying the English bowling for three sumptuous centuries. As a captain and dominant personality, he was the nearest thing Australia had to W. G. Grace. He was also the most sizeable cricketer of his age, or perhaps of any other age. The 'inoffensive chrysalis' first seen in England in 1902 had 'enlarged himself from 10 to 22 stone' (63 to 140 kg) by 1921.[28] Little wonder that he was known as 'Big Ship'.

Never was there a risk of mistaking Warwick Armstrong; pictures of him 'scarcely needed captioning'.[29] At around 12 inches

(30 cm) long and 7 inches (18 cm) wide, Armstrong's boots resembled 'small canoes'.[30] How, muses Gideon Haigh, can such a huge man ever have played cricket?[31] But he did, and paid little heed to others, being, as he was, peerless among cricketers willing to take on officialdom successfully.[32] 'A vessel more noted for tonnage than tact', the Big Ship was not above using 'gunboat diplomacy' when needed.[33] 'He wanted his own way' and 'he had it', but was 'kind-hearted' aside from 'the bossiness'.[34]

Skirmishes with the suits were regular. He refused to tour under an unpopular team manager and would not allow the authorities to billet his team with wealthy English fans. When Victorian cricket authorities proposed a ten-shilling daily allowance for players, he lobbied for a pound.[35] Once, during the 1920/21 Ashes series, he was reported to have padded up in the pavilion and killed time drinking whisky with his mates.[36] At Trent Bridge in May 1905 he refused to bowl because the crowd were noisy. In 1909 there was the infamous time-wasting at The Oval we have already heard about. During the Old Trafford Test in 1921 England declared when they weren't entitled to do so. When the match resumed after twenty minutes of deliberations between umpires and captains, nobody noticed that Armstrong had bowled the last over before the break and the first over after it. Another time, expressing frustration at the prospect of a turgid draw, he retired to the boundary and read a newspaper during play. Even the mild-mannered Jack Hobbs called him 'nasty and unsportsmanlike'.[37]

While he ruffled feathers, over 16,000 runs and eight hundred wickets across 24 seasons with an interruption for war says plenty. In his splendid biography, Haigh does not dodge the unsavoury elements of Armstrong's career, but places them within the context of Armstrong the successful player, captain and progressive thinker.[38] Cricket had moved into the roaring twenties, and men like Armstrong were doing the roaring.

# 9

# TOURING, TENNYSON AND ROLLO
## *Still Mainly in the 1920s*

Nobody beat Australia when Warwick Armstrong was the captain. After the 1920/21 series, the Big Ship travelled by big ship to deliver more punishment to England. Cricket tours are complicated, and perhaps only the travelling has got simpler. In their first-class seats, modern cricketers decide between chicken and fish and don headphones until touchdown. Unless you had no sea legs, in years gone by several weeks on a boat could have some benefits. The sharpest contrast is that on an aeroplane you might not even set eyes on your teammates, but during a boat trip you got to know every foible and failing. An upside of air travel, of course, is that if you've had an awful tour, you are home before recriminations gather momentum.

It's worth just pausing our timeline to consider how cricketers have travelled from A to a distant B. Sea travel wasn't for everyone. Legendary hitter Charles Thornton, for example, was invited by MCC to tour Canada and the USA in 1872, but before sailing he spotted a painting of a floundering ship in a shop window and promptly declined. On the *Peshawur* en route to Australia in 1882/3, England bowler Fred Morley broke some ribs in a collision with another ship. On his way to England in 1899, Victor Trumper nearly drowned after forgetting to close his cabin porthole. On the same voyage half a century later, Australian vice-captain Lindsay Hassett led community singing and orchestrated good-natured mayhem involving all on board. Sometimes the fun was rumoured to be happening behind cabin doors. The same ships carrying cricketers to play overseas were packed with 'prospective brides, mourning widows, young ladies escaping from broken love affairs' and some more obvious predators.[1] As a 'handsome bachelor', suggests Ian Wooldridge with a wink, England wicketkeeper Godfrey Evans might be 'the only English cricketer ever to score a century before he reached Australia'.[2]

Air travel also has its moments. Australian leg spinner Kerry O'Keefe recalls that during Australia's journey from Sydney to London in 1977, someone wondered how many beers could be consumed during the flight.[3] During the stop off at Bahrain, the eventual winner Doug Walters was 'in reasonable shape' despite having consumed 'thirty-five-odd cans of beer' and 'at least fifty cigarettes'.[4] Walters's final tally of 44 cans was beaten on later tours by Rod Marsh (45) and then David Boon (53). Marsh reportedly left the plane in a wheelchair while Boon spent two days in bed.

Travel, for England at least, often means Christmas away from home. In 1897/8, Yorkshire spinner Ted Wainwright poignantly wished he was back home 'turning the meat', and on Archie MacLaren's MCC 1922/3 tour to New Zealand, the Christmas Day fixture at Christchurch was interrupted by an earthquake.[5] More recently, England tourists Mike Selvey and Keith Fletcher sat down to a Christmas dinner of mutton curry in India. After they appealed for something more festive, the same food was presented, garnished with plastic holly. England's overseas Christmases have often been characterized by fancy-dress parties. Interesting costume choices include Michael Atherton's Robin Hood outfit in 1990/91. In 1994 Raymond Illingworth appeared as Ming the Merciless and Atherton reflected that when Illingworth assumed control of English cricket shortly afterwards, it was with the absolute power 'that even Ming might have envied'.[6]

But in 1921 there was more taking off than dressing up when Australia sailed to England. Skipper Armstrong and fast bowler Ted McDonald worked – presumably stripped to the waist – in the ship's engine room to get themselves into shape. It's unclear whether Armstrong's shape changed much, but it certainly did McDonald some good – he took 27 wickets as Australia recorded a 3–0 series win. Despite having been drubbed months previously, the hapless England were still led by Johnny Douglas. After two more heavy defeats, making seven successive thrashings by the Aussies, the selectors retained Douglas the player but replaced him at the helm.

The new skipper was Hampshire's the Hon. Lionel Tennyson. Others had been knighted or ennobled for their on-field endeavours, but Tennyson was to the manor born. His grandfather was Alfred, Lord Tennyson, and it is reported that the National Sound Archive's wax cylinder recording of the Poet Laureate reading *The Charge of the Light Brigade* in 1892 features the background gurglings of his infant grandson.[7] Even then, Lionel Tennyson was not easily suppressed.

Shortly after leaving Eton, Tennyson adopted a playboy lifestyle using money he usually didn't have. Once, while in the Coldstream Guards, he invited a bevy of chorus girls from the Gaiety Theatre to enliven guard duty at the Tower of London and avoided disciplinary action only because nobody could think of an appropriate punishment.[8] When Prime Minister Herbert Asquith wrote Tennyson a letter admonishing him for dallying with his married niece, the reply read, 'Dear Mr Asquith, you are an interfering old buger [sic].'[9] Young Lionel, it seems, had not inherited his grandfather's ability to spell. His life lurched continuously from famine to feast but he was also capable of masterminding the odd miracle. At Edgbaston against Warwickshire in 1922, his Hampshire side didn't simply revive, but jumped from the grave and ran screaming down the street.

The day before the match, young Hampshire batsman and England rugby international Harold Day drove Tennyson north towards Birmingham. Day was considered a responsible chaperone for his captain, who was famous for his 'nocturnal capers'.[10] Accordingly, Day was ordered to drop in at several country piles en route to the Midlands. The night before the match, the skipper retired to bed shortly before dawn, after assuring his nervous driver and subordinate that he would win the toss the next morning.

And he did. The mini procession of English sporting aristocracy (the other captain was the Hon. Frederick Somerset Gough Calthorpe) returned to the pavilion and Tennyson announced that the first victory was his. Seeing overcast skies and a damp wicket, Tennyson had decided his side would bowl first. It looked to be a good decision, as a solid Warwickshire top order faltered, recovering to 223 all out, which was reasonable given the conditions. With the wicket drying and losing its demons, Hampshire licked their lips. The first over was a maiden, giving no clue about what was to happen next.[11] Some forty minutes later, Hampshire's opening batsmen walked to the wicket for a second time. Were they resuming their innings after a rain break? No. They were following on, the whole of the first innings having lasted less than nine overs. Including four byes and an edge to the boundary, their first effort amounted to fifteen, 'the nadir of cricketing experience'.[12]

What made Hampshire's disaster inexplicable was that this was no team of second-raters. Sitting on his bat handle and watching the carnage from the non-striker's end was the man responsible for the only positive stroke of the innings – a hook for four. Phil Mead was a most accomplished batsman; only Hobbs, Woolley and Patsy Hendren made more first-class runs than his 55,061, and only Hobbs, Hendren and Hammond made more than his 153 centuries. But for such strong competition, he'd surely have played dozens of Test matches instead of just seventeen. Mead was unforgettable, asserted John Arlott, adding that he was as imposing as 'one of those lead-based, won't-fall-down dolls of our childhood'.[13] Like many others, Mead had his idiosyncrasies, touching his cap four times, tapping his bat four times and taking four mini-steps into position before each ball. If the procedure was disturbed, he started from the beginning. Such unhurriedness meant that he was often thought to bat slowly. So 'dull' was he, a Hampshire member once told Arlott, that Mead once stone-walled nearly all day to make 280.[14]

But he didn't get 280 this day in 1922 and had to settle for six not out. Eight teammates made ducks, and Warwickshire bowler Harry Howell took 6 for 7. At the end of day one, Mead was not out again with twelve, his team needing another 110 to make their opponents bat again. So confident was Calthorpe of winning that he suggested a golfing day for the amateurs from both sides. Tennyson apparently responded with some less-than-aristocratic language, betting his opposite number £10 (at huge odds) that Hampshire would win the match. Everyone thought he was mad. On day two, Mead went quickly, but Tennyson rallied with 45 and others chipped in. While it represented a marked improvement on the first innings, it still wasn't brilliant. When the eighth wicket fell, the Hampshire lead was only 66, with only the tail left. Not for the first or last time, Tennyson prepared to say a heartfelt farewell to a tenner he'd waged.

The last hope was George Brown, who was going well at one end. He made over 25,000 runs and took over six hundred wickets for Hampshire, acquiring legendary status along the way. In 1906 Brown walked sixty miles to Southampton for a trial with the county, hauling 'a tin trunk' containing everything he owned.[15] The eighteen-year-old had to succeed, since otherwise, he was going back the same way.[16] In this famous match, no doubt smarting about his first ball dismissal in the first innings, he made a snorting 172, ably assisted by wicketkeeper Walter Livsey (also Tennyson's valet) in a ninth-wicket stand of 177. Modern employment scholarship would describe working for Tennyson as 'precarious'. Wages were only forthcoming on the rare occasion His Lordship was flush, and often Livsey had to lend him back the money shortly afterwards.

Astonishingly, at the end of day two, Hampshire were 475 for 9 with a lead of 267. Livsey made his maiden first-class century the next day, and Hampshire finished with a frankly astounding 521. There was criticism of Calthorpe's captaincy, but whatever the peripheral factors, an improvement of over five hundred runs from first to second innings was unprecedented. It left Warwickshire facing an awkward-looking target of 303, and Kennedy and Newman soon made it impossible as they tore into the home side. Calthorpe made thirty and might have considered a personal match contribution of 100 runs and six wickets a decent return. But the scorebook told him that he'd lost by 158 runs after dismissing his opponents for fifteen. Then he had to find the cash to settle the bet with Tennyson. Unsurprisingly, the celebrations were as memorable as the match. The victors drank their Birmingham hotel dry and the occasion, understandably, was 'prodigiously expansive'.[17] Eighty years later, *The Observer* judged it the second-best sporting comeback ever, beaten only by Lasse Virén from Finland, who fell in the final of the 10,000 metres at the 1972 Olympics but recovered to win gold.[18]

Stories of Tennyson's shenanigans are legion. Aboard ship for a private tour to South Africa in 1924/5 managed by Archie MacLaren, Tennyson was playing percussion to enhance the evening's musical entertainment. However, he couldn't keep even the simplest tempo, and, supported by those watching, MacLaren threw the drum kit into the ocean.[19] Another time, Tennyson won the booby-prize pumpkin in a fancy-dress competition and playfully threw it at cricketing scribe Sir Home Gordon, only to miss and poleaxe the Lady Mayoress of Folkestone instead. An acting career in Hollywood was abandoned when he discovered it involved wearing make-up. His credentials as a toff, though, were impeccable: he insisted on being driven the 80 yards (70 metres) from his London pad to his club.

Financially speaking, his club was the scene of his best and worst moments. Tennyson regularly found himself financially embarrassed because of his inability to pass by any sort of wager. Once, it is claimed, he lost £12,000 in a week; most inflation calculators suggest that its contemporary value would be over half a million. Not that he always lost – he once arrived at a Lord's Test in a Rolls-Royce, winnings from a successful bet regarding the toileting activities of two flies.[20] Following one trip back to the family pile to sort out his debts – a visit as tense as a 'Tennessee Williams play' – he was sent to India, away from temptation.[21] Such a chaotic lifestyle was poor preparation for Tennyson's other major activities – war and cricket. Not that he would have found too much similarity between the two. Cricket was not war, and even war, according to Tennyson, was not always like war, as his reminiscences likened the Western Front to 'a grim but gentlemanly shooting party'.[22] During the conflict he was twice mentioned in dispatches and thrice wounded.

If he led his men as he led his cricketers, he would have received unstinting loyalty. But he was able to dish out the discipline when needed. Once, all-rounder Jack Newman famously found himself on the wrong side of his captain when, frustrated after appeal after appeal was turned down by the umpires, he threw the ball down in disgust. When he refused to pick it up, Tennyson sent him from the field. Afterwards, the skipper summoned Newman for a dressing down. Newman had disgraced Hampshire cricket – 'Hampshire cricket, mind you, the cradle of the game.'[23] Tennyson then dictated a letter of apology to opposing skipper Arthur Carr, and silently, Newman took down every word. Tennyson dictated a second letter, this time to himself, fully and formally addressed, beginning 'Dear Skipper, I humbly regret my behaviour, and so on ...'. Newman was finally sent on his way as a 'confounded old villain' who must never repeat such behaviour; 'Good evening to you, Jack,' added Tennyson, passing the miscreant a £5 note.[24] The skipper had a heart as big as his debts.

As a player, he also had his moments. He was a *Wisden* Cricketer of the Year in 1914, once hit a 140-yard (130 m) six at Southampton and another time flayed Gloucestershire for a century in less than an hour. But there were better players with more impressive records. Indeed, he was not even blessed with any special tactical skills as a captain; some even suggest that he wasn't a good enough player to merit selection in many of the teams he led. Nevertheless, as one of the most charismatic cricketers of all time, he brought to each something no one else could.

And so it was in 1921, when simply fed up with being thrashed by Australia, that England turned to Tennyson. Summoned from his St James's club on the eve of the second Test at Lord's, he responded by proclaiming that he was enjoying his second cigar and third bottle of bubbly, 'but, having informed you of that, I shall be delighted to play.'[25] One Test later, Tennyson was the captain. True, not even his infectious positivity could stop Australia, but he certainly slowed them down a bit. In three Tests with Tennyson at the helm, the visitors won one and two were drawn, but he characteristically led from the front. His 74 not out at Lord's was followed by two 'Falstaffian, semi-piratical' innings of 63 and 36 at Leeds after splitting the webbing between his fingers – all the while under the influence of painkillers.[26]

If ever a man embraced cricket's Corinthian spirit, it was Lionel Tennyson. Indeed, his life was 'one long cavalry charge' where

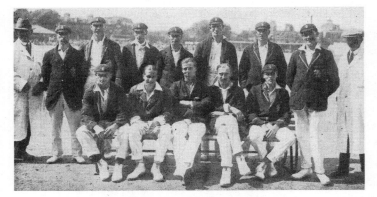

England Test team, 1921: Lionel Tennyson (sitting, centre), Andrew Sandham (standing, second from left), Phil Mead (standing, third from left), Johnny Douglas (sitting, second from left), Percy Fender (sitting, second from right), Frank Woolley (sitting, extreme right).

everything was done 'boldly, confidently, often waywardly, once or twice idiotically, but never meanly'.[27] He breathed his last at a hotel in Bexhill-on-Sea in 1951, the maid finding him sitting up in bed, cigar in mouth, with *The Times* opened at the racing page. 'What a wonderful man,' reflected Newman, adding that 'we loved him, every bone in his body.'[28] Another tribute was provided by Barbara Cartland, a lover of all things pink and romantic, but in later years fond of make-up so heavy that Tennyson would have certainly disapproved. He only had to walk into a room, she said, 'and it was like the sun coming out at Lord's'.[29] Modern cricket probably wouldn't have tolerated him. He would have had reserved seating in every casino in Las Vegas and private boxes at Lord's, Ascot and Epsom, and the tabloids would have photographs of him selling off silver spoons for petrol money.

Perhaps he was cricket's most eccentric captain until the emergence of Rollo John Oliver Meyer – 'Jack' to his friends, 'Boss' to his pupils. One of those pupils was the late Peter Roebuck, complex and enigmatic himself but ultimately tragic in a way his old headmaster was not. Roebuck described Meyer as 'gambler, golfer, chess player, scholar, scrounger and crossword solver'.[30] While a student at Cambridge, the first ever Kiwi Test skipper Tom Lowry introduced young Meyer to the 'Hellfire Club', whose initiation ceremony involved blowing three smoke rings and spitting through the middle of them.[31]

After university, Meyer went to India as a cotton trader, but made a name for himself trading racing tips, playing cards and hustling at pool.[32] If he earned a fortune, he also lost it. At the docks about to set sail home, he landed a job teaching the son of a man reportedly so lazy that he relied on a machine to transport him from his bath to his bed. Realizing he could bring the best out of his young charges, in 1935 Meyer founded Millfield, the Somerset boarding school famed for developing sporting talent 'without worrying too much about five good O-levels'.[33] With the only briefest of nightly sleeps in his chaotic study, Boss ran Millfield on a 'Robin Hood' philosophy where 'global plutocrats' subsidised the less privileged.[34] In other words, as Roebuck puts it more forthrightly, the 'stupid children of aristocrats paid double'.[35] One such lesser-off beneficiary was Welsh rugby legend Gareth Edwards, and other pupils included Ben Hollioake, Olympic swimmer Duncan Goodhew, hurdling gold medallist David Hemery and the children of Sean Connery, Omar Sharif and Oliver Reed. Perhaps some of those 'paid double', but nobody seems to have complained.

*Wisden* described Meyer as a 'mercurial' batsman and a bowler who delivered 'just about everything under the sun' at slow-medium pace.[36] He was asked to captain Somerset in 1947. Already afflicted with a bad back and poor eyesight, he found his county in a similarly poor condition. Always the innovator, one of his schemes was that everyone should hit England bowler Bill Bowes for six first ball. He theorized that the best way to handle Bradman was to load the leg side boundary and to bowl him full tosses.

Even the rain could not deny him. Meyer would use dressing-room furniture to plot on-field tactics. The 'musical chairs without the music' once went wrong in that when play restarted, it was discovered that the next batsman was a left-hander – 'something the schoolmaster had not taken into account'.[37] During Meyer's single season at the helm at Somerset, he enlivened dull days with 'idiosyncratic theories' and took a deep interest in his team's welfare.[38] Once, during rationing, Boss returned with six pounds of horse steak for ravenous first teamers. Another time he activated the communication cord on the train to Manchester so the guard could arrange for some refreshments at the next stop.

Like Tennyson, Meyer's Achilles heel was that he couldn't walk past a betting shop. Perhaps his taste for a flutter had been fuelled when he backed himself at 50-1 to win the Billiards handicap at the Royal Bombay Yacht Club and walked off with £1,000. Horse trainer Ian Balding recalls his brother Toby selling Meyer a horse called Milk Shake. So excited was Meyer that he took fifty pupils on a school trip to see the nag compete at Wincanton. It romped home, and Boss couldn't decide between giving a press conference or scooting off to pick up his winnings quickly before his bookie had the chance to double-cross him.[39] When his back pain was particularly incapacitating, he turned up at Cheltenham in a specially commissioned ambulance.[40] His fondness for the gaming tables meant his departure from Millfield was 'embarrassing', but, suggests David Foot, perhaps 'we shan't go into that.'[41] As a cricketer, perhaps his results weren't up to much, but his players, if wrong-footed by his eccentricity, nonetheless 'appreciated his concern for their well-being'. 'Surprise his weapon, experiment his fancy, dullness his enemy and inconsistency his weakness,' wrote Roebuck.[42] Imagine a team containing Tennyson and Meyer. They might not win, but it would be the hottest ticket in town.

# 10

# ROOT, TICH, LEARIE
# AND SANDHAM

*The 1920s Become the 1930s*

For Tennyson and others, the 1920s were bright and carefree. But for every privileged gentleman, there were pragmatists relying on cricket for a living. Fred Root was one such player who epitomized this more prosaic approach, not least because he wrote it all down. Seemingly no relation to Joe Root, with a modest annual income of about £300 per annum, Fred played cricket in a different world to his famous namesake, and had to pay for his own hotels, taxis, insurance, incidentals and even 'rubdowns'.[1] If there was any money in cricket, he mused, he hadn't found any in the worst-paid of professional games.[2]

Less fashionable counties were often reliant on one or two 'hard pressed' professionals, and Root was certainly one.[3] His career was largely spent in the shade, playing for Worcestershire between 1921 and 1932 when they were one of the weakest counties. During a miserable decade, Root carried their attack. In 1928 he did the cricketer's double of 100 wickets and 1,000 runs, although his batting belonged to the 'block and tackle' variety, without many frills.[4] His 207 wickets in 1925 are the most in a season for the county, and his 9 for 23 against Lancashire in 1923 are still the best figures for a Worcestershire bowler. Denzil Batchelor noted that Root was successful with a new ball and just as good on 'a humid day when the ball was as wizened as a Worcester pippin'.[5] Reverse swing? Sounds like it.

Root was nothing if not gritty: as a despatch rider in the First World War, he was shot in the chest and medical opinion determined his cricket career to be over. He negotiated a Bradford League contract while still in bed recovering. In 1937 he wrote *A Cricket Pro's Lot*, a warts-and-all account of life as a professional cricketer.[6] The book, notes Gideon Haigh, is 'occupational' rather than 'inspirational', and rather than trying to produce superstars, it aims to help journeymen 'with a lifetime of tradesman's tricks'.[7] Among the practical tips are recommendations to use talcum powder to ease chafing, methylated spirits for damaged fingers and extra socks for support. In this intriguing peep behind the curtain of county cricket, Root reveals that to ensure his prompt arrival at the train station, 'Nudger' Needham would wear civvies under his flannels so he didn't have to waste time getting properly changed. He also discussed some of cricket's quaint traditions, including handing a batsman a 'toffee ball' to get them safely from 99 to 100. He refers to cricket's 'freemasonry' and how sometimes the brotherly consideration prevailed, and at other times it didn't. One such example is when, as a young bowler, Root once played against Surrey and England veteran Tom Hayward. At lunch, tantalizingly poised on 94 not out, Hayward suggested to Root that since he had yet to take a first-class wicket, he'd make sure that he got himself out to Root's bowling in return for a safe passage through to 100. Hayward continued past one hundred, thrashing his way towards a second, with Root's bowling taking a fearful walloping.

Root believed in fair play and as such he was a professional who played like an amateur. Once, when two batsmen collided going for a run, he refused to break the wicket. Another time, he realized that he should have walked when he hit the ball, and everyone knew it apart from the umpires. He told his opponent that he'd get himself out to right the initial wrong. Thereafter, he 'slashed carelessly' but to his amazement (and no doubt the bowler's too), he scored 86. Root swore he was trying to get out, reflecting that perhaps Tom Hayward had been trying to do the same all those years before.[8] He was also a radical thinker, his prescriptions including an unwitting and yet visionary call for limited-overs cricket. Matches, he said, should be 'short and snappy'.[9] His most poignant advice to professional cricketers was that playing cricket didn't last forever, and they should brace themselves for a less exhilarating life in retirement. Much as he liked a gripe, he concluded that cricket is a 'great and glorious game' played by 'grand fellows'.[10]

While Root loved the game, it didn't always love him back. He was an early exponent of 'leg theory' bowling, where the ball was angled towards the batsmen's body in the hope they would tamely fend it off to a waiting fielder. Consequently, Root is tenuously connected to Bodyline, but his own relationship with Test cricket was fleeting. His debut against the 1926 Australian tourists was ruined by rain, but he finally got to bowl at Lord's, where he took 2 for 70 and 2 for 40. At Manchester, he returned a heroic 4 for 84 in 52 overs with 27 maidens. England skipper Arthur Carr filled the leg side with fielders, and the Aussies didn't like it. After four draws Root was dropped for the final Test, which England won by 289 runs, regaining the Ashes. The 'decoy duck' was needed for the first four Tests but not for the fifth.[11] England never called again, but to Worcestershire he was worth more than gold. He gave much to cricket and was the comical predecessor to 'Lillee c Willey b Dilley' and 'Cook c Mustard b Onions'. Even Fred must have cackled when George Beet kept wicket and victims were 'c Beet, b Root'.[12]

The fact that England was overrun with quality cricketers meant that there were limited chances for people like Root at the highest level. Similarly, Alfred Percy 'Tich' Freeman's first-class haul of 3,776 wickets somehow merited only a dozen Test matches. As the biggest of achievers but the smallest of men, the 5 ft 2 in. Freeman bowled leg spin for Kent between 1914 and 1936. In the eight seasons between 1928 and 1935 he took over two hundred wickets, and in the first of these, over three hundred. While his 304 wickets is the most ever taken in a season, he is also second, fifth and sixth on the list. Only Wilfred Rhodes took more first-class wickets – about two- or three-years' worth – but removing the First World War from the mix, Rhodes's career lasted 32 years compared to Freeman's 22. More astonishingly of all, while Rhodes was playing for England when he was 21, Freeman was five years older than that before he took his first wicket in county cricket. Freeman claimed five wickets in an innings 386 times and ten in a match 140 times. To put this in perspective, Shane Warne did those things 69 times and twelve times respectively.

The numbers are 'mind-boggling', and all achieved bowling leg spin, which by common consensus is the most difficult of bowling skills.[13] But Tich, with infinite patience and venom, hitched his trousers high and began plundering county batsmen. He barely relented until Kent released him in 1936, whereupon he became a professional in the Birmingham and District League with Walsall and, as you might expect, continued breaking records. With an emphatic message, he retired to a house called 'Dunbowlin'.[14] Eighty years after his last game for Kent, some new retirement flats near the St Lawrence Ground in Canterbury were named after him.

But Freeman was a paradox. County batsmen were terrified of him, but he, in turn, appeared terrified of his wife.[15] Test batsmen were not intimidated and on two tours to Australia, he was ineffectual: his leg-breaks captured only eight costly wickets.[16] A long-standing familiarity with leg spin enabled Australian batsmen to disarm him, since they had 'developed footcraft' in self-defence, 'as fish developed gills'.[17]

Like Freeman, there were other cricketers playing away from the wider public gaze. Much of the cricketing part of Learie

Constantine's life, for example, happened in Nelson, north of Burnley. But Lancashire is a long way from Trinidad, where his grandfather was a slave, one of the last to make the journey from Africa.[18] While the family surname was likely taken from his grandfather's owner, Learie was named after a 'gregarious Irishman' whom his father met in England in 1900.[19]

Constantine's father, Lebrun, was also a cricketer. Having made the trip to England in 1900, he was invited to do so again in 1906, but decided not to go, as he had four children to support. Keen to see his erstwhile teammates off, he made his way to Port of Spain, but arriving there before the players, he become 'lonely and iso-lated'.[20] He encountered a local businessman and cricket fan called Maillard, who was horrified to hear that Lebrun was unable to travel because he was financially strapped. Maillard quickly pro-vided enough money for the player to make the trip and for his family to manage without him, but the boat had left. 'Chartering a fast launch, they set out in chase,' reports Constantine Jr with more than a hint of relish, and before the steamer had made it to the open sea, they caught up. After climbing up a rope ladder, Constantine Sr joined his teammates on board.[21]

Learie was a better cricketer than his dad and became a 'cham-pagne cocktail' of a player.[22] As a batsman, he was unconventional and innovative, and on his day, 'virtually impossible to bowl at'.[23] To complement the 'considerable pace' of his bowling, as a fielder he was so 'acrobatic' he might have been made of 'springs and rubber'.[24] As a captain, he had 'subtlety, skill' and an infectious 'enthusiasm'.[25] So dominant was he within his team that when he failed, his colleagues couldn't take up the slack;[26] such was the case when the West Indies toured England in 1928, when he topped the charts as run scorer, wicket-taker and catcher.

Seldom less than 'dazzling', he beat Middlesex and Northamptonshire by himself.[27] In the Middlesex first innings,

Constantine's contribution was a solitary wicket. But he was just warming up. Batting at number 7, he made 86 out of the 107 scored while he was at the wicket. It took less than an hour, but there was still a 122-run deficit. Middlesex needed getting out, and so Constantine obliged, taking 7 for 57, clean-bowling five. His team requiring 259 to win, again Constantine took control, hitting a century in less than an hour, including two sixes and twelve fours. It was, wrote Ian Peebles – one of the hapless bowlers – 'the greatest all-round performance I was to see in my career – and possibly my life'.[28]

It was a different story in Test matches. England thrashed the visitors by an innings in each of the three games, Constantine scoring only 89 runs in six innings, and taking four England wickets for an inglorious 262. Indeed, his record in Tests is modest. Was Constantine just an average cricketer who masked his relative ordinariness by being industrious and energetic? Denzil Batchelor, for example, felt that Constantine was 'out of his element in Test cricket' and too good 'for the ponderous stuff'.[29]

But more importantly, he was one of cricket's great men, and an iconic figure who transcended its usual parameters.[30] As the first black player of real star quality to emerge from the colonial West Indies, he was a pioneer. As C.L.R. James explained, Constantine 'revolted against the revolting contrast between his first-class status as a cricketer and his third-class status as a man'.[31] Back in Trinidad, being black and from a humble background meant his legal career was never likely to flourish, since the best jobs went to whites.[32] Cricket was his route to a better life, and the professional leagues in the north of England enabled him to study law and 'to argue the causes of West Indian self-government and racial tolerance'.[33]

Like Sydney Barnes before him, Constantine's brilliance demonstrates that cricket legends can be built outside Test cricket,

Learie Constantine, 1930/31.

and even county cricket. Then as now, the leagues were populated by serious cricketers 'just short' of county standard, and professional players were engaged on the understanding that they would perform on the field and raise the standards of those around them.[34] The idea that such cricket is just friendly fun is very wide of the mark, and throughout the season, professionals are under pressure to perform.[35]

If Constantine felt such pressure at Nelson, it didn't show. The club had watched him during the 1928 tour, and shortly afterwards made him an offer. *The People* described him as 'the best all round cricketer in the world'.[36] Good as Constantine was, this was perhaps a stretch, though they were justified in thinking that signing him was the season's most sensational cricket news.[37] The remuneration was handsome and was enhanced by £1 for every fifty runs or five wickets, plus 'a collection from the spectators'.[38]

At the time he arrived at Nelson, the town's only other black man collected rags and bones.[39] If, for some reason, there were objections to his presence, Learie Constantine swept them aside. In league cricket, he was 'supreme'; he became the first Nelson player to score 1,000 runs in a season and made their highest individual score of 192 not out.[40] He took five wickets against every club on every ground. In 1934 his 10 for 10 dismissed Accrington for twelve runs. The club dominated the league in the thirteen seasons he played there. Michael Manley appositely quotes C.L.R. James's summary of Constantine's cricket; rather than a Test cricketer who played in the leagues, he was a 'league cricketer who played Test cricket'.[41]

But Constantine made an even greater impact on the world as a man than as a cricketer. Despite the people of Nelson showing their adoration by bestowing upon him the Freedom of the Town, not everyone was glad to see him, and his time in England was characterized by regular racist incidents and slights. The most notorious of these was in 1943, when he and his wife were asked to leave the Imperial Hotel in London because their presence offended other guests. Even though racial discrimination was not then illegal in Britain, he took the hotel to court and won the nominal damages he had sought. These events marked a moment for changing race relations in post-war Britain. Like Basil D'Oliveira after him, the calm with which Constantine conducted himself helped to expose racism to a wider audience, fighting as he did 'with a dignity firm but free of acrimony'.[42]

In the last twenty years of his life he built an astonishing curriculum vitae of public service. He received an MBE for his work during the war as a welfare officer in the Ministry of Labour and National Service. Called to the bar in 1954, he published his book about discrimination, *Colour Bar*, the same year. Back in Trinidad he became Minister of Works and Transport and then High Commissioner for Trinidad and Tobago in London. He was a member of the Race Relations Board, rector of St Andrews University and a governor of the BBC. He was knighted in 1967 and became Britain's first ever black life peer in 1969. All in all, he was a man of 'quiet manner, religious conviction and high principles'.[43]

In part, 1920s cricket was characterized by a sense of unfulfilled potential. There were plenty of star cricketers on whom the sun shone only briefly. Some, like Fred Root, were used and quickly discarded, while others, like Tich Freeman, were perceived to be not quite themselves at the top level. Learie Constantine's best cricket was played in more parochial surroundings. Others, like Surrey's Andrew Sandham, were denied the limelight simply because the quality of those around them drew it away.

One thing that Sandham will always be remembered for, though, is that he scored the first Test match triple century. When a batsman scores one at the highest level, the celebrations reflect its rarity. When Brian Lara passed Garry Sobers's world record 365 not out in 1994, Sobers himself walked to the middle to offer congratulations. A decade later, when Lara reached 400, the Prime Minister of Antigua did likewise. But the celebrations for Andrew Sandham's first Test triple were altogether more muted. Indeed, he seemingly spent his whole career under the radar. When, for example, he returned to The Oval shortly after retiring from almost six decades of service to Surrey as a player, coach and scorer, the gate steward didn't recognize him and wouldn't let him in.[44] In retirement as in work, he conducted his business quietly. David Frith reports meeting the 87-year-old Sandham in a Clapham pub, 'warm under his raincoat' and 'seeing a reduced version of the world around him through thick-lensed glasses'.[45] By then, he'd retired from Surrey after serving them, in some capacity, from 1911 to 1970. After playing, he became Surrey coach, and guided them to seven consecutive championship titles in the 1950s. With his Surrey teammate Herbert Strudwick, he started a cricket school in Wandsworth. Though they were both 'lovely fellows', Alf Gover reported that the two were commercially clueless, and eventually took the business over from them, turning it into the most famous cricket school anywhere in the world.[46]

As a player, Sandham attracted less than his share of attention because of who he opened the batting with. In any other team he would have been the senior partner, but not when he walked out with Jack Hobbs. While Hobbs's partnership with Herbert Sutcliffe was famous and enduring at Test level, the partnership with Sandham at county level was even more productive. They shared 66 opening partnerships of more than 100 in county matches, including an opening stand of 428 against the University of Oxford in 1926. How different it might have been if Sandham hadn't gone down with appendicitis just before the Battle of the Somme.

Those described as 'courtiers around a kingly presence' were often gifted, suggests Eric Midwinter.[47] One might understand the low-key aura of Andrew Sandham if he'd been a journeyman who'd had one startling day, like Ted Alletson, but Sandham was one of the greatest English batsmen. He made more than 41,000 runs for Surrey, including 107 centuries. Despite spending so much time in Jack Hobbs's shadow, he expressed no jealousy and remembered his old opening partner only with fondness. It seems that he played second fiddle in terms of headlines, but not style, possessing batting's 'silvery graces', and though no brute in terms of aggression, he was a 'sweet deflector' and a 'sort of exponent of judo-batsmanship'.[48]

In April 1930 the 39-year-old Sandham found himself opening the batting with fifty-year-old George Gunn in the final Test at Kingston. Both England and the West Indies hoped to break the series deadlock. England were determined not to lose, and as the first six batsmen all passed fifty in a Test innings for the first time, they plodded to 849 all out. Sandham borrowed a bat from his captain and boots from Patsy Hendren, which were so ill-fitting that they continually slipped off as he ran. He made 325 in ten hours, constantly contending with a succession of younger, sprightlier new partners insisting on quick singles. He hit 28 fours, a five and a seven, but overall, Sandham ran 213 of his 325 runs.[49]

It was all in vain. In the second innings he made a quick fifty, and after seven full days of play, hands were shaken, a draw was agreed upon and England headed for home. In the four Caribbean Tests, Sandham had made 583 runs while 'no one was looking'.[50] Back to The Oval he went, his fourteen-Test career over. Never had a cricketer been so deserving of an international career that was not forthcoming.

Then as now, Test cricket was the big event, populated by big names. But the likes of Fred Root, Freeman, Constantine and Sandham are no less part of cricket's narrative. Between them, these four players scored more than 58,000 runs, including 113 centuries and the first ever Test triple century, and took over 5,700 wickets, including the most wickets in a season by anyone. One was described as the best all-round cricketer in the world, but the four of them were worth a total of only 47 Test matches between them. Joe Root played more than that before his 26th birthday. They were all battlers, servers, sportsmen and artists, but if you were looking the other way, you might never have seen them.

# 11

# BRADMAN AND HAMMOND
*The Greatest, but for One Man*

The English cricket season of 1930 set the tone for the next two decades. Not in terms of one team dominating, but in terms of one man ruling supreme. Donald George Bradman had already played for Australia in the 1928/9 home series against England and scored enough runs (468, including two centuries) to indicate some merit. He had actually been dropped after his first Test and was only reprieved because of injuries. One cannot imagine how cricket might have evolved had the Australian selectors decided that scores of eighteen and one in his first Test match were insufficient for him ever to be picked again.

After 1930, there was never any doubt. Not yet 22 years old, he established himself at the pinnacle of cricketing achievement, with his own position in the 'pantheon of greats', looking down on everyone else from a pedestal 'built of record books and bowlers' broken spirits'.[1] In the series against England he made 974 runs in seven innings at an average of almost 140. It comprised a century, two doubles and – at Headingley in the third Test – a triple, when he became the third player to score a century before lunch on the first day of a Test. He added another between lunch and tea and scored 309 in one day. Across the tour he scored six double centuries, all helping him reach another rare landmark as he became the fifth man to score 1,000 runs in May. His 2,960 runs on that trip would be equivalent to a good season's work by three fine players. If Bradman's own recollections of the tour focused on the English countryside, meeting the royal family and a trip to the opera, his batting left England 'a pale, shaking shell'.[2]

While other sportsmen break records, Bradman smashed through barriers to set markers nobody would ever come near. His Test match batting average of 99.94 is almost 40 more than anyone else's. His career average of 95.14 is almost 40 more than anyone who played for a similar amount of time. It took him 295 innings to make a hundred hundreds while the next closest took well over five hundred. Nobody scored more double centuries in a career, or more triples. Crowds wanted records, wrote Raymond Robertson-Glasgow, and Bradman 'dressed his window accordingly'.[3] While Jack Nicklaus, Tiger Woods, Roger Federer, Michael Jordan, Serena Williams and Muhammad Ali all sat at the pinnacle of their sport for a while, Bradman perched on cricket's summit for almost two decades, a machine that turned out runs 'as other machines turn out screws or sausages'.[4]

He belonged to Australia, but his ancestry was European. In 1826 one Emanuel Sebastiano Neich left Genoa, thinking that the ship he was aboard was sailing to Holland. At some stage, presumably when it was too late, he discovered that he was actually going to New Holland, which is what they called Australia in those days. Despite the shock, and a far longer journey than he anticipated, Neich liked it there and settled, becoming a successful hotelier with major reserves of energy, his two marriages yielding 24 children.[5] He also had a daughter with another woman while his first wife was still alive.[6] The child in question was called Sophia and when of age, she married William Whatman. Their sixth child, Emily, married a chap called George Bradman. Neich's great-grandson was to become perhaps the most dominant cricketer of all time, his career meriting its own *Wisden* volume charting his every on-field heartbeat.[7]

Donald Bradman, 1930.

Beyond *Wisden*, so much has been written about Bradman. Only when statistics are set aside do we realize that unlike Bradman the batsman, Bradman the man had flaws. In *Bradman's War: How the 1948 Invincibles Turned the Cricket Pitch into a Battle Field* by Malcolm Knox, the 'war' does not refer to anything happening between 1939 and 1945 but instead describes the rather testy relationship between him and some of those who played alongside him.

That Bradman's reach extended beyond cricket came at a cost. He rarely partook of casual conversation and easy acquaintance, instead living a life akin to 'somewhere between that of an Emperor and an Ambassador'.[8] He was difficult to know, and difficult to keep knowing. While there were countless tributes recognizing his batting, sportsmanship and contributions as a cricketer, selector or administrator, tributes to Bradman the man are 'as rare as his runs were profuse'.[9] Australian leg spinner Bill 'Tiger' O'Reilly and Bradman, for example, walked onto the field many times as teammates, but never as friends. 'You could say we did not like each other, but it would be closer to the truth to say we chose to have little to do with each other,' observed O'Reilly, as precisely as if he was positioning a fielder.[10] Less precisely, he also suggested that the Bradman Appreciation Society held regular meetings 'in a telephone kiosk'.[11] There were rumours of a dressing-room split into religious factions and that Bradman (a teetotal Protestant) was intent on purging some Catholic teammates.[12] Thereafter two perceived targets, O'Reilly and Jack Fingleton (who also had something of a pathological dislike for Bradman), took belated revenge in their journalism.[13] Neither was Harold Larwood a fan, the bowler steadfastly believing that Bradman had nicked one to the keeper at the very start of the gargantuan innings at Headingley in 1930. He never changed his mind that Bradman 'wasn't a very likeable fellow'.[14]

Bradman outlived most of his critics, but there were others that viewed him differently. In 1980 he began a warm correspondence with a Welsh cricket fan. Doug Davies speculatively wrote to the great champion about his piano playing, and the two exchanged letters for over twenty years until Bradman's death. Davies was invited to Bradman's home on more than one occasion. He was just as Davies had imagined and hoped, Australia's most famous sportsman appearing 'ordinary and modest with no pretensions'.[15]

While nobody surpassed him as a cricketer in statistical terms, some came close. 'Our champion against your champion' has been a familiar dare since the Philistine kings challenged Saul. For all of the 1930s and much of what cricket was possible in the forties, the rivalry between England and Australia invariably polarized into a contest between Bradman and an equally eminent Englishman who had his own way of dividing opinion. In 'the olden, golden days', wrote Denzil Batchelor, cricketers were required to look the part, and while some looked like 'vikings' or 'crusaders', Walter Hammond had a torso 'majestic enough to make a ship's figure-head' and a face with 'a look of a lordship about it'.[16] A silk handkerchief in his hip pocket confirmed his superiority.

And it was justified. Hammond's record was also quite staggering. In first-class cricket between 1920 and 1951, he made more than 50,000 runs with an average of over 56 and took 732 wickets at around an average of 30. In Tests for England, he made 7,249 runs at 58.45. He is one of only nine cricketers to have made 1,000 runs in May; his 167 career centuries have only been bettered by Hobbs and Patsy Hendren; 36 times he passed 200, four times he passed 300. Such statistics reflect mammoth achievements but the key here was the way he went about his business.[17] As a batsman he was sublime, but he was also a fine bowler and might have made it simply for that alone. As a slip fielder he was peerless, and only three other outfielders took more than his 819 career catches.[18] Some of cricket's most sumptuous words are reserved for Hammond. His cover drive, for example, was 'sculpted in the mould of platonic perfection'.[19] Matches were influenced just by his presence, or how bowlers felt when they saw him taking strike, when 'lunch seemed far and the boundary near'.[20]

He played and lived as if to the manor born. Something of a social climber, he enjoyed the finer things in life and hobnobbing with the wealthy and influential. Attracted by the kudos of the England captaincy, he became an amateur, wore fine clothes and liked women who did the same. Driven by class and money, he had enough of the former but rarely sufficient of the latter. It might have partly explained his 'self-induced solitude' and 'uncommunicative nature'.[21] Apparently, when on tour in Australia, the sum total of Hammond's conversation with Len Hutton during a 700-mile car journey was 'Look out for a garage – we need petrol.' It meant fractious relationships with some of his Gloucestershire teammates. Charles Barnett had originally been friends with Hammond but took a dim view of his colleague's no show at Barnett's benefit match, and their rather cavalier extramarital socializing. The relationship between the two men deteriorated from 'shared transport and occasional shared suppers' to 'unmitigated contempt'.[22]

Despite his almost unparalleled ability, Hammond was 'tormented'.[23] David Foot's outstanding biography stands apart because of its attempts to explain how one of the most talented cricketers of all time could also be one of the moodiest. Foot proposes a legitimate if rather startling explanation. Hammond returned from MCC's tour of West Indies in 1925/6 with a serious illness apparently caused by a mosquito bite or blood poisoning; the details are unusually sparse, given that he was the nation's most promising sportsman. The reason for the mystery and reticence to discuss it, claims Foot, is that Hammond had contracted a sexually transmitted disease and its treatment by mercury had long-lasting effects on his mood and personality. Hammond, as described by England teammate Eddie Paynter, 'liked a good shag', and as 'the Hugh Hefner of interwar cricket', his lifestyle caught up with him. Indeed, seemingly it had almost killed him.[24]

When he recovered, his appearance shocked his teammates, few of whom realized how ill he had been. Eventually he resumed his life as a romancer, entering the 'bright and febrile world we know from Evelyn Waugh and *Brideshead Revisited*'.[25] But his love life was tumultuous, its awkward nadir coming during England's 1939 tour of South Africa, when he fell in love with a beauty queen (who eventually became his second wife) shortly before his current wife arrived to join the tour. Neither was the end of Hammond's career the lap of honour many might have hoped for. Aged 48 and out of shape, he was coaxed out of retirement for a match but despite a warm ovation his innings was 'brief and cruelly misplaced' as he scraped seven singles in fifty minutes. With Hammond's old elegance and coordination gone, Somerset spinner Horace Hazell encouraged him with some half-volleys. Seeing Hammond so powerless, the bowler admitted to shedding 'private tears'.[26]

To compound his problematic personal and professional relationships, he was a disastrous businessman. When he died in 1965, he was so financially stricken that his wife had to sell his cricketing memorabilia. Foot's description of the auction in 1969 is heartbreakingly detailed – inscribed gifts and artefacts were sold off for a few pounds as casual purchases for the curious. The sad denouement to this episode is an appeal from Hammond's daughter some time later. Her young son, it seemed, was showing promise as a cricketer but had no tangible memorabilia to remind him that his grandad was one of the greatest ever. Seemingly without notable cricketing talent, achievement or aesthetic charm, many cricketers found friends, fun and fellowship that Hammond never did.

In any other era Hammond would have been king of the cricketing castle. While he had choleric relationships with many, one of the most problematic professional relationships of his career – if 'relationship' is the word – was with Bradman. It was cruel luck that his career ran in parallel with Bradman's, and the greater part was spent 'in the shadow of the matchless Australian'.[27] Both were loners, and even if the rivalry was mainly driven by Hammond, it simmered along until 'one could smell the acrid fumes off the wicket'.[28] Whenever Bradman was involved, Hammond always seemed to be a day late and a dollar short. When in 1930, for example, the Englishman returned a respectable 306-run aggregate at an average of 34, Bradman – five years younger and in unfamiliar conditions – made 974 at almost 140. Hammond's 113 at Leeds looked trifling in response to Bradman's 334. The irritation was further compounded as Bradman's record series aggregate – still unsurpassed – consigned Hammond's 905 in the 1928/9 Ashes to second place. No sooner did Hammond set a mark than Bradman beat it.

Even when Bradman was blunted during the 1932/3 Bodyline series, Hammond was unable to put statistical daylight between them. He scored well enough, making 440 runs for 55 and taking nine wickets. In a quiet series for him, Bradman still managed 396 runs at an average better than Hammond's. He took a wicket too: with a filthy full toss he bowled an England batsman well set on 85. It was Hammond – of course it was. Around every corner, Bradman was there to scupper him. It is hardly surprising, then, that when Hammond beat Bradman's Test best of 334 in New Zealand a couple of months later, he was unusually and demonstratively pleased. A few years later, in the Adelaide Test of 1937, he got revenge of sorts, snaring his nemesis with a nifty caught and bowled. The Don, though, was on 212 at the time. Revenge comes at a price.

The rivalry gained an even sharper edge during the 1938 series in England. Hammond gave up his professional status – and the match fees accompanying it – in order to meet Bradman on equal terms as his country's captain. It was a tough call for one as money-minded as Hammond.[29] By the fifth Test, the Ashes had gone, but England still needed a face-saving win to square the series.

At The Oval, they took three days over 903 for 7 declared, Hammond ending the plunder only when it became clear that injury would prevent Bradman from batting. The Don never forgot the humiliation of losing a Test by an innings and 579 runs. It was bad news for England and Hammond when cricket resumed with the optimistically named 'Goodwill Tour' of 1946/7.

During the war, Hammond held a largely administrative role in the RAF, and despite his lack of combat, he saw the trip as some respite since Australia had escaped the worst of the conflict and food was plentiful. Hammond promised his team 'the happiest six months of your life'.[30] But for Bradman, memories of Bodyline and The Oval still stung. Bradman's war had consisted of 'selling stocks, playing golf and getting himself into committees' and a six-year break was merely a brief delay before the England pay-back began.[31] In the first innings of the first Test, the Australian edged one to slip at 28 but stayed put. Even the home crowd thought it was out, but the umpires – maybe nonplussed by his failure to walk – gave him not out. At The Oval, he went on to make 187, eventually leading his team to victory by an innings and 332 runs. 'Goodwill' was in short supply when Hammond told his rival it was 'a fine f****** way to start a Test series'.[32] Keith Miller described the series thereafter as more like 'a contest between Bradman and Hammond'.[33] Australia's comfortable series win all but ended Hammond's career. Homesick, out of shape and his enthusiasm for cricket gone, he became even more aloof, often travelling separately from his team in what Denis Compton called the worst mismanagement he ever saw.[34]

If off-field success is to be measured by wealth, stability and influence, then Bradman had the upper hand again. A fruitful business career was pursued in parallel with a happy 65-year marriage, and even in retirement he retained his grip on cricket, 'crippling it, issue by issue'.[35] His intransigence is thought to have driven international cricket into the welcoming arms of Kerry Packer. But even if he was not universally loved, his legend endures.

If Hammond ended his days forlorn and almost forgotten, Bradman lived more than thirty years longer and was honoured, adorned and mostly adored. When *Wisden* chose its greatest five cricketers of the twentieth century, the panel were given multiple votes and Hammond polled eighteen votes out of a hundred, but Bradman was selected by everyone. Most wise judges, though, had Hammond in front in one measure at least. As a batsman, Bradman was 'a millionaire practicing thrift'[36] and Len Hutton once apparently said that he preferred an hour of Walter Hammond to eight or ten of Don Bradman. The imperturbable Bradman probably wouldn't have cared. As for Hammond, he might have been the greatest, but for one man. Life is cruel and so is cricket.

# 12

# OLD FRIENDS FALL OUT

## *The 1930s*

Dealing with Bradman was the key cricketing conundrum for two decades. Consequently for England, the 1932/3 Ashes series in Australia looked to be a major problem. But nobody anticipated the lengths to which England would go to nullify cricket's greatest run machine. If any historical sporting relationship has been defined by just a few weeks, then this is it. It transcends cricket; in 2013 Australia's Deputy Prime Minister Wayne Swan referenced Bodyline in a renewed bid to establish an Australian Republic.[1] In 2016 England rugby union coach Eddie Jones played some footage of the Bodyline series before a match against Australia.[2] Short-pitched bowling in any club match will pejoratively be called 'Bodyline' by players who may not even understand why. For a while the British empire was threatened and a correspondent to the *Daily Telegraph* suggested that the series should have been abandoned, since some things were more important than cricket.[3] That was even more controversial.

It was cricket's biggest rumpus, the narrative consisting of a battle between nations, a plan, its execution, its reception and the inevitable tale of good versus evil. It was the story, suggests David Frith, of a 'Wild West shoot-out' between 'the smart young sheriff' and a 'narrow-eyed gunslinger'.[4] Jack Fingleton was an Australian batsman in three of the Bodyline Tests and claimed that no batsmen playing in the matches ever 'recaptured his love for cricket'.[5]

Bodyline begins, inevitably, with Bradman. Indeed, Australian cricket history is all about the letter B; Bradman and Bodyline.[6] The general plan to disarm him might have begun when Australia played Surrey during Australia's tour of England in 1930. Surrey captain Percy Fender had written that the Australian had batted 'like a schoolboy' when first part of the Test team.[7] In slow-burning revenge, Bradman 'murdered' Surrey with a double hundred, making a special point of ridiculing Fender by hitting the ball to the spot from where he'd just moved a fielder.[8] For Surrey fieldsman Douglas Jardine, it was the beginning of some deep theorizing about ways to thwart the Aussie champion.[9]

'Jardine' has become shorthand for ruthless single-mindedness. Indeed, Australians believe, 'rightly or wrongly', that in England Jardine is considered a hero, but think of him themselves as 'a pig-headed, cheating little grot'.[10] Having performed strongly as both captain and batsman in England's 1932 Test against India, he was chosen to lead MCC's tour to Australia in 1932/3. He soon took to referring to Bradman as 'the little bastard', vowing that in order to regain the Ashes, he had to be 'badly broken and beaten'.[11]

Jardine's 'Eureka moment' came as he watched film of Bradman batting against England fast bowler Harold Larwood.[12] The dazzling Australian seemed to flinch – as did others – against fast, short-pitched bowling. 'He's yellow,' concluded Jardine, and the plotting began. Before the tour, he met Larwood and fellow Nottinghamshire bowler Bill Voce at the Grill Room in London's Café Royal. As miners with simpler tastes, perhaps they would have preferred something less fancy, but Jardine was educated at Winchester and Oxford, so the meeting was never going to happen outside the local chippy. The two fast bowlers were essential to his plan; if the Australian batsmen were subjected to short bowling aimed at their bodies, they would be too busy preserving life and limb to score any runs. Continually forced to fend off deliveries, theorized Jardine, they would provide rich pickings for the waiting leg-side fielders.

Born in Bombay to Scottish parents, Jardine's talent emerged at school. Few great batsmen would have matured so early and at only seventeen, he could have moved on from the Winchester eleven into Test cricket 'and done reasonably well'.[13] However, also evident was a sense of functionality that eventually overwhelmed the carefree abandon of his earlier batting.[14] His cricket was imbued with a sense of duty, and perhaps it developed into an obsession; he wanted to beat an Australian team, and an Australian team containing Bradman. The Aussies hated him immediately, and he quickly alienated local journalists by refusing to reveal his team for an early warm-up match. While there was nothing unusual about players wearing university caps, Jardine's harlequin cap from Oxford drove Australian crowds potty. Panelled with segments of maroon, buff and dark blue, it connoted a rather haughty, aristocratic form of cricket, not necessarily the kind appreciated by earthier punters in Sydney, Melbourne and Adelaide.[15] The first glimpse of Jardine's cap on the 1928/9 tour begat Australia's hatred of Jardine, which in turn 'begat Jardine's hatred of Australia, which begat Bodyline'.[16] Decades later, businessman Nigel Wray paid £75,000 to make it part of his sporting memorabilia collection, alongside other items including the shirt worn by Stanley Matthews in the famous FA Cup final of 1953.[17]

In response to his assertion that Australians were 'uneducated and unruly', the *Melbourne Truth* speculated that as the only competitor in a hypothetical 'Most Popular Man in Australia' competition, Jardine would be unplaced.[18] This echoed the prophetic words of his cricket coach at Winchester. Upon hearing that Jardine would captain the tour, former England all-rounder Rockley Wilson reflected that while he might well win the Ashes, he might also lose a dominion.[19] Australian journalists were even less forgiving, suggesting that Jardine was the 'most notorious Englishman since Jack the Ripper'.[20]

As Bodyline developed, one famously demonstrative member of the crowd relentlessly pursued Jardine. So famous was 'Yabba' that other England skippers (not Jardine) used to shake his hand at the end of a series in Australia. Ironically, Yabba – or Stephen Harold Gascoigne, as he was christened – had an English father. Given the nickname on account of his incessant talking, he earned a living hawking rabbits door-to-door.[21] As a witty observer, Yabba 'had many imitators but no equals'.[22] A Boer War veteran, he had old-fashioned standards, and while his barracking was always earthy, it was never crude, though his wisecracks 'could shake trees in distant suburbs'.[23] In the early 1990s a new stand at the SGC was named after him, making him one of the few non-players or administrators to be so honoured.[24] Sculptress Cathy Weizmann created a bronze statue of him that stands at the Randwick End, facing the action and leaning forward to unleash his invective. Once or twice Yabba even called the match from the commentary box; he was inducted into the Australian Hall of Fame, and when he died in 1942, the New South Wales Cricket Association stood in silence.

Even though Yabba's banter may now seem rather pedestrian, at the time it was considered 'fresh and funny', with observations like 'send 'im down a piano, see if he can play that', and 'I wish you were a statue and I were a pigeon.'[25] A reminder that wit prevails over profanity, his most famous sledge was reserved for Jardine. As the imperious England skipper swatted away the flies on a steamy day, 'Jardine,' hollered Yabba, 'leave our flies alone!' With massive understatement, on the previous tour to Australia, England's clown-in-chief Patsy Hendren had observed that the local crowds didn't seem to like Jardine much. 'The feeling', he responded, 'is ******* mutual.'[26]

The Bodyline tour was an unhappy one, with plenty of dissenting voices from within. Tour manager Plum Warner described Jardine as 'difficult' and inclined to use 'poor language', and that when he came into contact with Australians, he had a tendency towards madness.[27] Gubby Allen felt the same, adding that Jardine was loathed 'more than any German who ever fought in any war'.[28]

The Nawab of Pataudi was another unhappy tourist. Also excelling at hockey and billiards, he played Test matches for both India and England. In 1931 he made five centuries in six innings for the University of Oxford and two years later, like princes Ranji and Duleep before him, he made a century on his Test debut against Australia just as Bodyline was beginning. But he disagreed with Jardine's tactics and refused to join the waiting ring of leg-side fielders. 'I see his Highness is a conscientious objector,' observed Jardine bitterly, and when the Indian did less well in the second Test, he was dropped.[29] 'I am told he has his good points,' said Pataudi of his captain, but 'in three months I have yet to see them.'[30]

All this contrasted starkly with reflections from Jardine's daughter, who remembers a man with a 'lovely dry sense of humour' who used to read her *The Jungle Book*.[31] He may have had a soft side, but not when it came to cricket. A few years before his death from cancer aged only 57, he appeared at Tilbury to wave off the England party touring Australia in 1954/5. His advice to a young Colin Cowdrey was to remember that when he arrived in Australia he should 'hate the bastards'.[32]

The part played by Bill Voce in Jardine's master plan is often marginalized as the story usually focuses on Larwood, the skipper and various antagonized Australians. But Voce's role was also important.[33] Slower than Larwood but taller and seemingly stronger, he could get the ball to rise steeply and even if batsmen worked out how to face the express pace of Larwood, they needed

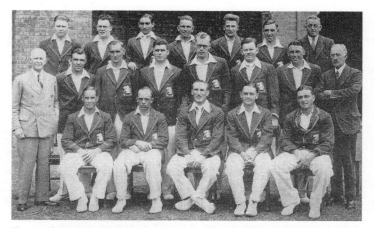

England's Bodyline Touring Party, 1932/3: Nawab of Pataudi (back row, third from left), Harold Larwood (back row, fifth from left), Eddie Paynter (back row, sixth from left), Bill Ferguson (back row, extreme right), Pelham Warner (middle row, extreme left), Leslie Ames (middle row, second from left), Hedley Verity (middle row, third from left), Bill Voce (middle row, fourth from left), Freddie Brown (middle row, sixth from left), Douglas Jardine (front row, centre), Gubby Allen (front row, fourth from left), Walter Hammond (front row, extreme right).

a different strategy for Voce. Statistically, his fifteen wickets in the series (he played in only four Tests) pale in comparison to Larwood's 33, but it was a proper double act.

Larwood and Voce had both worked as miners and were used to hard graft in hot conditions. Accordingly, they both liked their refreshments. England wicketkeeper Leslie Ames was appointed by Jardine as an unofficial minder for the pair to moderate their consumption. Clearly much better behind the stumps than as a chaperone, Ames simply joined in and became as drunk as his teammates.[34] Voce had a strong constitution and was still playing for England a decade and a half later. Larwood was cast aside after the final Test match, despite still being the fastest and most menacing option. Despite being the pivotal figure in a final Test win at Sydney (98 as nightwatchman and five wickets in the match), he never represented England again, as an embarrassed establishment laid the blame squarely at his door. Seen as even more guilty than Jardine, despite being required to apologize, he resolutely refused to do so for the rest of his long life.

There is no doubt as to why Larwood is considered the Rolls-Royce of fast bowlers. Based on fifteen seconds of video tape, it seems impossible to see any flaw in his action. Slow motion makes his action look dreamy and dramatic, and with shirt gently billowing, his strides lightly kiss the turf. Gathering into a menacing leap, he maintains his momentum during delivery. It is an action widely admired for its sleekness, but such perfection would be pointless if the product was insipid. But it wasn't. He was fast – 'you cannot imagine how fast,' claimed John Arlott.[35] Bill O'Reilly described facing him and just before he delivered the ball, 'something hit the middle of my bat with such force that it was almost dashed from my hands. It was the ball.'[36] Moreover, of those 33 Bodyline wickets, sixteen were clean bowled, so not everything reared up to hit the batsman. Most importantly of all, he is considered to be one of the few bowlers to ever seriously worry Bradman. For any other mortal, 396 runs at an average of over 56, including five fifties and a century, would have been perfectly respectable, but for Bradman it was seriously below par.

Fifteen or so years after Bodyline, Jack Fingleton – one of the terrorized batsmen – looked up his old adversary. He found Larwood living under the radar and struggling to make any money from his Blackpool corner shop.[37] Their conversation must have planted the seed of an idea. A couple of years later, Fingleton received a telegram: 'Leaving Orantes London tomorrow stop Can you arrange accommodation for self wife five daughters eldest daughters fiancee stop Also jobs signed Larwood.'[38] It seemed an enormous request, but Fingleton was well-connected and everything was arranged. An incredulous Denzil Batchelor suggested that there would be no story 'as dramatic and miraculous' as Larwood's return to Australia, and the welcome he received could only be eclipsed by the pope being applauded 'all the way round Moscow's Red Square'.[39]

Despite happy resettlement, Larwood maintained low-key links with England. Mike Selvey recalls that as a young player in 1968, he paid little attention to a courteous, bespectacled visitor leaving an autograph book for the players to sign. He found out later that it was Larwood, and regretted that he didn't recognize the old-timer: 'While he had my autograph, I didn't have his.'[40] But access to England cricket and its cricketers was not always as easy; when Larwood dropped in on England's tourists in 1950/51 and 1954/5, the dressing-room door was quite literally shut in his face.[41]

True, he held the odd grudge. He was no great fan of tour manager Pelham Warner, who tried his best to convince his charges that old-fashioned cricket protocols should prevail over the new tactics. As we have heard, neither was Larwood fond of Bradman, but he had huge admiration for Douglas Jardine, who was 'one of the finest men I have ever met . . . a magnificent captain, a great sportsman and a true friend'.[42] He was immeasurably proud of the inscribed ashtray 'from a grateful captain' and when he died in his 91st year, he was 'a man undefeated'.[43]

Besides Larwood's connection with Fingleton, he maintained a strong friendship with Bert Oldfield, ironically one of the batsmen he hit with his short-pitched bowling. The incident that inextricably joins them occurred in the third Test at Adelaide. Having made his way to a stubborn 41 not out, Oldfield hooked a ball from Larwood onto his skull, clutched his head and fell to his knees. At first, Larwood feared he was dead, and when he ran to the batsman's aid the crowd, of course, didn't hear Oldfield tell the bowler that he wasn't to blame.[44] Oldfield had sustained a linear fracture to the frontal bone that came within a whisker of proving fatal.[45] Afraid the crowd would invade the field, Larwood told wicketkeeper Les Ames to grab a stump for protection. The spectators didn't come, but the mother of all diplomatic rows certainly did.

The fact that Oldfield exonerated the bowler didn't placate anyone. Footage of him being hit was replayed to horrified audiences at home and abroad, the first such cricketer to be seen on the silver screen as a 'writhing, involuntary victim of violence'.[46] In 2000 actor Russell Crowe paid $28,000 for Oldfield's cap at auction, noting that judging by the way the peak had come away from the cap, something must have hit him 'with some force'.[47] One additional intriguing detail suggests that Douglas Jardine did, indeed, have a softer side when he contacted Oldfield's wife to express regret about her husband's injury, also arranging for their young daughters to receive Shirley Temple dolls.[48]

The Brisbane Test had been notable for another resounding win by England, who clinched the series. It was facilitated

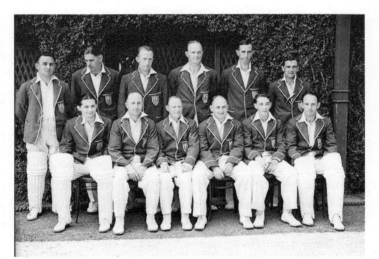

New South Wales team, 1936: Bill O'Reilly (standing, third from right), Bert Oldfield (sitting, third from left), Stan McCabe (sitting, third from right) and Jack Fingleton (sitting, extreme right).

by a Herculean effort by England batsman Eddie Paynter, a shy Lancastrian so innocent and clean-living that he had to be persuaded by Larwood to try a glass of shandy on the outward journey. At thirty years old, it was his first taste of alcohol.[49] Presumably unconnected, by the end of the second day of the Test, Paynter had come down with a sore throat serious enough to hospitalize him. Realizing it was no time to lose a batsman, Jardine pressurized Paynter to come back to the ground. 'What about those fellows who marched to Kandahar with fever on them?' suggested the skipper, reminding everyone of the momentous trek from Kabul led by General Roberts in 1880, when 10,000 thirsty British soldiers marched in the freezing dead of night to avoid the 100° heat.[50] It was only cricket, but for Jardine it had long since 'taken on the proportions of war'.[51]

After turning up to the dressing room in his pyjamas and going out to bat at number 8 with England six down but still over 120 runs short of Australia's first innings, Paynter made 24 not out on the first evening, before returning to hospital for some stern words from the ward sister.[52] The next day he made 83, ensuring a first-innings lead. England won the match, and on his return to Lancashire, his county captain threw a dinner in Paynter's honour and demanded the modest hero make a speech. 'Ah did me best at Brisbane for England an' for Lancashire,' he reflected, 'but as for talk about mi leavin' a sickbed at risk of mi dyin' – well, beggin' your pardon, Mr Eckersley, that were all rot. It were nowt more than a sore throat.'[53]

But Paynter, Larwood, Jardine, Bradman and all the action they provided could still be overshadowed. The hosts, of course, had a very different perspective of it all. In the first instance there was one Australian batsman that should have been there, skilfully facing the onslaught, and players from both sides were shattered by the death, during Bodyline, of Archie Jackson aged only 23.

After only eight Tests, it was clear that he was a special talent. If Bradman was Gulliver among the Lilliputians,[54] then many felt Jackson might have matched his achievements but would have eclipsed him in terms of style. Decades later, Harold Larwood talked about Jackson with huge fondness, clutching an ancient telegram: 'CONGRATULATIONS ... MAGNIFICENT ... BOWLING ... GOOD ... LUCK ... ALL ... MATCHES,' it said.[55] It had been sent by Jackson just a day or two before he died. The timing was doubly significant for Larwood, since Jackson's message arrived when he was being given 'the full treatment' by Australian crowds.[56]

Larwood no doubt recalled Jackson's Test debut at Adelaide in 1928/9. While the bowler toiled for 57 wicketless overs, twenty-year-old Jackson made a sensational first innings of 164, which was 'classical' for critics and 'magic' for any cricket lover.[57] His century was reached with a powerful square drive off Larwood, from a ball the bowler claimed was about as fast as anything he ever mustered.[58] In the next hour, he added another 64 runs and made Bradman look 'pedestrian'.[59] 'No one', noted Denzil Batchelor, looked at Bradman 'while Jackson was at the wicket'.[60]

Jackson was actually Scottish, his family having emigrated from Rutherglen to Sydney when he was a child. Early cricket in Balmain was spent under the tutelage of Arthur Mailey and the elegant batsman Alan Kippax. Despite rave reviews across Australia, his life was regularly punctuated with poor health. In 1931/2 he coughed up blood before a match and was sent to a sanatorium to recuperate. From there, he moved to Brisbane to be with his girlfriend and played some club cricket, but it became apparent that tuberculosis would claim him. Labour politician and eventual president of the United Nations General Assembly H. V. 'Doc' Evatt had been a regular sponsor of Jackson and paid for his parents to fly to his bedside. Jackson's gravestone simply proclaims, 'He played the game.' 'Ah well,' muses Batchelor, 'you

Archie Jackson,
*c.* 1930s.

would not have expected Keats to have been allowed to grow old.'[61]

Leading the pall-bearers at Jackson's funeral was Australian captain Bill Woodfull. Amid the tragedy of Jackson and the political furore, it was his job to keep order within his beleaguered team. It was fortunate that Woodfull was no hothead and without his measured dignity, Australia might never have welcomed back an England team. But there were times when even the 'stolid, reserved Victorian schoolmaster' was pushed to the limit.[62] Preferring discipline and fairness, great Aussie all-rounder Keith Miller recalls being castigated by him for some 'schoolyard misdemeanour'.[63]

The greatest challenge of Woodfull's career occurred during the third Test at Adelaide. It was mid-January, but the season of goodwill had bypassed cricket altogether. Indeed, *Wisden* called it probably the most 'unpleasant' of all Tests.[64] In retrospect, whoever scheduled it for Friday the 13th must have wondered whether

Thursday the 12th might have been a better idea. Responding to England's first innings of 341, Australia started badly before Woodfull was struck above the heart by Larwood. The skipper grabbed his chest in agony after the most serious of several blows sustained during his innings of 22.[65] The crowd became incensed and 'pandemonium reigned'.[66]

And it continued to reign. Plum Warner and assistant manager Dick Palairet ventured into the Australian dressing room to ask after the skipper's health, but Woodfull did not welcome their enquiry. He told them he didn't want to discuss it, since 'one side is playing cricket and the other is not.'[67] Further suggesting that England's tactics were damaging cricket, he went as far as saying that some involved in the game should get out of it.[68] For Warner, having the Australian skipper turn his back on him was his greatest cricketing humiliation; his humour was not improved when, after telling Jardine how angry Woodfull was, the England skipper's response was, 'I couldn't care less.'[69]

Australia Test team, 1930: Bill Woodfull (middle row, centre), Archie Jackson (back row, second from left), Clarrie Grimmett (back row, second from right), Donald Bradman (middle row, second from right) and Bert Oldfield (sitting on floor, extreme right).

Later in the Australian first innings, when wicketkeeper Oldfield was more seriously injured, Woodfull marched to the middle in his civvies, helped his teammate off the field and afterwards reflected that he should have closed the innings in disgust.[70] But Oldfield had faced worse than Larwood, having already come impossibly close to death while serving in the First World War in the 15th Field Ambulance. He was being transported on a stretcher and survived a German bomb that killed the four men carrying him.[71] Perhaps the consequent steel plate in his head provided that extra layer of protection against Larwood, but Oldfield certainly bore no grudge. Ian Wooldridge visited Larwood in the early 1970s and persuaded him to take a trip to Oldfield's sporting-goods store in Sydney. At first, reports Wooldridge, the old bowler was reluctant, but eventually relented. The reunion of the two old adversaries was 'very touching', noted Wooldridge, especially Oldfield's repeated refusal to blame the England bowler.[72]

There was a tangible sense of style and quality about Oldfield, who had an understated sense of humour and 'a genius for making friends'.[73] On the field, he was unobtrusive, appealed sparingly and usually only removed a single bail when breaking the stumps. There was minimal effort, minimal fuss and maximum performance from the most honest of wicketkeepers and also, for many, the best.[74] English umpire Frank Chester judged Oldfield the best wicket-keeper of all.[75] His Test record is exceptional and if stumpings are the connoisseur's measure of quality, then Oldfield was the ultimate keeper. In 54 Tests, 52 hapless batsmen were punished for straying out of their ground. Godfrey Evans claimed 46, but in almost twice many Tests. Oldfield was the first wicketkeeper to get to one hundred Test victims, and the first to make 1,000 runs. And to think, if things had turned out differently, he might easily have 'found an unknown grave in the bombardment of Polygon Wood'.[76]

In the meantime, after Adelaide in 1933, those running cricket in Australia and England began their own contest – not so much a war of words as a crossing of cables. Australian administrators described the Bodyline tactics as 'unsportsmanlike' and serious enough to undermine the game and threaten the relationship between the two countries. The cable was received with astonishment that anyone could challenge English sportsmanship.

In response, MCC were 'foggily resentful', but the official reply to Australia's 'hurried and ill-written complaint' began with one of the 'greatest cricketing sentences'.[77] 'We deplore your cable,' it said, and 'deprecate your suggestion that there has been unsportsmanlike play'.[78] They offered to call off the tour if the Australians wished. The exchange lasted for almost a month until the big guns – politicians – were wheeled out and finally, the Australian Board blinked first and backed down from their claims of unsportsmanlike behaviour. The tour continued amid 'a humiliating volte-face', since the Aussies assumed that the English tactics would change.[79] The assumption was wrong, which must have stung the Australian cricket hierarchy as much as losing the Ashes.

While the row often overshadowed the cricket, there were standout Australian performances. Foremost among these were the 27 wickets taken by Bill O'Reilly, who held a 'splendid animosity' towards opponents.[80] He was 'at his best when angry', which, it seems, was much of the time.[81] Hitting him to the boundary, for example, was like 'disturbing a hive of bees'.[82]

But Tiger O'Reilly's pantomime-villain truculence mustn't overshadow his brilliance, as he delivered spitting leg spinners at medium pace. Plenty considered him the best Australia had ever produced, and if Bradman describes you as 'the greatest bowler that I ever faced', then you were definitely good.[83] Bradman's opinion was especially significant since the two were never friends. During Bodyline, England had little clue as to how to deal with Tiger.

When he stopped playing, he didn't quietly fade away. The column he wrote in the *Sydney Morning Herald* for 42 years functioned as the 'fearless conscience' of Australian cricket.[84] Unafraid of voicing unpopular opinions, he claimed that there was nothing wrong with Bodyline, and that anyone imagining it was 'bad for cricket' should look at crowds and the interest it generated.[85] Fairness was everything; he told his employers that it should be the regular cricket correspondent who should go on tour to England after the war and not him. 'I have another job,' he told them, but 'Cricket-writing is his livelihood.'[86]

But O'Reilly was grumpy about modern cricket and had a 'trenchant dislike' for many of its fashions and gimmicks, including coloured clothing in limited-overs cricket.[87] His opinions about cricketers dyeing their hair and wearing jewellery were practically unprintable.[88] If he saw substandard quality, he called it out. When critical of Australian captain Ian Johnson, he was sidelined by *The Age*, and when an Australian wrote to him to protest at some stinging rebuke, O'Reilly pointed out '16 errors of spelling and syntax' and concluded that 'any of the eight-year-old children I used to teach could have done better'.[89] He never rated coaches much, either, and his advice to rookie leg spinners was that when they saw a coach approaching, they should 'run for their lives'.[90]

Next to O'Reilly (27 wickets) and paceman Tim Wall (sixteen wickets), Australia's next most effective bowler during Bodyline was left-arm spinner Bert Ironmonger. When picked for the second Test at Melbourne, he was nearing his 51st birthday. While others of his vintage were gently trundling away in club cricket, Ironmonger was thrust into the most contentious Test series of all time. He had something of a nomadic career and there was a theory that the selectors kept picking him because amid all the moving about, 'they lost track of his age'.[91] One newspaper described him as bowling with the joy of a 'rejuvenated pensioner'.[92]

But there was method in what initially looked like selectorial madness. Ironmonger had form at Melbourne and had taken 11 for 79 in the match there against the West Indies in 1930/31, and then 7 for 126 in the first Test against South Africa in 1931/2. A few weeks later, the Melbourne Cricket Ground played host as the South Africans tried their luck again. The match was affected by rain but only six hours of playing time were needed as Ironmonger – eleven in the match again – literally mopped up the visitors for 36 and 45. By time, it was the shortest completed match in Test history. In addition, Ironmonger's 11-fer was the cheapest ever Test match ten-plus wicket haul. His 4 for 26 in England's second innings in 1932/3 helped to secure the home side's only victory of the series.

Ironmonger didn't make his debut for Victoria until he was 33 but it might never have happened at all. As a kid, he lost part of his left forefinger while cutting chaff and his sister only prevented his blood loss from becoming fatal by thrusting his hand into a bag of flour.[93] It was messy, but her brother's life was saved, and he later developed a method of spinning the ball using the gnarled stump. Even then, Ironmonger was a throwback, and the Australia he knew was one of 'rural hardship'.[94] Everything about him was 'quaint', but no Aussie bowler has been so miserly or threatening on a wet wicket.[95] As a cricketer, they called him 'Dainty' in the same way you'd call a bald man 'Curly'. Other than his bowling, his general play was notable for its 'utter uselessness'.[96] He didn't even make 'a perfunctory gesture' towards batting and was completely useless as a fielder.[97] When Larwood made 98 as a nightwatchman in what proved to be his last Test innings, missing his century must have been especially bitter since he was caught by Ironmonger, the worst fielder on that or any other cricket field.

Bodyline was certainly not short of characters, which was no doubt something of a motivation for the makers of the ABC-BBC

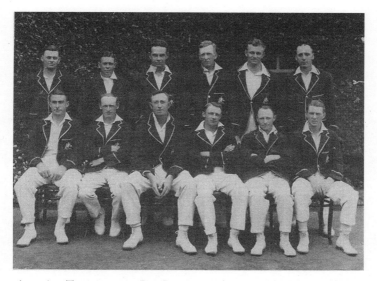

Australian Test team, 1928. Bert Ironmonger (back row, third from left), Bill
Woodfull (back row, extreme left), Clarrie Grimmett (front row, second from
left), Donald Bradman (front row, fourth from left) and Bert Oldfield (front
row, second from right).

jointly produced docudrama in 1984. *Bodyline* was unashamedly
xenophobic and a bizarre corruption of what happened in 1932/3.
David Frith eruditely details the charge sheet. Beside glaring conti-
nuity errors like the ship containing Jardine's team leaving England
with two funnels and arriving in Australia with three, the production took more audacious liberties than a Jos Buttler hundred.
The actors playing the balding Tiger O'Reilly and Stan McCabe
were erroneously hairy, Gubby Allen is much too tall, Bill Voce
much too short and Lord Harris much too fat.[98] Percy Fender is
depicted as 'some outrageous Bertie Wooster' type regularly surrounded by young women.[99] The 'hate' in Harold Larwood's eyes
was not recognized by anyone who knew him.[100] The series was
variously described as 'too ludicrous for words' (E. M. Wellings),
'trash' (Bob Wyatt) and 'repulsive' (Gubby Allen).[101] If ever given

the chance to watch it, Frith advises viewers to 'keep a sizeable pot of salt nearby'.[102]

Ultimately, few came out of the real Bodyline particularly well. Larwood was dumped at once and Jardine shortly afterwards. Warner was embarrassed and humiliated, and Woodfull's widow claimed that being struck on the body contributed to his untimely death aged 67. Perhaps the consequent competitive edge of every subsequent Ashes series has its origins in those steamy days when England's short-pitched bowling might have largely nullified Bradman, but, as predicted by Rockley Wilson, almost cost the long-term goodwill of its dominion.

# 13

# NAYUDU, VIZZY, VERITY, GRIMMETT, GIMBLETT AND SMITH

## More from the 1930s

It was money, and those who had it, that determined and perhaps overshadowed India's entrance to international cricket. Cricket in India is thought to have begun in 1721, when sailors off a trading ship pitched some stumps and began an impromptu game.[1] In 1792 cricket's status was elevated with the establishing of the Calcutta Cricket Club at Eden Gardens, which is still a Test match ground even now.[2] But India did not enter international cricket for another 140 years or so, and when it did, it was accompanied with controversy and a sense of the ridiculous.

In the 1920s and '30s India's royal princes were predominant in cricketing matters since their wealth attracted everything required to play the game, including English professionals and local talent.[3] Royal motives embraced 'self-interest, pragmatism and altruism'.[4] In 1932 India travelled to England to play their first Test match under their captain, the Maharaja of Porbandar. As a cricketer, he was enthusiastic but 'almost useless'.[5] Some pointed out that his princely total of two runs for the whole trip meant that he 'owned more Rolls-Royces than he had made runs'.[6]

India were soundly beaten in their first Test, but one or two players demonstrated considerable quality. English cricket fans knew nothing of the internal conflict created by the captaincy as it passed from Porbandar to stern commoner Cottari Nayudu, but were glad to have seen a side that won some games, 'fielded athletically' and put on 'a cheerful face'.[7] Plum Warner even suggested that England's bowlers didn't have the same 'sting' as the Indian bowlers. A number of the visitors stood out but Nayudu shone the brightest.[8] Playing every game of a long tour, his 1,600 runs included five hundreds and he was named one of *Wisden*'s Cricketers of the Year. His disciplinarian ways were not universally popular, but he was a natural leader and handled an indifferent side with 'skill, discretion and courage'.[9]

The other outstanding Indian cricketer across the trips in 1932 and 1936 was Amar Singh, and in his country's first Test he took four wickets and made India's first Test fifty, batting at number 9. Such was the quality of Singh's bowling that eminent judges described him as the best bowler seen in England since the First World War.[10] He enjoyed bowling at England's batsmen and batting against its bowlers. Chipping in with useful lower runs, he took 28 wickets in seven Tests, including 7 for 44. He died, aged only thirty, from typhoid thought to have developed from a fever following a swim during some wedding celebrations.

With Indian cricket at the mercy of those bidding to bankroll overseas tours, the Maharaja of Porbandar was only captain in 1932 because two other regal figures had withdrawn. The first was the Maharaja of Patiala, a striking figure. Cricket at his place involved 'elephants rolling the wicket', 'three hundred wives' and a 'deer-hunt' before play.[11] The second bidding nobleman was the Maharajkumar of Vizianagram – known as 'Vizzy'.

As India's captain when they returned to England in 1936, Vizzy was highly controversial. Unfortunately, he possessed none of the modesty that led Porbandar to gracefully step aside in 1932. The new captain lacked the ability to steward any team, let alone one divided by 'creed, wealth, culture and language'.[12] As the 'antithesis of Imran Khan', Vizzy couldn't 'bat, bowl, field or lead', and having bought his way to the top, he was completely exposed at the summit.[13] In one county match Vizzy gave a gold

C. K. Nayudu,
*c.* 1930s.

watch to the opposing captain in return for some friendly bowling, but nobody could be paid off in the three Test matches.[14] He
scored 33 runs in six innings.

He divided the Indian camp into supporters (showered with
gifts) and opponents (not showered with anything). He fell out
with his best players Nayudu and Armanath, sending the latter
home after a minor slight. A post-tour committee investigating

the debacle found Vizzy's captaincy 'disastrous' and seemingly lacking even basic appreciation of tactics or strategy.[15] Afterwards he moved into cricket administration and then on to broadcasting, where he was equally incompetent. Once he regaled listeners with a long, dull story about how he'd shot a tiger. West Indian batsman Rohan Kanhai, sitting alongside him, suggested that instead of being shot, the tiger might have died from boredom after listening to Vizzy's commentary.[16] Indian cricket has recovered well from him.

While India had their own problems, relations between England and Australia were still tetchy. Barely a year had passed since Bodyline when Bill Woodfull's men visited England in 1934. Revenge looked to be on the cards as Tiger O'Reilly bowled England out to win the first Test. The second was at Lord's, where Australia hadn't lost for 38 years. With Bradman, O'Reilly and Grimmett in the side, the happy trot looked set to continue. They were nicely set at 192 for 2 at the end of the second day, with Bill Brown on 103 not out and Stan McCabe on 24. Although 248 behind, a first-innings lead for Australia still looked possible, but on Sunday – a rest day – there was a thunderstorm. Few doubted that batting last on a wet wicket – 'a sticky dog' – would be disastrous for England. The Aussies needed winkling out, and quickly.

Salvation was at hand. The next morning Yorkshire left-arm spinner Hedley Verity surveyed the sodden streets and declared that the ball might turn in the damp conditions.[17] As understatements go, it was an Oscar winner. En route to the ground, Verity's taxi ran over a black cat just as the sun came out.[18] Terrible luck for the cat, but fortune was set to smile on Verity. Up to that point, Australia had found making runs straightforward on a dry wicket, but now it was different. The rain dramatically recast the course of the match. In those days, pitches were left to the mercy of the elements and on a drying pitch, Verity was at his most lethal.

His habitual pace – slightly faster than other spinners – was ideal. Australia capitulated for a further 92, with Verity adding six wickets to that of Bradman, caught and bowled on Saturday when it was dry. Australia missed the follow-on by seven runs.

Bradman's wicket was the prize, and his score when you took it generally determined who won the match. Following on in Australia's second innings, he had a rush of blood at thirteen and was again caught off Verity. 'Time seemed to stand still' as wicket-keeper Ames comfortably took the catch.[19] According to Walter Hammond, Verity remained expressionless, 'though he knew, as we all did, that the ball had won the match'.[20] With deadly efficiency, Verity despatched the tail and by 6 p.m., he had fourteen wickets in the day and England had triumphed by an innings and 38 runs. Not given to overstatement, Douglas Jardine suggested that in terms of executing a strategy, Verity's performance stood alone.[21]

Verity's astonishing day has its place in cricketing history but also in wider popular culture. Even Agatha Christie's mercurial sleuth Hercule Poirot was appreciative. In one ITV adaptation, the case of 'Four and Twenty Blackbirds' closed, Poirot dines with Inspector Japp and his friends Captain Hastings and Henry Bonnington. Throughout the case, Hastings had fretted about missing the Test match, his frustration exacerbated since the Belgian sleuth remained nonplussed about how anything lasting five days had still not reached a neat conclusion like one of his cases. The revelation that followed was therefore even more staggering as he castigated Hastings with a surprising appreciation of slow bowling. 'After the weekend rains you are surprised, mon ami?' he quizzed his companion, explaining that 'Australians are used to hard pitches. The Lord's wicket would have been decidedly sticky, no? So it's not a day for the stroke play. No. It's a day for the art of spin bowling, and Hedley Verity is the greatest exponent alive.'[22] The fun didn't last. England lost the series, and within days, Hitler orchestrated the Night of the Long Knives. Five years later, on the final day of county cricket before war, Verity took 7 for 9 for Yorkshire at Hove and wondered out loud whether he'd ever bowl there again.[23] Prophetic words indeed.

Cricket in the 1930s was dominated by the usual suspects. In the Ashes series of 1936/7, when Australia lost the first two Tests and won the following three, Bradman weighed in with 810 runs. Hammond contributed 468 but underlined his value as an all-round cricketer with twelve wickets. Other notable events, mid-decade, included Australia's visit to South Africa in 1935/6, when they thrashed their hosts 4–0. Three of the games were won by an innings, the South African batsmen having little answer to O'Reilly (27 wickets in the series) and his leg-spinning colleague Clarrie Grimmett, who took 44.

Grimmett, a diminutive figure who played 37 Tests for Australia between the wars, was actually a Kiwi. Quiet and understated, he was less of a box-office draw than O'Reilly and more careful than Arthur Mailey. Mailey, indeed, suggested that Grimmett judged a full toss to be 'cricket vandalism' and that a log hop was 'a legacy from prehistoric days when barbarians rolled boulders towards the enemy'.[24] His small head swamped by a huge, baggy green cap, Grimmett looked old before his time, as if he and the calendar had 'never reached any proper understanding'.[25] As 'a wizened little gnome', Grimmett's talents were not always appreciated by the selectors, but he had all the spinning tricks.[26]

Apparently he once played in a club match officiated by a rather starstruck umpire. Before one over, he told the official that he would describe each delivery before bowling it. Each ball spun this way or that, all as predicted. The last ball, advised Grimmett to an increasingly admiring umpire, would pitch straight and shape to move away like a leg break, but would cut back the other way to trap the batsman leg before wicket. As ball hit pad, Grimmett swung round with legs crossed, to be met by the umpire leaping in the air screaming 'OWWWZZZZAT!!'

An earnest cricketer, Grimmett was clearly not immune to fun. In contrast, for his almost-namesake Harold Gimblett, too often cricket meant torture and anguish. Today cricket is more forgiving for those struggling with their mental health. Several cricketers have sought refuge from its pressures, and when former England batsman Geoffrey Boycott suggested that one player's depression had arisen in response to criticism that he 'wasn't good enough', the world rightly winced.[27] But Harold Gimblett never quite came to terms with depression and what it did to him.

He was a sublime cricketer, bursting into prominence in 1935 in the most dramatic fashion – in a lorry. He had been discarded by Somerset after a trial lasting a couple of weeks but wasn't too perturbed. In fact, after being told he wasn't good enough, he told the chairman that it had been one of the best weeks of his life, as he had met all his heroes.[28] It was mid-May, and as the twenty-year-old prepared to return to village cricket, one of the regulars for the game against Essex at Frome was injured. In the ultimate case of 'right place, right time', Gimblett was selected, perhaps on the basis that he would run around and look lively in the field.

His mistake was to agree to find his own way to Frome. He planned to catch the bus to Bridgwater, where a car-driving team-mate would collect him for the final leg of the journey. Anyone who has slept through their alarm on the first day of a new job can imagine his panic when he missed the bus. With another not due for two hours, he began the brave but pointless walk, his embryonic cricket career saved only by a passing lorry driver who delivered him to Bridgwater. When he and his colleague arrived at the ground, the senior man was warmly received in the car park, but the anonymous youngster walked into the changing room 'without interruption'.[29]

If he was unfamiliar at the start of the match, soon Harold Gimblett was imprinted on everyone's memories. Arthur Wellard, Somerset's big hitter, told the youngster, 'I don't think much of your bat, cock,' and offered his own.[30] Appearing at 107 for 6, most expected the country boy to try to keep an end going while the seasoned professionals rebuilt the innings. When he whacked a boundary, some of those watching 'vaguely remembered' a lad with a reputation for big hitting in village cricket.[31] By the time he'd lofted a six to reach fifty less than half an hour later, the marquees had emptied of beer drinkers.[32] Gimblett was out for 123, and his century, including seventeen fours and three sixes in just under an hour, was the fastest scored by anyone all season. But even in his finest hour, dark clouds were looming as the new Somerset hero 'savoured the moment' but 'loathed the publicity' that followed.[33]

Gimblett played in three Tests for England. He made a fifty against India on his debut at Lord's in 1936, but not much else. It was as if the selectors never quite trusted him enough to pick him in a major Test against Australia. R. C. Robertson-Glasgow described Harold's batting as 'too daring' for the 'greybeards, blackbeards, brownbeards and the all-beards' who ran the game.[34] Robertson-Glasgow ends his 1943 essay with the hopeful coda that 'there is time yet.'[35] But there wasn't. Gimblett had already played his last Test match by then, and after the war, in between some sublime performances for Somerset, his own mental health overwhelmed him.

He actually dreaded being picked for England, and was once allegedly found sleepwalking, muttering to himself that he was scoring too many runs. By the start of 1954, he had been admitted to a psychiatric hospital to receive what is now termed electroconvulsive therapy.[36] He was there for four months, and it was hoped that when he returned to cricket, Gimblett would find the enjoyment that had been so elusive. In the match against Yorkshire at Taunton, Fred Trueman dismissed him for a duck and he simply went home. While the press knew something was amiss, Somerset's captain Ben Brocklehurst asked that nothing be reported while they investigated.[37] Grimblett showed up for the second innings, but failed again; it was his last act in a serious cricket match. Finding little solace in retirement, in 1978 he ended his own life in his mobile home in Dorset. The wider issue of the suicidal path taken by a seemingly inordinate number of cricketers is sensitively and brilliantly told by David Frith in *Silence of the Heart: Cricket Suicides*. Frith once admitted that it was a book that nobody should read more than once.[38]

During Harold Gimblett's innings at Frome, one Essex bowler got a particularly good look at him. Taking 1 for 89 off thirteen tortuous overs, Peter Smith might have concluded that the precocious young dasher looked a handful. Smith's Test career was no luckier than Gimblett's, but for distinctly different reasons. The experiences of both are reminders that besides battle, service, sport and art, cricket has always been a patchwork quilt of superstars, dilettantes, egos, emotionals and toilers. Throw a dozen or so disparate personalities into the cricketing sausage machine and the bangers emerging will be a mixture of competitiveness, feistiness and fooling about. Waiting to bat, and waiting for the rain to stop, there is plenty of time for cricketers to do nothing in particular. And the Devil, they say, finds work for idle hands.

More often, there is no malice, and many club cricketers are much better at larking about than batting and bowling. Cling film across the toilet, Deep Heat in the jockstrap, opening the bowling with an apple, mayonnaise in the keeper's gloves, exploding bails and telling someone they are on 49 when they aren't are not the cricket Harold Gimblett would have recognized. When Brad Hogg arrived as a replacement for Shane Warne on the 1996 trip to Sri Lanka, he was, by his own admission, very inexperienced and vulnerable to all sorts of wind-ups. When the team was handed out some pills, skipper Steve Waugh told Hogg that they were not to be swallowed but inserted where the sun don't shine. 'What I didn't know is they were simple vitamin C tablets and of course, they were meant to be taken the usual way.'[39] 'I felt uncomfortable for a few days,' he adds, 'but I never got a cold.'[40]

Other pranks are particularly well planned. Then rookie broadcaster Jonathan Agnew was on the wrong end of the joke, albeit a beautifully choreographed one. Agnew's commentating colleague Brian Johnston set up an interview with Fred Trueman and ex-Warwickshire bowler Jack Bannister to be conducted by Agnew, who assumed it was going out live. The topic of the discussion was the poor state of England's fast bowling, Vic Marks reporting that the two old stagers played a fine hand as they responded with replies that were either 'monosyllabic or irrelevant'.[41]

All these are small beer compared to the prank – nay, cruel trick – played on Peter Smith. Either side of the war, every county had a leg spinner, an obvious indulgence amid the austerity. Smith had somehow found his way into cricket, the game being a second choice after an arrangement to join the Rhodesian Mounted Police was delayed due to a family illness. He wistfully trialled for Essex as a batsman, and dutifully propelled the balls back to the bowler as is the custom in net practice. One of the established players noticed that he could spin it quite viciously, and he was hired. His education as a leggie was another triumph for Aubrey Faulkner, who knocked off the rough edges in return for Smith's long stints as a net bowler.

After some early eye-catching performances, Smith was considered as a future Test player but given the other talent available, he wasn't an immediate England prospect.[42] It must have been the last thing on his mind, when during an evening at the cinema in the summer of 1933, he was contacted via an on-screen message with a dramatic sense of urgency usually reserved for births or deaths. Outside, his father gave him a telegram purporting to be from the Secretary of Essex Cricket Club, telling him he'd been selected for the England team to face the West Indies at The Oval. He duly made his way to South London, excited about his England debut.

Upon arriving, Smith might have been surprised not to receive the 'thank-goodness-you've-come' welcome he might have anticipated. After some uncomfortable shuffling about and quizzical looks from his new teammates, England skipper Bob Wyatt confessed that he honestly had no idea why Smith was there. Someone had played a horrid joke, but fortunately, the story does not end there. Smith was summoned to play for England in 1946 – again at The Oval – when India were the visitors. Almost exactly thirteen years to the week after falling victim to the hoax, Smith made his Test debut. Bob Wyatt was 'almost as pleased as Smith' when he heard the news.[43]

Peter Smith shouldn't be remembered as a victim. He was a prolific bowler for Essex – nobody is likely to take more than his 1,610 career wickets. Furthermore, no Essex bowler is likely to take more wickets in a single season than his 172 in 1947. He did the all-rounder's double of a hundred wickets and a thousand runs that year too, the latter helped by his 163 against Derbyshire at Chesterfield. It remains the highest score by a number 11 batsmen in first-class cricket. He was a popular fellow and a fine cricketer, and those are things that some oik's warped sense of humour will never change.

# 14

# CRICKET ON THE CUSP OF WAR
## *Even More from the 1930s*

In the 1930s no venue was relished by batsmen as much as The Oval in southeast London. Traditionally it has the reputation of being a hard, flat wicket resembling a stretch of motorway. There has, of course, been the odd lapse, for example in 1882, when England perished against Australia and the bails were burnt to make the Ashes. The highest team score was 122, the four-innings aggregate was less than 370 and there were 29 single-figure scores, including nine ducks.

Thereafter, the wicket evolved from the 'spin-friendly pitches of the 1950s and '60s, to the dead pitches of the '70s, to the trampoline pitches of the '80s and '90s'.[1] While batsman-friendly featherbeds are not guaranteed at The Oval, many would agree it's nice to bat there and remains a place of 'final Tests in hazy September sun'.[2] Former England captain Alastair Cook was undoubtedly delighted to find a flat Oval wicket for his final Test against India in 2018, when he enjoyed a farewell century and a goodbye 'prolonged in its successive ovations'.[3]

More widely, it has long been thought that the batsmen's fortunes have eclipsed those of the bowlers. Bradman once suggested that you wouldn't expect champion billiards on a patched-up table, so batsmen should expect good wickets.[4] Ironically, two of his biggest career misses occurred at The Oval. One was damp squib of a final farewell, and the other was his failure to fill his boots on one of the flattest batting wickets of all time. In 1938 Australia had enjoyed a successful tour of England. Having won the fourth Test match, they retained the Ashes. New South Welshman Stan McCabe's 232 at Trent Bridge was widely acclaimed as one of the greatest Test innings of all time. Bradman himself instructed those teammates not already transfixed on the match to watch it as they would 'never see the like of this again', while Neville Cardus called it 'brilliance wearing the dress of culture' as McCabe savaged the English bowlers.[5] With a characteristic flourish, Cardus likened McCabe's commandeering of the English bowling to the way in which famously dashing seventeenth-century French highwayman Claude Duval charmingly took control of a stagecoach.[6]

Australia made their way to the final Test full of hope, but one major character needed to be factored in. His name was 'Bosser' Martin, and he had succeeded his brother as Oval groundsman in 1924. A stern disciplinarian, he was not above 'doping' his pitches, and his favourite treatment was a rustic blend of cow dung and clay that when baked in the sun produced pitches with the immovability of concrete and the veneer of glass.[7] Cricket, he felt, was about batsmen. The track prepared for The Oval in 1938 had Bosser's mark – if a mark were possible on something so hard – and you could smell his noxious treatment in the nearby streets.[8] Any remaining lumps and bumps had been squeezed into submission by 'Bosser's Pet' – an enormous heavy roller. With Australia's pace bowling attack of Waite (no Test wickets) and McCabe (36 wickets at over 40 each) looking as menacing as Grandma's knitting, the toss was important to facilitate batting first. England did just that, and when they reached 887 for 7, it became the highest ever team score in England.

More significantly, in a shocking development, after bringing himself on to bowl as the plunder continued, Bradman injured an ankle, preventing any further involvement. With Fingleton also injured during the match, 'Australia's cup was bitter full'.[9]

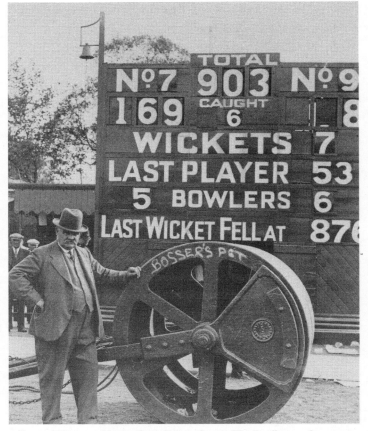

Bosser Martin and his 'pet' standing in front of England's record score at
The Oval, 1938.

For once, England captain Walter Hammond was in the ascendancy against Bradman, which perhaps explains why he might have emphasized the point and waited until the score reached 903 for 7 before declaring. Strolling in to bat when England were already beyond 500, England's wicketkeeper Arthur Wood noted that he had always been good in a crisis.[10] There was relief among the scoreboard operators, as there was no room for scores of four figures.[11] While by all accounts Bosser was livid his wicket didn't produce a thousand, Bill O'Reilly (3 for 178 in 85 overs) went looking for him, and not to shake his hand.

It stood as a Test record score for almost sixty years until Sri Lanka racked up 952 for 6 versus India at Colombo. England's score was especially unusual, since three of their top six batsmen (Edrich, Compton and Paynter) made thirteen between them. Maurice Leyland (187) and Joe Hardstaff (169 not out) made important contributions, and while English cricket was built on 'firm bone and muscle', Leyland was often its 'spinal column'.[12] Such efforts would usually ensure top billing, but that was reserved for 22-year-old Leonard Hutton. In only his sixth Test, his 364 set the bar at a new high in Test-match batting and destroyed the match as a contest.

This innings at The Oval cemented Hutton as one of England's batting greats. The whole thing lasted thirteen hours and seventeen minutes, beginning on Saturday and ending on Tuesday. Sunday was a rest day, which Hutton spent on Bognor Sands. At the end of Monday, 300 not out and within touching distance of Bradman's 334 and Hammond's 336 not out, he was advised to drink port and Guinness to get him to sleep.[13] He hit 35 boundaries, and eighty years later, of the 26 other individual Test scores where the number of balls were recorded, nobody else gets close to his 847. It was enough to keep Hitler off the front pages.[14]

When Hutton reached Bradman's score, a waiter in tails brought drinks, and despite their ongoing thrashing, the Australians were generous in their congratulations. A few runs later, Hutton passed his captain Walter Hammond's highest Test score. At the end of his momentous effort, the church bells in Pudsey pealed 364 times, and five hundred congratulatory telegrams arrived in one of the tea intervals.[15] But amid the adulation, there were some more reflective descriptions. Denzil Batchelor, usually ready to find the positive about which to eulogize, describes Hutton as a batsman who lacked 'colour', and suggested that though he had a full array of strokes, he didn't always seem to enjoy playing them.[16] *The Times* correspondent at the time seemed particularly underwhelmed; noting that Hutton had eliminated risk, he wondered whether it was the right way to play.[17] Further, those wanting excitement rather than statistics would have admired Hardstaff's innings more.[18] Such muted reports are perhaps a little unfair given that England won by an innings and 579 runs. As Hutton left the ground, a female fan wondered whether he might have made more effort to score one more run to match the number of days in the year. 'Can you ever please a woman?' he asked Denis Compton afterwards, in an age when such questions raised few eyebrows.[19]

Hutton was not a cricketer, or a man, to stir great emotional responses, despite his standing as England's first professional captain of the modern era. His record of personal achievement though, is immense. He made almost 7,000 Test runs at over 56 (including nineteen centuries), and over 40,000 career runs at over 55, including 129 first-class centuries. Only eight men scored more centuries, and all played more innings. As with Bradman, one can only imagine what Hutton might have achieved had the war not robbed him of five years of prime cricket.

Perhaps the reason Hutton never attracted plaudits as Hammond, Trumper or Archie Jackson did was his introversion. A 'compulsive' worrier, before long he thought of his record innings as an albatross around his neck, fearing that he might never satisfy expectations thereafter.[20] Everything about him was reserved. As a fifteen-year-old schoolboy, George Hirst had taken one look at him batting and declared, 'There's nowt I can teach this lad.'[21] Thereafter, the high standards and strong ethics established within the 'uncompromising' pre-war Yorkshire dressing-room

Leonard Hutton (left) with Donald Bradman, 1953.

became the guiding principles for his cricket.[22] Perhaps another key determining factor in Hutton's character lies in his upbringing in Pudsey's Moravian community.[23] Its inculcated characteristics embracing self-discipline, fortitude and always putting in a good shift were qualities that Hutton never lost.

His achievements – the majority of which were made after the war – were even more admirable given that while he was serving as a sergeant in the Army Physical Training Corps, a gymnasium accident resulted in a badly broken arm. Operated on three times, despite various bone grafts, his left arm was left two inches shorter than his right. He knew it was a serious threat to his cricket, recalling that when it emerged from the plaster, his arm was 'reduced to the size of a boy's'.[24] The batting adjustments he made thereafter, it is felt, enhanced the caution within his batting.

When he ascended to the England captaincy in 1952, he inherited a strong bowling attack, and the Ashes were regained in 1953.

Often, however, in addition to the extra pressure of captaincy, he was the best batsman in a weak line-up.[25] As his *Telegraph* obituary suggests, Hutton was 'quiet' and 'reticent', though capable of 'sudden shafts of humour'. He remained dignified and respectful of the game and was only critical of those who 'sullied it'.[26] When he discovered that his commitments as an England selector would interfere with his long-standing duties at the Hull company that had engaged him, he resigned as a selector.[27] Never ostentatious or overstated, he was 'as gritty as a half-finished road'.[28] His service to English cricket was recognized with a knighthood in 1956, three years after Sir Jack Hobbs was similarly honoured. Hutton was widely admired from many quarters; Jack Fingleton suggested that Australians didn't hate him, but 'just wished he were one of our own'.[29]

The 1938 Test match at The Oval was played without any time limit, and the idea was repeated a few months later, in March 1939, when England found themselves one up with one to play in the series against South Africa. The wicket at Durban was as hard as if not harder than The Oval, and those hoping for plenty of runs were not disappointed. Even if one feels that the slow roast of Test cricket is more satisfying than the microwaved offerings of Twenty20, perhaps even the most ardent cricket fan would concede that five days for a Test match is enough. Ironically, in the case of the match at Durban, eight days of cricket (with two rest days and one lost to rain) ended in the one result it was designed to avoid – a draw. It has become known simply as the 'Timeless Test'.

England were ahead in the series, but it hadn't been a straightforward trip. Skipper Walter Hammond's curmudgeonly nature and womanizing had created problems and even had some impact on team selection. Sussex batsman Hugh Bartlett had apparently scuppered any hopes of an England debut since during one earlier game, he had 'stolen' an 'attractive local society girl' whom Hammond had his eye on.[30]

The only nation to play Timeless Tests on a regular basis was Australia, but it had been agreed by both England and South Africa that if either side was one up or the series level, then the final match should be played until either won.[31] Nobody can have envisaged that the game would still be unresolved after ten days; Lady Jane Grey was Queen of England for less time. Amid huge interest in the match, Durban hotels were full, and the hosts sensed a chance to overturn England, now showing signs of raggedness after a long tour.[32] South African captain Alan Melville won the toss with a coin that fast bowler Norman Gordon had won off Hutton in a game of cards when the teams had travelled together. They took advantage of batting first on an 'iron-hard' wicket that suited all the batsmen but none of the bowlers.[33] It's almost as if Bosser Martin had relocated.

South Africa made two big scores at an excruciating two an over. In their first innings, Hedley Verity bowled 55.6 overs and the score was over 500 before he was hit for a boundary. The pitch was freshened twice by overnight rain and did not turn into the dustbowl that had been predicted.[34] Instead, it outlived the match and looked as if it might outlive all of the players and most of their grandchildren. Home batsman Ken Viljoen suggested that he needed two haircuts while it was still going on.[35] The England side walked to the ground every day and spinner Doug Wright suggested that by the end of the match, they were on first-name terms with everyone en route. Twelve new balls were taken. In his book about the match, John Lazenby devotes two and a half pages to the records that were established.[36] Among them were the longest ever first-class match, the most balls, the most runs, the slowest century by an Englishman, the slowest by a South African, the most scores over fifty, the most times a day's play ended for bad light and the most balls delivered by a single bowler in Tests. England's first innings had been comparatively modest, and they found themselves needing an enormous 696 to win. The target was 'beyond comprehension', given that only once before had a team made more than 400 in the final innings of a Test match.[37] They got off to a decent start, thanks to Hutton and his opening partner Paul Gibb, who was playing in only his fifth Test but already had some decent innings to his credit, including 106 and 93 on his England debut in the first Test of the series.

Bespectacled and balding, Gibb was one of the enigmatic and singular characters occasionally conjured up by the game of cricket. A decent county player but only a makeshift wicket-keeper, he started his cricketing life in Yorkshire and ended it in Essex, where he found his niche. His short Test career suggested that this was someone who could rise to the occasion, but off the field, he was his own man. Relatively slight, he nonetheless had an enormous appetite, and was as 'keen a trencherman' as any the game has produced, with a prodigious capacity for 'spare meals, leftovers and ice-cream'.[38] After playing, he became an umpire, travelling around the country in a caravan and finding himself in the middle of the miserable period when the authorities tried to eliminate throwing. Later he became a bus driver in Guildford. David Frith told Gibb of his plans to write a book about him, and while the player-turned-umpire-turned-busman agreed, it was on the understanding that any interviews could only happen while Gibb was driving his bus. Accordingly, Frith planned to travel the route with a tape recorder on his lap.[39]

Gibb enjoyed a level of anonymity inconceivable for a modern Test cricketer. When he appeared at the 1977 Centenary Test celebrations in Melbourne wearing a toupee, he was delighted that nobody recognized him. When he collapsed and died just before a driving shift a few months later, and before Frith had had the chance to interview him on the Guildford route, none of his bus depot colleagues had the faintest idea that he'd even played cricket, let alone represented England.

When England reached 78 in their mammoth quest, Gibb was joined at the wicket by Bill Edrich. Undeniably jolly, he was in the middle of a terrible trot of form. In eleven Tests to that point, he had amassed – if that's the word – 88 runs. When he joined Gibb, he'd made 21 runs in the series. His performances had been so bad that even Edrich's own biographer likened them to 'the currency of musical hall jokes'.[40]

The fact that on Day 7 it was he who was marching out at all was fortuitous. First, he had been scheduled to come in after Paynter, Hammond and Ames, and his first innings contribution of one run hardly inspired much confidence. Most, perhaps even Edrich himself, probably wondered why he was even in the team. Furthermore, the night before the match he'd gone to a party thrown by former South African Test player Tuppy Owen-Smith and had got absolutely hammered. Perhaps on the basis that it couldn't make his batting any worse, his worries lessened with every glass. But the next day, and to the surprise of everyone, Hammond promoted him up the order. Maybe the skipper didn't know about the raging hangover, but there were sniggers as Edrich went out to bat like a 'lamb to the slaughter'.[41]

But something had changed. Edrich smashed the first ball for a boundary, and before long had moved to fifty, and then a maiden Test hundred. Undoubtedly spurred on by a telegram from Middlesex teammate Denis Compton urging his friend to 'go for it', by the end of the day Edrich was unbeaten on a highly unexpected but extremely entertaining 107. Gibb, meanwhile, just went about his eccentric, idiosyncratic business at the other end and was still there on 78 not out.[42] But England were still 443 runs from their target.

The next day – Day 8 – was washed out owing to rain, which only compounded the looming problem of how and when the match would actually end, and how this would slot in with England's firm and irreversible travel plans. The *Athlone Castle* – England's boat home – had already sailed from Durban to Cape Town without the players. The two big questions were whether Edrich would get to 200, and how patient the ship's captain was prepared to be before he finally pulled up the gangplank. Ironically, as a South African journalist reported at the time, the Timeless Test was 'running out of time'.[43] By the end of Day 9, though, things were at least becoming clearer. Edrich was finally dismissed for a splendid 219, and England were within 200 runs of victory, their chances having moved from 'impossible' to 'odds on favourites'.[44] At the start of Day 10, nobody knew whether one side would win or whether the whole thing would peter out. When the rain came for the final time, England had made 654 for 5 and were 42 runs away from an astonishing victory. After sharing plenty of champagne with their hosts, they left to catch up with the *Athlone Castle* in Cape Town. The longest match of all time was over.

As they settled in for the voyage home, the players might have thought about the Europe they were returning to. Beware the Ides of March indeed; the day after the game ended, Hitler's army arrived in Czechoslovakia. Cricket was about to be bloodily stopped in its tracks again. Whether as battlers, servants, athletes or artists, it was all hands to the collective pump.

# 15

# VICTIMS, SURVIVORS
# AND INVINCIBLES
*The 1940s*

On 1 September 1939, about six months after England's crick-eters retreated from Cape Town, Germany's invasion of Poland triggered war. County cricket was abandoned at once but when a wire from Yorkshire's administrators suggested to skipper Brian Sellers that the game against Sussex at Hove should be called off, Sellers replied that it was a benefit match for opponent Jim Parks and the players would like to continue.[1]

Yorkshire certainly benefited from staying put. Happier in the rain than Gene Kelly, Hedley Verity was 'at his best when the wicket was at its worst', and took seven second wickets for nine runs in fewer than fifty balls.[2] At Leeds in 1932, he had taken every Nottinghamshire wicket for ten runs. No cricketer could do better on the cricket field in terms of 'mathematical perfec-tion or performance'.[3] Cricket was in the palm of his 'elegantly ruthless left hand'.[4]

Verity was entitled to think he had power to add to almost 2,000 first-class wickets. When he wondered out loud after the Hove match whether he would ever bowl there again, one won-ders whether it ever crossed his mind that he might not bowl *anywhere* again. In the second week of the invasion of Sicily, and as part of Montgomery's Eighth Army, Verity led his men towards a farm in Catania secured by German soldiers. Despite being shot in the chest, Verity urged his men on. As a POW 'in swelter-ing, overcrowded conditions', Verity travelled in an open railway truck across the Strait of Messina to Reggio, Italy.[5] Three days later, under local anaesthetic, he was operated on, but succumbed to his injuries. He rests in the military cemetery at Caserta. As good a slow bowler 'as anyone needed', Verity had been taken in his prime.[6] But the loss felt by Yorkshire and England was nothing compared to that felt by his family. His son Douglas recalled 'a lovely, warm, happy dad' who was popular with his peers despite having the bearing of a 'university professor'.[7] The Veritys were a churchgoing family, and one time when Hedley's father won a bottle of wine in a raffle, his mother poured the contents down the nearest drain.[8]

Verity was one of three players from the Timeless Test who fell in action. One of the others was Arthur 'Chud' Langton, a strapping fast bowler from Pietermaritzburg. Versatile enough to deliver pace or spin, he bowled 91 overs during the interminable draw at Durban. As a Flight Lieutenant in the South African Air Force, he was killed when his Ventura Bomber crashed in Nigeria. The other player lost was England's Ken Farnes. At 6 ft 6 in., the college shot-putter and body builder bowled ferociously quickly for Cambridge University and Essex. Even though he lacked the 'malice' that might have made him a world-beater, Farnes still had his moments.[9] His finest hour in an England sweater was his demolishing of Australia's top order (including Bradman) at Melbourne in 1937. He had signed off from cricket by capturing the last three wickets for the Gentlemen v Players at Lord's.[10] Originally intending to become a fighter pilot, he was too tall to fit into the cockpit. Instead he volunteered as a night bomber and was killed in a training accident aged only thirty.

Among Farnes's victims during his rampaging spell at Melbourne in 1937 was Ross Gregory, who made 80. While *Wisden* remained low-key about Gregory's innings, the ever-effusive Neville Cardus was considerably more enthusiastic.[11] Even with

Australian batting overflowing with quality, Gregory was a stand-out, and his omission from the 1938 tour to England was a shock. As a consequence, the youngster developed a more cynical opinion of administrators and selectors.[12] In what is now Bangladesh, it seems another plane flying above Gregory's erroneously dropped a bomb onto it.[13] Even if he was forced to grow up much faster than he might have been, his batting will forever be cherished as youthful and carefree.

Welshman Maurice Turnbull was killed by a sniper during the Normandy landings. A major in the Welsh Guards and a sporting polymath, he was born into a wealthy Cardiff family in 1906, confirming that the fortitude required to become a top-level sportsman was possible even for those born with a silver spoon in their mouth.[14] The Turnbull family home was a sumptuous eleven-bedroom affair, complete with 'cook, housemaid, kitchen maid, seamstress and charlady'.[15]

Turnbull was an outstanding all-round sportsman, winning rugby and cricket blues at Cambridge. But for injury, he'd also have received one for hockey. He founded the Cardiff Squash Club and became Welsh champion. He had already started playing cricket for Glamorgan when he began his rugby career for Cardiff, winning two caps for Wales at scrum-half. In nine Tests for England, his record was modest, but for Glamorgan he was a fine attacking batsman and a diligent and wily administrator. When he took over as club secretary, he rebuilt its financial base and took the club from almost certain ruin and a 'bedraggled flock without a shepherd' to a side worthy of seventh position in the championship table within seven years.[16]

Handsome and with film-star looks, he married Elizabeth, who when they first met had commented, 'I hear you're a budding cricketer.' 'Madam, I have budded,' he replied.[17] His sense of duty and sacrifice was evident when he turned down the chance to join an MCC tour of India, feeling instead that he should stay at home and raise cash for the county.[18] When Australia came to Swansea in 1938, as skipper, secretary and general factotum, Turnbull skilfully combined a competitive effort with carefully manipulating on-field events to keep Bradman not out overnight to maximize gate receipts the next day. The same day Hedley Verity bowled out Sussex at Hove, Turnbull was left unbeaten on no score when rain, rather than Hitler, stopped play at Leicester. He'd made 156 in the first innings, the last of his nineteen centuries for the Welsh county.

One of Turnbull's teammates in Wales's win at Twickenham in 1933 was Wilfred Wooller. Another titan of Welsh cricket, Wooller survived the war. Like Turnbull before him, he was a sporting multitasker, winning Cambridge blues at rugby and cricket, playing football briefly for Cardiff City and representing Wales at rugby, appearing eighteen times in the centre. As a cricketer he swung the ball, batted resolutely and excelled as a close fielder at a time when protective equipment was almost 'nonexistent'.[19] Indeed, his rationale was that while others had better batsmen and bowlers his teams would have the best fielders.

His 24-year career for Glamorgan straddled the war, and in 1948 he led the county to their first championship title. During the damp season he insisted his team be followed by a lorry containing blankets and a mangle. Only Wooller had the audacity to take on the weather and win; the players blotted waterlogged pitches with towels and squeezed them out with the mangle. They finished top mainly because they lost less time than anyone else. He made more than 13,000 runs and took almost 1,000 wickets for the county, achieving the all-rounder's double at the age of 42. He turned down two MCC tours because of other commitments, despite many feeling he would have been a shoo-in as England captain at some stage. He was captured by the Japanese in 1942,

and survived both Changi Prison and an unforgiving stint working on the notorious Burma Railway that many fellow prisoners
did not. Apparently thereafter he refused to use any 'Japanese-
made pocket calculator'.[20]

Towards the end of his playing career he served as an out-
spoken England selector. When he finally finished playing in 1961,
he became Glamorgan secretary, and then president. He directed
cricket in the Principality with uncompromising belligerence, and
as an administrator, he was a man of both 'charm' and 'arrogance'.[21]
Frank Keating reports that the first time he heard booing on a
sports field was at Cheltenham, when Wooller walked out to bat.[22]
Ruling his charges like 'a galley-slave skipper', any opponent by
default was 'a miserable specimen'.[23] To young Glamorgan supporters in the 1970s, he was a terrifying figure. Prowling around
the boundary in his sports jacket and brown suede lace-ups, he
had an iron fist within a velvet glove that had become rather
threadbare. Back then Cardiff's Sophia Gardens was a sprawling,
nooks-and-crannies affair and one day, a youngster spotted a
schoolboy-sized gap in the fence, masked by shrubbery. He bur-
rowed under the foliage and emerged headfirst, tortoise-like, into
the Promised Land. But the hapless young intruder was confronted with the famous suede lace-ups. After being helped to his
feet, the miscreant was asked for the price of admission.

Wooller rarely took a backward step. 'Bugger off, Tyson. You're
not fast enough to hurt me,' he told the world's fastest bowler as
the ball flew past his ears.[24] Notably elegant England batsman
Tom Graveney once scored 'the worst double-century' ever seen.[25]
There were other memorable moments when he commandeered
the public-address system. Once, disgusted with Brian Close for
refusing a run chase, he announced that because of Somerset's
perceived negative approach, he would refund the admission
money to anyone who called at the office.[26] As a broadcaster, his

voice is known to millions, many of whom perhaps do not realize it. It is Wooller excitedly exclaiming that 'He's done it! He's done it! And my goodness it's gone way down to Swansea!' as Garry Sobers sent the last of his six sixes in a single over on its way in 1968 when Glamorgan played host to Nottinghamshire. Wooller's journalism was also controversial, especially when advocating retaining sporting links with South Africa when most wanted the opposite. He polarized opinions, *Wisden* observing that those hating him did so 'with a tinge of affection' while those loving him did so with 'a touch of exasperation'.[27] To all he was 'that bloody Wilf Wooller'.[28]

But he was not the only player to suffer as a POW. The Edrich family are one of cricket's most distinguished families, and their experiences encompass most of the bad things the Second World War could muster. From the flat, fertile broads between Norwich and Great Yarmouth came four brothers. Eric, Brian and Geoff had stellar county careers, but elder brother Bill, as we have heard, made it to the highest level. He won a Distinguished Flying Cross as an RAF Squadron Leader, one raid involving 800 miles of excruciatingly low flying to evade radar. He survived the mission despite staring death in the face when an enemy pilot would have despatched him from 30 yards but for a jammed machine gun. It was an experience, Edrich recalled later, akin to 'two or three lifetimes rolled into one'.[29]

Thereafter, facing cricket balls was comparatively plain sailing, whoever was bowling them and however fast, so he played his cricket like a sailor with a 24-hour pass. Such an approach was exemplified by the 3,539 runs and twelve centuries he bludgeoned in his golden summer of 1947. He was no lover of authority and it felt the same way about him. The relationship wasn't helped by his rather 'macabre' lifestyle, which involved drinking and getting married and divorced with 'metronomic regularity'.[30] At the old boy's fifth wedding, old Middlesex colleague J. J. Warr was asked whether he was attached to the bride or the groom. 'Neither,' he responded, assuring the attendant that he had a 'season ticket'.[31]

They didn't break the mould after Bill. England bowler Brian Statham said of Bill's brother Geoff that he possessed the 'outstanding' Edrich characteristic of 'guts, guts and more guts'.[32] Despite 15,000 post-war runs and 26 centuries for Lancashire, he never played in Tests, but making it onto a cricket field at all is testament to the hardiness of the family DNA. Imprisoned after the fall of Singapore, eventually, like Wooller, he worked on Burma's notorious 'Railroad of Death'. Only six members of his platoon survived the experience. He sold his wedding ring to a guard to buy quinine in order to treat himself and other prisoners for malaria.[33]

Together with some resourceful comrades and Australian fellow captives, he somehow obtained some cricket gear. Extra physical exertion must have seemed ludicrous when rest days were limited to one every three weeks, but cricketers are cricketers, especially when they come from England and Australia. With hundreds of prisoners watching, they staged three Test matches. In the most unofficial, unrecognized and unknown Test series of all, Geoff Edrich made three centuries. You won't find them in *Wisden*, of course, yet they are among the most noble made in England's name. Though his wife thought he had long since died, somehow, he made it home, 6 stone (38 kg) of skin and bone.[34] Throughout the remainder of his long life, Geoff Edrich never mentioned his war horrors, but was always ready to talk cricket. The family pluck was inherited by cousin John; in case there is any doubt, watch how he faced down rampaging West Indies fast bowler Michael Holding alongside Brian Close at Old Trafford in 1976. The Edrich way seems to be to get on with life and make the most of it.

Besides the horrors experienced by Wooller, Geoff Edrich and others, the Second World War ended the lives of nine Test match cricketers and over a hundred first-class cricketers. But in contrast to the tragic Farnes, Verity and Langton, the man running into bowl when rain finally ended the Timeless Test became the first Test cricketer to bring up his own personal century. Quick bowler Norman Gordon took 1 for 256 and bowled 738 balls in the match. His return for such a mammoth effort reflected that it was a wicket that forgave nothing, and Gordon's trademark accuracy was nullified. But this was a man who knew what he wanted. In school he was so keen on cricket that he purposely flunked his exams to eke out another season.[35] Known for slicking down his floppy hair with Vaseline,[36] he played in the 1938/9 series against England after some sound Currie Cup performances. He played in all five Tests and was entitled to feel that he was due plenty more.

But like so many, Gordon's plans were scuppered by war. He served in the South African Army, although he still played cricket in some forces matches and struck up a friendly relationship with Walter Hammond.[37] By 1945, though, he was middle-aged for a fast bowler, and since there were more sprightly alternatives available, his Test career was over. His cricket had not been made easier by the anti-Semitism he regularly faced throughout his career, but Norman Gordon lived a long life. Very long, in fact. He ran a sports shop, became an accountant and only retired properly when he was 96. Two years later, he jacked in golf, despite recording his first career hole-in-one aged 87.[38]

On 6 August 2011 he became the first Test cricketer to bring up the happiest sort of century, and his birthday party at Wanderers Stadium in Johannesburg was attended by guests including Mike Procter, Shaun Pollock, Makhaya Ntini and others. In the days before, mindful that Gordon's century was approaching, former

South African Test skipper Ali Bacher cautioned the old stager against any 'flamboyant shots' and 'reverse sweeps', advising Gordon to 'take the odd single' placed carefully into a gap.[39] He made the metaphorical single, remaining at the crease until the Great Scorer finally gave him out on 103.

If Norman Gordon was seemingly almost invincible, shortly after the war a whole team were awarded the same epithet. In 1948 the UK was slowly returning to normal after war, austerity and shortages.[40] The country needed a pick-me-up, sporting or otherwise. Journalists are not usually noted for descriptive restraint, so any team nicknamed 'the Invincibles' might be thought special, but not necessarily unbeatable. By any measure, though, Bradman's 1948 Australian tourists were an exceptional cricket team. In 34 matches, 31 of them first-class, they won 25, drew nine and lost none. All in a damp summer, too. But it was not simply their record that was impressive, but the margin of their victories. Half of the games were won by an innings, and 24 times they passed 350. Seven of their batsmen completed 1,000 runs as the squad accumulated fifty centuries. *Wisden's* five Cricketers of the Year for 1949 were all Australian. They went about their business with 'a swagger' that 'grey, war-torn, still ration-booked old England' had never seen before.[41]

When the team landed at London's Tilbury Docks with a consignment of food parcels, 'red carpets' appeared, and at railway stations across the land, crowds would gather to see them, particularly 'the little emperor and captain'.[42] That, of course, was Bradman, whose fan mail alone necessitated an assistant. Invariably, to find some peace he had to spend more and more time indoors, and passed the time playing hotel pianos. Nothing, though, distracted him from scoring runs. Frank Keating recalls that a Benedictine monk called Father Fabian had promised to take him and some fellow prep-schoolers to see the tourists play at Worcester, but at the last minute he cancelled, judging the whole adventure too ambitious. The local rag claimed a moral victory with the blazing headline 'BRADMAN GOES CHEAPLY'.[43] He made only 107, which for him at the time was a comparatively modest contribution.

While for vice-captain Lindsay Hassett and a few fun-loving colleagues life was about Friday afternoons, Bradman was a Monday-morning, businesslike sort of chap. This was perhaps the only point of discord within one of the most successful sporting tours of all time. Despite assertions that Bradman had relaxed his usual autocratic approach, made no rules and imposed 'no curfews', the captain was determined that their opponents should be defeated, and where possible, 'annihilated'.[44] Accordingly, he had a 'deliberate, merciless, efficient plan' to establish a decisive psychological advantage over English bowlers.[45] Having recently served alongside each other versus a common enemy, cricketers from both sides appreciated the difference between sport and real conflict. If they had hoped to contest the Ashes under an overarching banner of bonhomie, Bradman did not, and many did not enjoy his ruthlessness against the ageing heroes of county cricket.[46]

The game at Southend in mid-May was indicative of Bradman's general approach as Essex were put to the sword to the tune of a staggering 721 in six hours. Four batsmen made centuries, including reserve keeper Ron Saggers, who registered his only first-class ton. So relentless was the slaughter that the crowd became equally interested in PA announcements about 'children searching for their aunts and wives wondering about their husbands'.[47] Victorian all-rounder Sam Loxton (who scored 120) suggested that the match was also noteworthy as it contained the tour's only sledge. The most offensive remark Essex keeper Frank Rist could muster after Bradman (who eventually made 187) had stroked three successive boundaries between square leg and mid-wicket was, 'Is that the only shot you've got?'[48] Bradman cracked a fourth to the fence and noted, 'There's another one,' dry as a desert.[49]

By the time of the first Test, Bradman was cooking. His scores at that stage were 107, 81, 146, 187, 98, 11, 43, 86 and 109 – in all 868 runs at an average of 96.44. The Tests were a procession; a draw in the third was preceded by Australian victories by eight wickets and 409 runs, and was followed by wins by seven wickets, and an innings and 149 runs. In fact, the only blip was when the Don played outside Eric Hollies's googly for 0 in his final Test innings at The Oval. 'Best f***ing ball I've bowled all season, and they're clapping him,' mumbled Hollies as Bradman left the Test stage, agonizingly short of a three-figure average but still a country mile ahead of anyone else.[50] In his 41st year, he'd made 2,428 runs on the tour, including eleven centuries.

In the days when Ashes tours were 'carnivals' lasting 'many months, meals, malts and matches', going home wasn't even possible after the final Test, and in mid-September the Aussies found themselves in Aberdeen.[51] It may not have been a glamour gig, but there were important matters afoot. By all accounts, the visit to Balmoral enabled King George VI to measure up Bradman for a knighthood. Some traditionalists took grievous offence that the Don was photographed strolling with the king with his hands in his pockets, but it didn't seem to be a problem for His Majesty and Bradman became 'Sir Donald' shortly afterwards.

The compelling consensus is that this was a team sprinkled with magic. They had world-beaters such as Keith Miller and Ray Lindwall, and cricketing statesmen like Lindsay Hassett and Arthur Morris. While Hassett was a fine player in his own right, perhaps his most important role was as a foil to Bradman, who lacked Hassett's soft skills. Morris was a man of quality and an elegant left-handed batsman with a particular fondness for English bowling, taking eight centuries off them across 24 Tests. Denzil Batchelor described Morris as 'the handsomest left-hand bat in the game today – and probably tomorrow'.[52] In the opinion of E. W. Swanton, few more charming men represented Australia, while John Arlott described him as the most popular cricketer of all time.[53]

Two other tourists typified the range of characters on show, from the youngster ready to take on the world to more seasoned protagonists who had taken it on already only to find it, and themselves, in some way wanting. In the latter category was Sidney Barnes from New South Wales. In the same way his almost English namesake Sydney had created havoc for teammates, opponents and administrators half a century before, the Australian was almost permanently out of step with authority. In fact, Barnes was 'over-confident' and 'bombastic', and at every club left behind 'a multitude of tales about his misdeeds'.[54] More recently, and perhaps with the benefit of hindsight, Barnes might be considered 'more prankster than gangster'.[55] He made three centuries (one a double) in only thirteen Tests and an average of over 63. In addition, so fearless was his short-leg fielding that they used to call him 'Suicide Sid'. The name proved sadly prophetic.

He was the class clown. During a storm at the Gabba in 1946, he overheard some England players ridiculing the size of the hailstones, so he raided the nearest kitchen and dropped a huge block of ice in front of their dressing room. In Bradman's testimonial, he is said to have walked to the wicket with a toy bat 10 inches (25 cm) long. Most famous of all, in 1952/3 as twelfth man in New South Wales's game against South Africa, he emerged for the first drinks interval in sunglasses, wearing a lounge suit and with a red carnation in his lapel. He brought drinks, a radio, a selection of cigars, scented spray and a hairbrush, comb and mirror and

Neil Harvey, 1951/2.

promptly set about giving batsman Keith Miller a makeover. But unlike English cricketing clown Patsy Hendren, who always knew 'when and at whom to throw the pie',[56] Barnes's joke went on too long and Miller's batting partner was dismissed, his concentration wrecked by the interval.

On the Invincibles tour, bad boy Barnes also developed a reputation for being a spiv who could spot money-making schemes at a considerable distance. Some worked, but most didn't. He was the only player not to appear in the official tour brochure, having refused the £5 fee and held out – unsuccessfully – for £50. Screenings of his home movies shot on tour became the hottest ticket in town, and while he claimed to have official permission for the appearance of royalty in his flickering footage, the authorities disagreed.[57] But others had different recollections. Alan Davidson recalls Barnes coming to his home when the younger man was picked to tour England in 1953. 'You'll need these for England,' explained Barnes, as he handed over his bat and cabin trunk from 1948. Barnes noticed that Davidson's wife was pregnant. When Davidson went to pay the bill for the birth, it had already been paid.[58] Such gestures mean that when, after having tried before, he finally took his own life, the tributes were often fond.

Among the sprightlier newcomers was Neil Harvey. When the young Victorian entered Test cricket with six centuries in his first thirteen innings, the critics mentioned him with the same hushed reverence as Bradman and Archie Jackson. He didn't disappoint, and with half a dozen centuries against the old enemy, his finest moments were reserved for Ashes matches; his 112 at Leeds in the 1948 tour is perhaps the highlight. He was the first left-hander to score a century on an Ashes debut. In a series Australia won so easily that few innings were 'crucial', this was one of them.[59] Short in stature and one of the first to make athletic fielding an important dimension of his game, he remained humble throughout. He didn't, for example, possess his own batting pads or gloves until he received them as gifts during the 1948 tour.[60] He was a special guest at the Ashes Test at Lord's in 2019. Over 58 years since he last played there, the 91-year-old reflected on some 'beautiful memories'.[61] 'I had to come back one last time,' he added, the last of the Invincibles.[62]

# 16

# NEW STARTS, NEW STARS AND CARIBBEAN SKIES

*The 1940s and 1950s*

Bradman's retirement at the end of the 1940s left a superstar-sized void, and to fill it there were several contenders from the Caribbean. Learie Constantine had been joined in the pantheon of great West Indian cricketers by George Headley, who lacked the same all-round skills but was a considerably greater batsman. A comparison between Headley and Bradman was fully justified, since only the two of them could be said to have never failed in a Test series between the wars.[1] Moreover, while Headley was just as nimble as the Don, not only was he a greater scorer 'on difficult wickets' in 'the hour of need' but his batting was considered more entertaining.[2] Further, while Bradman had all manner of high-quality colleagues around him, Headley usually carried the burden of his team's batting by himself. Accordingly, they called him 'Atlas'. His other nickname was 'the black Bradman', and the *Melbourne Sporting Globe* even described him as similar to Bradman but 'with more polish'.[3]

Headley was born in Panama to a Jamaican mother and Barbadian father who had relocated to work on the canal. Aged ten, he was sent to Jamaica to be educated in English rather than Spanish, and by eighteen, his batting was already earmarked as special. He scored a century in his debut Test match (against England in Bridgetown) and a century in each innings in his third. In his fourth, he made a second-innings 223 including 28 boundaries. But he could do it away from home, too: in Australia in 1930/31, Headley made another brace of centuries, impressive enough for Clarrie Grimmett to judge him as the best on-side batsman he ever bowled to, and better than both Hobbs and Bradman.[4] There were more unbeaten centuries at Old Trafford and Kingston (a double, no less), and just a few weeks before the outbreak of war, he made a century in each innings against England at Lord's.

After the war his powers had waned, but in 22 Tests across 24 years, Headley had scored ten of the West Indies' nineteen centuries and over 20 per cent of his team's runs. The first man to play for the West Indies who had been born outside the Caribbean, he also became the first Black player to lead the West Indies in a Test – albeit only once, versus England in 1948. He seemed able to move those watching as few others could. When Headley batted, the crowd watched 'in hope or fear' depending on which side they were on.[5] His son, Ron, was himself briefly a West Indian Test cricketer. Ron's son Dean played fifteen times for England, and remembers meeting his grandfather for the first time when the old man visited his English-based family in the West Midlands shortly before his death in 1983. Grandpa threw a few down to grandson, who took careful note. 'He was physically a small man . . . I felt I was as tall as him,' recalled Dean, not yet a teenager. He doesn't recall talking about cricket, but he confessed to having been delighted to have met his famous grandfather.[6]

Only four players with meaningful Test careers have higher averages than George Headley's 60.83. Others might have got there but for war, injury or bloody-minded selectors. Foremost among these is Trinidadian Andy Ganteaume. In 1948, against England at his home ground at Port of Spain, he made 112 in his only Test innings. True, it wasn't the best English bowling attack to have ever rolled up its sleeves, but you still have to hit the ball to the fence, which Ganteaume did, thirteen times. Responding

George Headley, 1930/31.

to England's first-innings 362, the home side were going nicely, albeit slowly. Once the debutant reached his century, skipper Gerry Gomez sent out a note to Ganteaume and batting partner Frank Worrell, giving them the hurry up. Ganteaume opened his shoulders and was out almost at once. 'That's not what I meant,' admonished Gomez, although it's hard to think how else you could interpret a note suggesting, 'We are behind the clock and need to score more quickly.'[7] The match was affected by rain, the home side didn't have time to win and the new opener paid with his Test career. No real explanation was given, but it was put about that he was 'simply too slow'.[8]

Unsurprisingly Ganteaume was no lover of the establishment. In the Caribbean, those running cricket were white, and only when the racial imbalance was corrected did the Trinidadian make any strides in cricket. In the early 1970s, for example, when the West Indies began to dominate Test cricket, Ganteaume was their manager. A cheery man with a sense of humour, reported *The Guardian*, he became an 'opinionated' newspaper columnist in Trinidad.[9] When he died in February 2016 aged 95, he was the West Indies' oldest former Test cricketer.

As Ganteaume would have undoubtedly confirmed, West Indian cricket has always been underpinned by colonialism and its associated implications. But as Professor Sir Hilary Beckles notes, when the game emerged from the colonies, in the hands of 'freed slaves and their progeny', it was 'refined, repackaged and re-exported'.[10] The first really show-stopping manifestation of the reboot was the team touring England in 1950. In short, they were sensational. 'Weekes, Worrell and Walcott' rolls off the tongue with alliterative ease, the trinity of superstars representing its most box-office element.

All three came from the same island. Of course, there have been other sporting fountainheads, such as Kirkheaton near Huddersfield, the home of Rhodes and Hirst. But Barbados is a warmer concentration of sporting brilliance and in the last ninety years or so, this island, only 21 miles long and 14 wide, has contributed at least nine Test cricket captains, over 60,000 Test runs and 2,400 Test wickets. The 'Three Ws', as they were called, were esteemed contributors to these tallies and remain the 'alpha and omega' of West Indies cricket, 'a tripartite of sheer lustre'.[11] Little wonder that they have a series of roundabouts named after them, but their impact extends beyond Caribbean traffic calming. In combination, they 'reconfigured West Indies history'.[12]

Weekes, Worrell and Walcott were born within eighteen months and a mile and a half of each other, yet retained clear points of stylistic, physical and temperamental difference.[13] Worrell was 'courteous' but simultaneously 'shrewd and strong-willed'; Weekes appeared to be the light-hearted one, while Walcott appeared 'almost melancholy' until he broke into an enormous grin.[14] While Clyde Walcott 'bludgeoned' bowlers, Everton Weekes 'dominated' them and Frank Worrell simply 'waved them away'.[15] Weekes 'pulled and whipped it', Worrell 'cut and caressed it' and Walcott 'stood up and flayed bowling off the back foot'.[16] While Worrell was of average height, Weekes was relatively short and Walcott was significantly more imposing than both.[17]

Walcott rejected a career in dentistry once he developed as a wicketkeeper, and, later, an inswing bowler. But this was no bits-and-pieces utility man – as a wicketkeeper, many felt he read the mystifying spin of Sonny Ramadhin better than anyone. As a batsman, he made fifteen centuries in 44 Tests at an average of almost 57. When he wasn't wearing the keeper's gloves, his average was 66, which was as high as anyone in the pack behind Bradman.[18] In the mid-1950s Walcott was not only the world's most explosive batsman, but one of the most elegant. An unforgettable mix of 'silk and gently rolling thunder', in 1953/4 he made 698 runs in a series against England; in 1955, against Lindwall, Miller, Benaud and other quality bowlers, he made 827, including five centuries.[19]

In retirement, Walcott became an administrator, holding himself with dignity and hating anything that approached 'showing-off'.[20] He was West Indies team manager and chairman of selectors during the 1970s and '80s, and in 1993 became chairman of the International Cricket Council. Later he became responsible for the code of conduct and umpiring standards but became frustrated with the lack of progress regarding match-fixing.[21] He was knighted in 1994 and died in 2006.

As the most diminutive of the Three Ws, Everton Weekes was as 'acquisitive' a 'run getter as Bradman'.[22] Possessing all the strokes, he could cut with 'the assurance of a Victorian dowager at a Church Parade'.[23] He played an 'annihilating' innings against Cambridge University on the 1950 tour, the game functioning as strong evidence for those feeling that benign wickets had eliminated an equitable contest between bat and ball.[24] The game also exemplifies cricket's occasional heroic pointlessness and everyone's reluctance to acknowledge it. Cambridge fielded a strong side, with batsmen Dewes, Sheppard, Doggart and Peter May all destined for international cricket. Dewes had already played in a Test match, but nobody could have anticipated that he would make 183, that opening partner David Sheppard would make 227, and that together they would put on 343 for the first wicket in less than five hours. Michael Stevenson – who also turned out for Cambridge – reports that the rest of the team 'chipped in' to allow a declaration at lunch on the second day at 594 for 4.[25]

The West Indians responded with an opening stand of 178 and when Christiani (111) and Stollmeyer (83) both departed, Weekes and Frank Worrell continued the gluttony. Their stand of 350 in three hours and fifty minutes was described by *Wisden* as 'entertaining',[26] which seems like describing the reign of Henry VIII as 'interesting' for his wives. It could have been more, too, since after a while the two stopped exerting themselves and dealt only in boundaries and leisurely singles. Out of a ridiculous 730 for 3, Weekes made 304 not out. All in all, he passed three figures seven times on that tour, five times nonchalantly powering on beyond 200.

Like Walcott before him, in retirement Weekes moved into cricket administration and was knighted in 1995. He played bridge for Barbados and was reported to enjoy regular swims in the sea almost until he died aged 95 in 2020. Author Michael Simkins recalls meeting Everton Weekes socially in 2008. Simkins didn't know to whom he was talking at first, but then the penny dropped. Having previously met such luminaries as Tony Blair and the boys from Abba, Simkins enthused that his encounter with the man who'd scored five consecutive Test match centuries eclipsed them all.[27]

Frank Worrell was the oldest of the Three Ws. It has been claimed by numerous commentators that he was the most important cricketer of all time. This is a big call, but not without foundation, since his contributions were so multidimensional. His mark was made as a batsman, captain and unifying cultural force. As a batsman he was very accomplished, very early. By the age of 22, he had participated in two partnerships exceeding 500, but this was no peacock preoccupied with his own feathers. He argued that conditions for both were loaded in favour of the batsmen. Notwithstanding such modesty, he was as 'elegant' as anyone who walked to the wicket' and a stylist incapable of ungainliness.[28]

On the 1950 tour of England, he made over 1,700 runs at an average of over 68, and in the Tests, 539 at an average of 88. When he made 261 at Trent Bridge, England skipper Norman Yardley ruefully concluded that setting any sort of field was impossible. It was a brilliant innings, and his 138 in the next Test was similarly classy.[29] E. W. Swanton called him a 'serene' leader who commanded supreme 'loyalty and affection', his name shining 'with a special lustre' in the history of the game.[30] More specifically, wrote John Arlott, as a skipper, Worrell was tactically sharp, and while quiet and measured, he could be firm 'to the brink of ruthlessness'.[31]

But Worrell was more than a world-class batsman. Sure, West Indian cricketers are celebrated like no others in their own parts of the Caribbean, but Worrell remains a beloved figure across all its disparate islands.[32] The 'awe-inspiring' team from the 1950 tour was, as protocol demanded, captained by a white man, C.L.R. James warning bleakly that London remained 'the capital of the West Indies' as he campaigned for the appointment of the first black captain.[33] The bitter debate was not resolved until 1960 and arguably only Worrell was able to appease both sides.[34]

If it was 'Frankie' before, now it was 'Frank'. Deposed skipper Gerry Alexander understood this was something transcending cricket, and to his great credit was supportive of his friend Worrell taking the helm. The colonials were initially 'appalled' but Worrell's 1960 tourists to Australia enchanted everyone, *Wisden* reporting that commerce in [Melbourne] 'stood almost still' as the visitors were given a send-off usually only laid on for 'Royalty and national heroes'.[35] Similarly, Worrell's 1963 team was 'probably the most disarmingly popular' ever to tour England.[36]

Upon retirement, Worrell became a warden at the University of the West Indies and a senator at the Jamaican Parliament. He was knighted in 1964 but was claimed by leukaemia in 1967, his 42 years packed full of good things.[37] Indeed, the consensus is that the world had been robbed of a future political superstar and one worthy of high office in an age where vocation often transcended personal fortune. After all, who, asks Telford Vice, 'would want Kevin Pietersen for an MP' or would 'entrust the tertiary education of their children to Shane Warne?'[38] It seems a little unfair to single out those two, but the point is made: Worrell was cricket's 'Nelson Mandela'.[39] With the batting poise of Hammond and Tennyson's ability to enthuse and encourage loyalty, Worrell possessed greater cultural significance than both. Even more, he quietly and diplomatically helped close a gaping racial wound without more blood being spilt.

But back to 1950. The tourists beat England by three Tests to one and while the Three Ws were heroes in a traditional sense, the two men responsible for regularly bowling England out certainly were not. In fact, never were there two more unlikely-looking sporting superstars. Sonny Ramadhin was mousy and moustachioed, while left-arm orthodox spinner Alf Valentine was bespectacled and bookish. Innocuous to look at, but lethal to play against, between them they took 59 of the 80 England wickets to fall in the four-Test series. Even more astonishingly, neither had played a Test before the series that cemented them into folklore. Commemorative material almost half a century later described how 'two colonial innocents', one descended from African slaves and the other from Indian labourers, tamed the 'imperial British lion' into 'docile submission'.[40]

The Trinidadian birth certificate of Ramadhin (26 wickets at 23.23 in the series) apparently gave his first name as 'Boy', from which evolved 'Sonny'. He probably wouldn't have approved of language about taming royal beasts, since he was famously reserved.[41] Having previously bowled only on matting wickets, Ramadhin was instantly recognizable, with his flopping fringe and shirt sleeves buttoned at the wrist. He was an early exponent of that high-currency enigma, 'mystery' spin. He himself explained the mystery as the combination of a quick arm and a mixture of off and leg spinners. Then as now, being able to do both is unusual. Years later he cast doubt over his own action by suggesting that nobody of his slight build could have bowled a faster ball without throwing it, but nobody in officialdom challenged its veracity, and he became one of cricket's legends rather than one of its 'outlaws'.[42] Legitimate or not, England's batsmen were flummoxed into hypnosis.

The Three Ws. From left in the foreground, Frank Worrell, Everton Weekes and Clyde Walcott. Sonny Ramadhin is in the background.

As with all magic tricks, though, eventually someone works out how it was done. Seven years later, when Ramadhin came back, England's batsmen were ready. By taking full advantage of the LBW law, Peter May and Colin Cowdrey in particular worked out that they could kick the ball away with impunity, bat safely tucked away out of danger. Ramadhin found it all too frustrating and, not wanting to go through it again, turned down the chance to tour England again in 1963.[43] He knew the spell had been broken. After a time in league cricket and a few seasons with Lancashire in the early 1960s, he settled locally and ran various pubs, one of them the splendidly named The Cloggers Arms on Saddleworth Moor.[44] He was no doubt both pleased and amused when grandson Kyle Hogg was picked to play for the England under-nineteens versus the West Indies, 51 years after his own finest hour.

Alf Valentine (33 series wickets at an average of 20.42) didn't look like a Test cricketer either. With a buck-toothed grin, he had already arrived in England for the 1950 tour when he realized his eyesight was so poor that he couldn't make out basic details on the scoreboard. Thanks to the brand-new NHS and the shiny spectacles they provided, he never looked back. With his fairly brisk left-arm spin and 'whirling action', he took 8 for 26 against Leicestershire in a warm-up and then 8 for 104 in fifty overs in the first innings of his Test debut at Manchester, five of them before lunch.[45]

He was an unusual bowler who did not bother marking out his run, his idiosyncratic approach to the wicket reminiscent of 'Groucho Marx getting into a lift before the door closes'.[46] Batsmen rarely seemed to laugh much, though, and for all his success he remained completely modest.[47] Amazed that cricket fans would be interested in him at all, he would tirelessly satisfy autograph hunters, with his only outward signs of extravagance being the shoes and jazz records that he collected as keenly as wickets.[48]

At Georgetown in February 1954 and in only three years and eight months, he became the first West Indian to reach a hundred Test wickets. In retirement, one might conclude that he was even more successful than he had been playing cricket. After an epiphany during a visit to a Sydney care home during West Indies' 1960/61 tour to Australia, he pledged to improve the lives of the children nobody seemed to want. After his first wife died (she bore four daughters), he set up home in Florida with his second wife and fostered children whose parents were in prison. Sometimes accommodating a dozen at a time, 'the couple ensured better lives for hundreds'.[49] He was immortalized in calypso as 'Those two little pals o' mine, Ramadhin and Valentine', but it seems as if there were many children in the southern states of the USA who might have adored him for reasons that had nothing to do with his bowling. It's full of good people, cricket.

# 17

## BRYLCREEM BOYS
### *More from the 1940s and 1950s*

The Three Ws were heroes whose fame transcended sport. Marketers and manufacturers had worked out that familiar, distinctive and recognizable faces had considerable commercial value. And while faces were the hook, to begin with at least, it was hair that could make the money; or, to be more specific, the stuff you put on it. Back in the 1940s and '50s, what is now called 'gel' was called 'grease',. and it's no surprise that manufacturers needed someone charismatic to endorse it. At the time, the two most alluring and magnetic cricketers on the planet were Denis Compton and Keith Miller.

When Tim Rice accepted his Best Song Oscar in 1994, he thanked Compton, calling him a 'boyhood hero'. It wrong-footed Disney, who concluded that Compton 'doesn't appear to be at Disney Studios or have anything to do with them'.[1] Even if the cultural reference didn't travel at that particular time, for a tired post-war nation desperate for entertainment, Compton was a national pin-up who was 'dangerously exalted yet never spoilt'.[2] Moreover, there was some merit in linking Compton with the film industry. In 1953 *The Final Test* became one the few feature films about cricket. It featured Compton alongside Len Hutton, Alec Bedser, Godfrey Evans, Jim Laker and Cyril Washbrook playing themselves, or at least a bunch of well-known English cricketers. Alongside them was proper actor Jack Warner, later of the BBC series *Dixon of Dock Green*. Warner represented a rather unlikely casting decision as a Test cricketer since he was 58 years old and looked even older. It is a curio worth watching for the excruciating self-consciousness of Compton and his teammates.

For young cricket fans of the 1940s, Compton was everything they wanted to be.[3] As a twelve-year-old, he played at Lord's for North London Schools and made 88.[4] He was a natural and didn't need much teaching. Lord's coach George Fenner was ambiguous about his part of Compton's development when he confessed, 'I wouldn't say I coached him, but I didn't mess him up.'[5] The youngster made a century for MCC at Suffolk, and when he debuted for Middlesex in 1936, he batted at 11 and scored 14, the umpire admitting later that he only gave Compton out because of an urgent call of nature. He passed fifty in each of his first three Test matches, and a century in the second of them against Australia in 1938 at Trent Bridge. *Wisden* was effusive – his style and confidence, they reported, impressed everyone.[6] It never disappeared thereafter.

The impact was never greater than in 1947, his *annus mirabilis*.[7] The season before had been fruitful enough, yielding 2,403 runs and ten centuries. But Latin doesn't do justice to what happened next. Following a bitter winter and alongside his jolly pal Bill Edrich, Compton put every bowler he encountered to the sword, making 3,816 runs with eighteen hundreds. Individually they were formidable; together they were unstoppable. The 'Gilbert and Sullivan' of English cricket were 'champions against dullness'.[8]

Compton made everyone feel better, embodying 'style and cool' even before such things were thought of.[9] He arrived at one match like a dishevelled James Bond with bow tie askew and borrowed a bat to make a century. Not arriving with everything he needed was a habit – a fellow Middlesex batsman describes once waiting to go in and suddenly realizing Compton was in the middle with his bat.[10] Compton is a cricketer about whom warm anecdotes and swashbuckling legends multiply and spread. Men wanted to be him, and while one half of the country's women wanted to mother him, the feelings of the other half towards him would certainly not be described as maternal.[11]

The brilliance was sustained across almost three decades. Only eleven men made more first-class centuries than his 123. W. G. Grace scored one more but played 639 – yes, 639 – more innings. Both his first-class and Test-match batting averages were over fifty, and his seventeen Test hundreds were among the most exciting ever made for England. Aside from his cricketing exploits, Compton played 54 times on the left wing for Arsenal either side of the war, and represented England eleven times during it, though these were deemed unofficial appearances.

His football career was impaired by a nasty collision with Charlton goalkeeper Sid Hobbins in 1938 and his knee was never the same again. Years later, when Compton's cricket career was threatened by it, 'a country mourned'.[12] Hobbins apologized, even though he was blameless. The kneecap, as we have heard, now resides in the Lord's museum.

Since he was the golden boy of English sport, manufacturers realized the potential value of his smiling face. By 1948 Compton was travelling with an extra suitcase just for fan mail and commercial offers. Press Association cricket correspondent Reg Hayter watched the developing administrative chaos, and, more pertinently, the opportunities being squandered. One of the letters in the case was from the *News of the World*, offering Compton £2,000 a year to be a columnist; another letter withdrew the offer because they'd had no reply. But Compton was 'a cavalier', not 'an accountant'.[13] Michael Parkinson reckoned that in later life, even when on a walking stick, Compton would still arrive 'in a cloud of dust'.[14] Hayter was among those bringing financial order, and quickly renegotiated another endorsement proposal discovered in the suitcase – from Brylcreem – from £300 a year to £1,000.[15]

Not that Compton seemed to care much, maintaining that he played cricket for fun, not money.[16]

One story about Compton reveals his multi-layered personality, his unwillingness to make a fuss, his popularity with the public, his undeniable and regular good fortune and his liking for a flutter. During a day's racing, Compton had a tenner on one of the runners in the day's final race. The bookmaker shook his head, helpfully suggested an alternative horse and handed Compton an 'indecipherable' bettering slip apparently referring to number seven. Despite being a local no-hoper, it stormed home at ten to one. Not really knowing whether he'd backed a winner or not, Compton sheepishly approached the bookie, who, beaming, handed him £100. As he walked off, the bookmaker sprinted after him, apologized for not handing back the original stake and made good the error. When a bookie first turns down your money and gives you the winning tip, pays you with a smile and then 'chases half a mile to give you more', reflected Trevor Bailey, you are fully deserving of the tag 'golden, eighteen carat'.[17]

If Compton made the English smile, then Keith Miller, with even more obvious masculinity – the most impossibly glamorous cricketer to have emerged from Australia – made Australians positively beam. Boys didn't bother trying to be like him since it was 'beyond them', concludes David Frith.[18] While Compton made £1,000 as a Brylcreem boy, Miller made £600, even though he was a far more obvious ambassador.[19] Many cricketers have idiosyncrasies, but Miller's hair, 'and what he managed to do with it', became so connected to his cricket that it is difficult to think of one without the other.[20] It was dark, reasonably long, fell over his face when he batted and flopped vigorously as he bowled.[21] Occasionally he'd sweep it back elaborately.[22]

Miller and Compton were mined from the same seam of flamboyance. Their approach to cricket – and to life – was that both should be vigorously enjoyed. It was inevitable that they became 'soul-mates', and for both, the notion of taking Ashes rivalry any further than an encounter on the cricket field was absurd.[23] K. R. Miller was born to be a flier, having been named after the Smith brothers – Keith and Ross – who at the time were midway through their maiden flight between England and Australia. During the Second World War, when Miller flew Mosquitos in the RAAF, the life expectancy for a fighter pilot was about a month.[24] The Aussie famously described 'pressure' as having a 'Messerschmitt up your arse at twenty thousand feet'.[25] The war redefined Miller's general approach to life and, like Bill Edrich, he dipped his bread in life's rich gravy thereafter.

Unlike Compton, Miller was not yet a Test cricketer when war came. He qualified as a pilot in 1942 and was posted to the UK in 1943. Stopping off in the U.S., he met Peg, who would become his first wife. Eventually he found himself in Bournemouth, and reality struck quickly as one of his regular drinking spots was bombed and several of his friends were killed. At the time he was playing cricket, otherwise he'd have been there himself. Not long afterwards, a plane he was flying malfunctioned, necessitating a return to base for repairs. Later that day the problem returned and the pilot flying it was killed. On another occasion, he crash-landed and walked away from his stricken plane as it became engulfed in flames. Another time, a bomb failed to drop from his plane and when Miller landed, it hit the ground with force but did not explode. If ever there was a man being saved for something later, it was him. For Miller the war provided 'a uniquely concentrated course in living and dying' and thereafter, he didn't 'give a bugger' about what happened on a cricket field because, quite simply, he was still alive.[26]

While Compton had a stellar football career with Arsenal, a growth spurt in his mid-teens ended Miller's aspirations to be a jockey, though his imposing new frame facilitated his short spell as a vigorous Australian Rules player at club and state level. But there were points of difference between him and his English pal. First, while Compton was only an occasional spinner in Tests (25 wickets at 56.40), Miller the fast bowler could boast 170 Test wickets (at 22.97) alongside his 2,958 runs at 36.97 (including seven hundreds). As well as being one of the most 'charismatic' and 'extrovert' all-rounders of all time, he was also among the best.[27]

Miller's most important collaboration was with Ray Lindwall. If Compton and Edrich were like Gilbert and Sullivan, Lindwall and Miller were Starsky and Hutch. In combination they formed Australia's most threatening pair of fast bowlers until Lillee and Thomson.[28] Lindwall was popular but 'quieter' than the 'more flamboyant' Miller.[29] Despite different temperaments, they were good friends, emphasizing that opposites attract.[30] While Miller was the life and soul of the party and liked a flutter, Lindwall enjoyed 'a beer and a chat'.[31] He was, in Ian Chappell's opinion, the humblest of men, and his silky-smooth bowling action provided a model to follow, especially to those who felt that cricket should be played as a side-on game, his simple, repeatable delivery being as fluent 'as running water'.[32] Lindwall's 27 wickets at less than 20 each was pivotal in the 0–4 thrashing of England in 1948. Miller played an important role, but for once only a supporting one, with thirteen wickets at 23. During that series, when Miller and Lindwall bowled to Compton and Hutton, with Bradman shrewdly watching from mid-off, cricket seemed to return to what it was before the war.[33]

Miller's sense of rebellion seemingly exceeded anything displayed by anyone else of that era. Frequent scrapes with military authorities were shrugged off. Taking detours during active missions to fly up the straight at Ascot, or to look down on the birthplace of his favourite classical composer (Beethoven), seem

Australian Test team, 1946: Lindsay Hassett (front row, third from left),
Sidney Barnes (front row, third from right), Ray Lindwall (front row,
extreme right), Keith Miller (back row, third from left), Bill O'Reilly
(back row, fourth from left).

inconceivable japes and drove the bigwigs absolutely potty. One
commanding officer stood out as a particularly fierce opponent,
and when Miller showed up to Royal Ascot in a Rolls-Royce
during the Ashes tour of 1953, the same CO was now a car park
attendant. 'Ah, my good fellow,' piped Miller, 'park my Rolls in the
shade, will you? That's a good chap.'[34] One imagines the flourish-
ing hand gesture that Miller made as he skipped off.

Falling out with former military commanders didn't matter
so much, but one cricketing adversary had a more negative and
long-lasting impact. Seemingly nobody who got on the wrong
side of Donald Bradman was left without a mark. Their relationship started off on the wrong foot and never really righted itself
until they were old men. It was a case of the 'roundhead of massive influence' versus the 'cavalier and maverick'.[35] Bradman had
his favourites, but Miller was some way down the list, perhaps
because they had such different approaches to cricket. For Bradman,

reflected Michael Parkinson, playing was 'business', but to Miller it was 'romance'.[36] The first time they met on a cricket field, Miller ran out Australia's great champion. Bradman was Australian captain when Miller played his first Ashes Test at Brisbane in 1946. Two particularly rapid deliveries from Miller almost 'decapitated' Bill Edrich.[37] When the bowler realized what might have happened, he reduced his pace, much to Bradman's disapproval. When he urged his bowler to crank it back up, Miller was adamant. 'This guy survived the war, Don,' he said as he tossed the ball back to the skipper, 'and I'm not going to kill him with a cricket ball.'[38]

During the Invincibles tour in 1948, matters came to a head. Miller thought that the complete annihilation of Essex at Southend was ridiculously excessive. Arriving at the crease at 364 for 2, he refused to take a guard and was bowled without making any effort to defend his wicket.[39] It was a pointed gesture to his captain, and later on the tour, when Bradman complained that one or two of his bowlers (including Miller) were taking it easy, Miller – suffering from a sore back – responded that not everyone had had the same sort of war experience as Bradman. The barbed comment implicitly suggested that Bradman's fibrosis had enabled him to escape the horrors many others had not.[40]

Although Bradman retired from serious cricket at the end of that tour, there were some farewell matches back home. In one, Miller released a flurry of bouncers, and one of them dismissed the champion batsman. For those expecting a victory lap by the great batsmen, the party was spoilt. Shortly afterwards the Australian selection committee (including Bradman) met to pick the team for South Africa and when it was announced, Miller was not in it. He did go in the end, but only when Bill Johnston sustained a minor injury in a car accident.

Looking back, Miller may have regretted his testy relationship with Bradman, who by the sheer weight of his runs and his strong character maintained his position as Australia's cricketing power broker for decades. It meant that Miller never captained Australia. Much has been made of the famous occasion when, finding that the team he was leading contained twelve men, his solution was, 'One of you bugger off and the rest of you, scatter.'[41] But Ian Chappell, who enjoyed – if that's the word – a similar relationship with Bradman, said that he was embarrassed to have captained Australia when Miller had not.[42]

Women loved Keith Miller. There were many romantic dalliances, including one, apparently, with the daughter of a duchess.[43] After he died, one of his sons suggested that Miller 'made Shane Warne look like an altar boy'.[44] Perhaps we'll leave that one there, but Miller was more complicated than his carefree cricket might have you believe. A man of paradoxes, he was as tough as teak yet struck up an unlikely friendship with fellow classical music buff Neville Cardus and another with the great conductor Sir John Barbirolli.[45] But for the man that John Arlott described as 'busy living life in case he ran out of it',[46] there were also scrapes with the law, gambling and other financial problems. Yet Miller was capable of great generosity, and never forgot those wartime friends he lost the night he was off playing cricket.[47] For more than fifty years, he returned regularly to England to visit their families.[48]

The last few years of his life were inglorious. He had alienated his family, more than one of his four sons had become dependent on drugs, his own health was failing and he had left his stricken wife of sixty years to marry his mistress.[49] His friendship with Compton, though, endured, and almost five decades since they first met, they still spoke on the phone every week, 'mostly swapping horse-racing tips'.[50] In the end, Miller outlived old pals Compton, Edrich, Lindwall and Godfrey Evans, and when his own time came in 2004, it was the end of an epic wartime adventure, comedy and romantic drama. But it was also the start of something. Cricket had long since been able to produce heroes, but now, amid burgeoning post-war capitalism, here was proof that its superstars could become recognizable beyond the game of cricket. And men's hair in England and Australia had never looked so good.

# 18

## SENSITIVE SPINNERS
### *The Mid-1950s*

When England took the Ashes in 1953 for the first time in almost two decades, Compton struck the winning runs in the final Test, but throughout the series, it was Hutton, Hassett, Morris and Harvey who shone with the bat and Lindwall and Bedser with the ball. In the next Ashes series in England in 1956, Compton made 94 in the final Test, helping England to the draw they needed to take the series 2–1. *Wisden* notes that Miller upped his pace to welcome Compton, who took a quarter of an hour to get off the mark.[1]

But one astonishing performance eclipsed everything in the series. Although what he did in the Manchester Test match was unprecedented, Jim Laker had form for bowling sides out by himself. Earlier in the season he'd taken all ten first-innings Australian wickets for 88 and six years previously, he'd done something equally dramatic in a Test trial. By the time England took on 'the Rest' in 1950, Laker's one standout performance was the 7 for 103 he'd taken against the West Indies in his first Test match. In the next seven Tests his best analysis was 4 for 78, his 23 wickets costing an unremarkable 32 runs apiece. Perhaps his most notable performance for England had been a brave innings of 63 in defiance of Bradman's all-conquering Invincibles.[2]

Accordingly, an audition for Laker at that stage was precarious, but every year until the mid-1970s, though, it was trials for everyone with aspirations to play cricket for England. Test selectors concluded that pitting England against eleven players on the fringes of selection – in other words, a notional second team – would help establish their best xi. 'The Rest' had more to gain than those in the Test team who were first picks until a first-baller or 0 for 150 might mean a demotion. No wonder these games were unpopular.

In the 1950 match Len Hutton turned out for England, though what extra the selectors felt they needed to know about a man with ten Test centuries (including a double and a triple) is moot. When 'the Rest' had first use of a damp Bradford wicket however, one thing they did learn about the second stringers was that they weren't very good against Jim Laker. Even the *New York Times* (not known for their cricket analysis) noted that Laker had made the match into a 'farce' by taking eight wickets for two runs.[3] Had he not made a deal allowing Surrey teammate Eric Bedser one off the mark on the journey to Bradford, his figures would have been even better. A nineteen-year-old Fred Trueman was responsible for the other run, off an inside edge. After the match, *Daily Express* reporter Pat Marshall was deadly serious when asking, 'Are those your best-ever figures, Jim?'[4] Laker was more ambivalent, suggesting that it had just been a day when things went his way.[5] Imagine how the selectors felt. Chairman and former England captain Bob Wyatt was having a bad couple of weeks. At the Manchester Test against the West Indies, he was woken up early on the last day to find Bill Edrich being helped to bed by a porter just before breakfast.

For those who understood his muted approach, Jim Laker was a straightforward Yorkshireman. For those who didn't, he was a 'tricky man' but a 'trickier bowler'.[6] Born illegitimately near Bradford but schooled in Saltaire, he started off as a pace-bowling batsman and once took six wickets for no runs as the opposition were dismissed for one. War interrupted everything, and

Laker gave up a spell with Barclays Bank to join the Royal Army Ordnance Corps. While serving in the Middle East, he developed his off spin, and when he returned, Surrey made more of a play for him than Yorkshire.[7] Perhaps, mused *Wisden*, his home county had forgotten about him.[8]

If that was the case, then they probably spent much of the 1950s wishing they'd kept him.[9] Surrey won the championship every year between 1952 and 1958 and no other county mounted any sustained challenge. When Laker bowled in harness with Tony Lock, they were called the 'Surrey spin twins', though this suggests at a mutual connection that never really existed despite their left-arm, right-arm combination being among the deadliest of all time.[10] In truth, they were always in competition and 'didn't really get on', albeit things eventually improved between them.[11]

Laker was brooding, undemonstrative, not given to emotional expression and considered something of a loner at Surrey.[12] Lock's career was tainted by regular suggestions that he threw his faster ball. At the time, cricket authorities were waging war against 'chuckers' and would seemingly pile no end of humiliation on culprits to eliminate them from the game. Lock could also be crotchety, but he could usually offset such grouchiness with an enthusiasm appreciated by those around him.[13] Indeed, as one of those 'big characters of his era', it seems clear that Lock had boundless enthusiasm for cricket.[14] County colleague Micky Stewart, for example, praised his full commitment to Surrey and the major part he played in the success of the 1950s.[15] As a close-to-the-wicket fielder, Lock had few peers: only Frank Woolley and W. G. Grace took more than his 831 first-class catches. His 2,844 first-class wickets put him eighth in the all-time list, and he made over 10,000 runs in the lower order.

An irrepressible competitor, once after being poleaxed while fielding, as he recovered in the pavilion, he noticed that the ball

MCC tour party to the West Indies 1953/4. Len Hutton, Godfrey Evans and Denis Compton (at the front). Jim Laker is at the top of the right-hand column, with Tony Lock immediately in front of him.

was spinning, and, 'still groggy', returned to the middle and took 6 for 24.[16] He resettled in Australia and captained West Australia, Leicestershire shrewdly securing his services during the Aussie winters. They thrived under his inspiring stewardship between

1965 and 1967, and so quick was he to congratulate those around him that the team's best slip fielder once dropped a simple catch on purpose simply because he couldn't face the thought of 'being kissed by Lockie at 11.32 in the morning'.[17]

But Lock's good humour was tested in 1956. Midway through Surrey's purple patch, the Australians arrived at The Oval. When Laker removed all ten batsmen, Lock bowled 33 fruitless overs. Adding to the humiliation, he grumpily moved past the bowler's unwanted century by conceding exactly 100. On any other day, a second-innings haul of 7 for 49 (which won the match) would have corralled the headlines, but that was the way that Lock's luck went in 1956. A few weeks later, on a wet wicket in Leeds, the Surrey pair bowled England to victory to square the series 1–1. In the first innings, Lock took four wickets. Laker took five. In the second innings, Lock took three. Laker, of course, took six. And so to Manchester.

England's victory was initially set up with first-innings centuries by David Sheppard and Peter Richardson. Later made the bishop of Liverpool, Sheppard is perhaps the most tangible intersection between cricket and religion. During that match in Manchester, however, Sheppard perhaps came the closest he ever did to witnessing a real-life miracle. When Australia began their reply at around 2.30 p.m. on the second day, there was no sign of what lay ahead. *Wisden* reported that while Laker had spun the ball sharply, the Australian batsmen capitulated too easily.[18] There was no answer to Laker's seven wickets for eight runs in 22 balls. In all, Tony Lock took one wicket and Laker took the other nine. Following on, Australia were 53 for 1 at the close, with McDonald (out with an injured knee) and Harvey (caught Cowdrey bowled Laker) both back in the pavilion.

Then it rained. Play was only possible in spells on Saturday, and with the storm continuing across a rest day, Monday was also a stop–start affair. On the final day, Australia resumed at 84 for 2 and McDonald – his knee better – and Ian Craig stood firm until lunchtime. With four hours left, England needed eight wickets for the win, and Australia needed a shade under 300 to make England bat again. Shortly before the interval the sun started to shine, and the ball to spin even more.[19] It was like shooting fish in a barrel: Laker took every Australian wicket in the match bar one.

Afterwards, there was a row about the wicket being designed to help Laker even before the rain, but Surrey old-timer Percy Fender wasn't having it. Either Lock and Laker were better than their Aussie opposite numbers Ian Johnson and Richie Benaud, he argued, or 'the last seven England batsmen are better than all the Australians put together'.[20] Australian captain Johnson was magnanimous enough to acknowledge Laker's feat, and over six decades later, 19 for 90 remained the best bowling analysis of all time in any first-class match.[21]

But not all Englishmen were celebrating. Lock was miffed that he had only one wicket to show for 63 overs on a pitch apparently perfect for spin bowling. He later regretted not being more pleased for his colleague, but at the time, Lock's mood would not have been helped by an intervention from Sydney Barnes (whose best bowling figures Laker had just beaten).[22] His bluntly acerbic analysis was a rather unhelpful 'No bugger ever got all 10 when I was at t'other end.'[23]

Laker was characteristically restrained. Never has a man achieved so much and celebrated so little. He 'simply flung his short-sleeved England sweater over his left shoulder and sauntered nonchalantly back to the pavilion'.[24] Thereafter, he changed and drove by himself back to London.[25] Motorways, like one-day cricket and colour television, were in the future. He stopped off in Lichfield for a sandwich and a quick pint, and sat in quiet anonymity while the patrons in the adjoining bar watched the highlights from Manchester. When he got home, his wife had no idea what he'd done.[26]

Laker's achievements did not obviously bring him satisfaction and peace. When he retired in 1960 his ghostwritten autobiography *Over to Me* was a 'surprisingly wooden and mild score-settling exercise' that swiped at some of English cricket's cherished names.[27] He was summarily disowned by Surrey and MCC and while he was eventually forgiven, the whole affair was, reflected Wooldridge, 'one of the saddest episodes I have known in sport'.[28] When Laker died prematurely in 1986, John Arlott, who often shared a BBC commentary box with him, observed that to work with Laker and to be accepted by him was 'an accolade and admission to a school of cricketing thought' sometimes 'quite bewildering in its depth'.[29] Spin bowlers, according to Arthur Mailey, were intriguing characters, and if they might be more temperamental than others, they were 'individuals' rather than 'civil servants'.[30] He surely meant it as a compliment to spinners rather than an insult to government officials, but Lock and Laker were exemplars of spin bowling individuality.

While Lock and Laker were fairly conventional, every modern team, we are told, must now have a mystery spinner. If they are good, even better, but the incomprehensible part seemingly trumps the impressive part. Even fairly average tweakers can appear as baffling as 'little green men from the planet Zog'.[31] Double-jointed elbows, hyper-flexible wrists and long, spidery fingers – if you are working any sort of sorcery, the grey suits are seemingly more likely to think you're Lord Voldemort than Harry Potter. But perhaps the mystery spinner's magic is not real magic at all. As John Gleeson (one of their number) pointed out, only three things can happen with a cricket ball: 'spin from the leg, spin from the off, or go in straight'.[32] It cannot, he added, 'disappear or explode'.[33] Gideon Haigh suggests that it's possible that the 'homogenising' influence of television and textbook coaching has accentuated the profiles of unusual cricketers.[34]

But nobody could ever accuse Jack Iverson of being homogenized. He was neither the best nor the most durable mystery spinner, but for a while he fooled just about everyone. Indeed, he 'zoomed' like a shooting star into the Australian team of 1950 before dropping out of it again.[35] Besides the fleeting ability to make the ball behave extremely oddly, the tall Victorian had seemingly no other discernible cricketing ability and nothing even approaching a cricket brain.[36] Iverson forgot the names of fielding positions, and it never occurred to him to move in as the bowler approached as everyone else did.[37] He was flaky, idiosyncratic and chronically lacking in self-confidence, but as a bowler he was 'metronome-repeatable' with 'cryptic' variations.[38]

Iverson's story is 'barely credible'.[39] He spent much of the war in Papua New Guinea idly messing around with ping-pong balls, coming up with a new grip that enabled him to spin them viciously.[40] The new method was reliant on his middle finger, reminiscent of a smoker flicking away a cigarette butt.[41] After the war, as a shy 31-year-old, he wandered into his local cricket club, looking for a match; on debut, he took fifteen wickets for 25 runs. After raising eyebrows and confounding numerous batsmen in the Sheffield Shield, he was picked for Australia. When England toured Australia in 1950/51, Iverson took 21 wickets at less than 16 and his 6 for 27 in the second innings at Sydney was instrumental in Australia retaining the Ashes. The Aussies began to contemplate 'the greatest match-winner since Bradman'.[42] Some even started calling him the best spinner in the world.[43]

But following the conclusion of that series, Iverson never played another Test. He mentioned giving up and soon, 'having wandered into the sunlit uplands of his sport, he wandered out again', retiring to work for his father's property business.[44] All in all, the whole thing might have been dreamt up by Disney – a tale of 'the cute farmhand who suddenly finds himself pitching for the World Series (with only his faithful pooch for company) before deciding to go and help Pa run the shop after all'.[45] Iverson was unlike any other mystery spinner, because every facet of his existence was arcane and puzzling. Indeed, he 'almost went out of his way to be unknown'.[46] Gideon Haigh reiterates the difficulty of researching a man whose life was spent under the radar.[47] What we do know for sure is that in 1973, Iverson shot himself in a shed in his garden while his wife did the housework.[48] In the end, he 'loved the game, but feared the stage'.[49]

Misanthropic, melancholy or just plain morose? Mysterious, magical or misunderstood? Spin bowlers may be all of those things, but, led by Laker's never-to-be-repeated day in the murky Manchester sunshine, they can put their names to some of the most astonishing events the game has ever witnessed.

# 19

# TIED TEST AND TUMULT
## *The 1960s*

According to the American humourist Dave Barry, the 1960s are now a historical period in their own right, 'just like the Roman Empire'.[1] They were certainly historic for cricket as it intersected with politics, the establishment, consumerism, race and international relations. If the West Indies featured prominently at the start of the 1950s, eventually a challenge to their reputation arrived in the form of a Jamaican fast bowler called Roy Gilchrist, a man 'capable of chilling the blood',[2] some of which was often left on the pitch.

In only thirteen Test matches, he made quite an impact. During the West Indies tour of India in 1958/9, alongside Wes Hall, Gilchrist established West Indian fast bowling as 'the fortress that repelled all challengers for two decades'.[3] If that was a high point of the tour, the low point was the ongoing conflict between Gilchrist and his captain Gerry Alexander.[4] After an incident with a knife, and a series of wilful bouncers and beamers in a tour match against North Zone, the bowler was sent home.[5]

He retired to the Lancashire leagues, but while the batting was less capable, it didn't matter to Gilchrist. While not the fastest or most physically commanding, he was 'completely lacking in conscience'.[6] The beamer is one of cricket's most distained taboos. Dangerous when accidental, it can be potentially fatal when used as a deliberate weapon. Thankfully Gilchrist didn't kill anyone, but while playing for Crompton in 1965, Gilchrist's volcanic temper erupted sensationally. Beamer after beamer was followed by bouncer, but the opposing batsmen evaded everything and even made some streaky runs. Eventually, Gilchrist charged through the crease and threw the ball at the batsmen as hard as he could. The game was abandoned and he was banned for three matches. Not above carrying on these clashes beyond the field, once he hit an Australian batsman on the head with a stump – in a charity match.[7] Another time, he allegedly thrust a hot iron into his wife's face.[8] Seemingly Mr Hyde had no Dr Jekyll to balance the unpleasantness.

Roy Gilchrist's antics were shaming, but the death of Collie Smith was desperate and tragic. An orphan born and raised in poverty, he made his way through willpower and strength of character. He became a popular and generous young man with a huge grin, and his personality won him many admirers.[9] He was also an accomplished Test cricketer and although he had curbed his natural instinct to thrash every ball, he was still capable of attacking assertively.[10] He made a century on his Test debut and became the first man to score centuries on his first appearances against both England and Australia. He was not a genius like Garry Sobers, but was nonetheless a God-fearing man with 'immense character'.[11]

In 1959, while representing Burnley, he made the first triple century in League history, but by early September he was dead, aged only 26. Since they were all based in Lancashire, Smith had joined fellow Jamaican Tom Dewdney – a fast bowler – and Sobers for a car journey to London for a charity match. Gilchrist was due to join them but didn't turn up. As Sobers reflected later, had they waited longer for the errant fast bowler, the subsequent tragedy might never had happened.[12] They drove through the night, and just before dawn, Sobers – whose turn it was to drive – was temporarily blinded by headlights and collided with a truck. At first it seemed that there were no real injuries; indeed, Smith suggested to a dazed Sobers that he should check on Dewdney. But while his colleagues sustained only mild injuries, Smith had damaged his spinal cord and died some days later. Depending on which report you read, his funeral in Jamaica was attended by between 60,000 and 100,000 people. Sobers described him as having an 'unquenchable ecstasy of spirit'.[13] With his closest cricketing friend gone, he reflected that Collie had been a calming influence who could have as much fun as anyone else but always knew when to go home.[14] By his own admission, Sobers's drinking and gambling increased thereafter.[15]

By the time the West Indies reached Australia in 1960/61, they could be forgiven for not being at the top of their game. Their first black captain, Frank Worrell, was under huge scrutiny. Those considering his leadership as being of political, social and humanistic significance prayed it would be successful. Praying just as hard that Worrell would fail were the less enlightened who felt the accession of any black man, however urbane, was a threat. Moreover, at that time, cricket was in 'the doldrums', having become increasingly defensive and sluggish and fallen victim to 'the convergence of professionalism and patriotism'.[16]

The West Indians also had something else to contend with. Their hosts were still enforcing their 'White Australia' policy, which, as it suggests, did not appear to extend a warm welcome to a team of black cricketers. In cricketing terms their tour was not successful, but in every other way it was a complete triumph. The *Sun Herald* effused that the relaxed, carefree approach of the West Indians charmed the home crowds, and while they lost the series, they 'won Australia'.[17] Half a million Australians gave them a ticker-tape parade as a send-off; it was, noted Sobers, 'so magnificent and so sincere, we shall treasure it to the end of our days'.[18]

While that was remarkable, it was only what the cricket deserved, as a competitive, entertaining tone was set from the very first Test. It will be known forever as the first tie and one of only two such results in the first 140 or so years of Test cricket. An expectant crowd at Brisbane realized there would be treats aplenty when Sobers smashed 21 fours in a lavish 132 on the first day. A total of 453 was a decent challenge, but the hosts returned it with interest, thanks to Bobby Simpson, Colin McDonald and 181 from Norm O'Neill. In reply, middle-order heroics from Worrell and Joe Solomon meant Australia needed 233. Many felt that Australia were favourites, but that was discounting Wes Hall, who promptly reduced the chase to a miserable-looking 57 for 5.[19]

Hall was more approachable and friendly than Roy Gilchrist, but was faster and approached the wicket from a run-up beginning somewhere 'in the next parish'.[20] Later, as a cricket administrator, high-ranking politician, ordained Pentecostal minister and knight of the realm, Hall quipped during his political career that those thinking his run-up was too long should listen to his speeches.[21] His philosophy for cricket was simply that batsmen wanted to bat, and his job was to stop them, but his philosophy for life was to have fun.[22] Tony Cozier recalls that his own fiftieth birthday party was running out of steam but when Hall arrived, it kept going 'for another four hours'.[23]

If the Aussies had underestimated Hall, in return the all-round mastery of Alan Davidson was a nasty surprise for the tourists. Becoming the first player to score a hundred runs and take ten wickets in a Test, his spectacular rearguard with Richie Benaud changed everything again. By getting the score to 226 for 6, a game which had looked lost now looked won.[24] Then Joe Solomon ran out Davidson with a direct hit – an eerie omen, as it turned out – and everything changed again. There were six to win, with three wickets left, and one final eight-ball over remaining. There was more chaotic scrambling and the scores were level. One wicket and two balls left. Kline tried an unlikely run and

Solomon's direct hit from a dozen yards ran out Ian Meckiff by a whisker. Match tied.

While it might be a stretch to say it was the greatest ever Test match, the final moments did generate a particularly memorable photograph, in which one of cricket's 'heart-stopping moments' was captured forever.[25] Shadows had started to dominate the landscape and Lindsay Kline turns around to see the mayhem at the other end, while Hall raises his arms 'in hope and desperation'.[26] Meanwhile, Rohan Kanhai jumps up excitedly, while at the non-striker's end, Frank Worrell backs up the stumps.[27] Convinced of a West Indian win, commentator Alan McGilvray and summarizer Keith Miller had left the ground before the final, breathless ball. Amid the chaos, those commentators who *had* stayed – Clive Harburg and Johnnie Moyes – didn't make it clear enough that the match was tied and had to re-record their vocal performances the following day.

Most photographers would agree that capturing such a moment represents the perfect intersection of anticipation and timing. While snappers all around him emptied their barrels during that last over, some professional sixth sense told Ron Lovitt of *The Age* to keep a shot back. He pressed the button at the exact moment Solomon's throw beat Meckiff to reach the crease.[28] Fellow *Age* photographer Bruce Postle called it the 'coolest effort by a photographer I have ever heard about'.[29] The notion that he'd captured something special wasn't lost on Lovitt himself. One of his sons recalls a phone call from his dad that evening: with 'a slight slur' in his voice, Lovitt announced that he'd taken 'the best cricket photo you've ever seen in your life'.[30] But more than that, Lovitt's image was indexical of a change in international cricket. When Test cricket's biggest challenge was the 'boredom' created by dull Test matches and cautious captains, Solomon's joyous leap was 'a harbinger of the cheerful spirit in which the rest of the series would be played'.[31]

Perhaps the affinity between the two teams has never reached such heights since, but for a while, they produced cricket that transcended natural partisanship and deep-seated racial scepticism. Worrell charmed the hosts with his manners and sophistication, but he was helped by a team that at times shone very brightly in a losing cause. The major contributors to the series were Hall (21 wickets at 29.3), off spinner Lance Gibbs (nineteen wickets at 20.8), batsman Rohan Kanhai (503 runs at 50.3, including two centuries at Adelaide) and, in his last first-class matches, wicketkeeper/batsman Gerry Alexander (sixteen catches and 484 runs at 60.5, including the only century of his whole first-class career).

With fifteen wickets, 430 runs and twelve catches, the predominant all-rounder in that series, and in many others, was Garry Sobers. Many observers suggested his 132 at Brisbane was the finest Test century ever made in Australia, the crowd remaining 'delirious' throughout.[32] The way he set about the bowling made some imagine it was as though Bradman's 'ruthlessness' and the 'artistry of a Kippax' were combined into one glorious batsman.[33]

There are three essential characters almost guaranteed to appear in any book purporting to provide even a rough chronology of cricket. W. G. Grace and Bradman are the first two; Garfield Sobers is the third. In 2000 a poll of one hundred eminent players and watchers of the game determined the five most prominent cricketers of the twentieth century. Even with a hundred people making five selections each, many breathtakingly good cricketers didn't feature. But the fact that voting was spread across only fifty different cricketers does suggest some degree of consensus. Indeed, everyone on the one-hundred-strong panel voted for Bradman, and only ten of them did not vote for Sobers. Undoubtedly each had a good reason for not doing so, but goodness knows what it was. Ian Chappell (joint 33rd, with one vote), called Sobers 'easily the best cricketer I've ever seen' but also 'the best batsman'.[34]

Bradman himself, whose opinion was always taken notice of, regarded Sobers as the best all-round cricketer he had ever seen.[35]

Born in Barbados, Sobers was one of seven children. A sibling died young in an accident and his merchant seaman father perished in 1942 when his ship was sunk by a U-boat.[36] Born with an extra finger on each hand, Sobers Jr was called 'a freak' by some. How right they were, but for all the wrong reasons. Sobers himself reports that the extra appendages didn't bother him and that the first extra digit fell off before he was ten. The other came off later with the help of 'a sharp knife'.[37] It isn't clear who was wielding it, but this is Garry Sobers we are talking about, so anything is possible.

At fourteen he was a gofer in a furniture factory, but at seventeen he was playing Test cricket. Besides the weight of raw statistics, he was 'unfeasibly cool', and a player who made you 'give thanks to any available god who happened to be listening for the invention of cricket'.[38] When overseas cricketers first enriched England's dreary domestic scene in 1968, Nottinghamshire won Sobers's signature after offering him a flat, a car and a salary of £7,000 for six months' work. No image rights or merchandising back then; just two sets of keys and £250 a week to revitalize a team who hadn't won a championship match at all in 1967. Sobers showed his worth as he racked up 1,600 runs and 84 wickets, helping Notts to fourth in the championship. The highlight came on the last day of August at Swansea. Chasing quick runs before declaring, and fortuitously choosing to do it with TV cameras present, he hit Glamorgan's Malcolm Nash for six sixes in an over. Books have been written about that one over.

He played golf, football and basketball for Barbados and held the record Test score of 365 not out until it was broken by Brian Lara. A perfect sportsman maybe, but perhaps there were flaws. His cricketing Achilles heel was his captaincy, in that he lacked insight and assumed everyone else could do what he could do. They couldn't, and while Sobers gave everything of himself on the field, often it wasn't enough.[39] His fondness for golf meant that when he might have been supervising team practice, he was elsewhere.[40] Also of concern was his tendency to travel by himself, Wally Hammond style.[41] He was also prone to on-field misjudgements. In 1967/8 at Port of Spain, Sobers set Colin Cowdrey's team a target of 215 in 165 minutes. The declaration was widely considered generous, 'absurdly' so, perhaps even 'suicidally' so.[42] England cruised it, and this single declaration perhaps reduced cavalier thinking on the part of all captains thereafter.[43] Effigies of Sobers were burnt in the streets, but he was unrepentant on the basis that to win, you must risk losing.

Neither was Sobers a believer in early bedtimes and temperance.[44] Besides being the world's finest player, he was also up there as a partygoer. Indeed, the man himself concedes that the last of his 26 Test centuries was made under the influence of more than adrenaline. Originally omitted from the tour and believing his international career was behind him, Sobers had been summoned as injury cover, but at Lord's in 1973 his century was an uncomfortable affair. On 31 not out overnight, he went clubbing with a former teammate, then remained in the hotel bar until breakfast.[45] Resuming his innings at the start of play, he missed his first five balls. Skipper Rohan Kanhai and the rest of the team were weak with laughter. He hit the sixth and on 132 retired with a stomach upset.[46] After recuperating with a large port and brandy, he returned and finally fell for 150. He wasn't as politically aware as others of the era either, having agreed to play in South Rhodesia during the angriest period of apartheid. The decision caused consternation in the Caribbean and certainly wasn't worth the £600 he was paid to appear in a double-wicket competition. Not a temperate man, not a diplomat, but what a player.

Besides Worrell's charm and Sobers's exuberance, the other reason Test cricket was lifted from its malaise was the Australian captain. It takes two to tango, and Worrell's opposite number in the 1960/61 series was Richie Benaud. The first Test player to achieve the double of 2,000 runs and 200 wickets, Benaud's contribution to cricket extended beyond his abilities as a hard-hitting batsman and a wily, innovative and attacking leg spinner. Indeed, his pioneering captaincy tends to be overlooked given that he later became a famous TV commentator and, in the opinion of some, 'arguably the most influential personality in cricket since the Second World War'.[47]

Like Bradman's, Benaud's ancestors came from Europe, his great-grandfather arriving in Sydney Harbour after a long trip from France's western coastline. Young Richie saw his first Sheffield Shield match at Sydney in 1940, and as one of an astonishing 75,000 spectators present, it was there that he first felt the 'urge' to bowl leg spin after watching Grimmett, O'Reilly and Cec Pepper.[48] The boy grew, the leg spin improved and in 1958/9, Benaud became Australian captain. Like Worrell, he realized that there was an important job to be done off the field, and the journalism training acquired while working crime and local affairs beats on the *Sydney Sun* meant that he understood what the media wanted from the game and its players. As a captain, he was successful in his 28 Tests as leader (won twelve, lost four, tied one, drawn eleven) and brought enterprise, daring and strategy where others looked for safety. He was shrewd enough to plan for life after cricket and in 1956 undertook broadcast training with the BBC to supplement his news-gathering and writing. Thereafter he was as much a part of televised cricket as the bat or ball, putting in stints with the BBC and Channel 4 in the UK and Channel 9 in Australia. Believing that cricket should be free to air and not hidden behind a paywall, when the game disappeared behind one, he disappeared with it.

For forty years or so, though, he was one of 'the mighty hand-ful' whose voices became the physical sound of their sports.[49] He was instantly recognizable and a gift to mimics. Imitating Benaud is done 'wearing an imaginary pastel jacket', with the body 'turned sideways at 45 degrees but head to the camera, with bottom lip protruding'.[50] But then comes the voice. Viewers were greeted with a characteristic 'morning everywunnn' and good play was deemed 'maaarvellush' before everyone hoped the batting side would make it to 72 for 2 just to hear him say 'siveny chew for chew'.[51] Even better, if that third-wicket stand should flourish and get past two hundred, everyone was willing it to get as far as 'chew twenty chew for chew'. Since then, things have changed in commentary boxes, where a 'celebrity band of brothers' simply never stop talking.[52] Shutting up, however, was something Benaud was good at: he gave us 'a master-class in the pregnant pause'.[53] If he had a fault, notes Michael Henderson, it was that he was inclined to 'bump up fairly ordinary performances', but looking for good when there might not be much doesn't seem so bad.[54]

During his time as Test captain, Benaud became involved in one of cricket's next great controversies. The game was gripped by its own witch-hunt, the enemy being not witches but crick-eters whose bowling actions were not as classical and correct as the laws insisted. 'Throwing' is the most serious of cricketing crimes, and even now, while ball-tampering, time-wasting, pitch-roughing and sledging are 'glossed over' in the name of 'competi-tion', 'chucking' is not.[55] Back then, it was a widespread problem and Bradman launched an almost personal crusade to get rid of it.[56] As a consequence of this unforgiving agenda, across England, Australia, the Caribbean and the subcontinent, sixteen bowlers were no-balled for throwing between 1960 and 1964.

Central to the denouement of the crisis in 1963/4 was Australian bowler Ian Meckiff. In more glorious days, he had

been pivotal to that joyous cricketing occasion when his failure
to beat Joe Solomon's throw resulted in the tied Test. At a 2000
reunion of those who played in the match, Meckiff's chair was
left empty as he struggled to make the venue on time. A wag
remarked that once again, he wasn't where Australia needed him
to be. Meckiff's left arm had 'a permanent bend', and there was
a whispered rumour that he was going to be called for throwing in the first Test against South Africa at Brisbane in 1963/4.[57]

Bizarrely, before the Test, Meckiff and umpire Col Egar had
won a lawn bowls competition together.[58] It comes as no surprise, then, that they were seen in convivial discussion at a cocktail
party on the eve of the match, with Egar giving no indication
that two days later he would be no-balling the second, third and
ninth deliveries of Meckiff's first over. But when Benaud walked
over to Meckiff at the end of the over to say, 'I'm afraid that's the
end, Dad,' he wasn't giving bad news to his father. Instead, he was
using his fast bowler's nickname to soften the public humiliation.
Meckiff had bowled one solitary excruciating over and Benaud
claimed he had no choice, having always maintained that if any
of his bowlers were called, he would withdraw them from the
attack.[59] Meckiff quit the game immediately, reflecting that even
in club cricket, there was always an umpire 'who wanted to get
his name in the paper'.[60] He accepted his fate, but ridicule followed and his health suffered.

Egar needed police protection at the ground, and it is claimed
he even received death threats. Remarkably, the umpire and the
bowler whose career he ended remained friendly until Egar's death.
Conspiracy theorists felt the on-field judgement seemed pre-
arranged, but throughout, Egar was resolute, saying he simply felt
obliged to act after being lectured by Bradman.[61] Some felt that
the 'witch-hunters' had created such a huge issue that administrators felt justified in throwing at least one career to the wolves

to save the game.[62] Benaud has the last word on how Meckiff's life changed so dramatically for the want of a straighter arm. It was, he said, 'an awful day'.[63]

Throwing had been lurking menacingly, but this was by no means the first public shaming of a bowler with an unusual action. Geoff Griffin was a highly controversial selection for South Africa when they toured England in 1960. Notwithstanding a child-hood accident that left his arm permanently bent, after watching a young Griffin from square leg, even Test keeper John Waite thought he threw it. John Arlott was among those warning the South African authorities that English umpires would take a dim view. When they picked him anyway, he called them 'utterly unsympathetic' towards cricket and Griffin as a human being.[64] Nobody was pragmatic enough to warn Griffin or Meckiff about their actions, and both remain 'guileless victims' of the imperative that something needed to be done.[65]

Up to that point, suspicious bowling actions among previous tourists were overlooked based on Plum Warner's diplomatic reminder that 'our guests' should not be publicly shamed.[66] Griffin, though, was a bent arm too far and it was no surprise when he was no-balled seventeen times by six different umpires in the county warm-ups. There was a widespread expectation that the selectors would sidestep the issue and not select him for the Tests. That he was picked was 'to the shame of the South African management'.[67]

Anticipating trouble, fast-bowling guru Alf Gover schooled Griffin and helped straighten his arm, even though it reduced the venom of his bowling. Even so, Griffin took four wickets at Edgbaston on his Test debut, celebrated his 21st birthday on the rest day and escaped official censure. Apart from a 100-run defeat for his team, all was good. In the next Test, though, Gover's magic dust wore off. England batted first and had hardly wiped the sleep from their eyes when Griffin was called by umpire Frank

Lee the first of five times that day. The second day it continued, and he was called for throwing eleven times altogether during England's innings. So distracting were these events that when amid the mayhem Griffin took the wickets of Mike Smith (99), Peter Walker (52) and Fred Trueman (0) in successive balls across two overs, it wasn't until skipper Jackie McGlew mentioned it that Griffin realized he had become the first to take a Test hat-trick at Lord's. That makes better reading than being the first to be called for throwing in a Lord's Test. That was Griffin, too.

His torment was not over. A resounding innings victory for England meant an early finish. Usually that wasn't a problem, except that this time the queen was visiting, so a twenty-overs-a-side match was hastily arranged. While many would have hidden, Griffin had the gumption to face his accusers and bowled again. He was promptly called again, switched to underarm and was no-balled for not telling the batsman. With no more ignominy possible, at the age of 21, it was the last time he was seen in a Test match, and a couple of years later after some more no-ball trouble, he gave up cricket for good. Griffin himself remained pragmatic throughout and shooed away lawyers promising huge damages because he felt it would hurt the game. The irony is that perhaps the most dignified figures within the whole of cricket's chucking row were probably the ones accused of doing the chucking.

# 20

## SMALL CHANGES,
## BIG CHARACTERS

*More from the 1960s*

A few months before Meckiff's excruciating exit, Lord's played host to another of those uplifting matches involving the West Indians. In 1963 Frank Worrell brought his team to England and the fact that he was batting at seven gives some indication as to the strength of a line-up including Hunte, Kanhai, Butcher, Sobers and Solomon. There was nothing shabby about the bowling, either; Sobers was a three-in-one, Charlie Griffith was terrifyingly fast and Lance Gibbs provided the spin. Spearheading it all was Wes Hall, accurate and menacing with a 'flying crucifix' around his neck.[1]

Arriving at Lord's 0–1 down, England's batting was strong (Edrich, Dexter, Barrington, Cowdrey) but their bowling looked rather frail, Fred Trueman being the only real match winner. Save for four runs, the first innings cancelled each other out but then came Basil Butcher's 133 out of 229, which was quite something on a tricky surface.[2] In response, requiring 234 to win and dodging the rain, England floundered to 31 for 3. Shortly afterwards, Hall struck Colin Cowdrey on the arm, the batsman recalling the 'awful noise' of ball against bone.[3] He was out of the game (or so he thought) with England needing 118 to win on the last day. The weather claimed the morning and both sides upped the urgency. Ken Barrington made 80, and Brian Close did what he often did – he used his body as a tactical weapon. Ignoring the danger, he danced down the wicket to put Hall and Griffith off their length.

Close saw opportunity where others saw danger. Once, at a Hollywood hotel, he heroically failed to dive into the swimming pool over three chairs and two tables, meaning that the hotel was temporarily short of poolside furniture.[4] Almost thirty years after his debut, when he was the youngest player to represent England, he played in 1976 as very nearly the oldest. His Yorkshire career was distinguished, and he led them to four championship victories in the early 1960s. Under Close, Yorkshire were 'argumentative, bloody-minded and disputatious', but everyone knew who the boss was.[5] His willingness to gamble secured the England captaincy but despite six wins from seven Tests at the helm, he was sacked for time-wasting in a championship match in 1967.

It was hardly the most heinous crime, but weeks before, then MCC secretary Billy Griffith had received a letter suggesting that it was wrong that 'third- or fourth-class types' from 'lower backgrounds' should captain England.[6] Behaviour could only improve, it continued, under the leadership of an 'aristocratic' gentleman.[7] The letter was annotated by someone with the initials 'DBC' who endorsed the sentiments therein. It doesn't take much deductive power to imagine that 'DBC' was Donald Bryce Carr, MCC's assistant secretary.[8] Close, who wasn't what most would imagine to be 'aristocratic', accordingly made way for Colin Cowdrey, who presumably was.

Aged forty, Close joined Somerset and turned them into a combative force, especially in the one-day formats that he apparently never really cared for. Aged 63, when most men were feeding their grandchildren boiled sweets and tall stories, he took over the captaincy of the Yorkshire county colts. He was, according to *The Guardian*, the 'spiciest' and 'most adventurous' captain the youngsters would have ever experienced; indeed, as one of his young charges observed, 'He doesn't half swear a lot.'[9] Perhaps Close is not remembered enough for almost 35,000 runs, 1,200 wickets and eight hundred catches. He will however, always be remembered for being tougher than teak. Derek Hodgson suggests that if Brian Close had been a Spartan, then 'Leonidas would not have needed 299 others to stop the Persians at Thermopylae.'[10]

In the match in 1963 at Lord's, Close perished for an insanely valiant 70, and after Parks, Titmus and Trueman came and went, England's fortunes rested with Derek Shackleton, playing his first Test for twelve years, and Gloucestershire off spinner David Allen. Neither were accomplished Test match batsmen. Eight were needed off the last over and a familiar figure with a crucifix stood in the way. After some Keystone Kops-style chaos, England needed six off three balls. A misjudged run resulted in Worrell beating Shackleton to the stumps in a race between 38 year olds.[11] Then, amazingly, his left arm in plaster, Cowdrey walked back into bat more gingerly than a parent coming home after a teenage party. David Allen was on strike, and discretion triumphed over valour as the penultimate ball was blocked. Last ball, six needed. The

Brian Close (right) presents Azeem Rafiq with the Yorkshire ccc Academy
Player of the Year award, 2008.

last delivery was 'as fast a ball' as Hall ever bowled, but it wasn't enough to beat Allen and the match was drawn.[12]

The result undoubtedly relieved England captain Ted Dexter, arguably the most charismatic England cricketer of the era.[13] In his pomp, he was worth 'at least double the admission price', batting as he did like 'a cavalier amateur'.[14] While he could be 'breath-taking and brilliant', his refusal to respect any kind of bowling often frustrated.[15] He was certainly his own man.

But cricket is only a part of Ted Dexter. 'Absorbing company', capable of playing golf as well as cricket to a high standard, he once 'piloted his family to Australia in a light aircraft'.[16] With his wife Sue, Dexter happily advertised Noilly Prat, which, besides being the name of T. S. Eliot's cat, was a tipple connoting the highest levels of 1970s sophistication. He came up with the idea of the ICC player rankings, but not everything he touched turned to gold. An eccentric reign as England's chairman of selectors was characterized by some odd decision-making, and he once famously put a misjudgement down to the 'the wrong juxtaposition' of the planets.[17]

Entering the world of thriller writing, he concocted an unlikely tale of an Aussie fast bowler expiring on the field after being poisoned. But he wasn't able to match the standard of his cricket, with a narrative 'weighed down' with a multitude of characters all suspected of the crime, including 'the press contingent, the officials of the MCC, several fans and a few glamorous women associated with the cricketing scene'.[18] Once put down, claimed some, it was hard to pick up again.

As the Conservative parliamentary candidate for Cardiff South East in the 1964 General Election, Dexter took on Labour Shadow Chancellor James Callaghan. But Dexter misjudged his pitch to the generally working-class folk of that part of the Welsh capital. 'While his minders despaired', reported local journalist Dan

O'Neill, Dexter explained that he recommended an Eton edu-cation for everyone, since it didn't only qualify you for 'politics or merchant banking'.[19] Seemingly oblivious to his audience, Dexter assured them that he himself knew old Etonians who worked as bookies. The noise that followed, notes O'Neill, wasn't applause, but the sound of Conservative hopes 'clattering to the floor'.[20] Callaghan increased his majority from 868 to almost 8,000.

'Lord Ted' had much the same luck when pushing cars. When his Jaguar ran out of petrol on the Chiswick flyover, he tried to push it and ran over his own leg, effectively ending his playing career. It was about the right time to give up anyway, reflected Dexter, since he had plenty of outside activities and still was able to keep fit by jogging and 'refusing the third gin & tonic'.[21] Politics, crime thrillers and car-pushing aside, if there was some-thing that Dexter turned his hand to like an expert, it was cricket's transition into a new one-day format. In the new competition – the Gillette Cup – Dexter led Sussex to victory in the first two Lord's finals in 1963 and 1964, his team working out how to adapt to the crash, bang, wallop faster than anyone else. The competi-tion began as 65 overs a side before eventually truncating this to 60; starting after breakfast, the matches had barely ended before the pubs stopped serving for the night.

Excitement was in short supply to begin with as the finals were low-scoring affairs. But the potential for mayhem was demon-strated in the 1965 showpiece when Yorkshire met Surrey. Batting first, Yorkshire made 317 for 4. This was 175 too many for Surrey and would still be an impressive score (albeit in far fewer overs) over fifty years later. The show-stopping performance for Yorkshire came from Geoffrey Boycott, his 146 containing fifteen fours and three sixes. To that point, Boycott was already one of the coun-try's top opening batsmen, albeit aggression was 'not among his plus points'.[22]

Boycott himself felt it was probably his greatest ever innings in terms of stroke play, but such aggression and risk taking were wholly uncharacteristic.[23] Writing afterwards, John Woodcock suggested it was likely that Boycott would be a Test opener for some while, but the prospect of his being so in his usual moribund fashion was difficult to imagine.[24] These were prophetic words, as Boycott off the pitch was invariably more entertaining than on it. When, for example, international cricket visited Swansea for the first time in 1973, few were exhilarated by his batting. It was only the sixth ever official ODI, and a strong New Zealand batting attack was no match for England, the visitors' 158 being not nearly enough, even in the days of more cautious batting. In response, Boycott's excruciating twenty took 88 balls. Spectators only eschewed the alternative entertainment provided by drying paint because of what was happening at the other end, where Dennis Amiss made a sumptuous 100 in 121 balls with fourteen fours and a six. Amiss was dismissed with the game all but won, *Wisden* reporting that 'it was a poor reward for him to be mobbed by unruly youngsters.'[25] Nobody, though, mobbed Boycott.

In a Test against India at Headingley in 1967, he made 246 not out but took nine and a half hours to do it. Brian Close broke the news to Boycott that he had been dropped for the next Test match during a car journey from Leeds to Bristol. What a trip it must have been – perhaps more eventful than the innings itself, remembered for its 'fist-gnawing, neuron-crushing dullness'.[26] *The Mirror* warned gravely that cricket could not afford to put such a 'joyless effort' in cricket's 'shop window',[27] but Boycott ploughed his own furrow and while the slings and arrows often wounded him, they never forced him to rethink his approach. He remained resolute and unburdened by self-doubt. When, in 2010, he was asked to pick his best England Ashes XI, he nominated Surrey's John Edrich to open the innings. If you were given three guesses who Boycott chose as the other opening batsman, you wouldn't need two of them.

Boycott's first-class and Test-match statistics, of course, are beyond challenge. Only seven batsmen made more career runs, and all played for longer. Fellow Yorkshireman Herbert Sutcliffe, for example, made 2,244 more runs than Boycott's 48,426, but played 145 more innings. His Test total of 8,114 runs marks him out as one of England's most prolific batsmen, but he did not collect admiring colleagues in the way that Hobbs or Sutcliffe did. Indeed, he had 'a facility for making enemies much faster than he made his runs'.[28]

Though Boycott denies it ever happened, while on one Ashes tour the rest of the England batsmen could not make head or tail of Australian mystery spinner John Gleeson, he allegedly told a teammate that he'd worked him out a while back but that the magic antidote was not for sharing with the rest of the team.[29] When picking up *Geoff Boycott: A Cricketing Hero* by Leo McKinstry, one shouldn't be fooled by the title – this is no hagiography and there are times when one wonders if the title is ironic. McKinstry does not shy away from establishing Boycott as a serious player with a serious record, but while Boycott's qualities are championed, he is eviscerated for his flaws. A groundsman described him as 'self-centred' and 'arrogant' with a 'vicious tongue'.[30] He could renege on a deal to pay a group of Pakistani boys to wash his car yet was capable of being sensitive enough to treat homesick England colleague Derek Randall to an English roast to cheer him up.

He did owe Randall, though. After a three-year hiatus from Test cricket, which seems to have been taken in protest at not being made England captain, Boycott made a comeback at Trent Bridge against Australia in 1977. It was Ian Botham's debut, but the Nottingham crowd only had eyes for local boy Randall, who

unwittingly drove his opponents 'barmy'.[31] During his staggering 174 against Australia in Melbourne a few months earlier, his
innocent singing of 'The sun has got its hat on' infuriated the
Aussies.[32] Dennis Lillee was eventually complimentary about the
innings, but at the time had not enjoyed Randall doffing his cap
in response to the meanest, maddest bouncers he could muster.
Though he suffered from 'selectorial inconsistency and unsupport-
ive captains', Randall was hugely popular; perhaps, for the people
of Nottingham, even more so than Robin Hood.[33]

Randall was everything Boycott wasn't. While the Yorkshireman
was organized and methodical, even down to the number of times
he folded his shirtsleeves, Randall had the perennial look of a
man who has just realized he has got off the train at the wrong
station with the wrong suitcase but has decided to make the best
of it anyway. As David Hopps notes, everything that Randall did
had 'a touch of dementia' about it.[34]

But at Trent Bridge in 1977, even Randall's humour was tested
when Boycott ran him out. Randall was 'done like a kipper' by
the Yorkshireman, who set off for a run without telling Randall.
Realizing that this one was all down to him, Boycott stood at the
non-striker's end with his head in his hands, apparently asking
himself, 'What have I done?'[35] Commentating for the BBC, John
Arlott had no doubts, exclaiming 'How tragic, how tragic, how
tragic.'[36]

Boycott went on to make the 98th century of his first-class
career but never was a Test century by an English batsman greeted
so indifferently.[37] Later that series, he chalked up first-class century number one hundred, in front of a TV audience and the more
forgiving patrons at Headingley. When Yorkshire decided to part
company with Boycott in 1986, club chairman Brian Close was
sadly earnest in summarizing the Boycott era that had lasted
since 1962. The dressing-room atmosphere had not been good,

he concluded, adding that a number of players had left to thrive elsewhere. One of Boycott's faults, added Close, was perhaps that he prioritized his own interest before that of the game or the club.[38] But Yorkshire colleague Don Wilson's summary was: 'Even though I don't like him, I would never deny that he was a great player.'[39]

Knighted in 2020, as a pundit, Boycott has divided his audience. While some love his bluntness, others cringe at the occasional gaucheness. Love him or loathe him, Boycott's insights have become famous beyond cricket. The 'corridor of uncertainty' is now a staple to describe the tempting channel outside a batsman's off stump. He is a regular exponent of the 'Yorkshire Apology', which is when a sentence starts with 'I'm sorry', but 'you're not actually sorry at all'.[40] Boycott's version is one that warms the hearts of cricketers worldwide but more likely the hearts of those splendid ladies that bore them. 'I'm sorry,' he puffs, 'but my mum could've

Geoffrey Boycott (left), 1979.

caught that in 'er pinny.'[41] Consequently, cricketing challenges are often ranked according to whether the late Mrs Boycott could have handled them in her pinny while simultaneously attending to everything else. Over the years, there have been suggestions that she might fancy 'Marlon Samuels' gentle off-spin', and in 2006, while bemoaning the quality of the Pakistani fielding, the *Yorkshire Post* claimed that Mrs Boycott could have taken four out of the five chances they spilled at Lord's 'without the aid of her apron'.[42] Apparently, her son was also on record saying that old Mrs Boycott 'could have handled subcontinental pitches as well as Ian Bell'.[43]

Even the quietest spell of Test cricket has been enlivened when BBC's cricket correspondent Jonathan Agnew was joined by Boycott as 'second voice'. Occasionally toe-curling and sometimes confrontational, Agnew gently pressed all the right buttons and Boycott never failed to deliver. His rather entrenched opinions about just about everything did occasionally make him vulnerable to the odd sophisticated wind-up. While on air together in 2017, for example, Agnew announced that one of Boycott's hundreds was being removed from the first-class records and that the celebratory dinner held to mark forty years since that unforgettable day at Headingley would therefore surely have to be cancelled. 'You've invited people under false pretences,' said Agnew, and when the commentator revealed it was a leg-pull, Boycott's relief was palpable. Close, Dexter and Boycott. What a dinner party that would be.

# 21

## SHORTER FORMATS,
## NEW STARS
### *The 1960s and 1970s*

Boycott was not the most obvious exponent of one-day cricket: on the face of it, he and many of his peers looked ill equipped for the requisite crash, bang, wallop. As would-be swashbucklers, they had the buckles, but not much of the swash. In 1969 the introduction of the John Player League on Sundays was a bewildering development for county stalwarts who participated as enthusiastically as anyone who'd just lost their day off. Brian Close waspishly suggested that cricket was reduced to 'sawdust', 'top hats' and 'red noses'.[1] Tom Graveney called it 'an act of cruelty' against old pros hoping to see out their days at second slip.[2]

Batsmen needed to do things sooner and faster, which was problematic for those already doing them as soon and as fast as they could. Now it was quick singles and an obscene new outrage called 'slogging'. Many games were played on out-grounds where wickets either kept low, bounced over your head or both. Bowlers had their run-ups limited, which was no good for long-limbed speedsters who got going by pushing off from the sightscreen. Initially only the good fielders enjoyed it, as they showcased skills that had previously gone unacknowledged.

While some counties took years to develop tactical strategies, others caught on quickly. Imagining that the new league was weekend club cricket 'on an elevated stage', Lancashire, for example, quickly realized that their players had actually been weaned on the format and so it shouldn't be a dramatic change.[3]

Statistics suggest that in the early days of the JPL 140 was a competitive score, and in the first four years of the competition only Lancashire – once – averaged over five runs per over. Scores over 200 were rare and individual centuries rarer. Anybody scoring as quickly as A. B. de Villiers would have been burned as a witch.

For those preferring to watch the JPL live rather than on TV, there was a liberating invitation 'to bring the family' – which was ideal, unless the cricket was where you went to avoid them. There was cash, too, and in the pre-decimalized days of 1969, for example, every six was worth the equivalent of £2.82 to the hitter, and every four-wicket haul earned the bowler £17.85. The hitter of most sixes in 1971 and 1974 was circus-loving Brian Close. True, it wasn't India Premier League money, but in 1970, a decent pint of beer cost twenty pence. It is a pertinent comparison, since that's probably where most of the bonuses went. Rudimentary and rustic, there was charm about the JPL's initial cluelessness. In those days one-day training consisted of the skipper poking his head around the door with a pithy 'batsmen – score faster; bowlers – don't run in so far; and fielders – do lots of diving. Good luck.'

Few, though, denied that one-day cricket was exciting and unforgettable. In the days when the BBC broadcast Test cricket, matches finished on a Tuesday. Imagining that the nation would be baying for more, the Corporation followed up with a full day of Gillette Cup action on Wednesdays. One semi-final at Old Trafford in 1971 lasted so long that most people watching at home did so in their dressing gowns, hugging their cocoa. Gloucestershire batted first, and the centrepiece of a decent 229 for 6 was a storming 65 by South African all-rounder Mike Procter.

Procter had an all-embracing relationship with his adopted county and fans recognized his dominance as Gloucestershire became 'Proctershire'.[4] As an all-round cricketer, comparisons with Sobers are justified.[5] His polished, attacking batting and his lethal fast bowling reminded people of Keith Miller, and during the 1970s, while Procter was comparable with Botham, Imran Khan, Hadlee and Kapil Dev in terms of statistics, in many ways he might have been the best of them.[6] He scored more first-class runs (21,936) than any of them, with an average second-best only to Imran, who beat him by a fraction. He also took more first-class wickets (1,417) than any of them apart from Hadlee, who took 73 more. Of the four, only the New Zealander had a better bowling average, but none of the four came within ten of his 48 career centuries. Botham took 29 more catches by virtue of a career spent in the slips. Throw in a run of six centuries in successive innings in 1970/71, and that puts him in a category with Bradman (of course) and C. B. Fry.

For Gloucestershire, his contribution was immeasurable, his batting complemented by 'lightning swing bowling' on the end of a 'vast, curving run' which gave the illusion of bowling off the wrong foot.[7] In the 1973 Gillette Cup final he made 94 and took 2 for 27; he made 109 not out from a team total of 135 in a JPL match in 1974, and in the County Championship in 1979 he made the season's fastest century and took an all-LBW hat-trick, having already bagged a similar hat-trick in 1972.[8] On that July day in 1971 at Old Trafford, his innings contributed to a challenging total, though it might have been more had it not been for some parsimonious off spin by Jack Simmons, who took 2 for 25. Even as a late starter plucked from the Lancashire leagues, Simmons only just missed the career double of 10,000 runs and 1,000 wickets. So miserly was his one-day bowling that in 1985 he completed a twelve-over spell for three runs. He was a *Wisden* Cricketer of the Year aged 44, and still an automatic choice for Lancashire at 48 years old. His huge influence on Tasmanian cricket made him as popular in Hobart as Haslingden.

Simmons also knew his business in the dining room: the nickname 'Flat Jack' described his low bowling trajectory and was nothing to do with a washboard stomach. As a 'spinner and gourmet', Simmons was always interested in where he could buy some decent fish and chips.[9] Skipper David Lloyd recalls once taking to the field with ten men at Southport because Jack was still negotiating his lunchtime pudding, adamant that it was the best gooseberry pie he'd ever encountered and 'he wasn't going to rush it for anybody.'[10] Another time, when Lloyd gave Simmons a lift home, the bowler asked to be dropped at the chip shop, from where he said he would walk home. Lloyd offered to wait, only to be told that it was okay, he'd eat his food on the way home as his wife would 'have the supper on'.[11] Few cricketers, surely, have ever had a meal named after them, but 'the Simmo' emerged from Great Harwood, halfway between Blackburn and Burnley. It was all because one night, Simmons couldn't decide between meat pie and fish, so he had both.[12] With chips and mushy peas.[13]

But back to 1971. Lancashire started sedately, and Gloucestershire undoubtedly hoped that Procter could follow his runs with some wickets. David Lloyd and Barry Wood got Lancashire off to a solid if slowish start, and cameos from Harry Pilling, Clive Lloyd and Simmons kept them in touch. Rain delayed the reply, but when all-rounder David Hughes marched in, Lancashire needed what looked like a straightforward 25 runs off five overs. The problem was that by now, it was 8.45 p.m. The light was murky and the BBC *Nine O'Clock News* was in serious danger of being delayed, the Corporation fearing uproar if they cut the live feed from Old Trafford. Procter wasn't exactly racing through his overs either, hoping for abandonment until the next day. The scene was increasingly chaotic, Lancashire having maximized the crowd to 25,000, meaning that hundreds were by now encroaching onto the field. The twitchiness of the hapless floor manager in the BBC Television

Centre was only matched by that of umpire Dickie Bird and his more experienced colleague Arthur Jepson.

Known as 'Jeppo', the former Nottinghamshire bowler and Stoke City and Lincoln City goalkeeper was a typical 'poacher turned gamekeeper' with a sense of humour that could be 'disconcerting' for those who had not met him before.[14] More experienced players realized that in between the caustic words, there was important intelligence to be collected, including what the pitch was doing, what the fielders were doing and the progress of 'the opposing captain's hangover'.[15] Lancashire skipper Jackie Bond realized that it might be better to conclude the game the next day when the batsmen could see the ball, a distinct advantage when facing Procter. Accordingly, he told Jepson that he couldn't see. It may have become the first ever day/night match, but Jepson was not budging. There was no way he was coming back the next day. 'You can see the moon. How far do you want to see?' was his last word on the matter.[16]

By this time, Hughes and Bond were communicating more by sound than vision and jointly concluded that the required runs were more likely to be scored off former England off spinner John Mortimore than Procter, who was now beginning his run-up five yards inside the boundary. In a few minutes of mayhem that are now part of folklore, David Hughes smashed the hapless Mortimore for 24 in one over, leaving Bond to take the winning run off what Brian Viner described as 'a scowling Procter', adding, 'at least, we had to assume he was scowling. We couldn't quite make out his face on our black-and-white telly.'[17]

David Lloyd reported later that when he and his teammates arrived home at 11 p.m. claiming to have just finished the match, suspicious wives asked for proof.[18] Nonetheless, he reflected, it was the game that put one-day cricket on the map, and there it remained.[19] Like women's skirts in the 1960s, cricket got progressively shorter. The Gillette Cup was sixty overs, the JPL was forty and now there are many worldwide twenty-over competitions and even a ten-over version – a 'fiery, fast and furious' game lasting an hour and a half.[20] Somewhere Brian Close is spinning in his grave. But twenty-over cricket is the new king of the jungle, especially in the subcontinent and the Indian Premier League. More of that later.

Even before the IPL, short-form cricket relied on overseas stars and it was the obvious platform for the new crop entering English county cricket in 1968. The game had already been enhanced by several players from elsewhere, and the prince among them – literally – was the 9th Nawab of Pataudi, known to the cricketing world as 'Tiger'. A cricketing prodigy, he was schooled at Winchester – Douglas Jardine's old school – and transitioned to first-class cricket with Sussex. The link with Jardine was bitterly historical. Young Pataudi's father had been 'the conscientious objector' to Jardine's Bodyline plans. His father combined regal duties with cricket and played Tests for England and India but died suddenly after playing polo on his son's eleventh birthday.

As a younger man, winked former Surrey and England stalwart Micky Stewart at a remembrance lunch for Tiger in 2012, the Indian 'led a fully active social life'.[21] The euphemism was both intentional and complimentary. Sussex teammate Jim Parks recalled that it was possible to turn up for the start of a match only to get a phone call from Tiger to say he was 'in Paris'.[22] That happened at least once, and Stewart was the opposing captain when it did. Delayed in the French capital, he asked Parks to deputize. Pataudi's widow Sharmila confessed with 'a little smile' that she was the reason for the skipper's tardiness.[23]

On the field, as captain of Oxford, Tiger's career as a batsman was sensationally kick-started by taking two centuries off Yorkshire that by all accounts even rendered Fred Truemen speechless. But then, tragedy struck – in a car accident in Hove, glass pierced his eye and rendered it useless. Astonishingly, only months later he became Indian Test skipper aged only 21. *Wisden* reported that he didn't merely add 'a whiff of the exotic' to monochrome 1960s cricket, but with a 'beguiling mixture of personal charm and tactical know-how', forced his team to leave behind their factional divides.[24] His batting was understandably never completely consistent but nonetheless retained its flamboyance and brought him six Test centuries at an average of 35. The pick of them – his 148 at Headingley in 1967 – 'would remain in TV viewers' minds forever'.[25]

As a man he had charm to spare.[26] Ian Chappell (hardly the easiest to impress) freely admits his everlasting admiration for Tiger. Long before the hyper-professional era in cricket, Chappell once asked Tiger what he did for a living. 'I'm a prince,' was the response. 'Not getting the point,' continued Chappell, 'I repeatedly asked him what he did between 9 and 5. He finally snapped and said, 'Ian, I'm a f*****g prince!'[27] But this was no egomaniac. He may have lost his title when India did away with such grandeur, but renamed Mansur Ali Khan, he remained 'a prince among men'.[28] *Wisden*'s claim that he was 'one of the most important figures in the history of Indian cricket' seems entirely justified.[29]

Other overseas players also made an impact. From 1968 players like Sobers (Nottinghamshire), Majid Khan (Glamorgan) Clive Lloyd and Farokh Engineer (both Lancashire), Procter (Gloucestershire) and Barry Richards and Gordon Greenidge (Hampshire) began long relationships with their adopted counties. Their longevity and loyalty sharply contrasts with notions of the modern era where overseas players 'dip in and out' as guns for hire with only a fleeting association with the counties employing them.[30] Even big supporters of the many Twenty20 competitions across the world would surely concede that they have fostered an easy come, easy go culture, meaning that players' suitcases often barely touch the floor.

Yorkshire were the only abstainers from the new international frontier, and while *Wisden*'s editor admired their 'recruit local' policy, he also judged newcomers to other counties a welcome change from the 'dour, safety-first' county cricket that had prevailed in the past.[31] Sobers was immediately successful, and the flamboyance of Majid Khan was loved by the Glamorgan public to the extent that his captain, Tony Lewis, called it 'catastrophic' when the Pakistani went back to Cambridge to finish his studies.[32] Such was his impact and charisma that Lewis suggested that had Majid been Welsh, they would have 'declared independence and made him our King'.[33] When Shane Warne joined 'Hampshheeer' in 2000, Vic Marks called him the biggest star to be attracted to county cricket since Sobers.[34]

Some, however, were wary of offering a ready-made platform for overseas talent and such concerns have remained. In 2003, speaking particularly about South African and Australian interlopers, England fast bowler Devon Malcolm suggested that county cricket was simply training them to understand the peculiarities of the English game so that they could come back as Test players with a big advantage.[35] True, the odd overseas player of questionable pedigree has arrived out of shape and out of form, but plenty have shown unquestionable commitment. West Indian Courtney Walsh, for example, took the Gloucestershire captaincy very seriously. Once, after requesting an overnight stay for his team ahead of the Cheltenham Festival, he was granted a budget for accommodation but not for food. Such was his commitment that Walsh paid for everyone's dinner himself.[36]

The epitome of the overseas professional becoming entirely wed to his adopted county was Keith Boyce. The West Indian all-rounder is remembered with affection in Essex for helping to fashion them into winners.[37] Originally a leg-spinning defensive batsman from Barbados, something peculiar must have happened to him, since everyone in Essex knew him for bowling like a train and hitting cricket balls into orbit. Plenty reckoned that he had the hardest, longest throw in the game's history. He made 'spectators duck' and 'batsmen quake', and after taking 9 for 61 on debut against Cambridge University, Essex simply loved him forever, appreciating his 'undimmed enthusiasm from the day he started to the day he finished'.[38] Spectators sobbed when he announced his injury-forced retirement over the PA system in 1977, and there was deep sadness when he collapsed and died in 1996 at his local pharmacy in Bridgetown, Barbados, on his 53rd birthday.

But not everyone was in awe of the influx of West Indian superstars. In 1969 – the season after Sobers joined Nottinghamshire – the then unlikely cricketing force of Ireland shocked the whole world of cricket. In fairness, the scheduling of the West Indies' visit to Northern Ireland for a two-innings-a-side, one-day match did them no favours. The day before, the tourists had been at Lord's, where England couldn't quite manage an audacious last-day win. The bizarre itinerary demanded the tourists be on parade the next day in Sion Mills, County Tyrone.

Heavy overnight rain had cleared and the pitch was sopping wet, but nobody wanted to disappoint the crowd of around 2,000. The tourists were without Sobers and Jackie Hendricks, who stayed in London with injuries, but they still fielded a side with six Test players, including Clive Lloyd and tour manager Clyde Walcott. With water covering their shoes, visiting and home skippers Basil Butcher and Doug Goodwin went out to toss. Butcher called correctly and decided to bat. He must have woken up screaming about his decision for years afterwards.

With his team 12 for 9 on a pitch described as 'green as an airsick leprechaun',[39] Butcher's colleagues quickly told the skipper that he may have got it wrong. A heroic 9 by tail-ender Grayson Shillingford elevated things a little, but even on a wet pitch, 25 all out was pitiful. Opening bowlers Alec O'Riordan and skipper Goodwin had bowled unchanged, taking 4 for 18 and 5 for 6 respectively. As per the pre-match agreement, the superior Irish first innings of 125 for 8 was enough for them to win.

There was plenty of talk that while Ireland had taken full advantage of a sporting wicket, the West Indians were all hungover. In the *Daily Telegraph*, Tom Peterkin confirms the inaccuracy, noting that Irish batsman Ivan Anderson described rumours of such excessive conviviality as an 'old wives' tale'.[40] Dignified in victory, Ireland had been calm throughout, O'Riordan explaining that there was no 'running up to each other, throwing the arms around and high-fiving'.[41] Apparently the tourists were not amused, and there were raised voices in the pavilion. Accounts of after-match events in the Irish dressing room are less fulsome, but one imagines it was hardly quick showers all round then home for supper.

# 22

# PARADISE LOST,
# PARADISE REGAINED

*From the 1960s to the 1990s*

Of all the cricketers that came to England in 1968, few generated more column inches than Barry Richards. Often we
heard of the 'tragedy' that he was never given a proper opportunity
to play at the highest level. As one of the most brilliant batsmen
of all time, he was also among the most enigmatic, simultaneously
appealing to 'both to the savage and the artist'.[1] In 1970 he scored
325 for South Australia in one day against a bowling attack featuring Dennis Lillee, Graham McKenzie and Tony Lock.[2] Although
the innings was covered by two TV stations, neither has archive
footage and the only permanent reminder is a three-minute film
shot by one of Richards's friends. Though it is not particularly
clear, it does at least include a shot of the scoreboard at the end
of the day.[3]

Such innings don't go unnoticed. Shortly before he died, Sir
Donald Bradman selected his greatest ever team and like all such
imaginary selections, it was contentious. Bradman himself, of
course, was in it, but Hutton, Viv Richards, Compton, Sydney
Barnes, Warne, Imran Khan, Gavaskar, Keith Miller, Richard
Hadlee, George Headley and Laker were not. Even Walter
Hammond only made twelfth man, but Barry Richards made
it into the final XI. *The Times* suggested that most critics 'collectively, and enthusiastically, dismantled it', the choice of the
South African ahead of Jack Hobbs, for example, leading people
to wonder whether Bradman might need some new spectacles.[4]

But others agreed about Richards. England bowler Bob Willis, for example, judged him to be 'among the top 10 players of all time'.[5]

Born into a Durban family with no discernible cricket connections, Richards was 'encouraged' rather than 'coached' by a doting grandfather. Not that it stopped Grandpa from tearing him off a strip when Richards made his first fifty for the under-thirteens and neither raised his bat nor touched his cap to the crowd.[6] Even with his sublime skills it was a bumpy ride for young Richards. After scoring a century for a representative XI against the touring Australians in 1966, he was refused entry to a nightclub for not wearing a tie. After Richards angrily kicked a flowerpot, the club manager complained, and Richards was demoted to number 8 in the second innings and left out of the Test team.[7]

When he arrived at Hampshire in 1968, his new colleagues were wary of a man who'd never played in a Test match and was picking up a big salary on the expectation of producing something extraordinary, rather than on the basis of already having done it. After telling a TV interviewer that he aimed to score 2,000 runs that season, he was dismissed fifth ball on his county debut. 'Just another 2,000 to go,' observed one of the Sussex fielders wryly.[8] At the hotel later, reacting to some teasing from his teammates, he kicked a hole in a door. His pay was docked, but nobody seemed unduly upset, since former county skipper Colin Ingleby-Mackenzie had set the bar impossibly high where vandalism was concerned by destroying a door at the same hotel 'with a spear'.[9] That season, Richards made his 2,000 runs, plus another 400 just to emphasize the point. Indeed, there were times during his Hampshire career when one could not imagine anyone ever batting any better.[10] With some regret, however, Richards reflected that at Hampshire he might have preferred 'fewer runs and more friends'.[11]

He was picked for South Africa in 1970 against Bill Lawry's Australians, joining other sublime talents including Procter,

Lee Irvine, the Pollock brothers and Eddie Barlow. Even within such company, Richards shone with scores of 29, 32, 140, 65, 35, 81 and 126. Shortly after the comprehensive dispatching of Australia, the South Africans were kitted out for their upcoming tour of England. It was due to begin on 1 June, but with nine days to go, it was cancelled.[12] Years later, Richards claimed that if he'd have known that four Tests would have been the full extent of his international career, the Australians would never have got him out.[13]

The reason the tour was cancelled was the ongoing row about – and public reaction to – South Africa's domestic policy. Mobilized by intensified nationalism and strong anti-immigration sentiments, South Africa had adopted a highly contentious regime of institutionalized segregation according to race. To consider apartheid through a narrow – and relatively insignificant – sporting lens seems trite, but for a while, cricket was in the eye of the storm. MCC Secretary Billy Griffith had warned South Africa that there was no guarantee that future England teams would be all-white, since in the UK multiculturalism was being facilitated in part by first-class cricketers who were becoming aspirational figures for first- and second-generation immigrants.[14] The man caught most specifically in the crosshairs of events in 1968 was Cape Coloured, and as a mixed-race citizen had few of the rights enjoyed by whites. With no opportunity to play cricket for South Africa, Basil D'Oliveira came to the UK, where he was deemed good enough first by Worcestershire and then by England. His selection was 'a testament to our inclusivity', noted Matthew Engel, and seemingly it was not an issue for anyone until England played South Africa.[15]

But after a moderate tour of the West Indies in 1967/8, D'Oliveira's international prospects were in the doldrums. While he might have partied a little too hard, the tour had been

catastrophic for England teammate Fred Titmus.[16] While relaxing in the Caribbean Sea, the Middlesex spinner's foot slid under
a boat. After 'a bang', he thought he'd cut it. Upon inspecting the
damage, however, he realized that he had a serious problem – he
had lost two toes and two others were hanging on by a thread.[17]
Skipper Colin Cowdrey (whose wife had been driving the speedboat), Robin Hobbs, Denis Compton and Brian Johnston used a
beach chair as a stretcher and raced him to hospital. Fortunately,
a Canadian surgeon interrupted his sunbathing nearby to make
good the bloody mess.[18] Only eight weeks later, Titmus played
against a British Army xi in Germany and followed an innings of
63 with 6 for 44. He took 111 wickets in the season that followed,
and finished top of the Middlesex batting averages. In 1982, and
in borrowed kit, 49-year-old Titmus took 3 for 43 to win a county
match for Middlesex, meaning that he had played cricket in five
decades, having first turned his arm over for Middlesex in 1949.
In all, he scored 21,588 first-class runs and took 2,830 first-class
wickets, and his story is one of 'good doctoring, good luck and
irrepressible spirit'.[19]

When Australia toured in 1968, D'Oliveira was selected for
the first Test and was the only batsman to put up much of a show
(with 87 not out) in a heavy defeat.[20] The selectors fiddled with the
side and he next appeared for the final Test, but only to replace
the injured Roger Prideaux. D'Oliveira was a contentious pick,
since it was the final Test before the party for South Africa was
selected. Implicitly, D'Oliveira was being given a clear chance
to be picked, even though South African prime minister John
Vorster had made it clear that the tour would be cancelled if the
England touring party was anything other than completely white.

D'Oliveira's first innings of 158 placed the cat well and truly
among the pigeons. It was hard for the tour selectors to ignore,
and yet still they ignored it. It was a case of '158 not in', and among

Basil D'Oliveira, 1975.

various peculiar decisions by England cricket selectors, D'Oliveira's
omission took the biscuit.[21]

The denouement of The Oval Test is captured by a famous
photograph of the entire England team, both Australian batsmen and one umpire clustered around the cut strip. The Ashes,

as far as England were concerned, were gone, but spectators had collectively mopped up the sodden playing arena to enable 75 minutes of play. One can't envisage such enthusiastic mangling and forking if the five remaining wickets had been English ones, but with only a few minutes left, and after a careful six-hour vigil, opener John Inverarity's concentration was breached. He kicked away Underwood's arm ball and umpire Charlie Elliott raised the finger.

While the exciting conclusion of the match was captured forever in the iconic photograph, there was bigger drama happening off the field. A tobacco company had previously offered D'Oliveira a big coaching contract if he opted out of the tour voluntarily. Resolutely ignoring such temptations, he was distraught when he wasn't picked.[22] Worcestershire teammate Tom Graveney recalled that D'Oliveira simply 'put his head in his hands and wept'.[23] There was ambivalence among the Lord's suits, since although those running the game wanted 'fair play', they loved the South African hospitality and had many friends and associates living there.[24] Matthew Engel ruefully notes how they always seemed to ignore the fact that the cheers emanating from 'blacks-only' parts of South African stadiums were not for the home team but for whoever they were playing.[25] Even more murkily, it was suggested that the inner sanctum of England's selectorial decision-making was shaped by some entrenched political leanings. Former England captain Arthur Gilligan and bowler Alec Bedser, for example, were both known to hold strong right-wing views and to have no appetite to change South Africa's political status quo.[26]

Justice, or at least moral justice, was seen to be done when D'Oliveira replaced Tom Cartwright, who dropped out of the tour party. It wasn't an obvious like-for-like swap since Cartwright was 'a bowler who batted' and D'Oliveira 'a batter who bowled'.[27] Cartwright's 'injury' may have been strategic, since the Warwickshire player was 'unusually radical' and hated South Africa and its injustices, making his views very clear to anyone who played there.[28] Choosing D'Oliveira meant that the tour was cancelled. Home Secretary James Callaghan sent a request to the Lord's powerbrokers to turn down the opportunity to tour, and that was that. The international careers of Richards, Procter and others were over. For them, it was a case of Napoleon's summation that while glory may be fleeting, 'obscurity is forever'.

Omitting D'Oliveira from the tour eventually had major consequences for sport and the lives of millions as it led first to South Africa's isolation and then, later, to the end of apartheid.[29] At the time, though, there were serious ramifications for the economic sustainability of English cricket. Then as now, the game was reliant on Test match revenue and in 1970, this lifeblood was removed at a stroke. A replacement series was hastily arranged against the 'Rest of the World'. Any such representative selection merits scrutiny, since the term has been applied with varying degrees of credibility. But the 'Rest of the World' team in 1970 contained Sobers, Procter and Barry Richards. They were joined by four West Indians, three other South Africans, an Australian, an Indian and two Pakistanis. The strong and richly multiracial team was managed by old England cricketer Freddie Brown.

Uniquely among Test captains, Brown was born in Peru. During MCC's South American tour in 1926/7, Brown's father Roger took 5 for 50 for the Lima Cricket and Football Club. Perhaps he proudly included the details when he next wrote to the teenage Freddie, who was being educated in Cambridge. Brown Jr's cricketing education was furthered by Aubrey Faulkner, who got the youngster switching between medium pacers and deadly looking leg spinners.[30] A first-class career with Surrey beckoned.

However big the world is, it's only a village. Six or so years after his father had played against them in that match in Lima,

Freddie Brown sailed with Plum Warner and Gubby Allen to Australia for what became the Bodyline tour. Brown had already played three home Tests without distinction, but had been picked after a terrific season for Surrey consisting of 1,135 runs and 120 wickets, including 'a glorious display of fearless hitting' when he made 212 in just over three hours, including seven seriously big sixes.[31] The selectors thought his energy and enthusiasm might add something to a tour party containing plenty of strong and intense teammates.

These qualities were evident even before the ship docked in Australia. Douglas Jardine enforced a soft-drink-only rule for the youngster, but Brown did a deal with wicketkeeper George Duckworth to add regular shots of gin to his orange juice.[32] Eventually he grew familiar with beverages of all types, since his tour comprised mainly of 'carrying out glasses of lemonade and spare bats' to those who were playing.[33] He didn't play in the Bodyline Tests, and generally speaking, Brown's pre-war cricket was a stop–start affair. Two weeks after he took 8 for 34 at Weston-Super-Mare, war was declared. As a member of the Royal Army Service Corps, he was captured alongside fellow Bodyline tourist Bill Bowes at Tobruk in 1942. The two arranged cricket matches in front of bewildered Italian and German guards who thought the batsman's blockhole might be the start of an escape tunnel. When the Americans rescued him in 1945, he'd shed over four stone (25 kg).

Having played no serious cricket for almost a decade, in 1949 he was persuaded to become captain of Northamptonshire. The county felt an immediate benefit, their fortunes revived by his 'rugged ebullience'.[34] With Brown in charge, the unfancied outfit soon became a potent force.[35] When England were looking for a captain to take them to Australia in 1950/51, their first two choices – Norman Yardley and George Mann – were unavailable, and so it was to Freddie Brown that the selectors turned. Rarely must a captain have ever begun a tour with such modest expectations. This feeling of foreboding was perhaps justified, since while the 1948 Invincibles had lost Bradman, they were otherwise mostly intact.

It was no shock when Australia went 4–0 up before England took the last Test to stop a whitewash. On paper, it looks a disaster, yet *Wisden* report that so inspirational was Brown as a captain that he became a 'smash hit'.[36] The Aussie crowds loved this 'rosy cheeked John Bull figure' who, with his 'white cravat and pipe', represented a throwback to the old amateur spirit.[37] When he made a brave 62 at Melbourne, the reception from the 60,000-strong crowd 'out-Bradmanned' the cheers for the great Australian in his prime.[38] One Aussie grocer advertised 'lovely lettuces with 'earts as big as Freddie Brown's'.[39] Popular Down Under, he nonetheless polarized opinion among his colleagues and charges. Fred Trueman and Brian Close weren't big fans, but as player, captain, commentator, tour manager, MCC President and Chairman of its Cricket Council, he filled many of the game's major roles and was awarded the CBE for his service.

Accordingly, Brown was a sensible choice to make the most of the impromptu Test series in 1970. The cricket had memorable moments, even if it lacked the intensity of nation versus nation. The visitors won the series 4–1, but it was a closer contest than the final scores suggest. The stars for England were skipper Illingworth, Tony Greig and, ironically, D'Oliveira with both bat and ball. There were bittersweet memories for Glamorgan opener Alan Jones. A prolific scorer at county level, he was selected for an England debut in the Lord's Test. True, he didn't cash in on his chance, making five and a duck, but official Test status was removed from the match some time later. John Arlott described it as 'a massive con trick – as cynical as any ever pulled in cricket'.[40] The injustice was finally righted in June 2020, when Jones was officially recognized as an England player, fifty years to the day after walking out to bat at Lord's.

For the Rest of the World, Sobers made a couple of centuries and took useful wickets. His contributions were rarely eclipsed, but this time South African all-rounder Eddie Barlow was the star of the show. 'If you have been driven into the last ditch, with 4,000 spearmen charging,' wrote Derek Hodgson, 'you would be happy to see Eddie Barlow in there with you.[41] With his barrel chest and spectacles, Barlow was an unlikely looking sportsman and was untidy as 'an unmade bed'.[42] They called him 'Bunter' after the fictional schoolboy Billy, but while Frank Richards's invention was always waiting in vain for a postal order that never turns up, Barlow would have taken the initiative and charged into the post office a long time since. With bags of determination, guts and 'an invincible optimism', Barlow had the traits common to many South Africans, but also one some others didn't have – a sense of humour.[43]

In the 1970 series he made a century in the first Test and another in the second, also taking 5 for 66 in England's first innings. He had a quiet third Test, but took twelve wickets in the fourth at Leeds, including a hat-trick which further developed into four wickets in five balls. Barlow's success was a pointed reminder that notwithstanding any of the political dimensions, international cricket was poorer without some outstanding South African cricketers. Derbyshire broke the bank in 1976 to sign him and he set about taking an unfashionable county to a Lord's final. As a coach and leader, he was inspirational – 'Clive Woodward, Duncan Fletcher and Alex Ferguson' rolled into one.[44]

The story of Eddie Barlow is a reminder that plenty of South African sportsmen – including Procter and Richards – were every bit as disgusted with apartheid as many of its external critics. Barlow stood as a parliamentary candidate for the anti-government

Rest of the World team, 1970: Barry Richards (standing, second from left), Clive Lloyd (standing, third from left), Mike Procter (standing, fourth from left), Intikhab Alam (standing, fifth from left), Rohan Kanhai (sitting, extreme left), Eddie Barlow (sitting, second from left), Garry Sobers (sitting, centre) and Graeme Pollock (sitting, extreme right).

Progressive Federal Party in 1980, only losing by a whisker. But apartheid was resilient, and for 22 years until 1992, South Africa had no official Test cricket. Even when it returned, there was still controversy. Nelson Mandela was free, but many felt that it was too soon for the country that had kept him captive to return to the sporting fold.

Their first Test match upon their return to international cricket was an inaugural contest versus the West Indies in Barbados. It was a baptism by fire, since the locals were acutely aware of the historical plight of black South Africans; 'Steve Biko stirs memories here', reflected Tony Cozier, 'not Graeme Pollock'.[45] However, Cozier also correctly predicted that it would be the West Indians themselves that had more trouble with hostile supporters.[46] If the match was a symbolic olive branch, it was reluctantly grasped and poorly attended because local boy Anderson Cummins had been overlooked in favour of Antiguan Kenny Benjamin. The ultimate irony was that South Africa's return was overshadowed by protests that for once 'had nothing to do with them'.[47]

Those staying away missed a treat. Replying to a modest 262, South Africa's reply was spearheaded by Andrew Hudson's 163. It was a Herculean effort, not least because of the occasion, but also because he became the first South African to score a debut Test century for South Africa. A University of Natal graduate in marketing and industrial psychology, Hudson had ample opportunity for self-analysis during a vigil lasting eight and a half hours and 384 balls.[48] Chasing 201 to win, Peter Kirsten and skipper Kepler Wessels guided the visitors to 123 for 3 before a strong West Indian rearguard.[49] The home attack had been muzzled by the new one-bouncer-per-over rule but the cavalry, in the form of Walsh (4 for 31) and Ambrose (6 for 34), emphasized to the visitors 'the harsh realities' of the Test match arena they had just re-entered.[50] Buying into the occasion, Everton Weekes announced Hudson and Ambrose as joint men of the match. All the South Africans bar Wessels were making their Test debuts, making their performance 'doubly meritorious'.[51]

But what of D'Oliveira, the man who had played an innings that 'changed the course of history'?[52] He continued to serve Worcestershire as a player and coach with distinction and was followed by son Damian and grandson Brett. He had a stand named after him at New Road and was posthumously made a Freeman of the City. In the meantime, John Vorster – the intransigent enforcer of apartheid – is remembered as a 'pariah' and thus some say that 'justice is done'.[53] But there was no justice for Barry Richards, Procter and a number of others. Instead of making headlines at Test level, they had to be content with county cricket amounting to 'quiet Mondays on empty grounds' and the odd televised game.[54] 'Sadness and regret' are associated with Richards in a way that they are not with Procter.[55] While Procter vigorously dedicated himself to transforming Gloucestershire, Richards seemed more prone to brood about how an accident of birth had denied him an international career commensurate with his talent. He scored a hundred before lunch nine times, and it was said that his own boredom was the only thing that could get him out.

Michael Atherton rightly points out the triteness of 'bemoaning the fate of a handful of white cricketers' when millions of black nationals were so degraded.[56] But one wonders what Barry Richards might have achieved with sustained motivation. If only there had been another Richards to illuminate cricket in the 1970s and '80s. More about him later.

## 23

# THE HOLY TRINITY
### *Nine Decades of Writers and Talkers*

I f Basil D'Oliveira changed cricket – and maybe the world – then
John Arlott helped to facilitate it. Capable of 'anger and passion',
Arlott had been to South Africa only once, but saw enough to be
outraged.[1] When completing the border-control declaration, he
declared his race to be neither Caucasian nor black, but 'human'.[2]
When he helped D'Oliveira relocate to Middleton, Lancashire,
it was the start of the player's distinguished career playing cricket
in England.

Arlott was multidimensional. He had been an office boy, a
clerk in a mental hospital, a policeman and a literary producer
for the BBC. He was confident in his role as wine correspondent
for *The Guardian* on the basis that he had a cellar containing
5,000 bottles.[3] As cricket's master wordsmith, he was eloquent
yet earthy enough for all fans, and versatile enough to operate
on both page and airwaves. A North Carolina-based cricket fan
reported that when he switched on his short-wave radio one day
in 1977, his American wife walked past and, upon hearing Arlott's
voice, noted that she now knew summer had begun.[4]

Arlott was guided by an unswerving adherence to his conscience. He stood twice for parliament, wrote for *The Guardian*
and was anchored by liberal values.[5] More specifically, in
invariably rooting for the underdog, he helped to establish the
Professional Cricketers' Association and to remove the inbuilt
class distinction differentiating 'gentlemen' from 'players'.[6] And

he was compassionate. A letter by Lawrence Thackray to *The Guardian* explained how he had been incarcerated as a conscientious objector in 1942. An unknown visitor to his cell spoke to him at length about various subjects, including Elizabethan poetry. The stranger was 'courteous', 'shrewd' and 'fair', and left the young man with some cigarettes and a book. Many years later the prisoner realized that his visitor had been Arlott.[7] He was a man, wrote Mike Brearley, with 'a deep hinterland'.[8]

At the BBC, he succeeded George Orwell as a producer of literary programmes, and in 1946 he found himself covering a couple of India's matches during their tour of England. On that basis, Arlott 'fluked' his way into cricket and became 'a national celebrity'.[9] His writing was rich and passionate and as a published poet, he counted Dylan Thomas and John Betjeman among his friends. Unsurprisingly, his words seemed better than those used by anyone else, and his description of 'a passing pigeon' seemed more compelling than those of others doing the same.[10] He had wit as well as wisdom. Among the gems are the explanation that a bat had 'as many holes in it as a Henry Moore sculpture', and when South Africa bowler Tufty Mann flummoxed England's George Mann, it was a clear case of 'Mann's inhumanity to Mann'.[11] In a match featuring Hampshire's John Rice and Irishman Andy Mutagh, a mundane dot ball was illuminated with 'Rice bowls . . . Paddy fields'.[12] Once a morning session was concluded with the summary that everyone present would 'willingly give Trevor Bailey every sandwich he possesses'.[13] Another was his nutshell characterization of Vintcent van der Bijl as a 'taller, stronger, healthier version of Lord Longford' but 'not so nearly as forgiving'.[14] All such beauties, though, are overshadowed by Arlott's description of cricket's first public nudity when England hosted Australia at Lord's in 1975.

The second Test of the series provided an England debut for silver-haired journeyman David Steele, dubbed 'the bank clerk who went to war'.[15] After finding himself in the Gents toilets instead of the Long Room on his way to bat, he and first-time skipper Tony Greig assertively set about the bowling of Dennis Lillee and Jeff Thomson as if they were kids on the beach. After a moderate reply by the Aussies, and thanks to 175 by John Edrich on the fourth day, England were happily building a mammoth target. It was all standard stuff until 3.20 p.m., when a navy chef ran onto the field dressed in 'nothing but his plimsolls and an XL sized smile'.[16] Fortunately for BBC *Test Match Special* listeners, Arlott was commentating. 'We've got a freaker,' he reported excitedly; gloriously out of touch with the transatlantic trend of running around in the nude, he'd created his own version of 'streaker'.

Egged on by the equally quaint Trevor Bailey, Arlott's suggestion that the intruder had 'seen the last of its cricket for the day' was completely accurate. After 'being embraced by a blond policeman', the intruder was paraded in the 'final exhibition' past a packed Mound Stand, where some of those watching, perhaps, had 'never seen anything quite like this before'.[17] Arlott concluded with delicious understatement that while it was the miscreant's last public appearance, it had nonetheless been 'a splendid one'.[18] The streaker/freaker was called Michael Angelow, and he was fined what he'd won from the drunken bet he had accepted to do it in the first place. He admitted to instant regret, perhaps echoing the sentiments of his father, a local councillor in St Albans whose own enjoyment of the afternoon's cricket on television had ended rather unexpectedly.

Arlott was cut some slack not afforded to others. He preferred a liquid lunch to a solid one and was often 'mellow' in the afternoon, when silences, wrote Mike Brearley, were not a sign of deep thought but more likely some 'post-prandial, post-Burgundy nodding off'.[19] His sign-off in the Lord's Centenary

Test in 1980 was understated. He just called the score. 'Nine runs off the over, 28 Boycott, fifteen Gower – 67 for 2, and after Trevor Bailey it will be Christopher Martin-Jenkins' and then he left his seat. Spontaneously everyone on the field stopped to applaud 'as a shirtsleeved, overweight figure high in the distance left the broadcast box in the pavilion turret for the final time'.[20] And that was it, Arlott himself concluding that 'there's nothing more romantic than a clean break.'[21]

But there was another, slightly more curmudgeonly side to John Arlott. Despite his poetic words, liberal outlook and railing against injustice, you would want to be on his right side. Brearley noted that while he was unstintingly loyal to those he liked, he had little time for those he didn't.[22] He could be acerbic: when introduced for a commentary stint with the words 'and now, as the sun sets in the West, here is John Arlott,' he responded that if the sun ever set anywhere else, his hapless colleague would be the first person to hear about it.[23]

One doesn't have to look too deeply to understand why he might have seemed 'lugubrious'.[24] There was professional tragedy, including his narrow escape when in February 1958 he was replaced as duty reporter on Manchester United's tragic trip to Belgrade when 23 people were killed in the Munich plane crash, including many of the 'Busby Babes'. His son Tim wrote a memoir about his father that divided opinion, but many might agree that grief was dominant in Arlott's life. He suffered the death of his son Jim in a car accident and lost an infant daughter and his second wife through illness. The first chapter of Tim Arlott's book is simply headed 'New Year 1965' and explains in visceral detail how his father woke him in the early hours to tell him his brother had been killed. Afterwards, in private correspondence, Arlott described how he thought about Jim constantly, and that 'there will be a well of sadness in me forever'.[25] He wore a black tie for the rest of his life.

His decline, due to illness, was painful. Brearley observes that even though Arlott had plenty of interests, even the good times were tinged with sadness because of the difficult end to his life.[26] An unlikely friendship with Ian Botham became a distraction for both men. The young Botham was only sixteen when he was asked to carry Arlott's lunch basket to the commentary box. Arlott explained the fleeting delights of Beaujolais Nouveau, and so began an enduring friendship. You wouldn't necessarily put a portly 56-year-old commentator together with an energetic sixteen-year-old Somerset rookie, but their relationship had little to do with cricket and everything to do with a mutual love of 'a good bottle of plonk'.[27] Later they became neighbours on Alderney, and Botham recalls regular phone calls at precisely 9.04 a.m. Botham was urged to come 'as soon as possible. And bring your thirst with you.' In 2018, Botham reported that whenever he was on Alderney he visited Arlott's grave to drink a toast, always leaving the cork.[28] In his final months, Arlott would struggle to walk the 100 yards or so from his front door to gaze across the sea to France, 'to make sure it's still there'.[29] While he knew about 'wit, delight, vividness, humour and humanity', for Arlott, cricket was not a matter of life and death, but 'just a matter of life'.[30]

Arlott was one-third of the holy trinity of influential cricket writers. Another was E. W. Swanton, but he and Arlott had seemingly vastly different approaches to life.[31] While Arlott was full of liberal introspection, Swanton was staunchly Conservative, defended the class system and wasn't 'plagued by self-doubt'.[32] Though they were not friends, they were united against racial injustice.[33] But while Arlott was all about art and elegant words, Leo McKinstry suggests that Swanton succeeded through ambition, graft, confidence and a 'ruthless exploitation of social and professional contacts'.[34] Stylistically, Swanton was no fancy dan. Indeed, England fast bowler J. J. Warr described his writing as

John Arlott, 1949.

'somewhere between the Ten Commandments and Enid Blyton'.[35] Even more damning was Arlott's wondering what it must be like not to leave 'one memorable sentence' from within a prolific corpus of work.[36]

But Swanton was an irrepressible cricketing grandee whose opinions made him one of English cricket's most influential figures. He was forthright in his opinions on who should be selected for the England Test team, and selection committees, it is rumoured, were ever mindful of what would please him. Known universally as 'Jim', perhaps Swanton was justified in his influence, as his experience spanned from watching W. G. Grace from his pram as a baby to the end of the twentieth century.[37] But he was a man with a 'complex and ambivalent personality'.[38] Even in the foreword of one of Swanton's numerous books, Lord Deedes noted the author's fluid attitude to fair play within sport: he was quick to condemn what he deemed bad manners on the cricket field, but prepared to insist an opponent hole a tiny putt when playing golf. While he could be helpful and supportive of rookie journalists, the word 'pompous' could easily have been dreamt up with Swanton in mind.[39] Ray Illingworth once suggested that Swanton was such a snob he wouldn't travel in the same car as his chauffeur. Once Swanton sent his secretary next door for his lunchtime gin and tonic and when she returned to explain they had run out of ice, his response was an incredulous 'But didn't you tell them who it was for?'[40] His entry into the radio commentary box, noted Henry Blofeld, seemed to merit 'a trumpet voluntary'.[41]

But he loved cricket. Even during a ghastly spell as a prisoner of war on the Burma–Siam railway, Swanton did not abandon the game, treasuring his 1939 *Wisden*, the cover stamped 'non-subversive' in Japanese.[42] Swanton had left for war 'a strapping 15-stoner' but when he returned, at the station, his mother walked right past her 'emaciated nine-stone son' without recognizing him.[43]

But he certainly wasn't everyone's cup of tea and Leo McKinstry admits that despite Swanton's opposition to apartheid and war service, after reading the biography written by David Rayvern Allen, he'd 'come to loathe the man'.[44] *Wisden*'s obituary was more generous, concluding that Swanton had 'applauded good, joyous, sporting cricket' and had contributed much to the game.[45]

The third – and oldest – member of cricket's holy trinity was Neville Cardus. The product of a fleeting liaison between a prostitute and an Italian musician, as a kid he was known as 'Fred'.[46] His early life was shaped by his grandfather and aunt, who encouraged and indulged him. He left school at thirteen, and after various jobs, including a stint as a pavement artist, he became the assistant music critic of the *Manchester Guardian*.[47] Eventually he simultaneously became its cricket correspondent and music critic, shaping both journalistic realms. When Cardus died in 1975, Alan Gibson reflected that all those writing about the game for the previous fifty years had been influenced by him, whether they copied him or 'tried to avoid copying him'.[48]

Eventually he became disillusioned at what he perceived to be the slipping standards at the newspaper he had 'worshipped' since he first read it.[49] Long after it dropped the 'Manchester', he refused to change the way he referred to it. Few possessed his literary style, which was characterized by almost perfect grammar.[50] What Cardus brought to cricket was what functional reports omitted, as he included details of 'the crowd, the atmosphere, the ambience' and the 'personalities'.[51] Readers were kept 'hovering between tears and laughter' as he elevated cricket writing to an art form 'fit for literary connoisseurs'.[52] Indeed, Cardus was a man of passion in all directions: though undoubtedly unfaithful to his long-suffering wife Edith, he remained 'an oddly considerate husband', visiting her every day long after adopting a life of 'bachelor seclusion [at] the National Liberal Club'.[53]

But this wasn't quite the neat story it might have been. It seems apparent that occasionally Cardus might have enjoyed a loose relationship with reality, not allowing the 'duller kind of fact' to ruin a story.[54] Indeed, Cardus often irked players by embellishing their remarks, and when they protested they hadn't actually said what he'd reported, they were gently appeased with a smiling assurance that he was sure they would have liked to have.[55] His biographer Christopher Brookes certainly had problems in 'reconciling' some of his work with 'fact'.[56] In 1929, for example, Cardus left the press box at Leeds before the end of South Africa's innings and missed a century stand for the last wicket. Discovering the unexpected news on his train home, he quickly filed a report from the station on the basis that 'I knew the bowlers, knew the batsmen and simply described the way they would have behaved.'[57] Brookes is clearly not alone in thinking that Cardus was capable of 'spinning a delightful yarn in days when looking up records was too difficult'.[58]

But perhaps we should be more forgiving. In his writing about cricket and music, Neville Cardus was a romantic who wrote from the heart.[59] Above all, while C.L.R. James, for example, combined cricket's technical aspects with wider societal context, for Cardus cricket was a 'self-contained aesthetic entity'.[60] His work is always joyful.[61] In contrast and for different reasons, the work of Arlott and Swanton never quite screamed such unbridled pleasure for such sustained periods. The colour, good cheer and enthusiasm that characterized the approach taken by Neville Cardus resonates with others who broadcasted and wrote about cricket. Brian Johnston, for example, was a consummate all-round broadcaster who, according to BBC colleague Henry Blofeld, was like a shaken-up bottle of champagne 'ready to froth furiously over the top'.[62] While Johnston's co-respondent shoes positioned him a dandy, he wasn't as dapper as Blofeld himself, who until his retirement from *Test Match Special* in 2017 brought an explosion of eccentric pastel shades to an otherwise conservatively dressed radio box. Any outfit, he says, can be 'jazzed up' by a 'flamboyant sock, an occasional cravat or perhaps even a sizzling waistcoat'.[63] They have been and continue to be a colourful lot, these writers and commentators, and we continue to owe them a debt: when cricket is inaccessible, unseen and obscure, their words can make it seem as real as if we'd been there ourselves.

# 24

# WORLD CUPS AND WORLD BEATERS
## *From the 1970s to the 1990s*

By 1975, even though purists clicked their tongues at the very
thought of it, one-day cricket was the format that marketers
recognized as capable of getting the blood pumping faster and
reaching new audiences. No doubt mindful how the whole world
paused every time there was a football World Cup, cricket wanted
some such global action itself. Although international one-day
cricket was only eighteen matches old, in 1975 cricket staged its
inaugural World Cup.

The eight-team tournament featured England, Australia,
India, Pakistan, New Zealand and the West Indies, the two final
places given to the less familiar Sri Lanka and East Africa. The
latter was an unlikely collection of Ugandans, Tanganyikans,
Rhodesians, Kenyans, exiled Indians, Pakistanis and a 43-year-
old Lancastrian expat called Don Pringle. He went wicketless
in his two matches and was killed in a road accident in Nairobi
a matter of weeks after the tournament. His son Derek was only
seventeen at the time, a year or two away from a Cambridge education and seven years from an England debut. He was noted
for his height, his 'slightly outré tastes in music' and the fact that
he was the first England Test cricketer to wear an earring.[1] He
became an erudite and insightful writer on the game.

The group stages began at Lord's, where England met India.
Given that in those days it was a 60-over competition, England
reached an unprecedented 334 for 4. A run rate over 5 was considered

supernatural, at least by Indian opening batsman Sunil Gavaskar. Judging the gargantuan total to be unreachable, and with a vapid personal contribution of 36 not out, Gavaskar shepherded his team to an inexplicably pitiful 132 for 3. Indian manager G. S. Ramchand later called it 'disgraceful and selfish',[2] dismissing Gavaskar's suggestions that the wicket was too slow to play shots, since England had just spent 60 overs doing nothing but.

England earned a semi-final against Australia at Leeds. At the time, the Headingley wicket was treated with more suspicion than an unexploded bomb, but England were buoyed by good form. Under the unyielding stewardship of Ian Chappell, Australia took no prisoners. Indeed, the conventional wisdom that England would be better prepared on a green wicket soon disappeared when they were fired out for 93 by a barrel-chested New South Welshman called Gary Gilmour, who took 6 for 14. Spectators bemoaning a home score under a hundred including only six boundaries soon perked up when the visitors found themselves in seemingly terminal decline at 39 for 6. Enter Gilmour, whose run-a-ball 28 not out saw his team home. With delicious restraint, *Wisden* noted that former West Indies captain Jeffery Stollmeyer 'had no difficulty in naming him Man of the Match'.[3] It must have been the easiest decision until 2019, when Krishnappa Gowtham made 134 not out and took 8 for 15 in a Karnataka Premier League Twenty20 match.[4]

Gilmour only played a few more ODIs and Tests, his *Daily Telegraph* obituary alluding to his 'carefree, high-living approach' to cricket and reluctance to keep in shape.[5] He survived a liver transplant in 2005 when Ian Chappell led the fundraising campaign. In the 1975 final, however, Gilmour was at the height of his short-lived powers. At Lord's in the blazing sunshine, his 5 for 48 included the wickets of Kallicharan, Lloyd, Kanhai and Richards. That, though, was only part of a much bigger story.

It was cricket from a different age. Lord's was packed, the players wore white with no names or numbers to identify them, there were no helmets and the captain of the West Indies wore glasses.[6] The drama began almost immediately as the West Indies found themselves at 50 for 3. The first man down was Roy Fredericks, who, with ultimate bittersweetness simultaneously hooked Dennis Lillee for six and stepped on his own wicket. It was enough to temporarily becalm the wearer of the jauntiest cap in cricket history, but Fredericks's dismissal simply cleared the stage for his captain.

Clive Lloyd's 102 was one of the most 'calculatedly brutal' World Cup innings ever, and a statement foretelling how his team would dominate world cricket for the next twenty years or so.[7] Such was his merciless flogging of the Australian bowlers that John Arlott described one stroke as being akin to a man 'knocking a thistle top off with a walking stick'.[8] Lloyd got to his 100 in 82 balls and the West Indies' total of 291 seemed challenging, though not insurmountable. Australia made a good fist of it too, finally falling 17 runs short just before 9 p.m. The crowd invaded, not for the first time, and trying to keep order at the end of an exhausting day were umpires Tom Spencer and Harold 'Dickie' Bird.

Formerly a 'fretful, twitching, modest first-class cricketer' for Yorkshire and Leicestershire, Bird became 'a fretful, twitching, top-quality first-class umpire' known across the world.[9] Indeed, Bird was more famous than most cricketers, in part because of a repertoire of 'idiosyncratic tics'.[10] 'Apart from holidaying at the Livermead Cliff Hotel and enjoying a breakfast of kippers', noted Derek Pringle, Bird relaxed 'by worrying'.[11] He was also the sort of umpire that attracted the unanticipated.[12] He was Arthur Jepson's partner when Lancashire beat Gloucestershire in 1971 and only the moon was visible. In 1973 he was officiating in England's Test match against the West Indies at Edgbaston when the other umpire – Arthur Fagg – refused to officiate until he'd had an apology from visiting captain Rohan Kanhai for his on-field behaviour.

The final Test match of the series at Lord's was interrupted by a bomb scare and subsequent urgent requests over the PA system for everyone to leave the ground. But instead of retreating, the crowd flooded the playing area. The covers were wheeled out to protect the wicket and Bird sat on top of them, since 'I knew there was no bomb under there.'[13] Then, at Headingley in 1988, he was forced to halt a Test match because an underground water pipe burst and flooded the bowler's run-up. In the denouement of that first World Cup final, as a jubilant West Indian crowd ran onto the field to celebrate, Bird ran off as if his life depended on it. Amid the chaos, his trademark white cap was pinched and the following year he noticed it on the head of a London bus driver, who readily admitted to taking it without realizing he was con-fessing to the victim of the crime.[14] He retired from umpiring in 1998, wise enough to recognize that he wasn't getting younger and that the game was changing, embracing – as it had to – the introduction of technological scrutiny. It ensured that Bird's legacy would be 'top-quality umpiring'.[15]

In the final of 1975 Bird and Spencer earned their money, since the Australian reply was blighted by some calamitous running between wickets and the rattlesnake speed of a junior member of the West Indies team called Isaac Vivian Alexander Richards. He was responsible for three of five run-outs, but, wrongfooted by all the 'newfangled excitement', *Wisden* mistakenly attributed them to Alvin Kallicharran.[16] It was an unusual way for the wider cricketing public to be introduced to Vivian Richards. Already a Somerset player, he hadn't pulled up many trees and had con-tributed just five to Australia's target. Removing Alan Turner and both Chappell brothers was a good day's work but gave no glimpse as to what lay ahead.

For the next two decades or so, Richards's wicket was the most valued in cricket. Not since Bradman, perhaps, was the appearance of a single batsman so excitedly anticipated by those watching, and so dreaded by those bowling. Batting helmets became universally used, but Richards never wore one. Strolling out – irrespective of how fast the bowling was – wearing just a cap might have encouraged bowlers, but instead seemed to intimidate them. It was a subliminal message that they had neither the skill nor speed to bother him, and that shortly they'd be wishing they'd never been picked to play.

In 1976, Richards was back with the West Indies when they toured England. Again under Lloyd's stewardship, they brought the usual venomous-looking bowling in the form of Andy Roberts, Wayne Daniel and the tall, lithe Michael Holding. Perhaps carried away with pre-season euphoria, in a widely watched TV interview England skipper Tony Greig promised to make the tourists 'grovel'.[17] People reacted quickly, wily England spinner Pat Pocock among them. 'You prat,' he exclaimed to his captain, 'what have you done?'[18] Everybody was upset at the choice of language, recalled Holding, and it was an insensitive promise for a white South African to make about a West Indian cricket team.[19] As the visitors fell just short of 500 in their first innings of the opening Test at Nottingham, the ones bowing and scraping were the English bowlers. With 232, the imperious Richards was everything neutral spectators had hoped for, and everything England had feared. England batted out the draw thanks to 39-year-old John Edrich and 45-year-old Brian Close, who was playing Test matches three years before Richards was born.

But Vivian Richards was not the only hot aspect of 1976. Despite empty reservoirs and fifteen consecutive days of 32°c (90°F) heat in the UK, confirmation that it was officially sweltering only came when for the first time in almost two hundred years, MCC members were allowed in the pavilion without jackets. Snowploughs sprayed sand onto roads to counteract bubbling asphalt and people fried eggs on pavements. We were urged to 'bathe with a friend' but the BBC suggested a shower would save water. 'A shower?' asked *The Telegraph*, adding that 'even then', the BBC was 'a conduit for metropolitan privilege'.[20]

Back at the cricket, it was mayhem. Richards missed the drawn second Test at Lord's through illness but returned for Old Trafford Test and weighed in with a century to supplement the efforts of Gordon Greenidge, who passed three figures in both innings. There was still no sign of West Indian grovelling as England perished to the tune of 425 runs. There was however some spirited resistance from Edrich and Close, who spent their Saturday evening trying to avoid decapitation on live television against some of the most hostile fast bowling ever seen. In the next Test at Leeds, England had a chance thanks to centuries from Greig and Knott. The visitors were skittled for 196 in the second innings, but more heroics from Greig weren't enough. A 0–3 series drubbing was inevitable when a relentless 291 from Richards contributed to a gargantuan 687 for 8 at The Oval. England brought back Dennis Amiss and a gutsy 203 suggested that the roughing up by the Aussies in 1974/5 was behind him. The headlines, though, were taken by Holding's 14 for 149 in the match. There had surely never been a silkier performance of destructive fast bowling by a better athlete. Nobody who ever saw it, or the 829 runs scored by Vivian Richards in that series, would ever forget it.

By the time of the 1979 World Cup, again held in England, Richards ruled the cricket world. In the final, his unbeaten century was perhaps overshadowed by a rampaging 86 by Collis King, but this only demonstrated that Richards was capable of playing whatever type of innings was needed. Even so, 138 not out in 157 balls is hardly sluggish. Five years later, in the first ODI of the tour of England, Richards did it again. The home attack of Willis, Botham, Foster, Miller and Pringle was good enough to initially overpower the visitors, reducing them to 102 for 7, and Richards was alone in resisting. The West Indies's hopes rallied when Eldine Baptiste joined him in a stand of 59. By the time Holding entered the fray, the score was an unthreatening 166 for 9, with Richards on 96. With fourteen overs left, Richards made his move; 84 balls later, their stand stood at 106.[21] Richards's 189 not out was typified by his final stroke – an off-drive from outside leg stump that would have taken Ian Botham's ear off had the bowler not taken evasive action.[22] Of the 35 centuries he scored at international level, it was among the most blistering, although another century in 56 balls against England in Antigua in 1985/6 more than matched it. Of his seven sixes, one 'smashed a bottle of rum in the grandstand' and another flew out of the stadium and into the nearby prison.[23]

Richards's relationship with Somerset ended in acrimony, and in 1987 he played for Rishton in the Lancashire League. It was the cricketing equivalent, asserted Tim Rich, of Richard Burton agreeing to play the Baron in the annual pantomime *Cinderella* in the Welsh seaside town of Porthcawl.[24] Using his own metaphor, Richards observed that his presence was a bit like being Jesse James where 'everyone wants to gun him down'.[25] But of course, he scored the runs and was more than willing to tell a few yarns and stand his round in the bar, the Rishton skipper noting that Richards particularly enjoyed his rum.[26]

But Richards's wider significance lay not in rum, or even runs. Like Frank Worrell before him, he was aware of a world beyond cricket and saw it as instrumental in fighting racism, especially apartheid.[27] It undoubtedly intensified his sense of competition and occasionally this drew criticism from those who felt he intimidated umpires, though he dismissed his sometimes maniacal

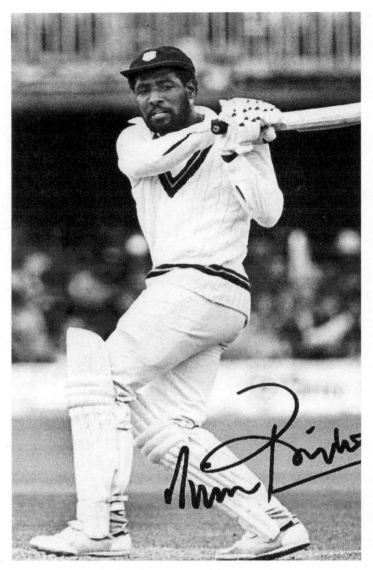

Vivian Richards, 1979.

appealing as a celebratory 'jig'.[28] When in 1990 English journalist James Lawton suggested that Richards's behaviour was excessive, instead of leading his team onto the field the following day, Richards confronted the journalist in the press box.[29] Lawton stood his ground and the next day's headline, 'Captain Viv blows his top', relegated the diplomatic tension between the USA and Russia to the status of a minor story.[30] When he was recruited by Glamorgan in 1990, the Welsh county loved him.[31] Teammate Matthew Maynard reflected that while up to that point he and his colleagues were paid to play cricket, 'it was Viv that made us professional cricketers'.[32] It was, he said, 'impossible to sum up his impact'.[33]

He had an unmatched swaggering self-assurance. His power and extraordinary eye were accompanied by an 'aura of cocksure invincibility'.[34] When he and Glamorgan teammate Adrian Dale put on 425 against Middlesex, Dale hit a boundary but still ran down the pitch to complete a run as a reflex action. He was castigated by Richards, who shouted from the other end that running simply just spoils the shot.[35] When Chris Cowdrey became England's third of four captains during the wretched home series against the West Indies in 1988, he recalled appearing for the toss in whites and an England blazer. Richards, he recalled, rocked up wearing 'a Bob Marley T-shirt, surfing shorts and flip-flops'.[36] As was the custom, Cowdrey began reading out the names of the final XI but was interrupted by Richards before finishing. 'Play who you want, man,' said the skipper, 'ain't gonna make any difference.'[37] And it didn't. The West Indies won by ten wickets.

Scyld Berry makes a big call but a difficult one to argue with. Richards, he claimed, 'was the most charismatic cricketer of his period, if not all time'.[38] When he retired from Tests in 1991, not only did cricket lose its biggest box-office draw, but the leadership of West Indian cricket lost its emphasis on civil rights and challenging injustice.[39] In 1983, though, not even Richards could save his team. The third World Cup was again held in England, reflecting the apparent balance of power in terms of money and administrative might. On paper and on the field, the West Indies were the world's most powerful team, and to nobody's surprise, they topped their group and made the final.

India also made the final, having lost one and won one against the favourites in the group stages. Most dramatically of all, India had diced with terminal danger against Zimbabwe at Tunbridge Wells. The unfancied Africans' bowling attack included the brisk medium pace of Kevin Curran, father of England players Sam and Tom, and Duncan Fletcher, later the successful England coach. Spin was delivered by Egypt-born John Traicos, who, having played in South Africa's last Test before exile in 1970, was well-preserved enough to play in Zimbabwe's first in 1992. It was an intriguing attack, but not one to keep batsmen awake at night. When India found themselves at 17 for 5, it must have seemed like a nightmare, but they were rescued in the most dramatic style by Kapil Dev with 175 not out off 138 balls, including sixteen boundaries and six sixes. They found themselves in the final, but surely they couldn't bring down Richards and his all-conquering West Indians. Could they?

The final started poorly for India. Roberts, Garner, Marshall and Holding blasted them away, and 184 was no score against the world's strongest batting line-up. What happened next is even more astonishing, given that these batting titans had no answer to the gentle medium pace of Madan Lal, Roger Binny and Mohinder Amarnath, who could only be described as 'dibbly dobblers' and as threatening as tea with your maiden aunt. But Clive Lloyd and company had no answer to their nagging persistence. The wicket of the Richards, as ever, was key. He had reached an assured 33 when he pulled Madan Lal to deep mid-wicket, the

BBC cameras panning to the grandstand, expecting the crowd to scatter.[40] But it didn't get that far. Watching the ball carefully over his shoulder as he ran towards the boundary, Kapil Dev safely pouched the catch. 'The King had fallen', and not even Clive Lloyd – batting with a runner – could rescue them.[41] The Caribbean dominance was interrupted, noted Kamran Abbasi, 'and an Asian giant was awake'.[42]

Kapil Dev was a type of vigorous all-rounder not generally produced by India – an attacking fast bowler and a swashbuckling middle-order batsman. He was the charisma in Indian cricket, bridging Gavaskar and Tendulkar, and while India might have been inconsistent under his leadership, they were no longer 'dull'.[43] His belligerence at Lord's in 1990 confirmed a willingness to take risks and reject the humdrum. In the match where Graham Gooch made 333 and 123, India were still 24 runs short of following on. Kapil Dev was joined by Narendra Hirwani, who was batting at number 11 only because there wasn't a number 12. Facing spinner Eddie Hemmings, Dev hit four successive sixes, Martin Johnson noting that they were 'huge ones, too'.[44]

Their World Cup triumph in 1983 shocked everyone, not least the Indians themselves. Having been ambivalent towards one-day cricket, India now 'made it her own'.[45] Such had been their muted ambition that only 20 per cent of cricket fans in India were even aware the World Cup was happening, while the Indian Board of Control for Cricket considered a Lord's final featuring their team so unlikely that 'they were late in applying for passes and did not receive their full allocation'.[46] But then drinks manufacturer Pepsi began recruiting actors and cricketers as brand ambassadors and cricket began to consume all the attention – and all the funding.[47] In the 2012 Olympics, other sports having been starved of investment, India finished 55th in the medal table, between Venezuela and Mongolia.[48] But India became the powerful epicentre of world cricket, perhaps all because Viv Richards mistimed one in the World Cup final.

Unsurprisingly, given the shift in cricket's global dynamic, the 1987 final was staged in Kolkata. Indian hopes of making the final were dashed by a fine semi-final century by Gooch and four wickets for Eddie Hemmings. With Australia and England contesting the final, there was to be a new World Cup winner, and for a while it seemed as if it would be England. Australia's 253 for 5 was not insurmountable, and England's top order set a firm base, but the turning point came when England skipper Mike Gatting tried a risky reverse sweep when risks were not needed. Australia won by seven runs. Gatting's wicket was taken by Australian captain Allan Border, only a fairly occasional slow left-arm spinner.

Though not a front-line bowler, Border was front-line in everything else. His tenure as Australian captain was characterized by a willingness to take cricket by the scruff of the neck after he ascended to Australian cricket's top job when Kim Hughes tearfully resigned mid-match at Brisbane in 1984/5. At the time Border's key role was to add the steel to a fragile-looking batting

Kapil Dev, early 1980s.

line-up and there was nobody else whom Australia's administrators could have asked.[49] The only player of the requisite quality and grit was the rather hot-headed fast bowler Rodney Hogg.[50]

As captain, Border recognized that until they could start winning, Australia needed to stop losing. And if they were going to lose, then the last man to disappear under the waves would be Border. Ian Botham asserted that Border had rejuvenated Australian cricket from the sorry mess he inherited, his leadership generating the ultimate loyalty from the players.[51] When Border retired, noted Botham, his team were second only to the West Indies.[52] Meanwhile, England had no such stability, as their leadership lurched 'from Gower to Gatting to Emburey to Cowdrey junior to Gooch to Gower again to Gooch again to Atherton, with occasional intervals of Lamb and Stewart'.[53]

As both cricketer and captain, Border was 'like a terrier out for a walk in a neighbourhood bristling with bigger dogs', fully prepared for a scrap.[54] But it was not a quality that came immediately. Indeed, he identified a bonhomie between England and Australia in the early to mid-1980s. He himself had been pivotal in encouraging beers with the opposition off the field, and a pleasant atmosphere on it. As Border hardened, the socializing ended.[55] While such a strategy might have lost him a few English friends, the Australians loved it.[56] He combined gritty, inspirational leadership with world-beating performances and over 11,000 runs at a Test average of over 50 was a major contribution.

The World Cup in 1992 was held in Australia and New Zealand. There were now nine teams involved, and when everyone played each other, if you got to the semi-final, then you certainly deserved it. By that measure, and by virtue of some generally wretched performances, Australia didn't deserve any more than finishing a frustrating fifth. When Pakistan beat them in the group stages at Perth, Border was wished luck for the remaining games at the

Allan Border, 1986.

after-match ceremony, and 'did well not to stick the microphone somewhere unmentionable'.[57]

Pakistan had edged Australia out of the semi-final spots by a single point. In the semi-final against New Zealand, Inzamam-ul-Haq steered his team to victory with a timely 60. The other semi-final between England and South Africa was affected by rain and ended in farce when the prevailing method for revising targets determined that when play resumed, instead of a comfortable 22 runs from thirteen balls, South Africa needed a ridiculous 21 runs from one. They wouldn't have garnered much cheer from the subsequent development on which the editor of the Royal Statistical Society's monthly magazine, Frank Duckworth, and a former lecturer and member of the Operational Research Society, Tony Lewis, soon began working. The resulting Duckworth–Lewis method has been the wet-weather reckoner ever since, albeit the

mathematics leave many none the wiser. 'Never pretend to understand it,' warns Jonathan Agnew; 'only two people do, and you're
not one of them.'[58]

Despite that chaotic semi-final, the tournament will be
remembered for Pakistan's momentous win in the final. It represented a personal triumph for their captain, Imran Khan. He
was the top scorer in the match, and although his 72 was not the
dashing innings one might have expected, nonetheless it was the
adhesive binding his team together. Neither were his 6.2 overs
especially world-beating, even though he took the final wicket.
He was, after all, 39 years old, and his legs lacked sprightliness
since the only cricket he'd played in the previous five years were
in internationals for Pakistan.

Khan had long planned the victory, and never doubted it,
despite his team's 'clumsy and clueless' passage to the final.[59] When
Ramez Raja took the catch to secure the trophy, Pakistan's team
manager Intikhab Alam raced onto the field, despite the fact
that nobody could remember the former leg spinner ever sprint-
ing during a long career at Surrey.[60] For Imran, winning the
Waterford Crystal trophy raised cricket's profile, Pakistan's profile
and Imran's personal profile as he embarked on a mission to build
a cancer hospital in the name of his late mother.[61] By 2015 he had
built two such hospitals. Much was made of his mid-tournament
pep talk when he said that his team should react to adversity like
a cornered tiger. Indeed, at the press conference after the game,
he wore a T-shirt showing a tiger embroidered in golden thread.
Irrespective of what had inspired his team, the streets of Pakistan
throbbed with happiness.[62]

But there is more to Imran Khan. At the time, Ian Wooldridge
called him 'one of the most interesting cricketers alive and, in
style, the very last of the princely amateurs'.[63] *The Independent*
agreed that he was a one-off, a man 'of social and environmental

commitment', 'a sex symbol in two countries' while Scyld Berry describes him as 'a bachelor more pinned up than down'.[64] Born to an upper-class family, he had ten cousins who each at some stage played in Tests for Pakistan. Since he was neither Sindi nor Punjabi, he was able to overcome the factions within Pakistan cricket and somehow persuade everyone to pull the same way at the same time. His cricketing education was finished in England, at Worcester and then Oxford. Moving to Sussex facilitated access to London society and a succession of high-profile girlfriends, but he has since moved on to yet grander things. Once linked with 'cricket and crumpet', reflects Scyld Berry, now he is associated with 'cancer and children'.[65]

Having suggested that Pakistani cricket is riddled with 'nepotism, inefficiency, corruption and constant bickering', Imran's opinion of the country's politics was similar.[66] He developed the ability to rattle governmental cages and his was a story of a famous sports star challenging the allegedly corrupt ways of those ruling Pakistan.[67] Homa Khaleeli noted that during an interview with Imran, they were interrupted by a butler serving coffee, just as Khan was discussing 'global injustice and world elites being able to siphon off money'.[68] He became Pakistan's prime minister in 2018, but there have been murmurs about his own integrity, including claims from his opponents that he is 'an opportunist' who benefited from 'back-door support' from Pakistan's influential military leadership.[69] Fast-forward to July 2019 and Imran, fast-medium bowler, stylish batsman and inspirational leader, meets President Donald Trump in Washington, DC. However overbearing his host might have been, the Pakistani prime minister had his own trump card; not even the president's most loyal supporters would believe that he had ever won a cricket World Cup.

## 25

# REVOLUTIONS AND REBELS
## *The 1970s to the New Millennium*

In 1975, with the first World Cup final still a fresh memory, Australia had taken a 1–0 lead in the Ashes, England captain Mike Denness had been replaced and Michael Angelow had appeared as God made him. In mid-August the teams convened at Headingley for the third Test, and England picked a new left-arm spinner debutant in Philippe-Henri Edmonds, born in Zambia to an English father and a Belgian mother.[1] It was a successful debut, as he took 5 for 28 in Australia's first innings, reducing the visitors to 135 all out.

Edmonds was his own man, and according to ex-wife Frances, had a reputation of being 'awkward and arrogant', mainly because 'he was awkward and arrogant'.[2] His skipper for Middlesex and England Mike Brearley found him 'unmanageable',[3] and in turn Edmonds favoured Geoffrey Boycott, described as possibly the 'worst captain' in history.[4] No wonder Simon Barnes called his biography of Edmonds *A Singular Man*. Barnes is in no doubt that while he was England's best spinner, their capricious selectors didn't fancy such an awkward cuss.

Barnes draws parallels with Kevin Pietersen – another self-confident African – but asserts that Edmonds had a dimension the younger man lacked, namely an interest in a world 'beyond himself'.[5] Indeed, such non-cricketing interests helped Edmonds build a personal fortune that by 2018 was estimated at £21 million.[6] His activities have been occasionally controversial, as he faced criticism for doing business deals in Zimbabwe and an apparent willingness to 'cosy up to Mugabe's government'.[7] In the boardroom he has been described as able to simultaneously enthral and terrify.[8]

He was desperate to play for Middlesex as an amateur, but management may have felt this would provide them with even less control than they had when he was being paid. In 1992, after a break of five years, he was recalled as an emergency spinner for Middlesex and apparently turned up in a Rolls-Royce and took four wickets. He hadn't changed much, still fielded 'aggravatingly close', still 'ostentatiously wore a watch' and still rubbed his hands in the dust before bowling.[9]

In 1975, though, such idiosyncrasies were a work in progress. Edmonds had helped England set Australia 445 to win. They started well, and moving into the last day, New South Welshman Rick McCosker was poised on 95 not out and Doug Walters, an old stager due a big score in England, was unbeaten on 25. But at 11 a.m. on the final day, play did not start as expected, and captains Tony Greig and Ian Chappell appeared in civvies to inspect deep gouges and puddles of engine oil that had appeared on the pitch. They agreed to abandon the game as a draw, meaning that everyone involved was denied a fascinating denouement.[10] Cricket fans were outraged, the Establishment was 'apoplectic' and one critic called for a return to capital punishment, without any obvious signs he was joking.[11]

Vandals Peter Chappell (no relation to Ian) and Colin Dean were supporters of a ne'er-do-well called George Davis, who was languishing in Albany Prison on the Isle of Wight doing twenty years for armed robbery. They believed him to be the victim of an outrageous injustice, and the eye-catching stunt at Headingley was intended to publicize his case. The accompanying graffiti – 'Sorry it had to be done, but George Davis is innocent' – was the work of Dean, Davis's brother-in-law. In 2007 he told *The Guardian* that he loved cricket and didn't want to ruin the Test match, but what other outcome he envisaged is moot.[12] Chappell and Dean received prison sentences, George Davis became a cause célèbre and cricket-loving inmates at Albany Prison wasted no time in telling him they weren't impressed. As it happened, Davis actually was innocent, and in 1976 his conviction was quashed. But the anti-climax experienced by cricket fans was perhaps also felt by Davis's supporters when, eighteen months later, 'he was caught red-handed robbing the Bank of Cyprus.'[13]

Ian Chappell and Tony Greig were hardly compromising cricketers, but on that day, consensus was possible. Chappell felt that England might want to play on a damaged pitch since it would increase their chance of winning, but Greig immediately agreed that the game should be abandoned. Two years later, they were on the same side of the argument again as both were pivotal in the revolution that rocked cricket to its traditional, apparently elitist core.

To give it some context, in 1976 the average weekly wage for a man was around £70 a week and the £200 Test-match fee for England players seemed fairly modest for five days of elite endeavour.[14] The Australians earned even less, and Chappell had grown frustrated that while the players were making almost nothing, the Australian Cricket Board were raking it in. His regular representations were rebuffed by Sir Donald Bradman, who, according to Chappell, treated board money 'as though it was almost his own'.[15] Chappell suggested that his frustration was intensified, since Bradman had always been very commercially active and financially aware during his own career.[16] The Don's intransigence and 'parsimony', suggests Chappell, triggered what happened next.[17]

By 1977 Kerry Packer, the owner of the Channel Nine TV station in Australia, had also grown tired of the cosy, apparently monopolistic relationship between the Australian Cricket Board (ACB) and the state broadcaster, the Australian Broadcasting Corporation (ABC). He wanted the TV rights for cricket, and despite offering a better deal, the status quo prevailed. But Packer was used to getting his own way and was enormously wealthy, famously belligerent and completely fearless. He decided that if he couldn't have someone else's cricket, then he'd have his own.

A legendary gambler, in 2000 Packer reportedly lost £13.6 million over three days playing baccarat in Las Vegas. It was like a man with £3,000 in his pocket losing £14.[18] Another time in Vegas, a brash Texan bragged about a $100 million fortune, and when Packer suggested that they toss for it, double or nothing, the man refused.[19] Once he took his ravenous polo team to an English pub only to be told that the kitchen was closed and wasn't opening for anyone. At the next pub, the landlord also declared the kitchen closed, but that he'd rustle up some sandwiches. The bill was a fairly steep £128, but Packer wrote a cheque for £100,128 and gave it to the astonished publican, insisting that he showed it to his less accommodating competitor on his way to the bank.[20]

Like media moguls before and since, he had the ears of political power brokers. Or perhaps they had his. Relaxing at home, once Packer was irritated by a ringing telephone that nobody was answering. Packer picked it up and immediately cradled the receiver. When it rang the next time, Packer's butler explained that the caller was Australian Prime Minister Paul Keating, upset he had been hung up on. Packer took the call and told Keating, 'If you don't smarten up the whole f***ing country will hang up on you.'[21]

But with great power, wealth and single-mindedness apparently came great sensitivity. Packer's generosity was 'magnificent'.[22] Among multifarious examples of his largesse was his habit of paying off the mortgages of waitresses in restaurants.

Shortly after he noticed two dozen children in wheelchairs on the touchline of a football match, the same children went on a magical trip to Disneyland in a plane specially modified to accommodate their wheelchairs.[23] His validation and favour were highly sought after, and supposedly he was even prepared to help a young business hopeful. A wannabe entrepreneur was about to meet a potential client at an airport and spotted Packer. He plucked up courage to ask the imposing figure whether he would mind coming over to say hello when the youngster had met his contact. As requested, Packer tapped the shoulder of the enthusiastic yet unknown younger man. 'G'day, Peter, good to see you,' he piped up cheerfully, to which Peter replied: '**** off, Packer, I'm in a meeting.'[24]

The cricket authorities soon wished that they could also dismiss Packer as easily. The notion of a parallel game – a so-called 'cricket circus' – seemed completely unfeasible, but Packer knew what he wanted: to be the host broadcaster for Australian cricket. Since nobody paid cricketers what they were worth, he argued, cricket was 'the easiest sport in the world to take over'.[25]

If Ian Chappell – coaxed out of retirement – was Raúl to Packer's Fidel Castro, then Tony Greig was Che Guevara. Recruiting the cream of Australian cricket was straightforward, and the South Africans didn't hesitate, since they were frozen out of international cricket. Greig had the toughest assignment, which was to sign up many of the same West Indians he'd recently promised to make grovel. As Chappell recalls, Greig never shirked a challenge, and after going to the market, Jack came home with some magic beans; or, in this case, a briefcase full of signed contracts.[26] World Series Cricket was on.

Of course, cricket's establishment were furious at having their box-office draws spirited away from under their noses. It all ended up in court, but the judge ruled that sanctions against the defectors would actually be restraint of trade. England's five rebels were not picked for England for a few years, but were still available for their counties.

But what of the cricket? The whole thing was given some credence by Richie Benaud's appointment as a consultant. It was a three-way contest between the West Indies, Australia and the Rest of the World, which rather confusingly meant anyone who wasn't Australian, including the West Indians. But that was possibly the most conventional element of the whole thing. Packer was prevented from using traditional terminology, so team names were prefixed by 'WSC'. There were sixteen 'Supertests' and 38 one-day games played over two seasons, contested by a total of seventy players. Also barred from cricket's traditional homes, Packer used large football stadiums and dropped-in pitches grown in greenhouses. These big stadiums had floodlights, and so day/night cricket was born.

There was coloured clothing, although what the macho West Indians thought about their pink kit was anyone's guess. Everyone, on Packer's orders, wore batting helmets, apart from Vivian Richards, who did his own thing. It was commercial rather than altruistic on Packer's part, as he reminded players that he wasn't paying them 'to lie around in hospital for six months'.[27] At a formal dinner, Packer noticed Australian rookie David Hookes wasn't wearing a tie. Hookes advised that he didn't wear ties, only to be told that he'd be wearing one when on duty for Packer.[28] Suggestions of exhibition cricket were quickly allayed, and the contests were of the 'hottest, hardest, highest-quality', amounting to 'a Darwinian struggle for a demanding boss courting a fickle public in an atmosphere of media scepticism'.[29]

Almost nobody turned up to watch, but that wasn't really the point, since it was the TV spectacle that mattered. Unsurprisingly, the non-Packer media sided with the ACB, and for a while neither

Tony Greig (left) with Kerry Packer, 1977.

Packer nor the cricket establishment blinked. But by the following year, Australia's official team – in reality, a second or even third XI – were being trounced, and the crowds realized that the real stars were elsewhere. Other countries knew that without their big names they had very little, and they began reselecting Packer players. Soon the ACB was 'haemorrhaging cash and goodwill' and were forced to the negotiating table, Packer emerging from discussions with a very favourable contract giving him exclusive rights for regular cricket, which is what he'd wanted all along.[30] Tony Greig was sacked by England but was promptly rewarded with a media job at Channel Nine. Packer passed away on Boxing Day in 2005, having survived a major heart attack in 1990 when he died, apparently, for six minutes. In a blow to clairvoyants everywhere, he declared at that time that, having visited 'the other side', he could assure everyone that 'there's nothing there.'[31]

*Wisden* – outraged by 'jet-age razzamatazz' cricket – forlornly hoped that the 1977 season would be remembered mostly for the Queen's Silver Jubilee.[32] But almost everything about cricket changed. Day/night matches became a norm, as did coloured clothing. Cricketers became better paid, and coverage was more innovative and engaged wider audiences. In sum, Packer had improved the lot of all cricketers in a game that had become 'exceedingly smug', and the much-improved rates of pay wouldn't have happened without his intervention.[33] Christopher Martin-Jenkins went as far to suggest that, W. G. Grace aside, 'there has been no more influential figure in the history of cricket.'[34] But such influence was not appreciated by everyone, and Matthew Engel claimed that if cricket ever built a statue of Packer, plenty might 'spit on it'.[35] Whatever Packer was, saviour or destroyer, the genie was out of the bottle. World Series Cricket showed that unofficial cricket could be staged and could function as political leverage.

The age of the rebel tour had begun, and it appealed especially to South Africa, who had nothing to lose by staging unofficial cricket. In 1981/2, English players were recruited to play a Test match and some one-day internationals against a formidable South African line-up hungry for top competition. Arrangements were made so secretly that the British press, who could smell 'a ripe fart from miles away', knew nothing about it.[36] Bankrolled by South African Breweries and paid depending on their reputation, most collected around £50,000, many times the usual remuneration for a four-week tour. But the touring squad was not quite star-studded. Indeed, it was described as Boycott, Graham Gooch, plus a collection of 'has-beens, hired hands and holidaymakers' that were no match for South Africa.[37]

Indeed, events off the field were considerably more notable than those on it. There was a political row between those condemning the players for accepting blood money, and others who saluted them for making a stand. Other countries, notably India, told the Test and Country Cricket Board that they could forget any future interaction if they didn't ban the players, which they did. There were various responses from the players, some addressing the obvious moral implications, others dodging them. Dennis Amiss, an honest, decent man, declared rather naively that while the players didn't agree with apartheid, they didn't want to 'get involved' in politics.[38] Tour skipper Graham Gooch argued later that Test cricket was precarious, and with a loss of form or fitness always possible, if big money was offered, you should take it.[39] But he also reflected that had he known he and his team would be banned from Tests for three years, he probably wouldn't have gone.[40]

There was still another unofficial England tour, in 1990. This time, the hapless captain was Mike Gatting, who, either by design or bad luck, always found himself in the middle of events where he definitely wasn't the star. As one of England's most accomplished batsmen and captains, one of Gatting's considerable strengths was 'a refusal to remain in the shadows', even if this was not always 'a pretty sight'.[41] It certainly wasn't pretty when Gatting was hit in the face by a Malcolm Marshall bouncer at Kingston in 1986. He later described it as like walking into a door, 'just slightly more painful'.[42] Marshall refused to bowl with the ball until a bone fragment was removed. Gatting was patched up back home in the UK before being shipped back to the Caribbean, where he promptly broke his thumb just before the third Test. In the 1987 World Cup final in Calcutta, when Gatting was caught from a reverse sweep, chairman of selectors Peter May was incandescent, having previously banned the team from playing the shot.[43]

A month after the World Cup final, there was more trouble. The first Test of England's tour of Pakistan had been blighted by some allegedly one-sided local umpiring. In the second Test at Faisalabad, umpire Shakoor Rana castigated Gatting for allegedly moving a fielder when bowler Eddie Hemmings had already begun running in. 'A testy conversation ensued,' further inflamed when, as Rana moved back to his position, he dropped in 'a parting shot'.[44] It was not, reflects Simon Briggs, a reminder about how many balls were left in the over, but notification to Gatting that he was a 'f***ing cheating b*****d'.[45] A furious finger-jabbing exchange ensued, and the outraged umpire stopped the match until Gatting had apologized.

Lord's insisted on the apology and Gatting obliged without enthusiasm. It is not known whether anyone pointed out that he'd misspelt 'Faisalabad' on his scruffy note but his team issued a statement strongly defending the skipper. Not everyone was as supportive, some critics advocating 'the guillotine' on the basis that no England captain should be a 'protagonist in a bar room brawl'.[46] Umpire Rana unedifyingly dined out on the written apology, claiming that as a historical document it would fetch a fortune. The only positive to emerge from the sorry affair was the eventual establishing of neutral umpiring.

The following season, on the eve of a Test match against the West Indies at Nottingham, Gatting made news again. There was no suggestion of anything untoward, but he was fired anyway, Peter May again voicing his disapproval, this time that the captain had irresponsibly invited female company to his room after dark. On such a basis, reflected Mike Brearley, it would be difficult to find eleven 'responsible' players, and the authorities might have instead stood up against the 'prying nastiness of this sensationalism'.[47] Less cerebrally, Ian Botham, referring to Gatting's voracious appetite, expressed disbelief that his skipper might be involved in anything dishonourable, since 'anything he takes up to his room after nine o'clock, he eats.'[48]

While Gatting hasn't always helped himself, he probably deserved more support from the cricketing establishment than he got, and when South Africa came in for him to lead the tour in 1990, he admitted he just 'felt like getting out'.[49] In the event, he was getting out of one hot kitchen and into an even hotter one. The 1990 tour was the 'most morally dubious of all', since apartheid was withering and this time the players were paid by the government rather than corporate sponsors. Against a febrile backdrop, protestors were angry that cricketers should be in league with a cruel white regime. Never one to dodge his responsibilities, it was always Gatting himself who 'emerged from the foxhole' to face the demonstrators.[50] Nelson Mandela was released the day after England's rebels were beaten in the only Test match within three days.

Gatting's redemption and return to the heart of cricket is therefore quite astonishing. He played for England again, albeit without enormous success, and it was his dubious luck to be on the receiving end of Shane Warne's 'ball of the century' in 1993. Since then he has at various times been ECB Managing Director of Cricket Partnerships and the president of MCC. As of 2019 he was on MCC World Cricket Committee, but perhaps his greatest validation as an establishment figure came in 2007, when he appeared in an episode of the legendary BBC radio soap opera *The Archers*.[51]

Redemption, however, was not readily available to the West Indian and Sri Lankan cricketers who toured South Africa on occasions between 1982 and 1984. Tours emanating from England and Australia had been contentious enough but lacked the additional racial conundrum of non-white cricketers apparently supporting a regime that was prejudiced against them. For many it was beyond the pale. Bandula Warnapura had captained Sri Lanka in their first Test and scored their first Test run in 1982, but when he led a tour of South Africa later that year, it was disastrous. Though 'charming ambassadors', the tourists were not afforded any special status and had to conform with the protocols of apartheid.[52] On the pitch the tourists were comprehensively outplayed, and on their return all fourteen players were given life bans.[53]

The West Indians who toured South Africa twice during that period were vilified even more. While the obvious discussion ensued about whether black sportsmen playing in South Africa would prolong apartheid or help dismantle it, one argument is that some who accepted the generous bounty did so simply out of dire financial need. When West Indian cricket was so strong, breaking into the Test team was all but impossible, and many good fringe cricketers had no realistic chance of international cricket. They were therefore vulnerable to such offers from wherever they came.

On some levels, the tours in 1982/3 and 1983/4 might be considered successful. The visitors did well on the field, with relatively comfortable wins in both the unofficial Tests and one-day games. Furthermore, the general consensus was that they were greeted as heroes in South Africa, although Colin Croft may not have agreed when he was barred from a 'whites only' railway carriage.[54] Indeed, at the start of the tour there was a reluctance within the team to go too close to the boundary for fear of a hostile reception.[55] But in a land where whites risked jail if found in the company of blacks, the visitors were welcomed.[56]

This was in strong contrast to their reception back in the Caribbean. A life ban was unsurprising, although it was relaxed a few years later. But some reputations and lives struggled to recover and in 2007 nine members of the 1983 team were living outside their home countries.[57] Among those who stuck around was left-handed batsman Herbert Chang, who fell on hard times and resorted to drugs. On a rare public sighting he was spotted 'standing listlessly in the middle of the road'.[58]

Another was David Murray, son of Everton Weekes and father of Barbadian first-class player Ricky Hoyte. In 2016 he was broke, 'reduced to a bone-and-skin frame, and still unable to overcome the menace of drugs'.[59] Another was Richard Austin, or 'Danny Germs' as everyone called him, who slept rough and lurked near the cricket 'looking for handouts'.[60] Things didn't change much for him until he died in 2015. Rebellion doesn't end well for everyone.

## 26

# ONE MAN'S SALVATION
## *1981*

Rebel tours left holes in many international teams, meaning opportunities for some who might otherwise never have expected a phone call from the selectors. In 1977/8, for example, Australia turned to former Test captain Bobby Simpson, who had last played Test cricket eleven years previously. When the shock announcement was made at a press conference, the assembled journalists applauded.

Among other players being considered for the limelight was Ian Botham. In 1975 *Wisden* editor Norman Preston suggested England should pick the nineteen-year-old Somerset all-rounder while he was youthful and exuberant, but the selectors resisted until 1977. Thereafter Botham's impact was enormous. If the ultimate test of an all-rounder is that they could be selected for either batting or bowling, then Botham passed it. Much like Garry Sobers and Ellyse Perry, at times Botham was even the best in his team at both and Bill Frindall rated him as 'undoubtedly the best to represent England in modern times'.[1] The Ashes series of 1981 dominates his cv, his two centuries and 24 wickets meaning that it will forever be known as 'Botham's Ashes', not least because he was the story at every point after a very poor start. Nobody, apart perhaps from Ben Stokes in 2019, has made such timely interventions on behalf of his team.

But of all the things Botham could do on a cricket field, captaincy was not his strongest suit. Like Andrew Flintoff and Kevin

Pietersen after him, Botham was an indifferent England captain on the basis that 'idiosyncratic genius works better set free rather than shackled by responsibility'.[2] But when the 1981 series began, for better or worse he was the captain, and his record of seven defeats and three draws to that point wasn't impressing anyone. Even worse, his personal form was dismal, and the selectors appointed him as skipper only for the first Test of the six-match series. Australia won by 4 wickets and England's catching in the game was so poor that without a sideways sexist glance, John Woodcock suggested it would have 'put a girls' school to shame'.[3] Botham nonetheless clung on to the captaincy for the second Test.

Meanwhile, the Australians had their own problems and were still smarting after the events of a few months previously. In one particular ODI against New Zealand at the Melbourne Cricket Ground and wearing their infamous beige kit, New Zealand needed six to tie off the final delivery and Aussie skipper Greg Chappell instructed the bowler (his younger brother Trevor) to roll the ball along the ground, thus preventing anything more than a block. 'This is possibly a little bit disappointing,' suggested commentator Bill Lawry in bemused embarrassment; wicketkeeper Rod Marsh shook his head and urged 'Don't do it,' which was an early indicator that the decision was controversial.[4]

But the protests were ignored, the ball was delivered underarm and Greg Chappell got some idea of how big the fuss would be when a young girl tugged at his sleeve as he walked off and told him, 'You cheated.'[5] Aussie selector Sam Loxton was so distressed that he confessed that on his homeward journey he was 'teary all the way', while the usually pragmatic Richie Benaud was incandescent, calling it 'one of the worst things I've ever seen done on a cricket field'.[6] But Chappell claimed that the underarm ball was a purposeful warning to administrators that cricket was returning to pre-Packer days when players were neither consulted nor considered.[7] He declined to tour England in 1981 and the party, including Trevor Chappell, was led by Kim Hughes. Old stagers Rodney Marsh and Dennis Lillee had no time whatsoever for their new captain and as Ashes preparations go, your best bowler trying to knock the captain's head off in net practice isn't ideal. Nonetheless, the focus was on Botham, the precariousness of his job and his place in the team.

The match at Lord's was a downbeat draw, and Botham made a pair. Steve McDowell recalled 'the dull thud' of his own heart breaking as his hero walked to the pavilion.[8] Traditionally captains are cut some slack by the members at Lord's, but there was no mercy for Botham, and he 'never forgot' their stony silence.[9] If only to preserve some personal dignity, Botham resigned before he was pushed out. England were 0–1 down after two Tests and needed a new captain.

Step forward Mike Brearley, the Middlesex captain who to that point had won fifteen of his 27 Tests as captain of England, including a resounding 5–1 series win in the 1978/9 Ashes series. Though perhaps not a Test-class batsman, as a captain Brearley was 'intuitive, resourceful, sympathetic and clear-thinking' and 'entirely without malice'.[10] Most importantly, Botham was among those he'd charmed. Brearley's impact, however, wasn't immediately apparent when England followed on at Headingley. The better news was that he seemed to have worked his magic on Botham, who took 6 for 95 in Australia's first innings and made 50 in a generally disastrous England first innings. When Graham Dilley joined him at the crease during England's follow-on, the hosts had three wickets intact, but 92 runs were still needed to avoid an innings defeat.

Expecting a swift conclusion, the England players checked out of their hotel. Botham's wearing of a long-sleeved sweater to bat suggested that he didn't anticipate sticking around for long, the notion seemingly confirmed by his suggestion to Dilley that they should 'give it some humpty'.[11] Within a day or so, hotels around Leeds were being hastily rebooked, since, ably assisted by Dilley, Chris Old and Bob Willis, Botham rewrote the story of the match by eventually making an astonishing 149 not out.[12]

But then it was time for Willis. Some thought that the old boy's body was generally starting to creak as he marked his run-up 'on that amazing morning'.[13] His 8 for 43 bowled out Australia for 111, 18 runs short of victory. Botham called it 'the greatest spell of fast bowling England had ever seen'.[14] The end of the match stretched 'logic and belief', and while Ben Stokes might have challenged the claim in 2019, the climax was as close to 'miraculous' as has been witnessed in any Test match.[15] Despite a crescendo of national fervour, in the same hangdog style that cricket viewers became familiar with, Willis described the prosaic aftermath – following the post-match interviews, he, Brearley and Botham returned to an empty dressing room as 'all the other players had gone off to play Gillette Cup games'.[16] But one suspects that neither he nor Botham bought their own drinks for a while afterwards.

In the next match Australia were faced with another relatively modest target when Brearley called on Botham. In a blistering spell, he took five wickets for one run, each batsman walking onto 'the point of the lance'.[17] Brearley suggested England had won both these two Tests with a cavalier, 'village cricket' approach of breaking loose to 'hit the ball as hard as you can', and if indeed it was 'blacksmith cricket', then 'what better cricketing blacksmith was there than Botham?'[18] In the next match at Old Trafford, England began better but needed Botham again. By common consensus, Botham's century eclipsed his efforts at Leeds. Brearley called it 'cultured brutality'.[19] Even more effusively, John Thicknesse asserted that Gilbert Jessop could not have bettered it.[20] England had won the Ashes, but Botham still managed to take ten wickets in the final Test at The Oval, which was drawn.

There were more days for him in the sunshine; taking the top spot as all time Test wicket taker in 1986, his savaging of Merv Hughes at Brisbane in his very next Test match, and a masterful all-round performance against Australia at the SCG in the 1992 World Cup. Such heroics raised his profile, which he then utilized for good. An unending commitment to charitable causes raised over £25 million as Botham walked every inch of eighteen sponsored walks, only stopping in 2017 because 'his knees [were] shot'.[21] His achievements have been accompanied by controversy, however, and besides his testy relationship with MCC members, his resignation from England and his angry departure from Somerset, there was a High Court skirmish with Imran Khan over the latter's comments regarding ball tampering. When he confessed to smoking a little cannabis now and then, the authorities banned him for a couple of months.

In the mid-1980s Botham was represented by the eccentric agent Lord Tim Hudson, who had left his native Cheshire to become a DJ in Hollywood, also appearing as a voiceover artist in *Jungle Book* and *The Aristocats*. Restyled with blonde hair, 'Panama hats, striped blazers and old school ties', if Botham looked the part, perhaps he didn't completely feel it.[22] Hudson expressed outrage that Botham wasn't earning a fortune from public appearances and set about making him a Hollywood star 'to rival Sylvester Stallone and Charles Bronson' with 'a pirate-style earring and a headband with the St George's flag on it'.[23] Botham's appetite for the Hollywood high life (and his collaboration with Hudson) disappeared when he discovered that before he could be taken seriously as an actor – and, it was reported, the next James Bond – he needed to forget a Caribbean tour with England and instead spend

Ian Botham, 1979.

six months in California learning how to act.[24] Controversy didn't
leave Botham alone for long. When he suggested that Pakistan
was the sort of place to send your mother-in-law for a month,
staff at the Hilton Hotel in Lahore, where the England team were
staying, threatened to strike.[25]

If that particular spat was eventually forgotten, the animosity between Botham and Ian Chappell has not been. With a first
name and an unwillingness to take a backward step in common,
time has not diminished the unpleasantness. On paper, they should
be a little friendlier as they seem to have plenty in common.[26]
Both are fiercely proud, and one might imagine the recognition
of something familiar within the other, yet they maintained their
feud well into its fourth decade.

The antipathy between them began in 1977 when Botham
was an ebullient 21-year-old continuing his education by playing
club cricket in Australia. Chappell's blunt assessment of English

cricket in a Melbourne bar was too much for him. 'I gave him three official warnings,' recalls Botham, and when Chappell didn't stop, 'I just flattened him.'[27]

Chappell contends that Botham threatened him with a broken glass, but neither can agree on a version of what actually happened, which has kept the rancour simmering.[28] In general, although they have often been in the same vicinity, 'for the good of world peace' they do all they can to keep out of each other's way.[29] If the on-field drama is ever lukewarm, 'these mangily superannuated stags' can always remind us why 'George Orwell defined international sport as war without weapons'.[30] Botham remains typical of 'middle-aged, Thatcher-era British males' in that he is 'patriotic, disdainful of political correctness' and 'wedded to free enterprise'.[31] Knighted in 2007 and made a cross-bench peer in 2020, across a range of issues he navigates the world 'as he navigated cricket'.[32] But the Englishman wasn't the only outstanding performer in 1981. Indeed, if it wasn't for Botham's heroics, the series might have otherwise been called 'Alderman's Ashes'.

When playing anywhere else, Terry Alderman's career might be summarized as 'honest toil with medium-pace and medium returns'.[33] But give him green wickets and British weather and he was as lethal as anything the West Indies could offer. In the 1981 series his returns in the six Tests were nine wickets in the first Test, followed by two, nine, eight, nine and five in the last. Only three men had taken more than 42 wickets in any Test series. By the time of the next Ashes in 1982/3, Australia were justified in thinking that they had a special bowler.

One of the by-products of Kerry Packer's involvement was that his Channel Nine network had secured exclusive rights to broadcast Tests in Australia. The marketing strategy whipped up xenophobia and television trailers consisted of bowler hats, London bobbies and 'know-alls' with 'bristling moustaches' suggesting Australia had no chance.[34] It was all designed to attract 'thousands more Australians – and British migrants – through the turnstiles and countless others into armchairs which might otherwise have stayed vacant'.[35]

If the plan was to get patriotic blood pumping faster, it worked. In the first Test at Perth, as England's first innings passed 400, some England fans waving Union flags invaded the playing area, including a nineteen-year-old local called Gary Donnison, originally from Yorkshire. After some pointless frolicking, he cuffed Alderman, who then gave chase and tackled the miscreant to the ground, dislocating a shoulder in the process. The players left the field, and subsequently 23 spectators appeared in court. Donnison's father Bill refused to stand bail for his son, bitterly reflecting that they must be the only working-class family who'd gone 'ex-directory'.[36] While Donnison was given probation and fined $500, for Alderman the consequences were equally serious, and many feared his bowling had been terminally compromised.

But after swimming a mile a day for eight months, Alderman rebuilt his shoulder and toured England again in 1989. Apparently Donnison became a born-again Christian and raised a family. In fact, the story ended well for everyone apart from Graham Gooch. Alderman planted a man at short mid-wicket to cut out a particularly fruitful area for the usually imposing Gooch, and more often than not the Essex man was trapped leg before wicket. So serious was the curse that Gooch apparently told the selectors he should be dropped. Alderman took 41 wickets in the series and even entered the realms of British political discourse and graffiti art. During the final chapter of her reign as prime minister, the familiar refrain 'THATCHER OUT' painted on walls the length of the country was now accompanied by 'LBW b Alderman' underneath it. She was ousted the following year, but for once it was an English removal that had nothing to do with Terry Alderman.

# 27

# WOMEN'S CRICKET
## *A Century of Inequality*

Researching this book has revealed a staggering imbalance in the attention paid to men's and women's cricket. On one level, this is just the regrettable way of the world; on another, it is difficult to understand given that England's women won four world cups before England's men did so for the first time in 2019. Thus the progression of women's cricket can only be measured in terms of incremental victories. There was one such significant triumph in June 2020 when Director of Women's Cricket in England Clare Connor was announced as the first women president in MCC history.

In 1992 *Wisden* included the match scores from two girls' teams – Roedean and Denstone College. True, it wasn't 'leaping in front of the King's horse on Derby day', but it was a mini-triumph nonetheless.[1] In 2009 England's Claire Taylor was named as one of the almanack's Cricketers of the Year, a decision pondered upon, apparently, 'as earnestly' as the Church considered women priests.[2] But it marked real progress from Len Hutton suggesting that women playing cricket was as 'absurd' as men knitting.[3] Following Taylor's notable achievement the Lord's pavilion was still standing, and 'life goes on'.[4] When in 2018 *Wisden* featured England bowler Anya Shrubsole on its cover, it was another 'moment of celebration'.[5]

In reality, of course, cricket belongs as much to women as it does to men. It starts, as do many cricketing sub-themes, with

W. G. Grace, whose mother Martha seems to have been just as formidable as her son. As a girl in Bristol in the early nineteenth century she was a guinea pig for her father, an enthusiastic inventor. Once, reports the *Western Daily Press*, he strapped her to a chair, attached some kites and 'flew her at a height of 300 feet'.[6]

Aviation aside, Mrs Grace became influential within Gloucestershire cricket. It was considered protocol that when dismissed the home team's batsmen pay their respects to the county's matriarch, who would pull no punches in telling them where they were going wrong.[7] Left-handed batting and returning the ball underarm were both on-field behaviours of which she disapproved. However, she wasn't able to convince her son that the fairer sex fitted into the game; women, he claimed, weren't 'constitutionally adapted' for it.[8]

From the same mould as Mrs Grace came Hedley Verity's mother, Edith. Although diminutive, she was a 'tigress' when defending her son.[9] While other mothers might be 'ironing shirts and making sandwiches', notes Max Davidson with a slightly gendered eye, Edith once summoned over a fielder 'like Queen Victoria giving orders to a footman' to pass a message to 'our Hedley' about a gap in the field.[10] We know about Mrs Boycott and her pinny, but other mothers have also made their mark on the game. During Bodyline, Stan McCabe warned his father that if he got hit, his mother should be prevented from jumping over the fence.[11] But homage to mothers does suggest a more passive role for cricketing women, when in reality their roll call for pioneering, playing and administration is wholly distinguished.

There's Betty Snowball, for example. Her 189 for England versus New Zealand at Christchurch in 1934/5 remained the highest individual score in women's Tests for over fifty years. Coached by Learie Constantine, she also played squash and lacrosse for England, and was the 'outstanding wicketkeeper of her generation'.[12] Her opening batting partnership with Myrtle Maclagan made them the female equivalents of Hobbs and Sutcliffe, but how frustrating it must have been that while they were worthy of comparison with their illustrious counterparts, their international opportunities were so limited.[13] Snowball, for example, played ten times for England in fifteen years while Maclagan played fourteen times in seventeen years. Then as now, women's Test matches were rare. Claire Taylor's ten-year Test career, for example, amounted to only fifteen matches.

Eileen Ash played seven Tests for England between 1937 and 1949. Born before the *Titanic* went down, she spent the war working for MI6, a period of her life about which she retains a 'patriotic silence'.[14] In 2020 Ash was still going strong well into her 109th year, having become a celebrity for regularly driving her yellow Mini, putting her longevity down to yoga, eating well and 'an apple a day'.[15] Determinedly independent, the signed bat next to her bed 'in case of burglars' was given to her by Bradman.[16] On her hundredth birthday her grandson delivered her to an airfield where a Tiger Moth was waiting to whisk her away on a commemorative flight. After she rang the bell at Lord's before the England women's World Cup final against India in 2017, she was seen 'flirting with John Major and drinking champagne'.[17]

Molly Hide also played lacrosse for England as well as cricket. She was the Test captain for seventeen of her twenty-year international career (fifteen Tests). Born in Shanghai, she returned to England as a child and studied agriculture at university. Her parents prevented her from touring Australia in 1939 on the basis that she shouldn't be off 'gallivanting'.[18] With Snowball, she added 235 for the second wicket against New Zealand in 1935, and a big innings win lifted women's cricket in England.[19] Hide was so dominant that even 'grudging male chauvinists' admired her.[20] With an 'almost lordly manner' as the 'quintessential Englishwoman', she spent her life dedicated to cricket as a player, captain, administrator, manager, selector and broadcaster.[21]

Prime among Australian champions of the era was Betty Wilson, the first cricketer – of either sex – to make a century and take ten wickets in a match. That happened in her ninth Test match, but in her first she made 90 and took ten wickets. In another she made a century and took nine. In all, a return of 862 runs at 57.46 including three centuries and 68 wickets at an astonishing 11.80 (including a hat-trick) in eleven matches makes you wonder what she might have achieved had she played as much as the men. The 'female Bradman' learned her cricket, like him, playing in the street and was similarly single-minded.[22] A sporting natural, she practised every day when most others did so weekly.[23] Accordingly, in the 1940s and '50s, everyone knew Betty Wilson. If 20,000 people attended a women's match, they'd all come to watch her.[24] In later life she was the first Aussie woman to be admitted to the Australian Sports Hall of Fame and to be given honorary membership of the Melbourne Cricket Club. Irrespective of whether she thought of herself as one, Wilson was 'an emancipist'.[25] After watching her play, even a crusty old hack like Bill O'Reilly was prepared to stop suggesting that anyone had batted or bowled 'like an old woman'.[26] She was engaged to be married at the time of her first tour in 1948, but the wedding was delayed at least twice to accommodate her cricket. When she was selected to tour England in 1951, she once again put the game first.[27] Thereafter she devoted her life to cricket.[28]

Enid Bakewell was similarly dedicated and, when given a chance, performed brilliantly. In order to make the trip to Australia and New Zealand for her first England tour in 1968, she raised the airfare by selling old books, holding coffee mornings and selling home-grown potatoes. Her record of twelve Test matches in eleven years seems par for the course, but she invariably rose to the occasion. With a batting average of just under 60 and fifty wickets at sixteen apiece, Bakewell's lifetime contribution has been recognized by both the *Sunday Times* and Sky Sports in their Sportswomen of the Year Award ceremonies.[29] As a 76-year-old 'in name only' she was still turning her arm over for Purley Redoubtables women's team.[30] Similar to her eminent predecessors, she simultaneously spun many plates: a mother of three and a PE teacher, she became a Labour councillor in the late 1980s.[31]

Having played in the first televised women's Test against Australia in 1976, Bakewell recalls the fuss regarding whether women could use the men's changing rooms.[32] The eventual resolution of such inequality was driven by the most influential woman cricketer of all. On the field, Rachael Heyhoe Flint was unbeaten as England captain across six series and led England to victory in the first World Cup in 1973. She hit the first six in a women's Test match, and when she retired had scored more Test runs than anyone else.[33] Of her three Test centuries, the 179 she scored at The Oval in 1976 in just under nine hours demonstrates a spirit not easily deterred.

Rachael Heyhoe Flint's influence extends further still. *Wisden* asserts that during the 1970s, alongside Mary Peters and Virginia Wade, she was Britain's most familiar sportswoman, even when women's cricket had 'no public profile'.[34] Besides being a successful captain and England's premier batsman,[35] Heyhoe Flint was also their manager and press officer. Not only did she devise the whole idea of the first women's World Cup in 1973, she secured sponsorship, sold tickets and wrote press releases.[36] In a process known affectionately by those on the receiving end as 'Rachaelizing', she used 'wit, charm and persuasion' to cajole people into contributing their effort and money.[37] Among those convinced by her compelling narrative was millionaire Jack Hayward, who sponsored two England women's tours to the West Indies. By making her a director of Wolverhampton Wanderers Football Club, Hayward ensured that others benefited from her enthusiasm and 'unquench-able desire to improve people's lives'.[38] When she died, the club's Vice-President, Led Zeppelin singer Robert Plant, described her as a 'wonderful lady' possessing 'energy, sensitivity and great humour'.[39]

Though eloquent and good-natured, she became a determined thorn in the side of cricket's establishment. As the 'last bastion' of male 'exclusivity', MCC had resolutely stood its ground amid accu-sations of chauvinism.[40] Prior to 1998 there were some parts of Lord's where women were not even allowed to venture.[41] While they were mainly engaged with tasks within the notoriously narrow range of 'caring, cashiering, catering, cleaning and clerical', a sixth 'c' – 'cricket' – was out of bounds.[42] Apparently, in a charity match at Sydney in 1994, Brian Lara was dismissed by Australian Test player Zoe Goss shortly after a steward had mistaken her for a groupie and had removed her from the dressing room.

There had been progress at Lord's when England's women played Australia in 1976, despite the *Evening News* reporting the 'shaking of heads' when it became clear the ladies would be walking through the Long Room.[43] Appropriately, Heyhoe Flint became the first female to enter the Lord's arena as a player, but cricketing emancipation remained elusive. In 1991, backed by Sir Jack Hayward, Dennis Amiss, Brian Johnston and Tim Rice, as plain 'R. Flint', she applied unsuccessfully for MCC membership.

Geoffrey Copinger, the owner of what is apparently the world's largest collection of cricket books, was a notable protestor against admitting women members. He conceded admiring the impas-sioned pleas for equality, and that there was 'an awful lot of claptrap from my side of the fence'.[44] Indeed, he also agreed that ladies' toilets could be easily installed and doubted whether 'women will talk loudly or behave badly once admitted'.[45] However, he

Rachael Heyhoe Flint, *c.* 1980s.

asserted, he wanted to watch the cricket 'in comparative peace' and considered women 'a threat' to his being able to do so. Rejecting suggestions that he was a 'cranky old chauvinist', his proof was that he'd been happily married for more than 35 years to a lady who wasn't, 'unfortunately, interested in cricket'.[46] Probably didn't have the time, what with all that cooking and cleaning.

Heyhoe Flint was determined that she wasn't there to dismantle the establishment but to join it.[47] In this regard MCC remained a little out of touch: after all, if you have to wait half your adult life to join something, noted Tim de Lisle, it is unsurprising if you are 'out of date when you get there'.[48] A letter to the *Daily Telegraph* in 2003 provided some light relief. It describes a club meeting where women umpires were suggested as a possible innovation. 'What about the language?' asked one concerned committeeman, the chairman replying, 'The players will just have to put up with it.'[49]

Fairness finally prevailed in 1999 when after two centuries of resistance, 70 per cent of those who voted approved admitting women to MCC. More gracious than some of those who opposed her, Heyhoe Flint reapplied, expressing no wish to make a fuss and reflecting that 'I may be the last one many people want as a member.'[50] But she duly became the first woman admitted to MCC, in addition to becoming television's first female sports commentator, the first woman inducted into the ICC Hall of Fame and one of the two first women appointed as members of the ECB.[51] Later Baroness Heyhoe Flint of Wolverhampton, she was responsible for ensuring that, in her words, mums and their daughters had their own cricket, 'instead of making cucumber sandwiches every weekend'.[52] When she died in 2017 the flag on the Lord's Clock Tower flew at half mast, a 'change in attitude' for which she herself was responsible.[53] Clare Connor becoming club president, one imagines, happened only because of Heyhoe Flint's cheerful and resolute determination. She made progress without militancy, noted Connor, but with 'charm, persistence and intellect'.[54]

Another positive emergence is the occasional double-header format of Twenty20 internationals, with women's and men's games held on the same day. Certainly, as the profile of women's cricket has increased, the scrutiny of players has intensified, much as it has for their male counterparts. When England's women won the Ashes in 2014, for example, some news outlets decided that the main story was skipper Charlotte Edwards announcing that the post-match celebrations involved 'getting smashed'.[55]

Indeed, after Rachael Heyhoe Flint, Edwards was the new lynchpin for women's cricket in England. Her 10,273 international runs for England reflect the opportunities to play different formats not available to Snowball, Bakewell and others. Edwards made her international debut aged sixteen, and before she was twenty she'd made three centuries for England and six fifties. She was England captain for a decade and at one stage in 2009 had led her team to win all the titles available – the Ashes, World Cup and World Twenty20. Her thirteen centuries and 67 fifties put her among the premier players in the world. Indeed, she was described by former England women's coach Mark Robinson as 'a once-in-a-generation cricketer'.[56] Robinson's praise, though, is tempered by the fact that his comments were made in 2016 as he discussed how he had dropped her as both England captain and England player. The rationale was that her dominance was such that Edwards would in some way inhibit the team's development.[57]

Edwards's removal reflects the 'brutal side of professionalism', and that women's cricket is increasingly falling in line with the men's game.[58] Other things have changed, too. Women wore skirts when Heyhoe Flint began playing, and she had to buy her own England blazer. The game developed to the extent that between 2003 and 2016, the number of clubs with women's teams in England grew from 93 to 693.[59] There are various Twenty20

Charlotte Edwards (left) with former England cricketers Lynne Thomas
(centre) and Enid Bakewell (right), 2017.

competitions around the world, but professionalism remains 'work
in progress'.[60] A 40 per cent increase in the England women's salary
pot and £20 million of investment between 2020 and 2024 are
positive moves, as is women's Twenty20 cricket being admitted to
the Commonwealth Games for Birmingham in 2022. Moreover, it
was estimated that England's victory over India in the 2017 World
Cup final attracted a global television audience of 'comfortably
in excess of 150 million viewers'.[61] Not only was this validation
that women's cricket could engage people across the world, it
was also confirmation that it has its own superstar players. While
Anya Shrubsole's 6 for 46 in the final was an eye-catching performance, it was perhaps eclipsed by something that happened
in the second semi-final between India and Australia at Derby.

The bare facts of Harmanpreet Kaur's innings are impressive
enough. Her 171 not out enabled India to post a challenging 281
for 4 in a match truncated to 42 overs per side. Her runs were
made from 115 balls and included twenty boundaries and seven

sixes. When she entered the action at 35 for 2 in the tenth over, her team's progress had been stuttering and sluggish. Thereafter Kaur was 'incendiary', 'flaming magnesium' and 'a solid-fuel cocktail of audacity and skill, a comet tail of ice and fire burning up on re-entry'.[62] So furious was her onslaught, and so intense was her scowling commitment to it, that when she reached her hundred following a rather risky run, Kaur castigated batting partner Deepti Sharma and then proceeded 'to take it out on the Australians'.[63]

That Australia were not able to seriously challenge the Indian total was of no consequence because it was all lost 'in the glare of The Greatest'.[64] Scyld Berry called it 'perhaps the finest innings by a woman outside Test matches' and one that will attract fans towards women's cricket.[65] Geoff Lemon wrote that the innings 'redefined' the possibilities for women's cricket while Charlotte Edwards simply judged it 'the best innings I've ever seen'.[66] *Wisden Cricket Monthly* concluded that pound-for-pound, Kaur's innings was the best innings of 2017 by a man or woman in any format.[67] Gratifyingly it was being judged in absolute terms, not just as an innings by a woman.

But the time has clearly arrived when this should happen. While in 2019, Jason Holder, Ravi Jadeja and Ben Stokes were among the best all-rounders in the men's game, it was perhaps a stretch to conclude that any of them were the best bowlers and the best batsmen in their respective international teams.[68] However, across international formats, Australian Ellyse Perry can justifiably claim to be just that. Indeed, she is not only the most valuable player in Australia's 'imperious' women's team but is probably the best in women's cricket, full stop.[69] Charlotte Edwards speculates that Perry is 'the greatest female player we're ever going to see'.[70]

Also a good enough footballer to play for Australia eighteen times and appear in the 2011 World Cup in Germany, Perry was named the leading woman cricketer in the world by *Wisden* in 2016 on the back of a season in which she scored seventeen half-centuries in 23 one-day international innings – 'the best such streak for any cricketer, man or woman, ever'.[71] She was the first male or female cricketer to score 1,000 runs and take a hundred wickets in Twenty20 internationals and Belinda Clark, who many believe to have been the best Australian female all-rounder, suggested that Perry was the most 'genuine Australian all-rounder of any gender or generation'.[72] The rubicon has been crossed, but not just by Perry. In 2018 England wicketkeeper Sarah Taylor was described by Adam Gilchrist as 'the best wicketkeeper in the world . . . male or female'.[73]

But the celebration comes with a proviso of 'What happens next'?[74] Everyone involved with women's cricket must help to perpetuate its momentum.[75] One heartening development is that

Ellyse Perry (left), 2014.

when watching cricket on TV or listening to it on the radio, you are as likely to hear a female commentator as you are a male. There is a purity about women's cricket too, since it 'eschews so many of the game's vices while embodying so many of its virtues.'[76] Until fairly recently, elite women cricketers raised money to play, paying for their own kit and blazers. They juggled playing with outside careers and, in some cases, the raising of young families. Everything they have has been hard-earned, but has often been given to them rather more reluctantly. Somehow, as well as being fully legitimate in terms of its skills, importance and audience, women's cricket also epitomizes the very best values in terms of what Jardine identified as battling and serving.

# 28

# CRICKET WILL NEVER DIE
## *A New Millennium*

I f in 1999 cricket took some time to reflect and celebrate that it was addressing the issue of gender imbalance, it was jolted out of its reverie pretty quickly. Indeed, the new millennium had barely had time to wipe the sleep from its eyes when something unusual – and sinister – happened at Centurion, South Africa, in January 2000.

As we've heard, the early days of cricket were blighted by a disregard for the rules, morals and the ethical dubiousness of manipulating results. Although there is no suggestion of any match-fixing, even the magnificence of the 1981 Test at Headingley did not escape from financial jiggery-pokery. With England 135 for 7, and before Ian Botham changed the complexion of the match, opponents Dennis Lillee and Rodney Marsh couldn't resist a wager at 500-1, Lillee suggesting that for a two-horse race, the odds were 'ludicrous'.[1] He asked the team bus driver to place a bet of £10, and when England won, the pair apparently collected £7,500 – but nobody for one moment felt that they had thrown the match.[2] Indeed, Lillee and Marsh are simply opportunist larrikins compared to events at Centurion.

England had struggled against a strong South African team and were 2–0 down going into the final Test. Three days were lost to weather, but the hapless tourists were unexpectedly given an opportunity to regain some pride. Home captain Hansie Cronje suggested that if England forfeited their first innings and South

Africa their second, both sides might go for the win. England Captain Nasser Hussain readily agreed, and in a thrilling denouement with minutes left, the tourists won by two wickets.[3]

The contrived conclusion was a throwback to cricket's Corinthian days, perhaps an old-fashioned gesture from an old-fashioned cricketer. Cronje was wholesome, religious and had progressed from the captaincy of Orange Free State at 21 to captain of the national side by the time he was 25. 'Young, good looking and articulate', he captained a team reflecting South Africa's new multiracial mix.[4] In partnership with coach Bob Woolmer, he was bold, adventurous and innovative. Absolutely respected by his team, Hansie Cronje seemed to epitomize the very best of South African sport.[5]

Except that he didn't. Weeks after the match, New Delhi police revealed that a phone-tapping operation had captured conversations where Cronje discussed fixing cricket matches. It appeared that in exchange for guaranteeing a positive result in the Test match, Cronje had accepted £5,000 and, 'bizarrely, a leather jacket'.[6] Stripped of the captaincy, Cronje tearfully revealed a wider involvement with bookmakers, and the world of cricket listened 'agog as much as aghast'.[7] Banned for life, the golden boy lost his lustre; having sold his reputation for 'many fistfuls of dollars', he was mistaken in thinking that 'a few manipulative words (and a slew of lawyers) could buy it back'.[8] Cronje's predecessor Kepler Wessels later revealed his own concerns about not all being as it should well before the Centurion match. During a one-day triangular series involving Australia and Pakistan in 1994, for example, Cronje made some on-field comments that Pakistan weren't trying to win, and Wessels smelled a rat.[9] Cronje's image was hardly helped when he engaged British publicist Max Clifford, who suggested that personal damage could be limited and the commercial potential of the story might be exploited.[10] Cronje died in a plane crash in 2002 and five years later, when his mentor Woolmer was found dead in uncertain circumstances during the 2007 World Cup in Jamaica, former South African all-rounder Clive Rice alleged both had been murdered by 'mafia betting syndicates'.[11] Noting the ambivalence when Cronje died, Michael Atherton suggested that the biggest tragedy of his death was that he was 'denied the redemption his Christianity would have demanded'.[12] But there was a wider tragedy, too. Cronje's corruption tainted several teammates who received shorter bans, and match-fixing – and its junior but no less contemptible partner, spot-fixing – developed into a global disease, resulting in bans for cricketers from England, Kenya, the West Indies, Bangladesh, New Zealand and Sri Lanka.

Cricket lurked in the doldrums for a bit and needed a lift. This came in 2005 when English cricketing blood pumped almost as quickly as it had in 1981. Truncate the explanatory phrase 'when England won the Ashes in 2005' to '2005' and everyone still knows you are referring to perhaps the best summer's cricket in living memory. *The Telegraph* recalled a series that completely captured the public imagination with an 'epic marathon' where almost every minute 'hypnotised' those watching.[13] Those with an ephemeral relationship with the game were suddenly asking if Flintoff was reversing it and by midsummer even cricketing agnostics were asking each other if England should declare or whether the middle order looked a bit brittle. England bowler Matthew Hoggard was one-quarter of England's once-in-a-generation pace attack alongside Steve Harmison, Flintoff and Simon Jones. He reflected that the bleary-eyed open-top bus celebration that followed the victory emphasized that the series had enthused millions, but he only fully realized the magnitude of what had happened a week or so later when staff at Burger King wouldn't accept payment for his supper.[14] Even the new football season couldn't match the Ashes as the biggest sporting story in town.[15]

But no sooner had the series ended with an epic, odd, euphoric final day at The Oval, and despite its huge new audience, cricket scuttled behind a televisual paywall, deciding that boosting revenue was its immediate priority.[16] For many, a subscription to satellite TV sport 'comes just below running water' in terms of domestic priorities, but those with more casual relationships with cricket were lost.[17] Cricket's live free-to-air coverage had gone, and like 'coastal erosion', concluded Jonathan Liew, 'the dwindling of terrestrial television's sporting portfolio has had a certain slow inevitability to it'.[18] Of course, the money provided by Sky Sports has in many ways saved cricket, and has elevated its broadcasting to the next technological level.[19] But after being bathed in the sunlight of joyous publicity, only cricket could celebrate by sliding back into the shade. After England's World Cup victory in 2019, it was hoped that a new audience might be attracted, but this may be the same audience 'it probably already had in 2005'.[20]

Audience size has never been an issue for the Indian Premier League. Since its inception in 2008, spectators, viewers, advertisers and everyone else have been drawn to it as if powered by magnets. Representing a new Indian 'festival', it is 'splashy, loud and full of colour'.[21] Some, of course, think the whole thing is distasteful, and a 'deadly disease' attacking cricket's nervous system, but while traditionalists detest Twenty20 cricket, purists seemingly no longer matter in a new cricketing world driven by rupees, dollars and sterling.[22]

Others are more optimistic. Besides providing a 'snackable capsule' of cricket action demanding a more fleeting commitment from spectators, the IPL is responsible for mending previously fractious relationships between players from across the globe.[23] Where else, for example, 'could you have seen Ricky Ponting and Sourav Ganguly share the same dressing room?'[24] Others go even further, claiming that there would have been no cricketer, ancient or modern, who wouldn't have wanted to play in it.[25] After all, it's all still about scoring runs and taking wickets.[26]

This book has chronicled how personalities have shaped the history of cricket, for good or for bad. But the advent of the IPL has ushered in the age of the truly global cricket superstar. In 2020, for example, Virat Kohli had a brand value of \$237.5 million, more than any other Indian celebrity, including any of the Bollywood powerhouses you'd care to mention.[27] But huge fortunes come with huge scrutiny. Many have found themselves falling short of the notional standards set by others.

For example, a simple Internet search for 'greatest bowler of all time' will generate sufficient reading about Shane Warne to keep you busy for weeks. He took the seemingly ancient art of leg spin from a dusty shelf, making it not only fashionable but sexy and lethal. Besides being a 'freak of nature' able to bowl beautiful, controlled, leg spin 'ball after ball with his eyes closed', he was also 'a glorious beast of a competitor'.[28] He was named one of the five greatest players of the century by *Wisden*, their only caveat being 'that he may yet figure in deliberations for the 21st'.[29] If such a discussion takes place in eighty or so years, whatever cricket might look like then, Shane Warne will still be on the agenda.

But the public gaze has not always revealed sunshine. Off the field, he missed the 2003 World Cup after being banned for taking an outlawed diuretic. His time in the IPL was punctuated by 'an ugly spat with a local cricket administrator' and 'a tiff with Indian superstar Sachin Tendulkar'.[30] He was fined \$50,000 after appearing on TV and blasting the secretary of the Rajasthan Cricket Association over his choice of wicket.[31] An advert featuring Warne's endorsement of a hair-restoring technique was considered misleading.[32] Moreover, he appears to have been particularly nocturnally active, a headline in 2019 describing the 'Noisy 2hr romp with 3 women' suggesting no major loss of form.[33] Shane Warne wasn't

Shane Warne, 2009.

your thing if you like your cricket heroes clean-cut like Trumper or Hobbs. But long lenses didn't exist back then.

Ben Stokes has also generated off-field headlines. A New Zealander who moved to the north of England with his family when he was twelve, England's premier all-rounder has hit many high points, including a century in his second Test match, almost making two hundreds in a Test at Lord's and a first-innings 92 followed by the fastest Test century for England since Jessop in 1902.[34] In 2016 at Cape Town he made the second fastest Test double century of all time, hitting the ball with 'rhythmic brutality'.[35] Ian Botham – amid the obvious comparisons – was ebullient, noting that Stokes's innings would 'change his life'.[36] A comment on the BBC's webpage suggested that rather than the other way around, Daniel Craig (of James Bond fame) was auditioning to be the next Ben Stokes.

But we were reminded of the other side of Stokes at Cape Town, when he was seen to aim 'foul language' at South African batsman Temba Bavuma.[37] Commentators clicked their tongues and added it to the late-night partying that got him sent home from the 2013 tour of Australia and the four speeding tickets in 2016.[38] A few weeks after scoring his double century, Stokes was handed the ball in the final of the T20 World Cup in Kolkata. The West Indies needed an unlikely 19 runs to win, and given his reputation as a death bowler, Stokes was a safe pair of hands. But four times Barbadian Carlos Brathwaite hit the ball miles into the cooling evening and England lost. Stokes was reduced to 'red-faced misty-eyed firebrand down on his haunches', and Mike Selvey suggested that this was a defeat that would take a while to recover from.[39]

In 2017 he was reprimanded for using 'obscene, offensive or insulting' language during a Test against the West Indies.[40] But worse was to come, and though he was cleared of affray after an incident outside a Bristol nightclub following an ODI, there was plenty for Stokes fans to defend. He was said to have consumed 'at least 10 drinks', and the CCTV footage also shows him throwing punches.[41] He was accused by a bouncer of offering £300 cash to get into a nightclub and was described as 'a very arrogant man who doesn't like to be told No'.[42] He was also filmed mocking the disabled son of celebrity Katie Price.[43] Locked in 'the behavioural patterns' of a twelve-year-old, wrote Janet Street-Porter, his 'maturity and personal development seems to have stalled at an adolescent phase' and any apology from him would be worthless until he learns 'respect, consideration and social skills'.[44] When a hefty fine and a ban followed, it seemed as if Stokes almost needed saving from himself.

But back he came. By the time of the 2019 World Cup, Stokes was once again England's lynchpin. Chasing an awkward-looking 242 to beat New Zealand in the final, England floundered, but Stokes did not. While some batsmen go at the ball using the bat face or a more wristy approach, others 'throw the kitchen sink at it'.[45] Ben Stokes, though, 'throws Ben Stokes at it'.[46] A super over that ended in a tie because the match itself had ended in a tie was won by England based on boundaries scored, and the whole thing was only possible because of Stokes's 84 not out. After the nightclub incident and everything else, by winning England's first ever men's World Cup, there was now something different to call Stokes's 'legacy'.[47] In the second Ashes Test that followed, he made a magnificently measured century at Lord's and the fact that Australia were required to hang on for a draw in a way they had not expected was largely Stokes's doing.

But everything was eclipsed by what he did next. The innings that Stokes played at Headingley on Sunday 25 August will be familiar to most people. Although it was similar statistically, it somehow eclipsed the last-wicket heroics by Kusal Perera that took Sri Lanka to victory against South Africa at Durban in February 2019. Stokes absorbed pressure and bided his time, then accelerated when required, picking off the runs with a mixture of power hitting and precision placement to capture the strike. It was England's highest ever fourth-innings target, notes Scyld Berry – though 'far beyond the limit of what had been done', Stokes, 'somehow, accomplished it'.[48] Former teammate Graeme Swann suggested that cricket in back gardens would henceforth forever be characterized by the 'bickering between siblings about who gets to pretend to be Ben Stokes'.[49] Geoffrey Boycott conceded that though he'd seen 'some remarkable cricket moments', what Stokes had achieved by winning the match with 135 not out eclipsed anything he'd seen in the previous 50 years.[50]

But then, in 2020, nothing. The game between the Karachi Kings and the Quetta Gladiators in Karachi on 15 March was the last elite cricket match anywhere before cricket, sport and most of regular life closed down as COVID-19 swept the globe. Thereafter cricket grounds from the village green upwards were populated

Ben Stokes during his sensational innings at the Ashes Test,
Headingley, 2019.

with tumbleweed and silence. Test cricket closed down for three
months but then, in early July, it tentatively restarted. Ireland, the
West Indies, Pakistan and Australia all toured England. There
were no spectators, but with new on-field protocols to observe,
the players emerged from their bio-bubbles and somehow produced joyous, uplifting cricket played in the right spirit and to a
high standard. But as cheered as we all felt, because of the loss
of revenue, English cricket, among others, was 'staring down the
barrel'.[51] Some other countries were a little safer, but Australia's
financial position was 'on a knife edge', and the West Indie's pre-
dicament was described as 'dire'.[52]

Notwithstanding these serious questions about money and how to attract more of it, cricket will return to full strength. If its history of battle, service, sport and art tells us anything, it is that the game has the characters to rebuild it. Cricket and its cricketers are not perfect, yet the game has emerged from war, scandal and political deadlock and will do so again. The traits shown by the cricket people in this book will be replicated all over the world. If it's not too inappropriate to conclude a cricket book with a baseball metaphor, all bases are covered:

### BATTLE

The belligerence of Grace, Warwick Armstrong, Sydney Barnes, O'Reilly and Boycott
The swashbuckling instincts of Tennyson and Headley
The strategizing of Jardine and Brearley
The pioneering spirit of Nayudu, Packer, Greig and Chappell

### SERVICE

The frontline sacrifice of Verity, Farnes, Blythe, Booth and all that fell
The patience of prisoners Geoff Edrich, Bowes, Brown and those who survived
The grit of Border, Close, Rhodes and Fred Root
The patient dignity of Sandham
The societal awareness of Constantine, Imran, Worrell and D'Oliveira
The administrative commitment of Warner and Allen
The statistical order of Bill Ferguson
The longevity of Norman Gordon and Eileen Ash
The dignity of Woodfull, Oldfield and Valentine
The emancipatory drive of Wilson and Heyhoe Flint
The every-level service of Hutton, Walcott, Benaud and Hide

**SPORT**

The all-round sporting brilliance of Fry, Stoddart, Turnbull and
Wooller

The cricketing brilliance of Mynn, Faulkner, Procter, Botham,
Kapil Dev, Sobers and Perry

The lasting dominance of Bradman and Hobbs

The intimidating power of Vivian Richards and Barry Richards

The star quality of Compton and Miller

The modest achievement of Laker and Getty

**ART**

The ingenuity and invention of Lumpy and Iverson

The beautiful rhythm of Larwood, Lindwall and Hall

The artistry of Mailey, Grimmett and Warne

The stylish brilliance of Ranji, Trumper, Hammond, Jackson,
Weekes and Mansur Ali Khan

The characterful legacies left by all these cricketers still have currency as examples for the future. The crowds will return, and cricket
will make a full, sensational comeback, like Lionel Tennyson's
Hampshire in 1922, and a Ben Stokes inspired England in 2019.
However long it takes to recover fully, in the meantime, we can
still dream about it, like John Arlott's 1950s imagined spectator
watching cricket at Worcester.

> Dozing in deck-chair's gentle curve,
> Through half-closed eyes I watched the cricket,
> Knowing the sporting press would say:
> 'Perks bowled well on a perfect wicket.'[53]

# APPENDIX:
## *The Laws of Cricket at a Glance*

They are 'laws', not 'rules'; get it wrong and expect forbidding looks. The laws most closely apply to proper professional cricket, where they are almost always applied with rigour and accuracy, and under the scrutiny of the watching public. Moving further away from first-class cricket, regulations might be applied with some flexibility.

Often in club cricket, for example, umpires are already-dismissed batsmen that re-enter the field of play to officiate. Sometimes harbouring a smouldering sense of injustice, they might make decisions on the basis of retribution rather than legitimacy. In club cricket, so long as everyone agrees, you can – within reason – be flexible and accommodating.

### The Preamble

The Spirit of Cricket is sacrosanct. Control yourself, respect your opponents, don't argue with the umpires. *It'll make you a better person.*

### LAW 1 Players and Captains

Captains announce their team. If the captain is indisposed, some-one else does it. They are responsible for making sure their side plays within the laws and spirit. *Power and responsibility.*

### LAW 2 The Umpires

There are two of them, and they are in charge. They make all the key decisions – if, where, when and how – and communicate with the scorers using semaphore-like actions. *Don't argue with them. Even when they are wrong, the Spirit of Cricket says that they're right.*

### LAW 3 The Scorers

Two of them officially record everything happening on the field of play. *The epitome of precision.*

### LAW 4 The Ball

Round, and of a consistent size, but different for women's and junior cricket. Made from cork, string and leather, a game usually starts with a new one and in longer matches it will be routinely renewed. *If it hits you, it hurts.*

### LAW 5 The Bat

Comprises a cane handle and a wooden blade. 'The bat', especially when a catch is being claimed, includes the bat itself and/or the hand or glove holding it. There are limits as to how big it can be and what you can repair it with. *Has to be made of wood.*

### LAW 6 The Pitch

It's 22 yards (20 m) long and 10 ft (305 cm) wide. Usually it's grass, but not always. *Some club cricket pitches appear to have been prepared by local sheep. Others might be guarded by proud groundsmen with guns.*

### LAW 7 The Creases

The lines showing you where to stand, run and land. *Depending on your role, you can be on the front line or behind it.*

### LAW 8 The Wickets

Three wooden stumps each end of the pitch, of a specified size depending on the type of cricket. There are grooves at the top of each for the bails, which fall off when the wicket is broken.

*Batsmen – protect them with your life.*

### LAW 9 The Preparation and Maintenance of the Playing Area

Can be rolled and mowed but there are rules about what with, when and for how long. During the match, the pitch can be cleared of dust, creases can be re-marked and footholds repaired.

*Make sure you have lots of sawdust.*

### LAW 10 Covering the Pitch

The pitch is covered before and during the match and on an ad hoc basis to protect it from the weather. *The covers coming on is cricket's saddest sight.*

### LAW 11 The Intervals

Play can stop for lunch, tea and drinks, and between innings when one side has finished batting. There is a break of ten minutes between innings. *Always the most-discussed ten minutes in cricket.*

### LAW 12 Start of Play and Cessation of Play

The umpires call 'play' to start and 'time' to end play. In certain formats, the last hour of play is specifically prescribed. *Usually the most exciting hour of the whole match.*

### LAW 13 Innings

There might be one per side, or two. Teams take it in turns. Innings are complete when all batsmen are out, when there is no time left or when the batting captain declares. *Two per side in longer cricket, one in the shorter form.*

## LAW 14 The Follow-on

In a two-innings match, when the team that is batting first establishes a specified lead, its captain can ask the other team to bat again – twice in a row – and out of sequence. *If a captain does this and loses, they will never be allowed to forget it.*

## LAW 15 Declaration and Forfeiture

Captains can declare their innings over or can even forfeit an innings. *Forfeiture is rare, and usually connected to the weather.*

## LAW 16 The Result

Either side can win by scoring more runs. Or the game might just run out of time with no result (draw). Very unusually the game might end in a tie, with the scores level. *This has only happened twice in over 140 years of Test cricket.*

## LAW 17 The Over

Six legitimate deliveries. Nobody can deliver successive overs, and overs must be completed. If the umpire miscounts, their mistake stands. *That's power.*

## LAW 18 Scoring Runs

Registered when the batsmen run and cross, or when the ball reaches the boundary. Umpires can award runs to the batting side for various transgressions by the fielding side, including non-legitimate deliveries or if the ball touches a discarded fielding helmet. *Runs are cricket's lifeblood.*

## LAW 19 Boundaries

The wider field of play is marked by something appropriate. If the ball is hit to the boundary and bounces first, that's four. If it doesn't bounce, it's six. *Clap the former, cheer the latter.*

## LAW 20 Dead Ball

This call divides the game into sections of play when the ball is 'live'. Most usually, the bowler running in signals that the ball is 'live'. When it's 'dead', nothing legitimate happens. *Not deceased, just out of commission.*

## LAW 21 No-ball

All about determining legitimate deliveries. Bowlers must deliver with a straight arm, making sure their feet are in the right place. Penalized by one run and a replacement delivery, and apart from specific instances, batsmen can't be dismissed from a no-ball. *'Throwing' is heinous.*

## LAW 22 Wide Ball

The ball must be delivered within certain parameters, giving batsmen a chance to hit it. The penalty is one run and a replacement delivery and again, unusual for batsmen to be dismissed. *The umpire holds their arms out, as if describing the fish that got away.*

## LAW 23 Bye and Leg Bye

Runs not off the bat. The ball might strike a batsman's pads or miss everything. *Neither are popular with bowlers.*

## LAW 24 Substitute Fielders

If a fielder is injured or ill, replacements might be allowed but might have limited involvement in the match. A recent concession allows replacements for players who were concussed while batting to take a much fuller part. *If you leave the field, don't come back on without telling the umpires.*

## LAW 25  Batsman's Innings

If a batsman is injured while batting, a previously dismissed batsman can run instead, wearing all the protective gear. *Hilarious when the original batsman forgets they are injured and runs anyway.*

## LAW 26  Practice on the field

No practice on the pitch but you can practice on the outfield. You can have a trial run-up during the match, but you can't obviously waste time. *There are consequences.*

## Law 27  The Wicketkeeper

The player most in the line of fire, they can protect themselves with appropriate pads and gloves. *But they mustn't get in the way of the batsman.*

## LAW 28  The Fielder

No over-clothing protective gear allowed. Can only use parts of their body to stop the ball. If the ball strikes a fielding helmet, penalty runs will result. *You can't have too many fielders behind square on the leg side any longer – see 'Bodyline'.*

## LAW 29  The Wicket is Down

The wicket is broken when one bail is disturbed by the ball, the batsman or any part thereof. If the wicket is already broken and needs to be broken again, the fielder pulls a stump out of the ground as a replacement action. *It's very messy when that happens.*

### LAW 30 The Batsman is Out of Their Ground

With the ball 'live', batsmen need something grounded behind the popping crease. If both batsmen are out of their ground and a wicket is broken, the batsmen nearest to the wicket is dismissed. *Learn how to stretch and keep one foot firmly anchored behind the line.*

### LAW 31 Appeals

If a bowler wants a decision in their favour, they appeal in a timely fashion. *Usually delivered in the form of 'how's that?' but in reality, it's a licence to legitimately scream at the umpire.*

### LAW 32 Bowled

If the ball hits the wicket, you're out and the bowler is credited. *Unequivocal.*

### LAW 33 Caught

When the ball travels from the bat safely to the hands of a fielder without bouncing, you're out and the bowler is credited. *Annoying.*

### LAW 34 Hit the Ball Twice

If you hit the ball twice before it gets to a fielder, you're a goner. You might get away with it if you were defending your wicket. No bowler credit. *Careless, but rare.*

### LAW 35 Hit Wicket

If the batsman breaks the wicket, it's goodbye. *Has been known to happen accidentally on purpose against particularly hostile bowlers.*

### LAW 36 Leg Before Wicket

If the ball hits the batsman (not their bat) on its way to hit the wicket, the batsman is out. They may escape depending on where the ball has pitched or if there is a genuine attempt to play the ball. *In club cricket, the biggest cause of bad language and bat throwing.*

### LAW 37 Obstructing the Field

If the batsman interferes with the fielders, they might be out. No bowler credit for this one. *Unusual.*

### LAW 38 Run Out

If, in going for a run, either batsman is out of their ground when the wicket is broken. No bowler credit. *Has rich comedic potential.*

### LAW 39 Stumped

If the facing batsman is out of their ground and the wicketkeeper removes the bails, the batsman goes. Credit for the bowler. *The ultimate mark of wicketkeeping dexterity.*

### LAW 40 Timed Out

Incoming batsmen can't take more than three minutes to get to the crease. *Otherwise, they might be asked to go back whence they came.*

### LAW 41 Unfair Play

The longest rule, demonstrating the importance of the Spirit of Cricket. No altering the ball's condition, no interfering with opponents, no trying to murder batsmen with dangerous bowling. No wasting time, no damaging anything, no non-striking batsmen attempting to steal runs. *Lots to remember, but lots of five-run penalties to remind you if you forget.*

### LAW 42 Players' Conduct

Best Sunday school behaviour and stay on the right side of the umpires. *Simple. Don't forget it.*

# REFERENCES

## INTRODUCTION

1 Philip Derriman, 'Tennis bucks trend but cricket must swing blokey bias', www.smh.com.au, 26 January 2008.
2 'The 50 most confusing things in the world', www.telegraph.co.uk, 7 October 2008.
3 David Lamming, 'Organised loafing', www.thetimes.co.uk, 2 May 2015; My Shout, 'Final true blue test for the fair dinkum', *Canberra Times*, 9 November 2005, p. 2.
4 Bill Bryson, *Down Under: Travels in a Sunburned Country* (London, 2016), pp. 155–6.
5 Paul Edwards, 'Essex sneak through; Northants, Lancashire in quarters after rain', www.espncricinfo.com, 24 July 2015.
6 'Kumar Sangakkara's 2011 MCC "Spirit of Cricket" Cowdrey Lecture in full', www.telegraph.co.uk, 5 July 2011.
7 Vic Marks, 'The climax to the county season is turning out to be a gripping affair', www.theguardian.com, 3 September 2011.
8 'Cricket was meant to be a game, not a life or death struggle', www.espncricinfo.com, 7 June 2016.
9 Lawrence Booth, *Cricket, Lovely Cricket?: An Addict's Guide to the World's Most Exasperating Game* (London, 2009), p. 119.

## 1 LUMPY, MYNN AND SILVER BILLY
### *Until the Mid-nineteenth Century*

1 P.C.C. Labouchere, T.A.J. Provis and P. S. Hargreaves, 'How it Started', in *All in a Day's Cricket*, ed. Brian Levison (London, 2012), pp. 8–9.
2 'A brief history of cricket', www.espncricinfo.com, 6 March 2006.
3 Satadru Sen, *Migrant Races: Empire, Identity and K. S. Ranjitsinhji* (Manchester, 2004), p. 38.
4 John Lichfield, 'French hamlet claims to be site of the first recorded cricket match', www.independent.co.uk, 30 August 2015.
5 'Even Chaucer had a word for it', www.telegraph.co.uk, 5 September 2003; Simon Hughes, *And God Created Cricket* (London, 2010), p. 11.
6 Hughes, *And God Created Cricket*, p. 13.
7 E.D.R. Eagar, 'Origins', in *Barclays World of Cricket*, ed. E. W. Swanton (London, 1980), p. 2.

8  Ibid.

9  Tim Rice, 'Letters: The silencing of Meirion Thomas; finding the Cross of St George in Tuscany; and healthy scepticism about NHS privatisation', www.spectator.co.uk, 10 January 2015.

10  Michael Henderson, 'Cricket has long been besmirched by cheats and rogues', www.telegraph.co.uk, 16 May 2014.

11  Hambledon Parish Council, 'Cricket History', www.hambledon-pc.gov. uk, n.d., accessed 10 January 2019.

12  Rob Light, 'Cricket in the Eighteenth Century', in *The Cambridge Companion to Cricket*, ed. Anthony Bateman and Jeffrey Hill (Cambridge, 2011), p. 34.

13  Michael Simkins, 'The village green is cricket's soul', www.telegraph. co.uk, 12 August 2011.

14  Martin Williamson, 'The cradle of cricket', www.espncricinfo.com, 13 October 2007.

15  Roger Protz, *The Beer Lover's Guide to Cricket* (St Albans, 2007), p. 6.

16  Steven Lynch, 'It began in Guildford?', www.espncricinfo.com, 6 September 2013.

17  'When cricket became a sport for both men and women', www. telegraph.co.uk, 26 July 2016.

18  Lynch, 'It began in Guildford?'.

19  Martin Williamson, 'John Nyren', www.espncricinfo.com, 6 September 2013.

20  Williamson, 'The cradle of cricket'.

21  Hambledon Cricket Club, 'Newsletter 20', www.thehambledonclub. co.uk, 5 October 2013.

22  Williamson, 'The cradle of cricket'.

23  Eagar, 'Origins', p. 5.

24  Arunabha Sengupta, '"Lumpy" Stevens: A supreme bowler and one of cricket's most durable nicknames', www.cricketcountry.com, 7 September 2016.

25  Thomas Penn, 'Cricket and History', in *The Authors XI: A Season of English Cricket from Hackney to Hambledon*, ed. Various (London, 2013), p. 145.

26  Ibid., pp. 144–5.

27  Sengupta, '"Lumpy" Stevens'.

28  Ibid.

29  John Nyren with Charles Cowden Clarke, 'Progress of Cricket', in *All in a Day's Cricket*, ed. Levison, pp. 78–9.

30  Jon Hotten, *The Meaning of Cricket* (London, 2016), p. 48.

31  Charles Condon Clarke, 'Young Cricketer's Tutor', in *The Gentleman's Magazine, and Historical Chronicle, for the Year 1833* (London, 1833), ed. Edward Cave and John Nichols, p. 44.

32  Rob Steen, *Floodlights and Touchlines: A History of Spectator Sport* (London, 2016), p. 118.

33  Andy Bull, 'Fixing games is nothing new – cricket lost its innocence years ago', www.theguardian.com, 8 November 2011.

34  Hotten, *The Meaning of Cricket*, p. 54.

35 'Billy Beldham', www.espncricinfo.com, accessed 10 December 2020.

36 'Graham Thorpe back home to open tribute to another England cricketer', www.haslemereherald.com, 6 July 2016.

37 'An invincible arrives', www.espncricinfo.com, n.d., accessed 18 July 2018.

38 A. A. Thomson, 'Lord's and the Early Champions, 1787–1865', in *Barclays World of Cricket*, ed. Swanton, p. 10.

39 Jon Henderson, *Best of British: Hendo's Sporting Heroes* (London, 2007), p. 17.

40 Samuel Reynolds Hole, 'The Memories of Dean Hole', in *All in a Day's Cricket*, ed. Levison, pp. 236.

41 Jon Hotten, 'The life of Alfred Mynn, cricket's first colossus and a master of single-wicket', www.guardian.com, 8 August 2016.

42 Abhishek Mukherjee, 'Alfred Mynn scores 125 on one leg: Pads come into vogue', www.cricketcountry.com, 24 August 2016.

43 Debashish Biswas, 'Mynn's majestic innings – and the birth of leg-guards', www.espncricinfo.com, 18 December 2004.

44 Arunabha Sengupta, 'Match-fixing before IPL: Alfred Mynn's misdemeanours in 1840s and 1850s', www.cricketcountry.com, 7 June 2013.

45 Simon Raven, 'Alfred the Great', http://archive.spectator.co.uk, 1 November 1963.

## 2 THE 'GOLDEN AGE', GRACE AND TRUMPER
### *The Turn of the Twentieth Century*

1 Ronald Mason, 'W. G. Grace and His Times, 1865–1899', in *Barclays World of Cricket*, ed. E. W. Swanton (London, 1980), p. 13.

2 Nabil Hassan, 'W. G. Grace: 100 years since death of England's cricketing icon', www.bbc.co.uk, 23 October 2015.

3 Jarrod Kimber, 'Cricket's greatest bastard', www.thecricketmonthly.com, April 2016.

4 Ibid.

5 Mason, 'W. G. Grace and His Times, 1865–1899', p. 12.

6 Ibid., p. 14.

7 David Frith, 'The greatest ever sports beard', www.theatlantic.com, 14 October 2010.

8 Donald Trelford, *W. G. Grace* (Stroud, 1998), p. 60.

9 Martin Williamson, 'Lord Harris', www.espncricinfo.com, n.d., accessed 25 August 2018.

10 Donald Trelford, 'More than one amazing Grace', www.espncricinfo.com, 21 July 1998.

11 R. C. Robertson-Glasgow, 'W. G.'s bad-tempered brother', www.espncricinfo.com, May 1962.

12 Ibid.

13 Abhishek Mukherjee, 'The death of 29-year-old Fred Grace', www.cricketcountry.com, 22 September 2016.

14 Peter Wilby, 'Amazing Grace: The Man Who Was WG by Richard Tomlinson – review', www.theguardian.com, 21 August 2015.

15  Ibid.
16  David Frith, 'Amazing Grace', www.espncricinfo.com, 2 August 2010.
17  Ibid.
18  Ibid.
19  Kimber, 'Cricket's greatest bastard'; Frith, 'Amazing Grace'.
20  Denzil Batchelor, *The Book of Cricket* (London, 1952), p. 8.
21  Trelford, *W. G. Grace*, p. 7.
22  Ibid., p. 66.
23  Ibid., pp. 65–6.
24  Sam Kitchener, 'Extraordinary life of the grand old man of English cricket; Amazing Grace by Richard Tomlinson; book review', www.independent.co.uk, 7 October 2015.
25  Frith, 'The greatest ever sports beard'.
26  Kimber, 'Cricket's greatest bastard'.
27  Wisden, 'Victor Trumper', www.espncricinfo.com, 1916.
28  Lionel Brown, *Victor Trumper and the 1902 Australians* (London, 1981), p. 7.
29  Richard H. Thomas, 'Gamechangers: Ancient and modern', www.wisden.com, 28 November 2017.
30  Sir Tim Rice, 'A Trumper of a story', www.telegraph.co.uk, 13 May 2002.
31  David Frith, 'Foreword', in Brown, *Victor Trumper and the 1902 Australians*, p. vii.
32  Harold Larwood, 'The Archie Jackson story', www.espncricinfo.com, 1983.
33  Gideon Haigh, *Game for Anything: Writings on Cricket* (Melbourne, 2004), p. 10.
34  Carl Bridge, 'Victor Trumper: The greatest batsman of the Golden Age – Almanack', www.wisden.com, 28 June 2019; Thomas, 'Gamechangers: Ancient and modern'.
35  Batchelor, *The Book of Cricket*, p. 42.
36  Gideon Haigh, 'Trumper, in light and shade', www.espncricinfo.com, 1 September 2016.
37  Batchelor, *The Book of Cricket*, p. 42.
38  Thomas, 'Gamechangers: Ancient and modern'.
39  Steven Lynch, 'Sydney's forgotten hero', www.espncricinfo.com, 2 December 2012; Steven Lynch, ed., *Wisden on the Ashes* (London, 2015), p. 99.
40  'Introduction', www.victortrumper.com, n.d., accessed 20 September 2018.
41  Thomas, 'Gamechangers: Ancient and modern'.
42  Batchelor, *The Book of Cricket*, p. 42.

## 3 MORE GOLDEN AGE CHAMPIONS
### *Victorians and Edwardians*

1  Jonathan Rice and Andrew Renshaw, *The Wisden Collector's Guide* (London, 2011), p. 111.
2  Denzil Batchelor, *The Book of Cricket* (London, 1952), p. 8.
3  James Lawton, 'The Twilight of the Gods', *The Independent*, 12 January 2002, p. 7.

4 Ibid.
5 Wisden, 'The definitive captain's innings', 1896.
6 Lawton, 'The Twilight of the Gods'.
7 Arunabha Sengupta, 'Andrew Stoddart: The first captain to declare an innings in Test cricket', www.cricketcountry.com, 24 February 2017.
8 Jeremy Malies, 'Mighty man of parts', www.espncricinfo.com, March 2004.
9 Jonty Winch, 'The tragic tales of Monty Bowden', http://rhodesianheritage.blogspot.com, 18 March 2014.
10 Martin Williamson, 'The ignorant internationals', www.espncricinfo.com, 28 November 2009.
11 Malies, 'Mighty man of parts'.
12 Steven Lynch, 'The cricketer who died on the *Titanic*', www.espncricinfo.com, 28 February 2005.
13 Martin Williamson, 'An Englishman abroad', www.espncricinfo.com, 27 September 2014.
14 'Caught Niven, bowled Flynn', www.espncricinfo.com, July 2001.
15 Malies, 'Mighty man of parts'.
16 Jack Young, 'From the nursery end', www.espncricinfo.com, June 1963.
17 Ibid.
18 Malies, 'Mighty man of parts'.
19 Scyld Berry, *Cricket: The Game of Life* (London, 2015), p. 135.
20 Ibid.
21 Batchelor, *The Book of Cricket*, pp. 28–9.
22 Martin Williamson, 'Ranji and racism', www.espncricinfo.com, 20 October 2007.
23 Ibid.
24 Ibid.
25 Rahul Bhattacharya, 'The light of the East', www.espn.co.uk, 6 February 2010.
26 A. S. Balakrishnan, 'The Wizard of the willow', www.espncricinfo.com, 29 October 1999.
27 Berry, *Cricket: The Game of Life*, p. 135.
28 Simon Barnes, 'Time Lords of the ring symbolised their era', www.thetimes.co.uk, 20 May 2011.
29 Denzil Batchelor, 'C. B. Fry', in *Great Cricketers*, ed. Denzil Batchelor (London, 1970), p. 35.
30 Marina Hyde, 'On your marks, sex, go . . . for the glamour Games', www.theguardian.com, 11 January 2012.
31 Batchelor, *The Book of Cricket*, pp. 28–9.
32 Batchelor, ed., 'C. B. Fry', *Great Cricketers*, p. 37.
33 Arunabha Sengupta, 'C. B. Fry: A life worth living', www.cricketcountry.com, 19 April 2016.
34 Ibid.
35 Batchelor, ed., 'C. B. Fry', *Great Cricketers*, p. 37.
36 Partha Bhaduri, 'Marriage helps Indian cricketers prosper', https://timesofindia.com, 17 July 2010.

37  David Robson, 'New light shed on C. B. Fry: A brilliant cricketer, a memorable character', www.espncricinfo.com, 20 September 1999.
38  Ibid.
39  Sengupta, 'C. B. Fry: A life worth living'.
40  Robson, 'New light shed on C. B. Fry'.
41  Simon Barnes and Alex Ralph, 'Quest for gold all about global suffering', *The Times*, 23 March 2012, pp. 54–5.
42  *Big Red Book*, 'C. B. Fry (1872–1956)', www.bigredbook.info.
43  Sengupta, 'C. B. Fry: A life worth living'.
44  Neville Cardus, 'Wilfred Rhodes – Yorkshire personified', www.espncricinfo.com, 1974.
45  Batchelor, *The Book of Cricket*, p. 40.
46  Frank Keating, 'Harold Larwood: Jardine told me to stand at short cover-point and just stare at Bradman', www.theguardian.com, 21 May 2014.
47  David Hopps, *Great Cricket Quotes* (London, 2006), p. 125.
48  Henry Cowen, 'The Ten: Irresistible comebacks', www.wisden.com, 17 January 2014.
49  Ibid.
50  Les Scott, *Bats, Balls and Bails: The Essential Cricket Book* (London, 2011).
51  George Plumptre, *The Golden Age of Cricket* (London, 1990), p. 8.
52  Ibid., p. 9.
53  Ibid., p. 11.
54  Anthony Bateman, *Cricket, Literature and Culture: Symbolising the Nation, Destabilising Empire* (Farnham, 2013), p. 115.

## 4 GENTLEMEN, PLAYERS, VARSITY AND ROSES
### Background Developments

1  Mike Savage, *Social Class in the 21st Century* (London, 2015).
2  Graham Ford, 'From the archive, 27 November 1962: Cricket ends distinction between Gents and Players', www.theguardian.com, 27 November 2012.
3  Michael Marshall, *Gentlemen and Players* (London, 1987), p. xx.
4  Ibid., p. 260.
5  Charles Williams, *Gentlemen and Players: The Death of Amateurism in Cricket* (London, 2013).
6  Michael Melford, 'University Match', in *Barclays World of Cricket*, ed. E. W. Swanton (London, 1980), p. 444.
7  Ibid.
8  John Ashdown, 'University games remain a valuable part of English cricket's heritage', www.theguardian.com, 28 March 2012.
9  Kevin Mitchell, 'Same as it ever was', www.theguardian.com, 14 April 2002.
10  Steve James, 'Nothing first class about a university match', *The Telegraph*, 17 April 2012, Sport, p. 20.
11  Michael Henderson, 'Enduring occasion honours game's debt to universities', www.thetimes.co.uk, 18 June 2012.
12  Ashdown, 'University games remain a valuable part of English cricket's heritage'.

13 Neil Squires, 'Cricket: What does this once great match tell us about the state of our cricket?', *The Express*, 9 August 2001, p. 72.

14 Jeanette Winterson, 'The War of the Roses revisited', www.countrylife. co.uk, 18 October 2014.

15 Ibid.

16 Editorial, 'Cricket and corruption: a sport that needs fixing', www. theguardian.com, 30 August 2010.

17 Graham Hardcastle, 'Ashwell Prince riled Yorkshire players says Adam Lyth', www.manchestereveningnews.co.uk, 20 November 2014.

18 Ibid.

19 Michael Parkinson, *Parky – My Autobiography: A Full and Funny Life* (London, 2009).

20 Neville Cardus, 'Beside the Roses the Ashes paled into insignificance', www.espncricinfo.com, 1968.

21 Rob Bagchi, 'Sachin Tendulkar's Yorkshire roots helped make him a master of modesty', www.theguardian.com, 29 June 2011.

22 Max Davidson, *We'll Get 'Em in Sequins: Manliness, Yorkshire Cricket and the Century that Changed Everything* (London, 2012), p. 186.

23 Geoffrey Boycott, 'History demands that I steer Yorkshire to the County Championship', www.telegraph.co.uk, 26 March 2012.

24 Bagchi, 'Sachin Tendulkar's Yorkshire roots helped make him a master of modesty'.

25 Ali Martin, 'Adil Rashid: "If I don't get a Test deal, I need to decide what to do next"', www.theguardian.com, 17 September 2019.

26 Fred Trueman, *As It Was: The Memoirs* (London, 2005), p. 253.

27 Tom Collomosse, 'The Ashes: Dopey cameo from David Warner inspires Roses rivalry truce', www.independent.co.uk, 2 August 2013.

28 Squires, 'Cricket: What does this once great match tell us about the state of our cricket?'.

## 5 THE GREATEST RIVALRY
### *Even Bigger Background Developments*

1 Denzil Batchelor, *The Book of Cricket* (London, 1952), p. 10.

2 Gideon Haigh, 'What do we know about the first Test cricketer?', www. espncricinfo.com, 7 August 2016.

3 Alfred Shaw, 'Alfred Shaw, Cricketer: His Career and Reminisces', in *All In a Day's Cricket*, ed. Brian Levison (London, 2012), p. 177.

4 Steven Lynch, ed., *Wisden on the Ashes* (London, 2015), p. 6.

5 Sport Australia Hall of Fame, 'Frederick Spofforth – Cricket', 2012, www.sahof.org.au.

6 Simon Burnton, '20 great Ashes moments No. 18: Ashes born as Spofforth slays England, 1882', www.theguardian.com, 27 June 2013.

7 Andrew Miller, 'Scattered stumps and hexed batsmen', www. espncricinfo.com, 29 July 2019.

8 'The birth of the Ashes', www.telegraph.co.uk, 17 July 2005.

9 Ibid.

10  Simon Hughes, *Cricket's Greatest Rivalry: Completely Revised and Updated for 2019* (London, 2019).

11  Batchelor, *The Book of Cricket*, p. 25.

12  Observer Sport Monthly, 'The 10 greatest bounders in the history of cricket', www.theguardian.com, 4 August 2002.

13  Jeffrey Hill and Anthony Bateman, 'Introduction', in *The Cambridge Companion to Cricket*, ed. Anthony Bateman and Jeffrey Hill (Cambridge, 2011), p. 34; Gideon Haigh, 'The majestic MacLaren that wasn't', www.espncricinfo.com, 18 July 2016.

14  Benny Green, *The Lord's Companion* (London, 1987), p. 144.

15  Haigh, 'The majestic MacLaren that wasn't'.

16  Jo Harman, *Cricketing Allsorts: The Good, the Bad, the Ugly (and the Downright Weird)* (London, 2017), p. 260.

17  Martin Williamson, 'England's one-off Test ground', www.espncricinfo.com, 18 June 2011.

18  Arunabha Sengupta, 'Bill Lockwood: Tormented genius, one of England's finest fast bowlers', www.cricketcountry.com, 23 March 2016.

19  Ibid.

20  Simon Burnton, '20 great Ashes moments No11: Last-gasp drama at Old Trafford, 1902', www.theguardian.com, 3 June 2013.

21  David Frith, *England v Australia: The Pictorial History of Test Matches since 1877* (London, 1984), p. 79.

22  Frank Keating, 'One-cap flops for whom the son shines', *The Guardian*, 5 June 1997, p. 28.

23  Burnton, '20 great Ashes moments No11: Last-gasp drama at Old Trafford, 1902'.

24  Frank Keating, 'Cricket (The Keating Column): Keeping up a family tradition', *The Guardian*, 16 February 1990.

25  A. A. Thomson, *Hirst and Rhodes* (London, 1960), p. 17.

26  Ibid., p. 54.

27  Almanack Archive, 'George Hirst: A legend of the Golden Age', www.wisden.com, 10 May 2019.

28  Thomson, *Hirst and Rhodes*, p. 191.

29  Gerald Brodribb, 'The legend of Gilbert Jessop', www.espncricinfo.com, May 1974.

30  Lionel Brown, *Victor Trumper and the 1902 Australians* (London, 1981), p. 156.

31  Martin Williamson, 'Crash, bang, wallop', www.espncricinfo.com, 16 December 2006.

32  Arunabha Sengupta, 'Ashes 1902: The Jessop Miracle', http://cricmash.com, 4 August 2019.

33  Thomson, *Hirst and Rhodes*, p. 198.

34  Steven Lynch, ed., *Wisden on the Ashes* (London, 2015), p. 102.

35  Batchelor, *The Book of Cricket*, p. 25.

36  Frank Keating, 'Ginny won in silver year. Now it's the golden one . . .', www.theguardian.com, 24 June 2002.

37  Ibid.

38  Batchelor, *The Book of Cricket*, p. 45.
39  Wisden, 'Arthur Jones', www.espncricinfo.com, accessed 10 December 2020.
40  Ibid.
41  Batchelor, *The Book of Cricket*, p. 45.
42  Wisden, 'Australia v England 1907–08', www.espncricinfo.com, 1909.
43  Bill Frindall, *England Test Cricketers* (London, 1989), p. 182.
44  Batchelor, *The Book of Cricket*, p. 49.
45  Wisden, 'Obituaries in 1937', www.espncricinfo.com, 1938.
46  Wisden, 'England v Australia 1909', www.espncricinfo.com, 2001.
47  Ibid.
48  Jack Pollard, *Australian Cricket: The Games and the Players* (North Ryde, 1988), p. 81.
49  Lynch, ed., *Wisden on the Ashes*, p. 133.
50  Arunabha Sengupta, 'Ashes 1909: Warwick Armstrong keeps debutant Frank Woolley waiting by bowling trial balls for 19 minutes!', www. cricketcountry.com, 13 August 2016.
51  Ibid.

## 6 GOOD FOR NOTHING AND NOBODY
### *The First World War*

 1  Denzil Batchelor, *The Book of Cricket* (London, 1952), p. 56.
 2  Graham Holborn, 'Aubrey Faulkner: Professional success hid personal tragedy', www.espncricinfo.com, 25 July 2001.
 3  Batchelor, *The Book of Cricket*, p. 56.
 4  Ian Peebles, *Spinner's Yarn* (Newton Abbot, 1978), p. 26.
 5  Holborn, 'Aubrey Faulkner: Professional success hid personal tragedy'.
 6  Peebles, *Spinner's Yarn*, p. 31.
 7  Ibid., p. 38.
 8  David Hopps, *Great Cricket Quotes* (London, 2006), p. 81.
 9  Vithushan Ehantharajah and Russell Jackson, 'Australia v New Zealand: day four of the first Test – as it happened', www.theguardian.com, 8 November 2015.
10  Batchelor, *The Book of Cricket*, p. 59.
11  Hopps, *Great Cricket Quotes*, p. 81.
12  Batchelor, *The Book of Cricket*, p. 58.
13  Ibid.
14  Suresh Menon, 'Portraits of Heroes', www.espncricinfo.com, 20 September 2009.
15  John Arlott, 'The Master', in *Arlott on Cricket*, ed. David Rayvern Allen (London, 1985), pp. 31, 32.
16  Bill Ricquier, 'Spin, Bounce and the Old Swingometer', https:// billpavilionend.com, 29 April 2017.
17  International Cricket Council, 'Top-ranked Anderson breaches coveted 900-point mark', www.icc-cricket.com, 13 August 2018.
18  John Arlott, 'Sydney Barnes: Cricket's living legend', www.espncricinfo. com, June 1963.

19  Ibid.
20  John Arlott, 'Sydney Barnes', in *Arlott on Cricket*, ed. Allen, p. 15.
21  Arlott, 'Sydney Barnes: Cricket's living legend'.
22  Batchelor, *The Book of Cricket*, p. 39.
23  Robert Winder, *The Little Wonder* (London, 2014), p. 133.
24  Hazel Carby, *Race Men* (Cambridge, MA, 2009), p. 117.
25  Rob Steen, 'Fiery Syd', www.espncricinfo.com, 18 December 2013.
26  Ibid.
27  Winder, *The Little Wonder*, p. 129.
28  David Frith, 'Was Barnes the greatest bowler of all time?', www.
    espncricinfo.com, n.d., accessed 20 September 2018.
29  Ibid.
30  Abhishek Mukherjee, 'Ted Alletson 189 in 90 minutes: Greatest
    onslaught by a tailender?', www.cricketcountry.com, 20 May 2016.
31  Andy Bull, 'Joy of six: Greatest tail-end innings', www.theguardian.com,
    28 March 2008.
32  Wisden Cricinfo Staff, 'Hove holocaust', www.espncricinfo.com,
    1 January 1984.
33  Wordsworth Reference, *Dictionary of Pub Names* (Ware, 2006), p. 199;
    Martin Williamson, 'Geoff Boycott's Indian bore', www.espncricinfo.
    com, 22 September 2012.
34  Martin Williamson, 'Duty calls', www.espncricinfo.com, 4 August 2014.
35  Andrew Renshaw, *Wisden on the Great War: The Lives of Cricket's Fallen,
    1914–1918* (London, 2014), p. 51.
36  Katie Smith, 'The Story of Major Booth', www.ww1playingthegame.org.uk,
    27 June 2016.
37  Mike Atherton, 'Pals for ever linked by horror of the Somme', *The
    Times*, 1 May 2014, p. 66.
38  Smith, 'The Story of Major Booth'.
39  A. A. Thomson, *Cricketers of My Times* (London, 1967), p. 202.
40  Scyld Berry, 'Why England v South Africa at Headingley is a fixture
    with a famous pedigree', www.telegraph.co.uk, 1 August 2002.
41  Ibid.
42  Ibid.
43  Neville Cardus, *Good Days* (London, 1937), p. 51.
44  Ibid.
45  Martin Williamson, 'A Canterbury tale', www.espncricinfo.com,
    9 December 2005.
46  Arunabha Sengupta, 'Story of a cricket painting: *Kent vs Lancashire
    at Canterbury 1906*', www.cricketcountry.com, 4 May 2016; Williamson,
    'A Canterbury tale'.
47  Winder, *The Little Wonder*, p. 117.
48  Cardus, *Good Days*, pp. 54–5.
49  Ibid.
50  Winder, *The Little Wonder*, p. 117.
51  Nigel McCrery, *Final Wicket: Test and First Class Cricketers Killed in the
    Great War* (Barnsley, 2015), p. 326.

52  Liam Coventry-Poole, 'Cricket and the Anzac Spirit', www.auscricket.
    com.au, 24 April 2014.
53  Nikita Bastian, 'wwi death of Australian Test hero Cotter revealed',
    www.espncricinfo.com, 26 April 2012.
54  Samanth Subramanian, 'Percy Jeeves', www.espncricinfo.com, n.d.,
    accessed 18 June 2019.

## 7 GOVERNANCE, GROUNDS, GRANDEES, BOOKS AND BENEFACTORS
### *Three Hundred Years of Organization and Altruism*

1  E.D.R. Eagar, 'Early Days in Kent', in *Barclays World of Cricket*, ed.
   E. W. Swanton (London, 1980), p. 3.
2  Marylebone Cricket Club, 'The law of cricket 2017 code (2nd edition –
   2019)', www.lords.org, n.d., accessed 10 July 2019.
3  James Elwes, 'It is the law of cricket, not rules', *Financial Times*,
   14 September 2010, p. 12; David Fraser, *Cricket and the Law: The Man
   in White is Always Right* (New York, 2005), p. 30.
4  Richard Williams, 'We know what the mcc does, but we can't
   understand why', *The Guardian*, 10 October 2006, p. 7.
5  Ivo Tennant, 'Benches are a sore point for mcc ', *The Times*, 22 April 2016, p. 5.
6  Williams, 'We know what the mcc does, but we can't understand why'.
7  The debate about gender is covered in more detail later; Marylebone
   Cricket Club, 'How to Join', www.lords.org, n.d., accessed 10 July 2019.
8  Richard Thomas, 'The Ashes: Jofra Archer, Steve Smith and
   cricket's dilemma of balancing safety with media spectacle', https://
   theconversation.com, 21 August 2019.
9  'Fake Lord's cricket card: James Lattimer fined £10k', www.bbc.co.uk,
   11 March 2020.
10  Christopher Hope, 'Theresa May jumps 26-year waiting list as mcc
    membership fast-tracked', www.telegraph.co.uk, 24 May 2018.
11  Jonathan Liew, 'My dear old ding! Lord's is a leaping; The Saturday of
    the Test at Lord's has an atmosphere of its own, an experience to savour,
    not to guzzle', *Sunday Telegraph*, 9 July 2017, p. 11.
12  Scyld Berry, 'Plenty of fizz and pop on display at Lord's - and that's just
    the fans', www.telegraph.co.uk, 16 July 2016.
13  Sandy Balfour, *What I Love about Cricket* (London, 2010), p. 150.
14  Ibid.
15  Marylebone Cricket Club, 'The History of Lord's', www.lords.org, n.d.,
    accessed 10 July 2019.
16  Stephen Green, *Lord's: The Cathedral of Cricket* (Stroud, 2003), p. 85.
17  Ibid., p. 88.
18  Mike Atherton, 'Swing King James Anderson hits right notes to join
    the England chart toppers', www.thetimes.co.uk, 18 May 2013.
19  Wisden, 'Obituaries index: A-E', www.espncricinfo.com, 2006.
20  Simon Briggs, 'McGrath's long run drives him to distraction', www.
    telegraph.co.uk, 14 July 2005.

21  Mike Selvey, 'Vaughan orders fungus on the side', www.theguardian. com, 19 June 2004.

22  David Hopps, 'An alternative five', www.espncricinfo.com, 1995.

23  Ibid.

24  David Lacey, 'Is there a new Hurst or Platt out there?', www. theguardian.com, 13th April 2002.

25  Qamar Ahmed, 'Gavaskar rejects MCC life membership', *The Times*, 30 July 1990.

26  Tennant, 'Benches are a sore point for MCC'.

27  Ibid.

28  Marylebone Cricket Club, 'The Masterplan', www.lords.org, n.d., accessed 15 March 2020; Hayley Dixon, 'Three former England captains wade into row over future of Lord's', www.telegraph.co.uk, 4 September 2017.

29  'Australia have won the Ashes, now they want to knock down Lord's and rebuild it in the mould of the MCG', www.dailymail.co.uk, 28 December 2017.

30  Ibid.

31  Bill Frindall, *England Test Cricketers* (London, 1989), p. 194.

32  Michael Henderson, 'Enduring occasion honours game's debt to universities', *The Times*, 18 June 2012, pp. 54–5.

33  Mark Hodgkinson, 'The top 10 hapless officials', *Sunday Times*, 15 December 2002, Sport, p. 14.

34  Graham Stewart, 'For thirty minutes or more I was surrounded by a howling mob', *The Times*, 8 August 2009, p. 89.

35  Simon Barnes, 'Aussie cricketers have always been world class cheats (and whingers!)', www.dailymail.co.uk, 25 March 2018.

36  Dean Nelson, 'House of the peer who gave cricket to India "left to crumble by authorities"', *Daily Telegraph*, 10 September 2014, p. 16.

37  R. L. Arrowsmith, 'Harris, 4 Lord (George Robert Canning)', in *Barclays World of Cricket*, ed. E. W. Swanton (London, 1980), p. 3.

38  Wisden, 'Plum Warner', www.espncricinfo.com, 1964.

39  Ivo Tennant, 'Woodcock at 90', www.espncricinfo.com, 6 August 2016.

40  Wisden, 'Plum Warner'.

41  Denzil Batchelor, *The Book of Cricket* (London, 1952), p. 33.

42  John Arlott, 'Sir Gubby Allen', www.espncricinfo.com, 1989.

43  Ibid.

44  Batchelor, *The Book of Cricket*, p. 118.

45  E. W. Swanton, 'Wisdom from beyond the boundary', www. espncricinfo.com, 13 January 1997.

46  Simon Hughes, *And God Created Cricket* (London, 2010), p. 102.

47  Arunabha Sengupta, 'Gubby Allen's horror at the Oval Test of 1968 and the beginning of cricket sponsorship in England', www.cricketcountry. com, 18 May 2015.

48  Arunabha Sengupta, '18 father-son pairs who have appeared in the same match', www.cricketcountry.com, 19 November 2015.

49  Martin Williamson, 'You've been asking for a punch all night', www. espncricinfo.com, 26 August 2005.

50  Ibid.
51  Ibid.
52  Robert Winder, *The Little Wonder* (London, 2014), p. 1.
53  Ibid.
54  Emma John, 'Nothing dusty about Wisden – the cricket tome with a radical edge', www.theguardian.com, 16 April 2016.
55  Winder, *The Little Wonder*, p. 81.
56  'Sydney Pardon', www.espncricinfo.com, 1926.
57  Lawrence Booth, ed., *Wisden Cricketers' Almanack* (London, 2015), p. 708.
58  Simon Briggs, 'Wisden's return to monthly action is welcome; Final whistle Cricket's famous marque is back to fight for readers in a glossy battle waged against an old foe', *Daily Telegraph*, 7 October 2017, p. 24.
59  Alison Flood and Sian Cain, 'Beatrix Potter-pinching and Zizekian swipes: the strange world of book thefts; Booksellers explain some of the reasons why certain titles won't stay on the shelves, and remember some of their most eccentric thieves', www.theguardian.com, 24 July 2017.
60  Mike Atherton, 'Wisden echoes old warning but the moment has passed', *The Times*, 10 April 2014, p. 67.
61  John, 'Nothing dusty about Wisden – the cricket tome with a radical edge'.
62  Ibid.
63  John Mehaffey, 'Wisden Almanack endures as conscience of the game', https://uk.reuters.com, 10 April 2010.
64  Simon Briggs, 'Just watch – the T20 revolution has only just begun; Final whistle Soon, the beefiest batsmen will be on a yearround carousel of short-form cricket', *Daily Telegraph*, 11 February 2017, p. 24.
65  Winder, *The Little Wonder*, p. 300.
66  John Willcock, 'Tycoon "almost paranoid over way empire was run"; The Maxwell Trial; Day 10', *The Independent*, 14 June 1995, p. 8.
67  William Rees-Mogg, 'A natural man, built on an unnatural scale', *The Independent*, 11 November 1991, p. 23.
68  Winder, *The Little Wonder*, p. 301.
69  John Woodcock, 'Wisden's return is friendship renewed', *The Times*, 12 April 1990, Sport.
70  Ivo Tennant, 'Wisden front cover', *The Times*, 9 May 2003, p. 47.
71  'Wisden tradition knocked for six by Getty', *Daily Telegraph*, 23 April 2003, p. 25.
72  'Sir Paul Getty', www.telegraph.co.uk, 18 April 2003.
73  Simon Rocker, 'The Yiddle in the middle', www.thejc.com, 1 April 2010.
74  Stephen Chalke, 'The unlikely philanthropist', www.espncricinfo.com, September 2005.
75  Laura Connor, 'As his 12-year-old son lay dying of cancer, billionaire Getty moaned about the hospital bills . . . he was "too busy" to attend the funeral', *Daily Mirror*, 18 January 2018, pp. 20–21.
76  Peter Sheridan, 'Jean Paul Getty: Cold-hearted tycoon who refused to buy his grandson's freedom', www.express.co.uk, 6 January 2018; Olivia

Petter, 'John Paul Getty: True story of the billionaire who refused to pay kidnappers $17m to save grandson's life', www.independent.co.uk, 4 December 2017.

77  Sheridan, 'Jean Paul Getty: Cold-hearted tycoon who refused to buy his grandson's freedom'.

78  Roya Nikkhah, 'Garsington Opera: Behind the Getty gates', www.telegraph.co.uk, 29 May 2011.

79  Graeme Wright, 'He loved cricket because it drew him out of his reclusive world', *The Independent*, 18 April 2003, p. 3.

80  Huw Turbervill, 'Getty a genuine lover of the game', www.telegraph.co.uk, 20 April 2003.

81  Wright, 'He loved cricket because it drew him out of his reclusive world'.

82  Associated Press, 'Stanford gets 110 years for role in $7B swindle', www.foxnews.com, 20 November 2014.

83  Stephen Brenkley, '"I am not going to walk away when people start shouting"; ECB chairman Giles Clarke has come under intense fire over the Stanford debacle but he is defiant in his refusal to quit', *The Independent*, 25 February 2009, p. 58.

84  Steve James, 'Ghost of Allen Stanford haunts ICC corridors of power', www.telegraph.co.uk, 3 March 2014.

85  Simon Hughes, 'Enriched by a cricket obsession', www.telegraph.co.uk, 24 April 2003.

## 8 BOXING, SOUND THRASHINGS AND THE BIG SHIP
### *The 1920s*

1  Simon John, '"A Different Kind of Test Match": Cricket, English Society and the First World War', *Sport in History*, XXXIII/1 (2013), pp. 19–48.

2  Ibid.

3  Ibid.

4  Derek Pringle, 'Whitewash for the wizards of Oz', *The Times* (South Africa), 6 January 2014, Sport.

5  Denzil Batchelor, *The Book of Cricket* (London, 1952), p. 16.

6  Graham Otway, 'The sorry tale of England's last 5–0 flops', *Daily Mail*, 2 January 2003, p. 65.

7  Bill Frindall, *England Test Cricketers* (London, 1989), p. 112.

8  Jo Harman, *Cricketing Allsorts: The Good, the Bad, the Ugly (and the Downright Weird)* (London, 2017), p. 242.

9  Batchelor, *The Book of Cricket*, p. 16.

10  David Foot, 'Johnny will hit today', www.espncricinfo.com, April 2004.

11  Otway, 'The sorry tale of England's last 5–0 flops'.

12  Ashley Mallett, 'Fergie's wagon wheel', www.espncricinfo.com, 22 December 2012.

13  Arunabha Sengupta, 'Ashes 1905: Fergie appointed a scorer and baggage master after visiting the dentist', www.cricketcountry.com, 19 February 2016.

14 Mallett, 'Fergie's wagon wheel'.

15 Ibid.

16 'When the pen is mighty as the bat', www.theguardian.com, 14 April 2009.

17 Wisden, 'Obituaries in 1957', www.espncricinfo.com, 1958.

18 Suresh Menon, '10 for 66 and All That by Arthur Mailey', in 'Which are the finest cricket books?', www.espncricinfo.com, 5 November 2012.

19 Arunabha Sengupta, 'Arthur Mailey: Australia's first celebrated leg-spinner, who was also a cartoonist, painter and writer', www.cricketcountry.com, 17 September 2015; Batchelor, *The Book of Cricket*, p. 73.

20 Jack Pollard, *Australian Cricket: The Games and the Players* (North Ryde, 1988), p. 717.

21 Peter Roebuck, 'In a freakish league of his own', www.espncricinfo.com, 14 July 2010.

22 Batchelor, *The Book of Cricket*, p. 74.

23 David Hopps, *Great Cricket Quotes* (London, 2006), p. 100.

24 Ashley Mallett, 'The literal art of cricket', www.espncricinfo.com, 3 February 2014.

25 Pollard, *Australian Cricket: The Games and the Players*, p. 716.

26 Arthur Mailey, 'Trumper: Opposing my hero', in *Best Cricket Stories*, ed. Denzil Batchelor (London, 1967), p. 171.

27 Ibid., p. 174.

28 Batchelor, *The Book of Cricket*, p. 53.

29 Gideon Haigh, 'A giant of his time', www.espncricinfo.com, 19 September 2009.

30 Ibid.

31 Ibid.

32 Pollard, *Australian Cricket: The Games and the Players*, p. 40.

33 Pradip Dhole, 'Warwick Armstrong becomes first to score 100 and 200 in same Sheffield Shield match', www.cricketcountry.com, 13 August 2016.

34 Ibid.; Pollard, *Australian Cricket: The Games and the Players*, p. 40.

35 '39. Warwick Armstrong, 1879–1947', *Weekly Times*, 12 October 2011, p. 3.

36 Ibid.

37 Simon Briggs, 'No chat, no Ashes', www.espncricinfo.com, 21 November 2006.

38 Gideon Haigh, *The Big Ship: Warwick Armstrong and the Making of Modern Cricket* (Sydney, 2012).

## 9 TOURING, TENNYSON AND ROLLO
### *Still Mainly in the 1920s*

1 Ian Wooldridge, 'Why I won't shed a tear for Godders, a star who lived for life', www.dailymail.co.uk, 5 May 1999.

2 Ibid.

3 Kerry O'Keefe, 'O'Keefe reveals how a great tradition was born', www.smh.com.au, 27 November 2004.

4 Ibid.

5 Frank Keating, 'Raking over the Ashes in search of Christmas', *The Guardian*, 24 December 1994, Sports, p. 17.

6 Mike Atherton, 'Some like it hot', *The Spectator*, 18 December 2004, p. 44.

7 Jeremy Malies, *Great Characters from Cricket's Golden Age* (London, 2000), p. 166.

8 Ibid., p. 167.

9 Sue Arnold, 'The week in Reviews: Books: "Mr Asquith, you're an interfering old bugger"', *Observer Review*, 29 March 1998, p. 16.

10 Alan Edwards, *Lionel Tennyson: Regency Buck* (London, 2001), pp. 112–13.

11 Ibid., p. 113.

12 Arunabha Sengupta, 'Hampshire beat Warwickshire after being bowled out for 15', www.cricketcountry.com, 5 November 2015.

13 John Arlott, 'The man who never encouraged bowlers', www.espncricinfo.com, n.d., accessed 17 August 2019.

14 Ibid.

15 Pat Symes, 'Hampshire cult heroes', www.espncricinfo.com, December 2005.

16 Ibid.

17 Edwards, *Lionel Tennyson: Regency Buck*, p. 120.

18 Jon Henderson, 'The 10 greatest comebacks of all time', www.theguardian.com, 7 October 2001.

19 Malies, *Great Characters from Cricket's Golden Age*, p. 175.

20 Ibid., p. 166.

21 Ibid., p. 169.

22 Ibid., p. 171.

23 Martin Williamson, 'You have disgraced the annals of Hampshire cricket', www.espncricinfo.com, 24 September 2005.

24 Ibid.

25 Frank Keating, 'Cricket hard nut with a soft side; Captain says he'll wait until the end of season', *The Guardian*, 29 July 1997, p. 21.

26 Henry Blofeld, 'Atherton adds to Headingley roll of honour', www.independent.co.uk, 10 July 1995.

27 Edwards, *Lionel Tennyson: Regency Buck*, p. 188.

28 Williamson, 'You have disgraced the annals of Hampshire cricket'.

29 John May, 'A hero on and off the field', www.dailyecho.co.uk, 23 July 2001.

30 Pradip Dhole, 'Jack "Boss" Meyer: Eccentric schoolmaster, Somerset cricketer, Ranji Trophy captain', www.cricketcountry.com, 23 August 2018.

31 Peter Roebuck, 'A cad, inspired genius and a fox with a flair for the unexpected', *Sydney Morning Herald*, 28 December 1989, p. 34.

32 Ibid.

33 Matthew Gwyther, 'Victor Chandler', *Management Today*, 10 July 2008, p. 44.

34 P. J. Lennon, 'Rollo Meyer, visionary and founder of Millfield School', http://lastwordoncricket.com, 7 September 2016.

35 Ibid.

36 Wisden, 'Jack Meyer', www.espncricinfo.com, n.d., accessed 16 October 2018.

37  Lennon, 'Rollo Meyer, visionary and founder of Millfield School'.
38  Ibid.
39  Ibid.
40  David Foot, 'The endearing eccentric', www.espncricinfo.com, July 1991.
41  Ibid.
42  Roebuck, 'A cad, inspired genius and a fox with a flair for the unexpected'.


## 10 ROOT, TICH, LEARIE AND SANDHAM
### *The 1920s Become the 1930s*

 1  Gideon Haigh, 'The cries of a cricket pro', www.espncricinfo.com, 17 January 2006.
 2  Ibid.
 3  Eric Midwinter, *The Illustrated History of County Cricket* (London, 1992), p. 224.
 4  Bill Frindall, *England Test Cricketers* (London, 1989), p. 380.
 5  Denzil Batchelor, *The Book of Cricket* (London, 1952), p. 85.
 6  Haigh, 'The cries of a cricket pro'.
 7  Ibid.
 8  Fred Root, 'A Cricket Pro's Lot', in *All in a Day's Cricket* (London, 2012), ed. Brian Levison, p. 143.
 9  Abhishek Mukherjee, 'Fred Root: Innovator on the field, radical off it', www.cricketcountry.com, 1 August 2016.
10  Haigh, 'The cries of a cricket pro'.
11  Batchelor, *The Book of Cricket*, p. 85.
12  Brian McLean, 'The day Cook was caught by Mustard off Onions', *Daily Dispatch* (South Africa), 4 October 2012, Sport.
13  Abhishek Mukherjee, '"Tich" Freeman: Colossus who ruled the County Championship for Kent', www.cricketcountry.com, 10 January 2015; David Taylor, 'Tich Freeman and the Decline of the Leg-break Bowler', www.cricketweb.net, 8 March 2010.
14  Mukherjee, '"Tich" Freeman: Colossus who ruled the County Championship for Kent'.
15  Stephen Chalke, *Summer's Crown: The Story of Cricket's County Championship* (Bath, 2015), p. 140.
16  Scyld Berry, 'England wrist-spinner Mason Crane aiming to rewrite history Down Under', www.telegraph.co.uk, 6 November 2017.
17  Batchelor, *The Book of Cricket*, p. 78.
18  Ibid., p. 116.
19  Abhishek Mukherjee, 'Learie Constantine: 25 things about a slave's grandson who became a Baron', www.cricketcountry.com, 21 September 2017.
20  'L. S. Constantine', in *Great Cricketers*, ed. Denzil Batchelor (London, 1970), p. 58.
21  Ibid., p. 59.
22  Batchelor, *The Book of Cricket*, p. 116.
23  Wisden, 'Baron Constantine', www.espncricinfo.com, 1972.

24 Ibid.
25 Batchelor, *The Book of Cricket*, p. 116.
26 Tony Cozier, *The West Indies: Fifty Years of Test Cricket* (Newton Abbot, 1978), p. 5.
27 Ibid.
28 Ian Peebles, *Spinner's Yarn* (Newton Abbot, 1978), p. 56.
29 Batchelor, *The Book of Cricket*, p. 116.
30 Michael Manley, *History of West Indies Cricket* (Bury St Edmunds, 1988), p. 50.
31 John Mehaffey, 'Extraordinary anti-racist book celebrates 50th anniversary', www.reuters.com, 31 December 2013.
32 Mukherjee, 'Learie Constantine: 25 things about a slave's grandson who became a Baron'.
33 John Arlott, 'Lord Constantine', in *Arlott on Cricket*, ed. David Rayvern Allen (London, 1985), p. 282.
34 Manley, *History of West Indies Cricket*, p. 51.
35 Ibid.
36 Nelson Cricket Club, 'Chapter Six: Constantine – The Legend', www.nelsoncricketclub.co.uk, n.d., accessed 20 August 2019.
37 Ibid.
38 Ibid.
39 Mike Amos, 'Backtrack: Pro's and Constantine', *Northern Echo*, 7 September 2017, Opinion.
40 Manley, *History of West Indies Cricket*, p. 51.
41 Ibid., p. 52.
42 Peter Oborne, 'Cricketer Learie Constantine who managed to hit racism for six while batting at the crease', www.dailymail.co.uk, 24 August 2017; John Arlott, 'Lord Constantine: The Spontaneous Cricketer', www.espncricinfo.com, 1972.
43 Arlott, 'Lord Constantine', in *Arlott on Cricket*, ed. Allen, p. 282.
44 Frindall, *England Test Cricketers*, p. 385.
45 David Frith, 'The first member of the 300 club', www.espncricinfo.com, December 2007.
46 John Woodcock, 'Old school that stood the test of time; Gover Cricket School', *The Times*, 10 November 1989.
47 Midwinter, *The Illustrated History of County Cricket*, p. 197.
48 Batchelor, *The Book of Cricket*, p. 183.
49 'Cricket: Competition: Vote for the greatest ever knock against the Windies', *Birmingham Post*, 12 July 2004, p. 23.
50 Batchelor, *The Book of Cricket*, p. 183.

## II BRADMAN AND HAMMOND
### *The Greatest, but for One Man*

1 John Ashdown, 'Great Ashes moments No16: Don Bradman's 334 at Headingley', www.theguardian.com, 20 June 2013.
2 Ibid.

3  R. C. Robertson-Glasgow, *Cricket Prints* (Norwich, 1943), p. 127.
4  Ibid.
5  Daniel Lane and Andrew Wu, 'Joe Burns' family folklore about Donald Bradman finally set straight', www.smh.com.au, 27 December 2014.
6  Abhishek Mukherjee, 'Don Bradman: 15 lesser-known facts about the 99.94 dude', www.cricketcountry.com, 27 August 2017.
7  Graeme Wright, ed., *Wisden on Bradman* (South Yarra, 1998).
8  R. C. Robertson-Glasgow, 'Sir Donald Bradman', in *Wisden on Bradman*, ed. Wright, p. 15.
9  Scyld Berry, 'The other side of Don Bradman', 3 March 2001, www. telegraph.co.uk.
10  Swaranjeet Singh, '"Tiger" O'Reilly – 60 Years in Cricket', www. cricketweb.net, 6 October 2008.
11  Berry, 'The other side of Don Bradman'.
12  Denis Campbell, 'The 10 most bitter sporting feuds of all time', www. theguardian.com, 8 April 2001.
13  Ibid.
14  Duncan Hamilton, 'An Ashes feud that lasted for life', www. theguardian.com, 5 July 2009.
15  Wales Online, 'The Don and I', www.walesonline.co.uk, 29 May 2013.
16  Denzil Batchelor, *The Book of Cricket* (London, 1952), p. 119.
17  David Frith, 'The lonely colossus', www.espncricinfo.com, 22 November 2010.
18  John Arlott, 'Hammond', in *Arlott on Cricket*, ed. David Rayvern Allen (London, 1985), p. 38.
19  Arunabha Sengupta, 'Cricketing Rifts – 3: The intense animosity between Don Bradman and Wally Hammond', www.cricketcountry. com, 2 September 2014.
20  Robertson-Glasgow, *Cricket Prints*, p. 15.
21  David Foot, *Wally Hammond: The Reasons Why* (London, 1998), p. 7.
22  Ibid., p. 162.
23  Arunabha Sengupta, 'The day Wally Hammond passed away', www. cricketcountry.com, 1 July 2016.
24  Arunabha Sengupta, 'Hugh Bartlett and the perils of eyeing the same girl as the captain', www.cricketcountry.com, 11 December 2017; Simon Briggs, 'The Ashes 2010: Wally Hammond's records still stand but talented cricketer was eaten up by envy of "The Don"', www.telegraph. co.uk, 14 December 2010.
25  Derek Hodgson, 'Hammond under the microscope', www.independent. co.uk, 22 July 1996.
26  David Foot, 'Wally Hammond's sad reprise was one of cricket's many bad judgments', www.theguardian.com, 24 June 2009.
27  Frith, 'The lonely colossus'.
28  Sengupta, 'Cricketing Rifts – 3: The intense animosity between Don Bradman and Wally Hammond'.
29  Briggs, 'The Ashes 2010: Wally Hammond's records still stand but talented cricketer was eaten up by envy of "The Don"'.

30 Arunabha Sengupta, 'Ashes 1946–47: Don Bradman refuses to walk at Brisbane', www.cricketcountry.com, 9 February 2016.
31 Ibid.
32 Ibid.
33 Sengupta, 'Cricketing Rifts – 3: The intense animosity between Don Bradman and Wally Hammond'.
34 Briggs, 'The Ashes 2010: Wally Hammond's records still stand but talented cricketer was eaten up by envy of "The Don"'.
35 Sharm de Alwis, 'The mean, lean Bradman – The other side of the man', www.island.lk, 11 September 2012.
36 Ibid.

## 12 OLD FRIENDS FALL OUT
### *The 1930s*

1 Jonathan Pearlman, 'Bodyline cricket scandal is proof Australia should become a republic, says Deputy PM', www.telegraph.co.uk, 25 January 2013.
2 Chris Jones, 'Australia v England: Eddie Jones uses Bodyline footage before Brisbane Test', www.bbc.co.uk, 8 June 2016.
3 W. de Burgh Whyte, 'Test Match Tactics', in *Not in My Day, Sir: Letters to the Daily Telegraph*, ed. Martin Smith (London, 2011), p. 21.
4 David Frith, *Bodyline Autopsy* (London, 2003), p. 7.
5 'Cricket's biggest moment', www.theage.com.au, 11 February 2004.
6 Chris Ryan, 'Cricket Ashes special: Bodyline spectre that will not pass on', *The Guardian*, 21 October 2002, p. 5.
7 Phil Derriman, 'Australian cricket's 25 biggest moments', *The Age*, 11 February 2004, p. 21.
8 Ibid.
9 Ibid.
10 Ryan, 'Cricket Ashes special: Bodyline spectre that will not pass on'.
11 Duncan Hamilton, 'An Ashes feud that lasted for life', www.theguardian.com, 5 July 2009.
12 Ibid.
13 R. C. Robertson-Glasgow, *Cricket Prints* (Norwich, 1943), p. 20.
14 Ibid., p. 21.
15 Frith, *Bodyline Autopsy*, p. 71; Denzil Batchelor, *The Book of Cricket* (London, 1952), p. 108.
16 Markus Berkmann, *Rain Men* (London, 1995), p. 84.
17 Live Reporter, 'This sporting life: One of the world's most valuable collections of sports memorabilia', www.dailymail.co.uk, 12 May 2012.
18 Frith, *Bodyline Autopsy*, p. 71; Martin Williamson, 'Bodyline quotes', www.espncricinfo.com, 19 October 2007.
19 Frith, *Bodyline Autopsy*, p. 70.
20 Ibid., p. 72.
21 Martin Williamson, 'Yabba', www.espncricinfo.com, n.d., accessed 18 November 2018.
22 Ibid.

23  Rohit Brijnath, 'Spectators' freedom should not embrace culture of jeering', www.straitstimes.com, 4 August 2015.

24  Williamson, 'Yabba'.

25  Sriram Vera, 'Leave those flies alone', www.espncricinfo.com, 2 January 2007.

26  Frith, *Bodyline Autopsy*, p. 71.

27  Williamson, 'Bodyline quotes'.

28  Ibid.

29  Ibid.

30  Dileep Premachandran, 'Pataudi changed India's focus to spin and fielding', www.thenational.ae, 26 September 2011.

31  Jake Perry, 'Douglas Jardine – the English hero who was always a Scot at heart', www.cricketscotland.com, 8 June 2018.

32  Stephen Brenkley, 'The good ship Flintoff sets sail for dreamland', www.independent.co.uk, 8 October 2006.

33  Abhishek Mukherjee, 'Brutal Bill Voce dismisses and disorients "Box" Case with pace', www.cricketcountry.com, 3 March 2016.

34  Brian Viner, 'Raise a glass to Voce; his century is up', www.independent.co.uk, 8 August 2009.

35  Duncan Hamilton, 'From pit-pony boy to fastest bowler ever', www.theguardian.com, 5 July 2009.

36  Ibid.

37  Frank Keating, 'Ashes and sackcloth: Obituary: Harold Larwood', *The Guardian*, 24 July 1995, p. 12.

38  Ibid.

39  Batchelor, *The Book of Cricket*, p. 122.

40  Mike Selvey, 'I owe Harold Larwood a belated apology for an ignorant youthful snub', www.theguardian.com, 7 July 2009.

41  Ibid.

42  Duncan Hamilton, 'An Ashes feud that lasted for life', www.theguardian.com, 5 July 2009.

43  Peter Roebuck, 'A man undefeated', www.espncricinfo.com, 29 March 2005.

44  Marea Donnelly, 'Angry crowds decided it "just wasn't cricket"', *Daily Telegraph* (Australia), 16 January 2018, p. 21.

45  Frith, *Bodyline Autopsy*, p. 197.

46  Ibid., p. 201.

47  Andrew Webster, 'Why Crowe is selling Bodyline series' most iconic Baggy Green', *Sydney Morning Herald*, 23 March 2018, p. 46.

48  Arunabha Sengupta, 'Bodyline series: The day Bill Woodfull was struck on his heart by Harold Larwood', www.cricketcountry.com, 8 January 2016.

49  Patrick Kidd, 'Paynter's masterstrokes in Brisbane left Australia reeling', *The Times*, 4 December 2007, p. 64.

50  Arunabha Sengupta, 'Eddie Paynter gets out of hospital bed and scores a match-changing 83 in an Ashes Test', www.cricketcountry.com, 13 February 2013.

51  Ibid.
52  Kidd, 'Paynter's masterstrokes in Brisbane left Australia reeling'.
53  Sengupta, 'Eddie Paynter gets out of hospital bed and scores a match-changing 83 in an Ashes Test'.
54  Gerald Howat, *Cricket's Second Golden Age* (London, 1989), p. 172.
55  Daniel Lane, 'No romance, just heartbreak as Phillip Hughes joins sport's most tragic figures', *Sydney Morning Herald*, 29 November 2014, p. 59.
56  Ibid.
57  Batchelor, *The Book of Cricket*, p. 141.
58  Steven Lynch, ed., *Wisden on the Ashes* (London, 2015), p. 211; Greg Buckle, 'Crik: Archie Jackson; a batting artist, taken at 23', AAP Newsfeed, 4 September 2009, Sports News.
59  Jack Pollard, *Australian Cricket: The Games and the Players* (North Ryde, 1988), p. 594.
60  Batchelor, *The Book of Cricket*, p. 141.
61  Ibid.
62  Pollard, *Australian Cricket: The Games and the Players*, p. 1196.
63  Ibid., p. 1198.
64  Lynch, ed., *Wisden on the Ashes*, p. 206.
65  Sengupta, 'Bodyline series: The day Bill Woodfull was struck on his heart by Harold Larwood'.
66  Lynch, ed., *Wisden on the Ashes*, p. 206.
67  David Frith, 'Cricket: The Don and the Bodyline Mystery', *The Observer*, 4 March 2001, p. 14.
68  Ibid.
69  Frith, *Bodyline Autopsy*, pp. 185, 193.
70  Ibid., p. 198.
71  Suvajit Mustafi, 'Bert Oldfield: 10 interesting facts about one of the finest wicketkeepers in cricket history', www.cricketcountry.com, 9 September 2016.
72  Ian Woolridge, 'Bodyline tag clean bowled shy, honourable man', *Daily Telegraph* (Australia), 28 July 1995, p. 45.
73  Wisden, 'W. A. Oldfield – the star keeper', www.espncricinfo.com, 1977.
74  Batchelor, *The Book of Cricket*, p. 103.
75  Rowland Ryder, 'The great wicket-keepers', www.espncricinfo.com, 1972.
76  Wisden, 'W. A. Oldfield – the star keeper'.
77  Alan Gibson, 'Cricket: Pillars of society saluted in style', *The Times*, 3 June 1987.
78  Ibid.
79  Simon Wilde, 'Bitter sweet victory', *Sunday Times*, 18 July 1999.
80  Batchelor, *The Book of Cricket*, p. 129.
81  Pollard, *Australian Cricket: The Games and the Players*, p. 821.
82  Sir Donald Bradman, 'W. J. O'Reilly', in *Great Cricketers*, ed. Denzil Batchelor (London, 1970), p. 173.
83  Scyld Berry, 'Obituary: Bill O'Reilly', www.independent.co.uk, 7 October 1992.

84 Matthew Engel, 'Testing Times against the Tiger; Obituary: W. J. O'Reilly', *The Guardian*, 7 October 1992, p. 37.
85 Ian Wooldridge, 'O'Reilly, a master of his trade as Test spin bowler and critic', *Daily Mail*, 7 October 1992, p. 52.
86 Ibid.
87 Peter McFarline, 'O'Reilly cheering form the celestial stands', *The Age*, 10 June 1993, p. 28.
88 Ibid.
89 John Stevens, 'O'Reilly a giant from cricket's golden age', *The Age*, 7 October 1992, p. 1.
90 Richard H. Thomas, 'A terribly awkward romance', www.espncricinfo. com, 14 May 2014.
91 Pollard, *Australian Cricket: The Games and the Players*, p. 588.
92 Grantlee Kieza, 'Old and wonky but Dainty passed Test', *Courier Mail*, 27 November 2016, p. 68.
93 Gideon Haigh, 'Tough in life and cricket', www.espncricinfo.com, 3 January 2006.
94 Ibid.
95 Ibid.
96 JGK, 'Cricket's all-time alphabetical 1 team', www.theroar.com.au, 6 June 2013.
97 Batchelor, *The Book of Cricket*, p. 72.
98 Frith, *Bodyline Autopsy*, p. 386.
99 Ibid.
100 Ibid., p. 387.
101 Ibid.
102 Ibid.

## 13 NAYUDU, VIZZY, VERITY, GRIMMETT, GIMBLETT AND SMITH
### *More from the 1930s*

1 R. A. Roberts and D. J Ratnugar, 'India', in *Barclays World of Cricket* (London, 1980), ed. E. W. Swanton, p. 79.
2 Ibid.
3 Gerald Howat, *Cricket's Second Golden Age* (London, 1989), p. 227.
4 Ibid.
5 Martin Williamson, 'Maharaja of Porbandar', www.espncricinfo.com, n.d., accessed 28 August 2019.
6 Ibid.
7 Howat, *Cricket's Second Golden Age*, p. 233.
8 Sir Pelham Warner, *Lord's, 1787–1945* (London, 1946), p. 212.
9 Denzil Batchelor, *The Book of Cricket* (London, 1952), p. 102.
10 S. J. Southerton, 'The All India team in England 1932', www. espncricinfo.com, 1933.
11 Howat, *Cricket's Second Golden Age*, p. 227.
12 Ibid., p. 237.

13 Abhishek Mukherjee, 'Vizzy: The most undeserving of all Indian cricketers who brought shame and ridicule to the nation', www. cricketcountry.com, 24 June 2016.

14 H. Natarajan, 'Indian skipper takes bribery to a new level in cricket!', www.cricketcountry.com, 1 December 2014.

15 Mukherjee, 'Vizzy: The most undeserving of all Indian cricketers who brought shame and ridicule to the nation'.

16 Nishad Pai Vaidya, 'Vizzy: 15 things to know about the controversial Indian captain', www.cricketcountry.com, 28 December 2016.

17 'Verity the last man to bring some Lord's joy to England', *Yorkshire Post*, www.yorkshirepost.co.uk, 15 July 2009.

18 Frank Keating, 'I cannot remember a feebler show by England', www. theguardian.com, 16 July 2001.

19 Stephen Brenkley, 'When Verity destroyed the Aussies', www. independent.co.uk, 15 July 2009.

20 Lawrence Booth, 'Hedley Verity: Star of England's 1934 Lord's win who led from the front', www.theguardian.com, 19 July 2009.

21 Brenkley, 'When Verity destroyed the Aussies'.

22 ITV, 'Four and Twenty Blackbirds', *Agatha Christie's Poirot*, first broadcast 29 January 1989.

23 Alan Hill, 'Rock of Yorkshire', www.espncricinfo.com, 10 October 2009.

24 Arthur Mailey, *10 for 66 and All That* (Crow's Nest, 1958), p. 105.

25 R. C. Robertson-Glasgow, *Cricket Prints* (Norwich, 1943), p. 114.

26 Jack Pollard, *Australian Cricket: The Games and the Players* (North Ryde, 1988), p. 496.

27 Stephen Brenkley, 'One more victim of modern cricket's constant demands', www.independent.co.uk, 25 March 2011.

28 Arunabha Sengupta, 'Harold Gimblett's incredible debut for Somerset', www.cricketcountry.com, 13 January 2016.

29 Steve Jennings, 'The legends: Harold Gimblett – "Folklore formed in freezing Frome!"', www.thein-cider.co.uk, 28 October 2014.

30 Martin Williamson, 'When the game became too much', www. espncricinfo.com, 24 September 2011.

31 Sengupta, 'Harold Gimblett's incredible debut for Somerset'.

32 Ibid.

33 Williamson, 'When the game became too much'.

34 Robertson-Glasgow, *Cricket Prints*, p. 108.

35 Ibid., p. 109.

36 Williamson, 'When the game became too much'.

37 Ibid.

38 In discussion with the author.

39 Abhishek Kumar, '11 hilarious stories from Australian dressing room revealed in Brad Hogg's book – The Wrong 'Un', www.cricketcountry. com, 13 November 2016.

40 Ibid.

41 Vic Marks, 'Jack Bannister – game mourns a cricketing man for all seasons', www.theguardian.com, 23 January 2016.

42 Martin Williamson, 'The cruellest hoax', www.espncricinfo.com, 24 November 2007.

43 Ibid.

## 14 CRICKET ON THE CUSP OF WAR
### *Even More from the 1930s*

1 Mike Atherton, 'Great Test venue deserves its century', *The Times*, 27 July 2017, p. 73.

2 Barney Ronay, 'A Viking farewell for Alastair Cook, England's unflashy seducer of crowds', *The Guardian*, 10 September 2018, Sport.

3 Ibid.

4 Tim Rich, 'Arsene Wenger fevered by Wigan Athletic pitch', www.telegraph.co.uk, 10 March 2008.

5 Arunabha Sengupta, 'Stan McCabe: A glorious batsman remembered for three immortal innings', www.cricketcountry.com, 14 July 2016.

6 Arunabha Sengupta, 'Neville Cardus performed the alchemy of changing reportage to literature', www.cricketcountry.com, 2 April 2017.

7 Roger Evans, *Cricket Grounds: The Evolution, Maintenance and Construction of National Turf Tables and Outfields* (Bingley, 1991), p. 29.

8 Martin Williamson, 'The Oval grind of 1938', www.espncricinfo.com, 22 August 2015.

9 Neville Cardus, 'The archive: 24.08.1938: Cricket: Heroic Hutton leads England to 903: "A match taken out of the realm of cricket" Bradman injury a blow to all concerned: Scorecard – Correction Appended', *The Guardian*, 6 November 2007, p. 12.

10 Richard Hobson, 'Bopara fails to make most of no-win situation', *The Times*, 13 August 2011, p. 16.

11 Ibid.

12 Alan Tyers, 'Final Test centurions: the elite club Alastair Cook could join by signing off with a hundred', www.telegraph.co.uk, 5 September 2018, Cricket.

13 Stephen Brenkley, 'Cricket: Pudsey's proudest hour; Sporting anniversary: Len Hutton made his Test record 364 against Australia at The Oval 60 years ago today', *The Independent*, 23 August 1998, p. S2.

14 Alex Bannister, 'Mantle of the master', *Guardian Weekly*, 16 September 1990, p. 32.

15 Brenkley, 'Cricket: Pudsey's proudest hour'.

16 Denzil Batchelor, *The Book of Cricket* (London, 1952), p. 172.

17 Cricket Correspondent, 'Hutton betters Bradman as England pass 900', *The Times*, 24 August 2001.

18 Ibid.

19 Brenkley, 'Cricket: Pudsey's proudest hour'.

20 Bannister, 'Mantle of the master'.

21 Ibid.

22  Ibid.
23  Christopher Sandford, 'True grit of Len Hutton a century after master batsman's birth', *Yorkshire Evening Post*, 21 June 2016.
24  John Lazenby, *Edging Towards Darkness: The Story of the Last Timeless Test* (London, 2017), p. 249.
25  Bannister, 'Mantle of the master'.
26  Martin Smith, ed., *The Daily Telegraph Book of Obituaries* (London, 2000), p. 104.
27  Ibid.
28  Sandford, 'True grit of Len Hutton a century after master batsman's birth'.
29  Ibid.
30  Frank Keating, 'Way back when; Frank Keating looks back to the "Timeless Test" of 1939 and an innings', *The Guardian*, 15 March 1999, p. 6.
31  Douglas Alexander, 'When 10 days were not enough', www.espncricinfo.com, 7 March 2009.
32  Lazenby, *Edging Towards Darkness*, p. 103.
33  Alexander, 'When 10 days were not enough'.
34  Ibid.
35  Ibid.
36  Lazenby, *Edging Towards Darkness*, pp. 280–82.
37  Keating, 'Way back when; Frank Keating looks back to the "Timeless Test" of 1939 and an innings'.
38  Bill Frindall, *England Test Cricketers* (London, 1989), p. 158.
39  Pradip Dhole, 'Paul Gibb: The bespectacled wicketkeeper', www.cricketcountry.com, 14 February 2017.
40  Andy Bull, 'The Test match that went on and on and on. Without a winner but with meaning', www.theguardian.com, 22 December 2015.
41  Lazenby, *Edging Towards Darkness*, p. 154.
42  Bull, 'The Test match that went on and on and on'.
43  Lazenby, *Edging Towards Darkness*, p. 161.
44  Ibid., p. 167.

## 15 VICTIMS, SURVIVORS AND INVINCIBLES
### *The 1940s*

 1  Paul Weaver, 'Sussex honour Hedley Verity and a game the outbreak of war could not stop', www.theguardian.com, 16 September 2009.
 2  Denzil Batchelor, *The Book of Cricket* (London, 1952), p. 127.
 3  Scyld Berry, 'Inside Cricket: Forget Don Bradman or Brian Lara – Hedley Verity lays claim to the only perfect 10', 29 May 2014, www.telegraph.co.uk.
 4  Lawrence Booth, 'Cricket: The Ashes: 2 nPower Test: The star of Lord's who led from the front: Nine years after inspiring England's last Lord's win against Australia, Hedley Verity was killed in the war', *The Observer*, 19 July 2009, p. 5.

5  Simon Austin, 'Hedley Verity: Ashes legend who died for his country', www.bbc.co.uk, 20 July 2013.

6  Batchelor, *The Book of Cricket*, p. 126.

7  Weaver, 'Sussex honour Hedley Verity and a game the outbreak of war could not stop'; Nick Britten and Richard Edwards, 'The officer and the trooper, two giants of Lord's; Englishmen; who triumphed 75 years apart in the Ashes are images of a different world', *Daily Telegraph*, 21 July 2009, p. 3.

8  Britten and Edwards, 'The officer and the trooper'.

9  Batchelor, *The Book of Cricket*, p. 156.

10 Frank Keating, 'A final glorious flurry with bat and ball before the upping of stumps – for six years; Way back when', *The Guardian*, 23 August 1999, p. 7.

11 Jack Pollard, *Australian Cricket: The Games and the Players* (North Ryde, 1988), p. 489.

12 Robert Hands, 'Frith digs deep in tribute to Gregory', *The Times*, 13 May 2004, p. 48.

13 David Frith, *The Ross Gregory Story* (South Melbourne, 2003).

14 John Hopkins, 'Tribute to life of Welsh sporting stalwart', *The Times*, 19 January 2002, Sport.

15 Ibid.

16 E. W. Swanton, *Cricketers of My Time: Heroes to Remember* (London, 2000), p. 62.

17 Keating, 'A final glorious flurry with bat and ball before the upping of stumps – for six years; Way back when'.

18 Andrew Hignell, *Cricket in Wales: An Illustrated History* (Cardiff, 2008), p. 115.

19 Tony Heath, 'Obituary: Wilf Wooller', www.independent.co.uk, 12 March 1997.

20 Ibid.

21 Ibid.

22 Frank Keating, 'Madcap Wilf Wooller created my Glamorgan angst', www.theguardian.com, 20 April 2011.

23 Ibid.

24 Wisden, 'Wilfred Wooller', www.espncricinfo.com, 1998.

25 Ibid.

26 Ibid.

27 Ibid.

28 Ibid.

29 Observer Sport Monthly, 'Fields of Glory', 6 November 2005, online at www.theguardian.com.

30 Arunabha Sengupta, 'Bill Edrich: Success, failure, drinks and divorces', www.cricketcountry.com, 26 March 2016.

31 'John Warr, cricketer – obituary', www.telegraph.co.uk, 10 May 2016.

32 'Geoff Edrich', www.telegraph.co.uk, 10 January 2004.

33 'Geoff Edrich', www.independent.co.uk, 10 January 2004.

34 Ibid.

35  'Norman Gordon – obituary', www.telegraph.co.uk, 2 September 2014.
36  Martin Williamson, 'Norman Gordon', www.espncricinfo.com, n.d.,
    accessed 14 September 2019.
37  'Norman Gordon – obituary'.
38  Ibid.
39  Sport 24 Archives, 'SA legend celebrates century', www.sport24.co.za,
    5 August 2011.
40  Frank Crook, 'Invincibles' tour was true triumph of spirit', *Daily
    Telegraph*, 22 June 2005, p. 57.
41  Frank Keating, 'Invincible', www.espncricinfo.com, 12th May 2003.
42  Ibid.
43  Ibid.
44  Crook, 'Invincibles' tour was true triumph of spirit'; Martin Williamson,
    '721 all out . . . in a day', www.espncricinfo.com, 30 June 2012.
45  Ibid.
46  Malcolm Knox, *Bradman's War: How the 1948 Invincibles Turned the
    Cricket Pitch into a Battlefield* (London, 2013).
47  Williamson, '721 all out . . . in a day'.
48  Lawrence Booth, 'In the stands veterans of Ashes series past relive old
    battles', www.guardian.com, 18 July 2009.
49  Ibid.
50  Abhishek Mukherjee, 'Don Bradman and his ducks', www.
    cricketcountry.com, 16 February 2016.
51  Greg Baum, 'When they were Kings: The Invincibles – The 1948
    Australians', *The Age*, 14 August 1998, p. 4.
52  Batchelor, *The Book of Cricket*, p. 198.
53  Tony Stephens, 'Obituary: Arthur Morris 1922–2015', www.smh.com.au,
    22 August 2015.
54  Pollard, *Australian Cricket: The Games and the Players*, p. 86.
55  Daniel Lane, 'Sid Barnes: more prankster than gangster', www.smh.
    com.au, 15 December 2013.
56  R. C. Robertson-Glasgow, *Cricket Prints* (Norwich, 1943), p. 16.
57  Lane, 'Sid Barnes: more prankster than gangster'.
58  Ibid.
59  Batchelor, *The Book of Cricket*, p. 208.
60  Daniel Lane, 'The last Invincible: Neil Harvey moves quietly into the
    90s', www.smh.com.au, 6 October 2018.
61  Andrew Ramsey, 'Invincible Harvey salutes for final Lord's innings',
    www.cricket.com.au, 17 August 2019.
62  Ibid.

## 16 NEW STARTS, NEW STARS AND CARIBBEAN SKIES
### *The 1940s and 1950s*

1  C.L.R. James, 'George Headley', in *Great Cricketers*, ed. Denzil
   Batchelor (London, 1970), p. 199.
2  Denzil Batchelor, *The Book of Cricket* (London, 1952), p. 144.

3  Russell Jackson, 'West Indies cricket cause is hopeless but inspiration could come from pioneers', www.theguardian.com, 31 December 2015.

4  James, 'George Headley', p. 201.

5  R. C. Robertson-Glasgow, *Cricket Prints* (Norwich, 1943), p. 131.

6  Chris Lander, 'The Spirit of George will keep an eye on my son Dean', *The Mirror*, 27 January 1998, p. 29.

7  'Andy Ganteaume, cricketer – obituary', www.telegraph.co.uk, 24 February 2016.

8  Peter Mason, 'Andy Ganteaume obituary', www.theguardian.com, 18 February 2016.

9  Ibid.

10  Hilary M.C.D. Beckles, 'The detachment of West Indies cricket from the nationalist scaffold', in *The Cambridge Companion to Cricket*, ed. Anthony Bateman and Jeffrey Hill (Cambridge, 2011), p. 161.

11  Frank Keating, 'My salad days with West Indies' summer knights', www.theguardian.com, 13 March 2007.

12  Vaneisa Baksh, 'The power of three', www.espncricinfo.com, 27 August 2006.

13  B. C. Pires, 'Obituaries: Sir Clyde Walcott: Batsman and manager who made the West Indies a winning side', *The Guardian*, 28 August 2006, p. 31.

14  Ibid.

15  Sir Learie Constantine, 'Sir Frank Worrell', www.espncricinfo.com, 1968.

16  Scyld Berry, 'West Indies mourn great ambassador Walcott', *Sunday Telegraph*, 27 August 2006, p. 4.

17  Pires, 'Obituaries: Sir Clyde Walcott'.

18  Berry, 'West Indies mourn great ambassador Walcott'.

19  David Frith, 'Sir Clyde Walcott', www.espncricinfo.com, n.d., accessed 29 September 2019.

20  'Sir Clyde Walcott', www.telegraph.co.uk, 28 August 2006.

21  Ibid.

22  Batchelor, *The Book of Cricket*, p. 206.

23  Ibid.

24  Ibid.; Michael Stevenson, 'Cricket: A match batsmen couldn't fail in', *The Times*, 23 December 1986.

25  Stevenson, 'Cricket'.

26  Ibid.

27  Michael Simkins, 'Meeting Weekes left me weak at the knees', *Daily Telegraph*, 21 June 2008, p. 30.

28  E. W. Swanton, *Cricketers of My Time: Heroes to Remember* (London, 2000), pp. 79, 80.

29  Batchelor, *The Book of Cricket*, p. 206.

30  Swanton, *Cricketers of My Time*, p. 79.

31  John Arlott, 'Sir Frank Worrell', in *Arlott on Cricket*, ed. David Rayvern Allen (London, 1985), p. 266.

32  Beckles, 'The detachment of West Indies cricket from the nationalist scaffold', p. 163.

33  Keating, 'My salad days with West Indies' summer knights'; Mark
    Whitaker, 'Worrell's tortured path to West Indies' top job', www.
    independent.co.uk, 24 August 2000.

34  Swanton, *Cricketers of My Time*, p. 79.

35  Keating, 'My salad days with West Indies' summer knights'; Dileep
    Premachandran, 'Australia's recent tour a blast from the past', www.
    thenational.ae, 29 April 2012.

36  Keating, 'My salad days with West Indies' summer knights'.

37  Telford Vice, 'Mover and shaker', www.espncricinfo.com, 1 January 2000.

38  Ibid.

39  Albert Baldeo, 'Sir Frank Worrell's Legacy – The West Indies should
    learn from its Elder Statesman', https://guyaneseonline, 17 May 2018.

40  David Hopps, 'Old pals do another turn; David Hopps recalls
    how Ramadhin and Valentine once shook the Empire', *The Guardian*,
    17 June 1995, p. 21.

41  Ibid.

42  Peter Johnson, 'Ramadhin owns up at last: I used to chuck it', *Daily
    Mail*, 1 March 1999, p. 59.

43  Hopps, 'Old pals do another turn'.

44  Johnson, 'Ramadhin owns up at last: I used to chuck it'.

45  Martin Williamson, 'Off to a flier', www.espncricinfo.com, 14 June 2007.

46  'Alf Valentine West Indian spin bowler who distinguished himself
    in partnership with Sonny Ramadhin during the 1950 tour', *Daily
    Telegraph*, 13 May 2004, p. 27.

47  B. C. Pires, 'Obituary: Alf Valentine: Spin bowler who, with Sonny
    Ramadhin, ensured the West Indies' first Test victory over England
    outside the Caribbean', www.theguardian.com, 13 May 2004.

48  Ibid.

49  Ibid.

## 17 BRYLCREEM BOYS
### *More from the 1940s and 1950s*

 1  Abhishek Mukherjee, 'Cricket at Academy Awards? Tim Rice
    acknowledges Denis Compton in his Oscar speech', www.
    cricketcountry.com, 29 February 2016.

 2  'Denis Compton', in *The Daily Telegraph Book of Sports Obituaries*, ed.
    Martin Smith (London, 2000), p. 250.

 3  Jack Bailey, 'Denis Compton', in *Cricket Heroes*, ed. Peter Hayter
    (London, 1990), p. 50.

 4  Arunabha Sengupta, 'Denis Compton: The knight in shining armour of
    English cricket', www.cricketcountry.com, 20 November 2015.

 5  David Hopps, *Great Cricket Quotes* (London, 2006), p. 48.

 6  Steven Lynch, ed., *Wisden on the Ashes* (London, 2015), p. 234.

 7  'Denis Compton', in *The Daily Telegraph Book of Sports Obituaries*,
    p. 250.

 8  Robert Winder, *The Little Wonder* (London, 2014), p. 223.

9   Stephen Brenkley, 'When Compton made everyone feel good again', *The Independent*, 14 May 2012, p. 24.

10  Stephen Brenkley, 'Obituary: Denis Compton, 1918–1997: The sporting idol we knew', *The Independent*, 27 April 1997, p. 51.

11  Brenkley, 'When Compton made everyone feel good again'.

12  Ibid.

13  Lawrence Booth, 'Denis Compton the cavalier: 100 years ago this week England cricket's biggest star since W. G. Grace was born', www.dailymail.co.uk, 21 May 2018.

14  Ibid.

15  Nick Varley, 'Bat and Fad', *The Guardian*, 24 April 1997, p. T2.

16  Ibid.

17  Trevor Bailey, 'Denis Compton', in *Great Cricketers*, ed. Denzil Batchelor (London, 1970), pp. 237–8.

18  David Frith, 'Keith Miller', www.independent.co.uk, 12 October 2004.

19  Philip Derriman, 'Bet you 6–4 Miller gets 80 not out tomorrow', *Sydney Morning Herald*, 7 November 1999, p. 62.

20  Mihir Bose, *Keith Miller* (Newton Abbot, 1980), p. 34.

21  Ibid.

22  Ibid.

23  Stephen Brenkley, 'Obituary: Denis Compton, 1918–1997: The sporting idol we knew', *The Independent*, 27 April 1997, p. 51.

24  Olivia Blair, 'Battle of Britain flypast: Five things you didn't know about the Battle of Britain', www.independent.co.uk, 14 September 2015.

25  Michael Parkinson, *Parky – My Autobiography: A Full and Funny Life* (London, 2009), p. 295.

26  Bose, *Keith Miller*, p. 18; Ian Wooldridge, 'How the war set Miller's dashing innings alight: Runs didn't matter', *Daily Mail*, 6 May 1995, p. 75.

27  Mike Selvey, 'Keith Miller', www.theguardian.com, 12 October 2004.

28  Ian Wooldridge, 'Keith Miller . . . True great and a great friend', *Daily Mail*, 12 October 2004, p. 73.

29  Wisden, 'Ray Lindwall', www.espncricinfo.com, 8 October 2019.

30  Ian Chappell, 'Keith Miller was my sporting idol, a war hero, a sharp thinker and the best captain Australia never had', www.smh.com.au, 26 October 2011.

31  Ibid.

32  Ibid.; Jack Pollard, *Australian Cricket: The Games and the Players* (North Ryde, 1988), p. 665; Robert Craddock, 'Death of cricketer Ray Lindwall a loss to the world', www.couriermail.com.au, 20 June 2013.

33  John Woodcock, 'Mosquito pilot by night, cricketer by day', *The Times*, 12 October 2004, p. 65.

34  Ashley Mallett, 'The swashbuckling flight lieutenant', www.espncricinfo.com, 3 November 2015.

35  Selvey, 'Keith Miller'.

36  'A gentleman and a skoller to the very end', www.smh.com.au, 16 October 2004.

37 Ahmed Rizvi, 'Keith Miller was more than just a cricketer for Australia', www.thenational.ae, 31 October 2011.
38 Ibid.
39 Ibid.
40 Malcolm Knox, 'The Don's war', www.smh.com.au, 23 September 2012.
41 'Keith Miller 1919–2004', www.smh.com.au, 16 October 2004.
42 Chappell, 'Keith Miller was my sporting idol, a war hero, a sharp thinker and the best captain Australia never had'.
43 David Llewellyn, 'Keith Miller – The Life of a Great All-rounder; Book of the week by Roland Perry', *The Independent*, 19 February 2007, p. 44.
44 Roger Patching, 'The Private Lives of Australian Cricket Stars: A Study of Newspaper Coverage, 1945–2010', PhD thesis, Bond University, Queensland, 2014, p. 153.
45 Mallett, 'The swashbuckling flight lieutenant'.
46 Ibid.
47 Llewellyn, 'Keith Miller – The Life of a Great All-rounder'.
48 Mallett, 'The swashbuckling flight lieutenant'.
49 Spiro Zavos, 'The glorious but sad story of Keith Miller', www.theroar. com.au, 28 April 2009.
50 Wooldridge, 'How the war set Miller's dashing innings alight'.

## 18 SENSITIVE SPINNERS
### *The Mid–1950s*

1 Steven Lynch, ed., *Wisden on the Ashes* (London, 2015), p. 306.
2 Denzil Batchelor, *The Book of Cricket* (London, 1952), p. 199.
3 Huw Richards, 'Cricket: England celebrates Laker's match – Sports – International Herald Tribune', www.nytimes.com, 26 July 2006.
4 Frank Keating, 'Put the lot of them on trial after the Lord's tribulation', www.theguardian.com, 29 July 1999.
5 Martin Williamson, 'It was just one of those days', www.espncricinfo. com, 26 February 2005.
6 Stephen Brenkley, 'Book review: Jim Laker: A Biography – Tricky man, trickier bowler', www.independent.co.uk, 16 August 1998.
7 Wisden, 'Jim Laker', www.espncricinfo.com, 1952.
8 Ibid.
9 Simon Briggs, 'Life behind legend of Jim's 19–90 It is 50 years since Laker launched a legend but his career endured as many lows', *Daily Telegraph*, 13 July 2006, p. 4.
10 Brenkley, 'Book review: Jim Laker: A Biography – Tricky man, trickier bowler'.
11 Rob Steen, 'Heroes and Villains: Jim Laker', *The Observer*, 30 July 2006, p. 65.
12 Brenkley, 'Book review: Jim Laker: A Biography – Tricky man, trickier bowler'.
13 David Foot, 'Obituary: A bowler with bite; Tony Lock', *The Guardian*, 31 March 1995, p. T19.

14 Arunabha Sengupta, 'Tony Lock: A colourful character and an excellent left-arm spinner', www.cricketcountry.com, 5 July 2016.

15 Derek Hodgson, 'Obituary: Tony Lock', *The Independent*, 31 March 1995, p. 20.

16 Ibid.

17 'Tony Lock' , *The Times*, 31 March 1995, Features.

18 Lynch, ed., *Wisden on the Ashes*, p. 303.

19 Ibid., p. 304.

20 Percy G. H. Fender, 'Test wickets', in *Not in My Day, Sir: Letters to the Daily Telegraph*, ed. Martin Smith (London, 2011), p. 59.

21 Lynch, ed., *Wisden on the Ashes*, p. 304.


22 Brenkley, 'Book review: Jim Laker: A Biography – Tricky man, trickier bowler'.

23 Simon Wilde, 'Laker the destroyer', *Sunday Times*, 21 March 1999, Sport.

24 Ian Wooldridge, 'Hero Laker, a victim of spin', *Daily Mail*, 8 July 2006, p. 95.

25 Ibid.

26 Ibid.; Steen, 'Heroes and Villains: Jim Laker'.

27 Barney Ronay, 'Confessions of a sports personality: six autobiographies worth reading', www.theguardian.com, 6 October 2009.

28 Wooldridge, 'Hero Laker, a victim of spin'.

29 John Arlott, 'Bewildering spinner with the twisted grin', *The Guardian Weekly*, 24 April 1986, p. 23.

30 Amol Raja, *Twirlymen: The Unlikely History of Cricket's Greatest Spin Bowlers* (London, 2011), p. 95.

31 Simon Wilde, 'The history of mystery', www.espncricinfo.com, 1999.

32 Ibid.

33 Ibid.

34 Gideon Haigh, 'International men of mystery', www.espncricinfo.com, 28 April 2008.

35 Robert Winder, 'A dying game. Why would a cricketer commit suicide? Robert Winder reads the lives of three great former players and is bewildered by their self-absorption and petty obsessions', www.newstatesman.com, 19 June 2000.

36 Malcolm Knox, 'The greatest Ashes Test', www.thecricketmonthly.com, July 2015.

37 Steven Lynch, 'Uncovered', www.espncricinfo.com, 18 October 2008.

38 Knox, 'The greatest Ashes Test'.

39 Nicholas Lezard, 'Leather on willow', www.theguardian.com, 20 April 2002.

40 Ibid.

41 Arunabha Sengupta, 'Four mystery spinners before Sunil Narine's arrival', www.cricketcountry.com, 8 August 2014.

42 Richard Whitehead and Patrick Kidd, '50 greatest sports books', *The Times*, 7 December 2010, pp. 64–5.

43 Lezard, 'Leather on willow'.

44 Winder, 'A dying game'.

45 Ibid.
46 Lezard, 'Leather on willow'.
47 Will Buckley, 'Peaking at a low point: You might as well shortlist the annual report of Man United plc', *The Observer*, 26 November 2000, p. 15.
48 Lezard, 'Leather on willow'.
49 Robert Winder, 'A dying game'.

## 19 TIED TEST AND TUMULT
### *The 1960s*

1 Dave Barry, *'My Teenage Son's Goal In Life Is To Make Me Feel 3,500 Years Old' and Other Thoughts On Parenting From Dave Barry* (Kansas City, MO, 2001), p. 103.
2 David Frith, 'Obituary: Roy Gilchrist', *The Independent*, 21 July 2001, p. 7.
3 B. C. Pires, 'Obituary: Roy Gilchrist: West Indian cricketer renowned for fast bowling and quick temper', *The Guardian*, 24 July 2001, p. 20.
4 Ibid.
5 Paul Coupar, 'The Awkward XI', www.espncricinfo.com, 13 October 2005.
6 Frith, 'Obituary: Roy Gilchrist'.
7 Abhishek Mukherjee, 'Roy Gilchrist: A fast-bowling terror whose career was cut short by his mercurial nature', www.cricketcountry.com, 28 June 2016.
8 Frith, 'Obituary: Roy Gilchrist'.
9 'Cricket robbed of so much superb talent', *Whitsunday Coast Guardian*, 28 January 2015, p. 23.
10 John Stern and Marcus Williams, eds, *The Essential Wisden: An Anthology of 150 Years of Wisden Cricketers' Almanack* (London, 2013), p. 934.
11 Michael Manley, *History of West Indies Cricket* (Bury St Edmunds, 1988), p. 141.
12 Arunabha Sengupta, 'Collie Smith dies in a tragic car accident at the peak of his cricket career', www.cricketcountry.com, 2 September 2015.
13 Richard H. Thomas, 'The Ten: Cut Off In Their Prime', www.wisden.com, 12 September 2014.
14 Frank Keating, 'An authentic West Indies hero, Smith's death plunged Sobers into the despair of drink and gambling; Way back when', *The Guardian*, 6 September 1999, p. 7.
15 Ibid.
16 Manley, *History of West Indies Cricket*, pp. 150–51.
17 Tom Wald, 'Kings of the Caribbean add spice to any series', *The Sun Herald*, 23 October 2005, p. 72.
18 'Tied Test more than just cricket', *Canberra Times*, 25 November 2010, p. 23.
19 Tim Lane, 'A test in time', *Sunday Age*, 5 December 2010, p. 8.
20 Tony Cozier, 'Wes Hall', in *My Favourite Cricketer*, ed. John Stern (London, 2010), p. 74.
21 David Hopps, *Great Cricket Quotes* (London, 2006), p. 198.
22 Lokendra Pratap Sah, 'Wes Hall: Fast bowling is 50 per cent perspiration, the rest is inspiration', *The Telegraph* (India), 10 May 2010.

23  Cozier, 'Wes Hall', p. 77.
24  Lane, 'A test in time'.
25  Russell Jackson, 'The Joy of Six: Australian sport's most memorable photographs', www.theguardian.com, 11 March 2014.
26  Ibid.
27  Ibid.
28  Ibid.
29  Time Lane, 'A test in time'.
30  Chloe Saltau, 'How the players saw that moment . . . when cricket played out its most famous finish', *The Age*, 21 November 2000, p. 6.
31  Daniel Williams, 'All the Way to the Wire', http://content.time.com, 13 November 2000; Paul Daffey, 'The Ten – Most iconic Australian Sporting photos', *Sunday Age* (Melbourne), 17 April 2005, p. 31.
32  Arunabha Sengupta, 'West Indies tour of Australia 1960–61: The first-ever Tied Test', www.cricketcountry.com, 15 December 2016.
33  'Sobers to the fore', *Sunday Observer*, 24 July 2011.
34  Ian Chappell, 'Who's the next-best batsman after Bradman?', www.espncricinfo.com, 1 April 2013.
35  Ian Wooldridge, 'Garry Sobers: Cricketers of the Century tribute – Almanack', www.wisden.com, 28 July 2019.
36  Ibid.
37  Arunabha Sengupta, '12 little-known facts about Garry Sobers', www.cricketcountry.com, 27 July 2016.
38  Andy Zaltzman, 'The Sobers-Kallis debate resolved for the final time ever', www.espncricinfo.com, 15 May 2012.
39  Manley, *History of West Indies Cricket*, p. 190.
40  Ibid.
41  Ibid.
42  Matthew Engel, 'Third Test: How the jokers came up trumps: A triumph for our cricketers and even the umpire gives radio listeners a warm glow from somewhere hot and far away', *The Guardian*, 12 December 2000, p. 3; James Lawton, 'Cricket: Cowdrey a true great in any era: Mild-mannered, iron-willed but diffident England test batsman never grasped quite how good he was', *The Independent*, 6 December 2000, p. 27.
43  Ivo Tennant, 'Sporting Sobers would be crying in his rum punch', *The Times*, 18 July 2006, p. 69.
44  Chappell, 'Who's the next-best batsman after Bradman?'.
45  Martin Williamson, 'A Test hundred with a hangover', www.espncricinfo.com, 21 January 2012.
46  Ibid.
47  'Richie Benaud; Celebrated cricket commentator who was in his time an outstanding and versatile Test player', *Daily Telegraph*, 11 April 2015, p. 29.
48  Richie Benaud, *Anything But . . . an Autobiography* (London, 1998), p. 18.
49  Michael Henderson, 'Cricket will never see another like Richie Benaud. He had the modesty of a prince', www.telegraph.co.uk, 11 April 2015.
50  Mike Selvey, 'Ambassadorial Richie Benaud would always fight shy of criticising players', www.theguardian.com, 10 April 2015.

51  Ibid.
52  Ibid.
53  Barney Ronay, 'G'day Richie, back in the commentary box again', www.theguardian.com, 3 July 2009.
54  Henderson, 'Cricket will never see another like Richie Benaud'.
55  Stephen Bierley, 'Throw cricket open to the chuckers', www.theguardian.com, 23 May 2002.
56  Malcolm Conn, 'Mystery of 1960s "chucker" goes to grave with umpire', *The Australian*, 6 September 2008, p. 53.
57  Jack Pollard, *Australian Cricket: The Games and the Players* (North Ryde, 1988), p. 745.
58  Chris Barrett, 'The one over that ended a career', www.smh.com.au, 27 October 2012.
59  Ron Reed, 'Meckiff relives nightmare dismal day for Aussie "chucker"', *The Advertiser*, 27 December 1995.
60  Barrett, 'The one over that ended a career'.
61  Robert Craddock, 'Cricket's straight shooter', *Courier Mail*, 4 October 2008, p. 94.
62  Pollard, *Australian Cricket: The Games and the Players*, p. 745.
63  Simon Lister, 'The XI worst overs', www.espncricinfo.com, August 2005.
64  Luke Alfred, *Testing Times: The Story of the Men who Made SA Cricket* (Claremont, South Africa, 2003), p. 152.
65  Gideon Haigh, 'It's just not cricket', *Sunday Age*, 5 November 1995, p. 18.
66  'Obituary of Geoff Griffin South African bowler whose throwing action brought a premature end to his career', *Daily Telegraph*, 23 November 2006, p. 29.
67  Martin Williamson, 'No-balled out of the game', www.espncricinfo.com, 11 August 2012.

## 20 SMALL CHANGES, BIG CHARACTERS
### More from the 1960s

1  Tony Cozier, 'From fire to friendship', www.espncricinfo.com, 10 February 2009.
2  Ted Dexter, 'On a knife's edge', www.espncricinfo.com, 30 May 2010.
3  Abhishek Mukherjee, 'West Indies vs England, Lord's 1963: A thriller where all four results were possible till the very end', www.cricketcountry.com, 25 June 2016.
4  Michael Parkinson, 'Close still battling on at 70', www.telegraph.co.uk, 25 February 2001.
5  Ibid.
6  Simon Wilde, 'MCC stripped Close of captaincy in upper-class coup: Newly released files show Cowdrey was brought in because he went to "right" university', *Sunday Times*, 13 November 2011, p. 13.
7  Ibid.
8  Ibid.

9  'Cricket: Close Makes a Yorkshire Comeback aged 63', *The Guardian*, 25 April 1994, Sport, p. 19; David Hopps, *Great Cricket Quotes* (London, 2006), p. 54.

10  Derek Hodgson, 'Book of the Week; Brian Close: Cricket's Lionheart by Alan Hill', *The Independent*, 23 December 2002, p. 12.

11  Mukherjee, 'West Indies vs England, Lord's 1963'.

12  Ibid.

13  Mike Selvey, 'Kevin Pietersen power show a reminder of Ted Dexter's outrageous dominance', www.theguardian.com, 19 May 2015.

14  Martin Chandler, 'Lord Ted', www.cricketweb.net, 17 April 2014; Arunabha Sengupta, 'Ted Dexter: One of the most colourful characters to grace English cricket', www.cricketcountry.com, 15 May 2013.

15  Ibid.

16  Selvey, 'Kevin Pietersen power show a reminder of Ted Dexter's outrageous dominance'.

17  Sengupta, 'Ted Dexter: One of the most colourful characters to grace English cricket'.

18  Arunabha Sengupta, 'Ted Dexter ventures into the world of crime, pens murder mystery "Testkill"', www.cricketcountry.com, 20 July 2016.

19  Dan O'Neill, 'How "Lord" Ted found himself on a sticky city wicket', www.walesonline.co.uk, 4 July 2012.

20  Ibid.

21  Ted Dexter, 'When youth has flown', www.espncricinfo.com, September 1991.

22  Abhishek Mukherjee, 'Geoff Boycott muscles his way to win Gillette Cup 1965 for Yorkshire', www.cricketcountry.com, 17 April 2017.

23  Craig Salmon, 'Big Interview: Geoffrey Boycott', *Lancashire Evening Post*, 22 April 2017.

24  John Woodcock, 'A startling performance by Boycott', www. espncricinfo.com, 1965.

25  Wisden, 'England v New Zealand', www.espncricinfo.com, 1974.

26  Marina Hyde, 'In Stoke, May marches on with familiar neuron-crushing dullness', www.theguardian.com, 16 May 2017.

27  Arunabha Sengupta, 'England drop "selfish" Geoff Boycott after the opener crawls to an unbeaten 246', www.cricketcountry.com, 9 June 2013.

28  Derek Hodgson, 'Geoffrey Boycott: Impactful cricketer, trenchant voice', www.wisden.com, 21 October 2019.

29  'John Gleeson; Australian cricketer whose mystery spin bowling was admired by Don Bradman and bamboozled Geoffrey Boycott', *The Times*, 14 October 2016, p. 59.

30  Richard H. Thomas, 'The Ten: Cricket Books', www.wisden.com, 17 October 2014.

31  Marcus Berkmann, 'Heroes and Villains: Marcus Berkmann on Derek Randall', *The Independent*, 23 July 2005, p. 62.

32  Ibid.

33  Ibid.; Andrew Nickolds, 'Cricket: Spirit of Trent Bridge passes tests of time and doldrums', *The Guardian*, 4 August 2001, p. 5.

34  David Hopps, 'Cricket: Memories are made of rags the Twasack', *The Guardian*, 17 September 1993, p. 23.

35  Vic Marks, 'Cricket: First Investec Test: "Selfish Shiv" puts calamity behind him to perform another rescue act', *The Guardian*, 18 May 2012, p. 39.

36  Peter Hayter, 'Self-minded Boycott riled up his team-mates not just opposition bowlers', https://thecricketpaper.com, 9 August 2017.

37  Kevin Marriott, 'Ignorance is no defence for Boycott', *Cornish Guardian*, 30 March 2011, p. 98.

38  Peter Ball, 'Cricket: Yorkshire calm as Boycott era comes to a close', *The Times*, 25 September 1986.

39  Thomas, 'The Ten: Cricket Books'.

40  Ian Martin, 'G2: I'm sorry, but our apologising has reached ridiculous extremes. Who are these toddlers who need to be affronted to feel alive?', *The Guardian*, 16 December 2013, p. 5.

41  Ibid.

42  Robin Scott-Elliot, 'So far outside the box that it moves the goalposts, in a post-ironic way', www.independent.co.uk, 28 May 2012; 'Collingwood earns honour', *Yorkshire Post*, 14 July 2006.

43  'Cricket: First Test: Test Notebook', *The Observer*, 18 November 2012, p. 14.

## 21 SHORTER FORMATS, NEW STARS
### *The 1960s and 1970s*

1  Martin Johnson, 'Will T20 slog fest soon be a thing of the past?', www.thecricketpaper.com, 13 June 2017.

2  'Tom Graveney, cricketer – obituary', *Daily Telegraph*, 3 November 2015.

3  Derek Pringle, 'One-day odyssey hits new frontier Packer showed everyone how to market the new bite-sized game as a product', *Daily Telegraph*, 24 June 2002, p. 13.

4  Jon Hotten, 'Exiles on Main Street', *The Nightwatchman* (Summer 2018), p. 40.

5  Arunabha Sengupta, 'Mike Procter: A supreme all-rounder who enjoyed the shortest of stints on the world stage', www.cricketcountry.com, 15 September 2013.

6  Ibid.

7  Hotten, 'Exiles on Main Street', p. 39.

8  Pradip Dhole, 'Horace Fisher takes a hat-trick of LBWs', www.cricketcountry.com, 7 August 2016.

9  Robin Marlar, 'Flat Jack and the Lancashire hot-pot', *Sunday Times*, 23 June 1991, Sport; Abhishek Mukherjee, 'Mike Gatting vs Jack Simmons: The platter battles', www.cricketcountry.com, 22 September 2017.

10  David Lloyd, 'Energy drinks? We had bitter or Double Diamond . . . David Lloyd spills the beans on the regime in his playing days', www.dailymail.co.uk, 8 November 2013.

11  'The Big Interview: Jack Simmons', www.lep.co.uk, 30 June 2003.

12  Marlar, 'Flat Jack and the Lancashire hot-pot'.

13  Ibid.
14  Derek Hodgson, 'Obituary: Arthur Jepson', *The Independent*, 8 August 1997, p. 18.
15  Ibid.
16  Martin Johnson, 'Cricket: Dissent driving umpires out of the game', *The Independent*, 22 July 1992, p. 30.
17  Brian Viner, 'Red rose-tinted memories of the 1970s when Lancashire ruled one-day game', www.independent.co.uk, 26 August 2006.
18  Martin Kelner, 'Sport: Screen Break: Bumble's naan breads have won me over', *The Guardian*, 2 August 2010, p. 14.
19  Ibid.
20  Emirates News Agency, 'Abu Dhabi Cricket to host T10 League from 2019–2023', https://ttsports.com, 18 March 2019.
21  Amit Ray, 'In honour of 'Tiger'', www.mid-day.com, 19 June 2012.
22  Wisden, 'Mansur Ali Khan Pataudi', www.espncricinfo.com, 2012.
23  Ray, 'In honour of 'Tiger'.
24  Wisden, 'Mansur Ali Khan Pataudi'.
25  David Frith, 'Mansur Ali Khan Pataudi obituary', www.theguardian.com, 25 September 2001.
26  The author offers a small personal embellishment. A number of years ago at Lord's, a distinguished-looking man took a neighbouring seat in the Long Room and chatted to me enthusiastically about the match. We'd never met, but I knew him to be Shahryar Khan, former President of the Pakistan Cricket Board and a familiar on-screen figure. 'Tiger' Pataudi approached – the two were cousins and the greetings were warm. I was acknowledged with equal solicitude but took my leave, a little embarrassed but nevertheless convinced that as a humble comprehensive schoolboy from Cardiff, I would have been completely welcome to stay and chew the fat with the two of them, a senior Pakistani politician and an Indian cricketing superstar.
27  Nitin Naik, 'Pataudi's bat was always the one near the dressing room door', https://timesofindia.com, 21 December 2011.
28  Frith, 'Mansur Ali Khan Pataudi obituary'.
29  Wisden, 'Mansur Ali Khan Pataudi'.
30  Jon Hotten, 'A brief history of overseas players in county cricket', www.wisden.com, 4 June 2018.
31  Jonathan Rice and Andrew Renshaw, *The Wisden Collector's Guide* (London, 2011), p. 215.
32  Richard Thomas, 'Majid Moments', *The Nightwatchman* (Summer 2018), p. 55.
33  Ibid., p. 57.
34  Vic Marks, 'Dozen from down under', www.theguardian.com, 30 April 2000.
35  BBC, 'Malcolm Bows Out', www.news.bbc.co.uk, 19 September 2003.
36  Martin Searby, 'Courtney gesture', *Sunday Times*, 8 August 1993, Sport.
37  Derek Hodgson, 'Obituary: Keith Boyce', *The Independent*, 22 October 1996, p. 14.

38 David Foot, 'Making the day for Essex; Obituary: Keith Boyce', *The Guardian*, 14 October 1996, p. 11; Mike Selvey, 'Keith Boyce', www. espncricinfo.com, 1996.

39 Martin Birtle, 'Irish cricket eyes were smiling back in the summer of 69', www.thenorthernecho.co.uk, 30 June 2005.

40 Tom Peterkin, 'Irish cricketer on a mission for England Batsman's role in World Cup means divided loyalties for his sporting family', *Daily Telegraph*, 30 March 2007, p. 9.

41 Paul Rowan, 'When Ireland bowled out West Indies for 25', *Sunday Times*, 29 June 2003, Sport 7.

## 22 PARADISE LOST, PARADISE REGAINED
### From the 1960s to the 1990s

1 Jack Pollard, *Australian Cricket: The Games and the Players* (North Ryde, 1988), p. 884; 'Barry Richards, a moody maverick', www.thehindu.com, 22 July 2000.

2 Paul Hayward, 'Farewell to the Waca, after a century of fierce conflict', *Daily Telegraph*, 11 December 2017, pp. 18–19.

3 H. Natarajan, 'Barry Richards's epic 325 not out in a single day's play against Dennis Lillee and Graham McKenzie', www.cricketcountry. com, 13 July 2014.

4 'Bradman's XI', *The Times*, 17 August 2001, Sport.

5 Bob Willis, 'My dream team', *Sunday Times*, 15 October 2006, p. 26.

6 Barry Richards, *The Barry Richards Story* (Newton Abbot, 1978), p. 27.

7 Wisden Staff, 'The Definitive: Barry Richards', www.wisden.com, 20 January 2016.

8 Jon Hotten, 'Exiles on Main Street', *The Nightwatchman* (Summer 2018), p. 37.

9 Ibid., pp. 37–8.

10 Ivo Tennant, 'Richards serves past reminder', *The Times*, 26 June 1991, Sport.

11 David Llewellyn, 'Cricket: Books for Christmas: The life and times of a master craftsman', *The Independent*, 17 December 1998, p. 25.

12 Richards, *The Barry Richards Story*, p. 105.

13 Tennant, 'Richards serves past reminder'.

14 Simon Wilde, 'New England', *The Nightwatchman* (Summer 2018), p. 44.

15 Matthew Engel, 'Basil D'Oliveira's 158 not in was a bodged job that changed history', *The Guardian*, 23 August 2018, Sport.

16 'Basil D'Oliveira; Obituaries Cape Coloured cricketer who overcame racism with dignity and brilliance to represent England', *Daily Telegraph*, 21 November 2011, p. 33.

17 Martin Williamson, 'The speedboat and the toes', www.espncricinfo. com, 3 December 2011.

18 'Fred Titmus; Obituaries Outstanding off-spin bowler for Middlesex and England who was known for his economy in Test matches and

his ability to keep a perfect length', *Daily Telegraph*, 24 March 2011, p. 33.

19 Williamson, 'The speedboat and the toes'.

20 'Basil D'Oliveira; Obituaries Cape Coloured cricketer who overcame racism with dignity and brilliance to represent England'.

21 Engel, 'Basil D'Oliveira's 158 not in was a bodged job that changed history'.

22 'Basil D'Oliveira; Obituaries Cape Coloured cricketer who overcame racism with dignity and brilliance to represent England'.

23 Rich Evans, 'Dropping Dolly: The D'Oliveira affair 50 years on', www.wisden.com, 27 July 2018.

24 Engel, 'Basil D'Oliveira's 158 not in was a bodged job that changed history'.

25 Ibid.

26 Evans, 'Dropping Dolly: The D'Oliveira affair 50 years on'.

27 Engel, 'Basil D'Oliveira's 158 not in was a bodged job that changed history'.

28 Ibid.; Abhishek Mukherjee, 'Easier Said than Done – a review: Alan Wilkins, in flesh and blood, finally', www.cricketcountry.com, 5 June 2018.

29 Mike Selvey, 'Mopping up the tail – and just about everything else', www.theguardian.com, 3 September 2005.

30 Denzil Batchelor, *The Book of Cricket* (London, 1952), p. 146.

31 Wisden, 'Freddie Brown', www.espncricinfo.com, 1992.

32 David Frith, *Bodyline Autopsy* (London, 2003), p. 63.

33 Batchelor, *The Book of Cricket*, p. 146.

34 Bill Frindall, *England Test Cricketers* (London, 1989), p. 68.

35 Batchelor, *The Book of Cricket*, p. 146.

36 Ibid.

37 Frith, *Bodyline Autopsy*, p. 63.

38 Wisden, 'F. R. Brown: leader of men'.

39 Steven Lynch, ed., *Wisden on the Ashes* (London, 2015), p. 276.

40 Steve James, 'England cricket team's most vital statistic in 2011? Nought', www.telegraph.co.uk, 3 January 2012.

41 Derek Hodgson, 'Obituary: Eddie Barlow; "Powerhouse" cricketer', *The Independent*, 4 January 2006, p. 32.

42 'Obituary of Eddie Barlow Combative all-rounder for South Africa who kept his best performances for Tests against Australia', *Daily Telegraph*, 31 December 2005, p. 23.

43 Hodgson, 'Obituary: Eddie Barlow'.

44 Ibid.

45 Tony Cozier, 'Cricket: West Indies lay tourist traps', *The Independent*, 3 April 1992, p. 34.

46 Ibid.

47 Richard Streeton, 'Patient Hudson hits century for South Africa', *The Times*, 20 April 1992, Sport.

48 David Miller, 'Hudson equal to cricket's greatest test', *The Times*, 22 April 1992, Sport.

49 Mike Selvey, 'Cricket: South Africa shattered at a pace', *The Guardian*, 24 April 1992, p. 17.

50 Ibid.

51 Scyld Berry, 'Cricket: South Africans deserve better of history', *The Independent*, 26 April 1992, p.27.

52 Geoffrey Boycott, 'A lovely man who changed the course of history', *Daily Telegraph*, 21 June 2011, pp. 14, 15.

53 Engel, 'Basil D'Oliveira's 158 not in was a bodged job that changed history'.

54 Hotten, 'Exiles on Main Street', p. 39.

55 Ibid.

56 Mike Atherton, 'Great players betrayed by colour blindness', *The Times*, 6 September 2012, p. 71.

## 23 THE HOLY TRINITY
### Nine Decades of Writers and Talkers

1 Mike Brearley, 'Arlott: poetic voice of our time; Mike Brearley, on the centenary of the late commentator's birth, places him on a high pedestal', *The Times*, 25 February 2014, p. 56.

2 David Rayvern Allen, 'My hero: David Rayvern Allen on John Arlott', www.theguardian.com, 28 February 2014.

3 Ibid.

4 'Poetic policeman: Letters: John Arlott', *The Guardian*, 24 December 1991.

5 John Barclay, 'What a good sport; BOOK REVIEWS: John Barclay on two great cricket pundits who didn't see eye to eye but both fought for the spirit of the game', *Daily Telegraph*, 5 May 2018, pp. 28, 29.

6 Ibid.

7 'Poetic policeman: Letters: John Arlott'.

8 Brearley, 'Arlott: poetic voice of our time'.

9 Matthew Engel, 'Forever in the Mind's Ear: Arlott was the voice of summer, his cricket commentaries a form of instant poetry. But a new memoir by his son shows a grimmer side of loss and desolation', *The Guardian*, 15 February 1994, p. 2.

10 Brearley, 'Arlott: poetic voice of our time'.

11 Allen, 'My hero: David Rayvern Allen on John Arlott'; Brearley, 'Arlott: poetic voice of our time'.

12 Geoff Wijesinghe, 'Rice bowls . . . and Paddy fields', http://archives. dailynews.lk, 15 June 2002.

13 Simon Barnes, 'Voice that was the sound of summer', *The Times*, 16 December 1991, Home News.

14 Arunabha Sengupta, '19 super-talented cricketers who never played Test cricket', www.cricketcountry.com, 7 August 2014.

15 Ben Dirs, 'Ashes 2015: David Steele became an unlikely England hero in 1975', www.bbc.co.uk, 5 July 2015.

16 Arunabha Sengupta, 'The first streaker at Lord's cricket ground', www. cricketcountry.com, 2 March 2017.

17 Henry Blofeld, 'From "mellow" Arlott to the bubbly Johnners, ours was an all-star cast', *Sunday Telegraph*, 15 October 2017, p. 7.

18 Adam Sherwin, 'Cricket's big question: as Ashes battle resumes 38 years on, where is streaker Michael Angelow?', www.independent.co.uk, 9 July 2013.

19 Blofeld, 'From "mellow" Arlott to the bubbly Johnners, ours was an all-star cast'; Brearley, 'Arlott: poetic voice of our time'.

20 Frank Keating, 'Arlott's imperishable voice will never be forgotten', *The Guardian*, 10 December 2001, p. 18.

21 Ibid.

22 Brearley, 'Arlott: poetic voice of our time'.

23 Ibid.

24 Ibid.

25 Timothy Arlott, *John Arlott: A Memoir* (London, 1994), p. 150.

26 Brearley, 'Arlott: poetic voice of our time'.

27 Richard Siddle, 'Launching my own wine range feels better than scoring a hundred at Lord's', *Daily Express*, 13 October 2018, pp. 24–5.

28 Ibid.

29 Arlott, *John Arlott: A Memoir*, p. 211.

30 Barnes, 'Voice that was the sound of summer'.

31 Barclay, 'What a good sport'.

32 Ibid.

33 Ibid.

34 Leo McKinstry, 'Not how the game should be played: Jim Swanton was the doyen of the press box but his behaviour, well, it just wasn't cricket', *Sunday Telegraph*, 8 August 2004, p. 12.

35 Wisden, 'E. W. Swanton', www.espncricinfo.com, 2001.

36 McKinstry, 'Not how the game should be played'.

37 Mike Selvey, 'Jim Swanton dies at 92', www.theguardian.com, 24 January 2000.

38 Christopher Martin-Jenkins, 'Cricket Society's book of the year', *The Times*, 22 April 2005, Sport p. 88.

39 Selvey, 'Jim Swanton dies at 92'.

40 Frank Keating, 'Heroic efforts cannot stop snickers at the Marathon', www.theguardian.com, 17 April 2007.

41 Blofeld, 'From "mellow" Arlott to the bubbly Johnners, ours was an all-star cast'.

42 Keating, 'How the R&A made its mark at Stalag Luft III', www.theguardian.com, 3 January 2012.

43 Ibid.

44 McKinstry, 'Not how the game should be played'.

45 Wisden, 'E. W. Swanton'.

46 John Arlott, 'Cardus at the crease: Centenary of the greatest of cricket', *The Guardian*, 2 April 1988.

47 Ibid.

48 Gavin Mortimer, *A History of Cricket in 100 Objects* (London, 2013), p. 113.

49  'Books: A man of spirit / Review of "His Own Man – The Life
    of Neville Cardus" by Christopher Brookes', *The Guardian*, 6 June 1985.
50  Scyld Berry, *Cricket: The Game of Life* (London, 2015), p. 239.
51  Scyld Berry, 'Neville Cardus' writing', www.espncricinfo.com, 13 March
    2010.
52  Alan Gibson, 'Sir Neville Cardus', www.espncricinfo.com, 1976;
    Arunabha Sengupta, 'William Attewell: Yet another Neville Cardus lie',
    www.cricketcountry.com, 11 July 2017.
53  Arlott, 'Cardus at the crease: Centenary of the greatest of cricket'.
54  'Books: A man of spirit / Review of "His Own Man – The Life
    of Neville Cardus" by Christopher Brookes'.
55  Paul Weaver, 'Sport: Cardus was proud to put words in others' mouths',
    *The Guardian*, 7 July 2009, p. 12.
56  'Books: A man of spirit / Review of "His Own Man – The Life of
    Neville Cardus" by Christopher Brookes'.
57  Ibid.
58  Sengupta, 'William Attewell: Yet another Neville Cardus lie'.
59  Rupert Christiansen, 'Cardus: a man whose prose was poetry', *Daily
    Telegraph*, 20 July 2009, p. 26.
60  Kenneth Surin, 'C.L.R. James and cricket', in *The Cambridge Companion
    to Cricket*, ed. Anthony Bateman and Jeffrey Hill (Cambridge, 2011), p. 133.
61  Christiansen, 'Cardus: a man whose prose was poetry'.
62  Blofeld, 'From "mellow" Arlott to the bubbly Johnners, ours was an all-
    star cast'.
63  Henry Blofeld, 'Dress Sense: In association with Peter Christian
    Cricket buff and bon viveur Henry Blofeld knows a thing or two about
    sartorial finery. Here are some of his favourites from the Peter Christian
    range', *Daily Telegraph*, 11 January 2014, p. 6.

## 24 WORLD CUPS AND WORLD BEATERS
### From the 1970s to the 1990s

1  'Derek Pringle', www.espncricinfo.com, n.d., accessed 27 September
   2019.
2  ICC, 'What they have said about the World Cup', www.cricketworldcup.
   com, 25 May 2019.
3  'The Prudential World Cup 1975, first semi-final: England v Australia',
   www.espncricinfo.com, 1976.
4  '"Krishnappa Premier League": 134 Not Out and 8 Wickets in One T20
   Match', https://heraldpublicist.com, 24 August 2019.
5  'Gary Gilmour; Obituaries High-living Australian all-rounder who
   took six wickets against England at the inaugural World Cup in 1975',
   *Daily Telegraph*, 22 July 2014, p. 23.
6  Tim de Lisle, '"Everything we wished for": Boyhood memories of
   the first Cricket World Cup final', www.theguardian.com, 13 July 2019.
7  Mike Selvey, 'Mike Selvey's top World Cup innings', *The Guardian*,
   14 May 1999, p. 117.

8  Tony Cozier, 'Cricket World Cup: Innings that shook the World', *The Independent*, 9 May 1999, Sport.

9  Vic Marks, 'Cricket: An eye view not strictly for bird', *The Observer*, 14 January 1996, p. 8.

10  Derek Pringle, 'Lord's the perfect place for "Dickie" to bid adieu', *The Independent*, 12 June 1996, p. s9.

11  Ibid.

12  Marks, 'Cricket: An eye view not strictly for bird'.

13  Dickie Bird, *My Autobiography* (London, 1998), pp. 71–2.

14  Ibid., p. 80.

15  Wisden, 'Dickie Bird', www.espncricinfo.com, n.d., accessed 3 October 2019.

16  De Lisle, 'Everything we wished for'.

17  Martin Williamson, 'Who's grovelling now?', www.espncricinfo.com, 19 May 2007.

18  Ibid.

19  Simon Briggs, 'Catch a Fire: When England's captain threatened to make the West Indies grovel 35 years ago he sparked a cricketing revolution that saw the rest of the world ruthlessly humbled', *Daily Telegraph*, 30 April 2011, pp. 42, 43, 45, 47, 49.

20  Graeme Archer, 'Drought? The summer of 1976 was glorious', www.telegraph.co.uk, 18 April 2012.

21  Rob Bagchi, 'Martin Guptill's unbeaten 189 edged by Viv Richards's 1984 brilliance', www.theguardian.com, 4 June 2013.

22  Ibid.

23  Rod Gilmour, 'Cricket: The five fastest centuries of all time; From Viv Richards' 56-ball century to David Warner's 69 ball effort against the hapless Indians, Telegraph Sport looks back at the five fastest Test centuries of all time', www.telegraph.co.uk, 13 January 2012.

24  Tim Rich, 'The golden summer when a small Lancashire town signed Viv Richards', https://inews.co.uk, 6 September 2019.

25  Ibid.

26  Ibid.

27  Scyld Berry, *Cricket: The Game of Life* (London, 2015), p. 192.

28  David Hopps, *Great Cricket Quotes* (London, 2006), p. 295.

29  Paul Newman, 'Passionate, devoted and fearlessly honest – a true giant of sports writing'; James Lawton, *The Independent*'s former chief sports writer, has died aged 75', *The Independent*, 29 September 2018, p. 14.

30  Ibid.

31  Vic Marks, 'Botham, Richards and Garner's dramatic Somerset exit: The inside story', *The Observer*, 23 June 2019, Sport.

32  Richard H. Thomas, 'State of the Nation', *Wisden Cricket Monthly* (April 2019), p. 47.

33  Ibid.

34  Bagchi, 'Martin Guptill's unbeaten 189 edged by Viv Richards's 1984 brilliance'.

35  Steve James, *The Art of Centuries* (London, 2015), p. 236.

36  Les Scott, *Bats, Balls and Bails: The Essential Cricket Book* (London, 2011).
37  Ibid.
38  Scyld Berry, 'Misbah-ul-Haq equals record for fastest ever Test century as Pakistan head for rout of Australia', www.telegraph.co.uk, 2 November 2014.
39  Robin Marlar, 'Stumped', *Sunday Times*, 4 July 1993, Features.
40  Tim Rich, 'The shot that made India cricket kings', www.independent. co.uk, 22 June 2013.
41  Kamran Abbasi, 'Kapil gets Viv', www.espncricinfo.com, 19 February 2019.
42  Ibid.
43  David Lemmon, ed., *Wisden Book of Cricket Quotations* (London, 1990), p. 233.
44  Martin Johnson, 'Cricket First Test: Gooch treats himself to a second helping; Batting records keep on tumbling while India avert the follow-on with a spectacular assault by Kapil Dev, *The Independent*, 31 July 1990, p. 30.
45  '200 not out: As Lord's celebrates its bicentenary, our writers select their personal memories', www.telegraph.co.uk, 4 July 2014.
46  Rich, 'The shot that made India cricket kings'.
47  Ibid.
48  Ibid.
49  Glenn Moore, 'Cricket: One of the boys yet a man apart; Allan Border, Australian cricket captain, is one of the game's all-time greats', *The Independent*, 15 August 1993, p. 22.
50  Matthew Engel, 'Cricket: The Border line from amiability to rock hardness', *The Guardian*, 19 August 1993, p. 12.
51  Brian Scovell, 'Cricket Legend Quits: Captain Grumpy goes with heavy heart and parting shot', *Daily Mail*, 12 May 1994, p. 76.
52  Ibid.
53  Engel, 'Cricket: The border line from amiability to rock hardness'.
54  Lemmon, ed., *Wisden Book of Cricket Quotations*, p. 168.
55  Engel, 'Cricket: The border line from amiability to rock hardness'.
56  Derek Pringle, 'The Ashes 2005: Border created Australian Dynasty', *Daily Telegraph*, 19 July 2005, p. 4.
57  Martin Johnson, 'Cricket/World Cup 1992: Pakistan's panache pulls Australia's world apart', *The Independent*, 12 March 1992, p. 38.
58  Jonathan Agnew, with Nick Constable, *Aggers' Special Delivery* (London, 2005), p. 72.
59  Alan Lee, 'Pakistan crowned champions', *The Times*, 26 March 1992, Sport.
60  Mike Selvey, 'Cricket: English Journeymen travel a match too far', *The Guardian*, 26 March 1992, p. 19.
61  Ibid.
62  'Cricket / World Cup Final 1992: Explosion of joy on the streets', *The Independent*, 26 March 1992, p. 40.
63  Ian Wooldridge, 'Imran, prince of the crease', *Daily Mail*, 12 March 1992, p. 54.

64 'Profile: Finally, the importance of being Imran', *The Independent*, 28 March 1992, p. 16; Scyld Berry, 'Cricket: A man with a mission', *The Independent*, 29 March 1992, p. 32.

65 Berry, 'Cricket'.

66 Alan Lee, 'Imran rises above the modern mire; Pakistan captain's newly published autobiography', *The Times*, 4 July 1988.

67 Homa Khaleeli, 'Imran Khan on the Panama Papers: "The coalition of the corrupt help each other"', www.theguardian.com, 19 April 2016.

68 Ibid.

69 Steve Coll, 'Can Imran Khan Really Reform Pakistan?', *New Yorker*, 27 July 2018.

## 25 REVOLUTIONS AND REBELS
### *The 1970s to the New Millennium*

1 Peter Klinger, 'Philippe-Henri Edmonds', *The Times*, 28 April 2005, p. 51.

2 David Hopps, *Great Cricket Quotes* (London, 2006), p. 35.

3 Ben Macintyre, 'The business big-game hunter out to spin his way to an African empire', *The Times*, 14 July 2007, p. 32.

4 Spiro Zavos, 'Why Phil Edmonds is so contrary; Sports Books Review', *Sydney Morning Herald*, 29 October 1986, p. 53.

5 Simon Barnes, 'Time opens all wounds, leaving Pietersen marooned on island of egotism', *Weekend Australian*, 10 January 2009, p. 42.

6 Celebrity Net Worth, 'Phil Edmonds Net Worth', www.celebritynetworth.com, 2018.

7 Andrew Alderson and Russell Hotten, 'Business and morality: Is Edmonds right to trade with Mugabe?', *Sunday Telegraph*, 15 June 2008, p. 5.

8 Ibid.

9 Peter Roebuck, 'Edmonds has high old time in comeback', *Sunday Times*, 7 June 1992, Sport.

10 Robert Winder, *The Little Wonder* (London, 2014), p. 283.

11 Andrew Malone, 'George Davis is not innocent', *Daily Mail*, 7 February 2009.

12 Colin Dean, 'On this day: 18.08.1975: Protesters dig up the Headingley pitch: "We used knives and forks from a service station", *The Guardian*, 18 August 2007, p. 2.

13 Ibid.

14 'Back when money was worth something', http://news.bbc.co.uk, 13 February 2001.

15 'Bradman accused by Chappell over Packer's rebel series', *The Times*, 28 November 2002, Sport 52.

16 Ibid.

17 Ibid.

18 Simon Davis, 'Gambler Packer loses £13m in 3 days', www.telegraph.co.uk, 31 August 2000.

19 Zoe Brennan, 'How does it feel to lose £2million in a night's gambling? After a casino sues a billionaire for not paying a vast debt, the secret

and decadent world of the really high-rollers', *Daily Mail*, 3 March 2007, p. 58.

20 Tim Lane, 'Slow, hostile beginnings to TV bonanza', *Sunday Age*, 23 August 2015, p. 10.

21 'Kerry has last (f) word', *Australian Financial Review*, 26 November 2012, p. 44.

22 Mike Hedge, 'Big fella; has left the building', *Northern Territory News*, 31 December 2005, p. 16.

23 Ibid.

24 Peter FitzSimons, 'The fitz files', *Sydney Morning Herald* (Australia), 17 June 2000, p. 80.

25 Martin Williamson, 'A dummy's guide to World Series Cricket', www.espncricinfo.com, 4 December 2007.

26 Ian Chappell, 'Tony's passion for cricket always came through', www.espncricinfo.com, 29 December 2012.

27 Andy Bull, 'Tall tales and a big vision: Kerry Packer's World Series Cricket 40 years on', www.theguardian.com, 2 May 2017.

28 'First blooming was Hookes' finest moment', www.telegraph.co.uk, 20 January 2004.

29 Gideon Haigh, 'The night when cricket left the dark ages', *The Australian*, 26 November 2015, p. 15.

30 Martin Williamson, 'World Series Cricket', www.espncricinfo.com, 21 November 2007.

31 'Obituary: Kerry Packer: Australian media tycoon who built on his family fortune and made his mark on world cricket', *The Guardian Weekly*, 6 January 2006.

32 Winder, *The Little Wonder*, p. 277.

33 Christopher Zinn, 'Kerry Packer', www.theguardian.com, 28 December 2005; 'Lillee goes in to bat for Packer but some argue his methods were just not cricket', www.smh.com.au, 28 December 2005.

34 Christopher Martin-Jenkins, 'Ruthless visionary who understood game's true value', *The Times*, 28 December 2005, p. 62.

35 Robert Winder, *The Little Wonder* (London, 2014), p. 279.

36 Sambeet Dash, 'The story behind the South African rebel tour', www.theroar.com.au, 14 February 2016.

37 Greg Struthers, 'English rebel cricket tour of South Africa, 1982', *Sunday Times*, 26 December 2004, p. 20.

38 R. W. Apple Jr, 'British Cricketers defy ban to play in South Africa', *New York Times*, 3 March 1982, p. 3.

39 Graham Gooch, 'Why I was wrong to tour South Africa', *Mail on Sunday*, 10 July 1994, p. 83.

40 Ibid.

41 Ivo Tennant, 'Gatting expects testing spell in office', *The Times*, 30 September 2013, p. 51.

42 'Mike Gatting feels force of Malcolm Marshall: "There was a bit of bone stuck in the ball"', *The Guardian*, 17 February 2007, p. 2.

43  Matthew Pryor, 'Gatting's bad timing ushers in era of Australian dominance', *The Times*, 21 July 2005, p. 82.

44  Simon Briggs, 'Jabbing finger is still a sore point, 30 years on; Final whistle; Mike Gatting's angry reaction to the slur on him by Pakistani umpire Shakoor Rana had a lasting legacy', *Daily Telegraph*, 9 December 2017, p. 24.

45  Ibid.

46  Alan Lee, 'Thursday Spectrum: The reign that stopped play – Profile of Mike Gatting', *The Times*, 10 December 1987.

47  Mike Brearley, 'Siding with hypocrites; Mike Gatting and the barmaid scandal', *Sunday Times*, 12 June 1988.

48  Jerome Starkey, 'Botham fired up over BBC "ambush"; Former cricketer threatens to boycott corporation after radio interview turns sour', *The Times*, 3 August 2017, p. 3.

49  Martin Johnson, 'Cricket: Gatting batting on good wicket', *The Independent*, 27 May 1992, p. 30.

50  Richard Edmondson, 'Monday Cricket: Confessions of an unrepentant patriot', *The Independent*, 24 March 1997, p. s1.

51  Camilla Redmond, 'Radio: A month in Ambridge', *The Guardian*, 21 September 2007, p. 31.

52  Luke Alfred, 'When Sri Lanka went to cuckoo land', www.espncricinfo.com, 2 February 2017.

53  Ibid.

54  David Hopps, 'Cricket: S. Africa head for W Indies', *The Guardian*, 3 March 1992, p. 1.

55  Daniel Schofield, '"If being a mercenary is fighting for someone's cause, then I was": Rebel West Indian tours helped to end apartheid', *The Times*, 21 March 2013, p. 74.

56  Siddhartha Vaidyanathan, 'The unforgiven', www.espncricinfo.com, 20 March 2007.

57  Ibid.

58  Abhishek Mukherjee, 'Herbert Chang: The Jamaican of Chinese origin who wasted his life in South Africa', www.cricketcountry.com, 2 July 2016.

59  Abhishek Mukherjee, 'David Murray: Promising career reduced to wreck by drugs and South Africa tour', www.cricketcountry.com, 28 May 2016.

60  Mike Atherton, 'Hard times for a West Indies outcast', *The Times*, 5 February 2009, p. 79.

## 26 ONE MAN'S SALVATION
### *1981*

1  Bill Frindall, *England Test Cricketers* (London, 1989), p. 47.

2  Tom Fordyce, 'Kevin Pietersen: An idiosyncratic genius who could be both divisive and dazzling', www.bbc.co.uk, 18 March 2018.

3  Steven Pye, 'Ashes 1981: How Captain Beefy became Butterfingers Botham at Trent Bridge', www.theguardian.com, 9 July 2013.

4 Paul Connolly, 'The Joy of Six: Australia v New Zealand', www. theguardian.com, 2 December 2013; Clayton Murzello, 'Marshy blow adds to Oz woes', www.mid-day.com, 25 October 2018.

5 Martin Williamson, 'Underhand, underarm', www.espncricinfo.com, 29 January 2011.

6 ESPNcricinfo staff, 'Sam Loxton dies aged 90', www.espncricinfo.com, 3 December 2011; Connolly, 'The Joy of Six: Australia v New Zealand'.

7 Wisden Cricinfo staff, 'Grubber was a "cry for help"', www.espncricinfo. com, 16 November 2004.

8 Steve McDowell, 'My Golden Summer: 1981', www.wisden.com, 9 March 2017.

9 Michael Henderson, 'Centre stage: It was 20 years ago that a young man played the innings of his life to help England turn a Test on its head and beat Australia', *Daily Telegraph*, 14 August 2001.

10 Siddhartha Vaidyanathan, 'You need to work by intelligent hunches', www.espncricinfo.com, 11 August 2007; Lawrence Booth, 'Inside the mind of the thinking man's captain: Ben Stokes to open, why Jos Buttler can be better than Ian Botham, what Joe Root did wrong – nearly 40 years on, you can't stop Mike Brearley's original ideas about cricket', www.dailymail.co.uk, 6 October 2018.

11 Steve James, *The Art of Centuries* (London, 2015), p. 97; John Stern, 'Ian Botham, Headingley, July 20, 1981; The burden of English Cricket captaincy hindered Ian Botham in the first two Tests of the 1981 Ashes, but his performance in the third would firmly cement his icon status', www.telegraph.co.uk, 12 July 2012.

12 Steven Lynch, ed., *Wisden on the Ashes* (London, 2015), p. 432.

13 Matthew Engel, 'Bob Willis obituary', www.theguardian.com, 4 December 2019.

14 Dean Wilson, 'Ian's Ashes; The match that changed my life . . . Headingley 1981. Thirty years on by Sir Ian Botham', *The Mirror*, 14 July 2011, pp. 16, 17.

15 Lynch, ed., *Wisden on the Ashes*, pp. 430, 431.

16 'Time to capture the big moment; Cricket: The Ashes; Exclusive Bob Willis', *The Express*, 9 July 2013, p. 58.

17 Lynch, ed., *Wisden on the Ashes*, p. 436.

18 Mike Brearley, '"Ian Botham's Ashes": The myths, the legends and me', www.theguardian.com, 2 July 2011.

19 Mike Brearley, 'Lucky captain? I was fortunate to be picked by England at all; From a rival's injury to Botham's brutality, Mike Brearley admits good luck helped him become a great leader', *The Times*, 6 July 2013, p. 7.

20 Lynch, ed., *Wisden on the Ashes*, p. 437.

21 Oliver Holt, 'England cricket legend Sir Ian Botham calls time on the epic charity walks that have raised over £30m for charity', www.dailymail. co.uk, 2 December 2017.

22 Michael Horsnell, 'Former hippy draws stumps on his cricketing idyll', *The Times*, 8 November 2004, p. 9.

23 Nick Greenslade, 'Bang goes Beefy', *The Observer*, 30 September 2007.

24  'Botham, Hollywood and James Bond', www.espncricinfo.com,
    26 January 2013.
25  'Ian Botham at 60 – controversies, best quotes, career highs and 9
    things you didn't know about England star', www.telegraph.co.uk,
    24 November 2015.
26  Kevin Michell, 'Botham v Chappell: time for a drink', www.
    espncricinfo.com, December 2007.
27  'Chappelli slams Botham's honour', *The Australian*, 24 October 2007, p. 23.
28  Martin Johnson, 'Grudges thrive in bad-blood sport; Anderson-Jadeja
    tiff is just latest in a long line of bitter cricketing feuds', *Sunday Times*,
    20 July 2014, p. 8; Martin Williamson, 'The thirty-year feud', www.
    espncricinfo.com, 11 December 2010.
29  Alan Tyers, 'Tales of England vs Australia mischief and misconduct',
    www.nzherald.co.nz, 12 December 2017.
30  Matthew Norman, 'This feud has more fire than the Ashes; The
    Botham-Chappell animosity shows the true essence of sport', *Daily
    Telegraph*, 11 December 2010, p. 27.
31  Jonathan Liew, 'Sir Ian Botham ready to thrive in time of great
    uncertainty and hit the EU for six', www.telegraph.co.uk, 1 June 2016.
32  Ibid.
33  Arunabha Sengupta, 'Terry Alderman: Enduring Ashes hero', www.
    cricketcountry.com, 12 June 2013.
34  David Frith, 'The Alderman incident', www.espncricinfo.com, January 1983.
35  Ibid.
36  Hopps, *Great Cricket Quotes*, p. 149.

## 27 WOMEN'S CRICKET
### *A Century of Inequality*

1   Robert Winder, *The Little Wonder* (London, 2014), p. 313.
2   David Hopps, 'Wisden accolade heralds a new era in the women's
    game', www.theguardian.com, 3 April 2009.
3   Ibid.
4   Scyld Berry, 'Cricket survives Claire Taylor shock', www.telegraph.co.uk,
    7 May 2009.
5   Isabelle Westbury, 'Female recognition in sport is a work in progress, but
    momentum is shifting – as Wisden has shown', www.independent.co.uk,
    11 April 2018.
6   'Recycling good ideas from our engineering past', *Western Daily Press*,
    17 June 2014, pp. 18–19.
7   Robert Low, *W. G. Grace: An Intimate Biography* (London, 2010).
8   Tessa McLaren, 'Women in Cricket', www.espncricinfo.com, 1992.
9   Max Davidson, *We'll Get 'Em in Sequins: Manliness, Yorkshire Cricket and
    the Century that Changed Everything* (London, 2012), p. 68.
10  Ibid.
11  Harry Pearson, 'Watch out for mums on the warpath', www.
    theguardian.com, 31 July 2009.

12  Wisden, 'Betty Snowball', www.espncricinfo.com, n.d., accessed
    9 October 2019.
13  Abhishek Mukherjee, 'Betty Snowball: one of the earliest female cricket
    superstars', www.cricketcountry.com, 18 September 2015.
14  Simon Briggs, 'The oldest Test player cruises on past her century; Final
    whistle celebrity has come late to Eileen Ash but, at 106, she is relishing
    the spotlight', *Daily Telegraph*, 4 November 2017, p. 24.
15  Will Humphries, 'Driver, 105, takes test after eight decades on the road',
    *The Times*, 21 September 2017, p. 15.
16  Ibid.
17  Briggs, 'The oldest Test player cruises on past her century'.
18  Rachael Heyhoe Flint, 'Obituary: Molly Hide; A flashing blade in far
    pavilions', *The Guardian*, 14 September 1995, p. 15.
19  David Frith, 'Obituary: Molly Hide', *The Independent*, 13 September
    1995, p. 14.
20  'Molly Hide', *The Times*, 14 September 1995, Features.
21  Frith, 'Obituary: Molly Hide'.
22  Adam Cooper, 'Legend Wilson dies', *Sunday Mail*, 24 January 2010, p.
    47.
23  'Betty Wilson; Obituaries: Australian cricketer hailed as the female
    Bradman who hit a century and took 10 wickets in the same Test', *Daily
    Telegraph*, 26 January 2010, p. 29.
24  Cooper, 'Legend Wilson dies'.
25  Greg Baum, 'Wilson's sporting legacy', *The Age*, 30 January 2010, p. 10.
26  Ibid.
27  'Betty Wilson; Australian cricketer dubbed "the female Bradman" who
    was equally effective with the bat and the ball', *The Times*, 15 February
    2010, p. 55.
28  Ibid.
29  Andrew Longmore, 'Saturday Ultimate accolade is icing on the cake
    for Bakewell; A record-breaking trailblazer for women's cricket is
    rewarded for deeds', www.thetimes.co.uk, 7 November 2015.
30  Ibid.; Richard Edwards, 'I sold potatoes to raise enough money for the
    plane fare to tour Australia'; CRICKET Women's cricket pioneer Enid
    Bakewell talks to Richard Edwards about how times have changed',
    *i-Independent*, 29 June 2017, p. 48.
31  Cathy Harris, 'Bakewell returns to England sphere; Enid Bakewell;
    Cricket', *The Times*, 11 July 1988.
32  'Newstead cricket legend Enid Bakewell inducted into Hall of Fame',
    *Hucknall Dispatch*, 21 February 2013.
33  Martin Williamson, 'Rachael Heyhoe Flint', www.espncricinfo.com,
    n.d., accessed 10 October 2019.
34  Wisden, 'Rachael Heyhoe Flint', www.espncricinfo.com, 2018.
35  Not a sexist comment – the word 'batsman' is used to refer to both men
    and women.
36  Clare Connor, 'Heyhoe Flint the tireless worker for equality', *Daily
    Telegraph*, 3 April 2017, p. 22.

37  Eleanor Oldroyd, 'I was Rachaelised – and proud of it; The late, great women's sport pioneer Rachael Heyhoe Flint was a master of persuasion', www.thetimes.co.uk, 22 January 2017.

38  Scyld Berry, 'Heyhoe Flint the WG of women's cricket; Sport Cricket Game mourns death of trailblazer at age of 77 England captain created first World Cup in 1973', *Daily Telegraph*, 19 January 2017, pp. 12, 13.

39  'Rachael Heyhoe Flint dies: Robert Plant and Steve Bull lead tributes to a Wolverhampton sporting legend', www.expressandstar.com, 18 January 2017.

40  'Sport: Cricket: MCC to vote on women members', http://news.bbc.co.uk, 25 August 1998; Ian Burrell, 'MCC in new vote to admit women', *The Independent*, 5 August 1998, p. 8.

41  Emily Dugan, 'Women cricketers fail to break through old boys' defensive block', *The Independent*, 28 September 2008.

42  Gabrielle Monaghan, 'Gender off the agenda; Women are popping up everywhere in male-dominated professions, and there are still plenty of other "macho" jobs they can break into', *Sunday Times*, 25 March 2012, pp. 4, 5.

43  Abhishek Mukherjee, 'Rachael Heyhoe Flint: The woman who was cricket', www.cricketcountry.com, 18 January 2017.

44  Geoffrey Copinger, 'Cricket Viewpoint: History men stay on guard', *The Independent*, 3 May 1991, p. 32.

45  Ibid.

46  Ibid.

47  Andy Bull, 'Rachael Heyhoe Flint: The reluctant feminist who could talk Lord's language', www.theguardian.com, 25 January 2017.

48  Tim de Lisle, 'A membership inclined to stuffiness at the best of times is further stuffed by its own waiting list', www.independent.co.uk, 28 June 1995.

49  Martin Smith, ed., *Not in My Day, Sir: Letters to the Daily Telegraph* (London, 2011), p. 197.

50  Vivek Chaudhary, 'MCC votes to lift ban on women members; MCC's record 211-year stand against women broken at last', *The Guardian*, 29 September 1998, p. 1.

51  Anna Kessel, 'Rachael Heyhoe Flint: "It's amazing . . . women are almost on parity with men"', www.theguardian.com, 10 May 2014.

52  Emily Dugan, 'Still knocking them for six; The former cricket star, now a member of the House of Lords, is right behind the *IoS* campaign to build recognition for women's sport', *The Independent*, 11 August 2013, p. 18.

53  Berry, 'Heyhoe Flint the WG of women's cricket'.

54  Connor, 'Heyhoe Flint the tireless worker for equality'.

55  Izzy Westbury, 'The sisterhood of the England captains', www.espncricinfo.com, 24 August 2014.

56  Scyld Berry, 'Mark Robinson: Why "outstanding" Charlotte Edwards had to go as England captain', www.telegraph.co.uk, 3 June 2016.

57  Will Gore, 'Edwards' retirement is desperately unsatisfactory', *The Independent*, 13 May 2016, p. 71.
58  Berry, 'Mark Robinson: Why "outstanding" Charlotte Edwards had to go as England captain'.
59  Nick Hoult, 'Edwards left in tears as England cut short international career; Captain wanted to carry on her 20-year stint Robinson seeking more "hard-nosed" approach', *Daily Telegraph*, 12 May 2016, pp. 14, 15.
60  Isabelle Westbury, '"My generation don't need to do a normal job" – How professional cricket has changed the landscape for England Women's team', www.telegraph.co.uk, 1 July 2019.
61  'Women's Cricket World Cup Watched By Record TV Audience', www.sportsbusinessdaily.com, 26 July 2017.
62  Geoff Lemon, 'Women's World Cup: Harmanpreet Kaur destroys Australia en route to securing India a final spot', www.abc.net.au, 21 July 2017.
63  Abhishek Mukherjee, 'The day Harmanpreet Kaur descended upon Derby', www.cricketcountry.com, 20 July 2018.
64  Lemon, 'Women's World Cup'.
65  Scyld Berry, 'England must curb Kaur to rule world and spark revolution; Sport Women's World Cup final; Final can lead to major growth in women's game Indian hit seven sixes in epic semi-final century', *Daily Telegraph*, 22 July 2017, pp. 10, 11.
66  Lemon, 'Women's World Cup'; Callum Davis, 'Introducing Harmanpreet Kaur: India's new cricket superstar', 21 July 2017.
67  '2017 in review: Harmanpreet slays Australia', www.wisden.com, 2 January 2018.
68  'ICC Rankings', www.icc-cricket.com, 23 December 2019.
69  Tim Wigmore, 'Why the world's best female player just wants to get better and better; Australia's Ellyse Perry tells Tim Wigmore that there are no limits for her or women's sport', *Daily Telegraph*, 18 July 2019, p. 9.
70  Christopher Devine, 'Ellyse Perry "the greatest female player we're ever going to see", says Charlotte Edwards', www.sportingnews.com, 1 August 2019.
71  Konrad Marshall, 'Ellyse Perry: "Hopefully we're almost at a point where women's sport is, just, sport"', www.smh.com.au, 6 July 2019.
72  Peter Lalor, 'Is Perry the world's greatest all-rounder?', *The Australian*, 9 July 2019, p. 31.
73  ESPNcricinfostaff, 'Adam Gilchrist: Sarah Taylor is the best wicketkeeper in the world', www.espncricinfo.com, 22 June 2018.
74  Westbury, 'Female recognition in sport is a work in progress'.
75  Ibid.
76  Rob Steen, 'Why I am enamoured of: Women's cricket', *The Guardian*, 21 August 1999, Sport, p. 14.

## 28 CRICKET WILL NEVER DIE
### *A New Millennium*

1 ESPN staff, 'Lillee casts light on "infamous betting scandal"', www.espncricinfo.com, 1 December 1998.
2 Ashley Mallett, 'A bat, a ball and a bet – cricket's dirty little secret', *The Advertiser*, 16 December 2017, p. 83.
3 Richard Edwards, 'Darkest day as Cronje went to hell for leather; Sixteen years ago South Africa's cautious captain sold his soul at Centurion and launched the great match-fixing scandal by giving England a chance', *The Independent*, 22 January 2016, p. 66; Michael Atherton, 'Tough battles with a passionate captain Cronje's mistake may have been to think of himself as invincible', *Sunday Telegraph*, 2 June 2002, p. 9.
4 Atherton, 'Tough battles'.
5 Ibid.
6 Edwards, 'Darkest day as Cronje went to hell for leather'.
7 Wisden, 'Hansie Cronje', www.espncricinfo.com, 2003.
8 Daniel Murt, 'Was Hansie Cronje murdered?', www.theguardian.com, 3 August 2003.
9 Asian News International, 'Kepler suspected Cronje of fixing matches long before getting caught in 2000', www.business-standard.com, 23 February 2017.
10 Bill Bradshaw, 'Exclusive: Cronje signs up with Max Clifford', *The Observer*, 2 July 2000, p. 13.
11 Lucy Carne, 'Hansie Cronje, Bob Woolmer murdered by mafia betting syndicates: Clive Rice', www.foxsports.com.au, 7 September 2010.
12 Atherton, 'Tough battles with a passionate captain'.
13 Ian Chadband, 'The Ashes 2005: remembering the greatest series', www.telegraph.co.uk, 4 July 2009.
14 Matthew Hoggard, 'I walked out to an eerie silence as if the crowd dared not draw breath', *The Independent*, 1 August 2009, p. 8.
15 Martin Samuel, 'Murray can be a messiah – if he keeps his eye on the ball', www.dailymail.co.uk, 1 July 2009.
16 Richard Thomas, 'England win Men's Cricket World Cup in a last-ball thriller – now will the country see more matches on free TV?', https://theconversation.com, 14 July 2019.
17 Peter Orchard, 'ECB and Sky Sports deserve credit, but . . .', *Gloucestershire Echo*, 18 August 2014, p. 7.
18 Jonathan Liew, 'Australia shatters the pay-TV myth; British fears that sports will suffer dire consequences if denied best broadcast deals proven false Down Under', *Daily Telegraph*, 21 January 2015, p. 20.
19 Orchard, 'ECB and Sky Sports deserve credit, but . . .',
20 Thomas, 'England win Men's Cricket World Cup in a last-ball thriller'.
21 'IPL: ODI and Test Cricket stand to lose', *Kashmir Times* (India), 3 April 2015; Amrit Mathur, 'IPL is cricket's holi: loud, splashy and colourful affair', *Hindustan Times*, 20 March 2019, online at: www.pressreader.com.

22 'IPL: ODI and Test Cricket stand to lose'; Vijay Lokapally, 'IPL–7: Taking Guard Afresh', www.thehindubusinessline.com, 15 April 2014.

23 'IPL: Indian cricket's Dr Jekyll and Mr Hyde', *The Pioneer* (India), 15 April 2018.

24 Ibid.

25 Lokapally, 'IPL–7: Taking Guard Afresh'.

26 Power Politics, 'Will IPL consume cricket, the gentlemen's game?', 11 July 2012.

27 'Virat Kohli remains India's most valuable celebrity, MS Dhoni on ninth position', *Economic Times*, 7 February 2020, online at: https://economictimes.indiatimes.com.

28 Richard H. Thomas, 'A terribly awkward romance', www.espncricinfo.com, 14 May 2014; Hugh McIlvanney, 'Warne was always a warrior wizard', *Sunday Times*, 10 December 2006, p. 11.

29 Greg Baum, 'Shane Warne: The cricketer of and for his times – Almanack', www.wisden.com, 13 September 2020.

30 'Cricket: Warne bows out on a low', *New Zealand Herald*, 19 May 2011, Sport.

31 Ibid.

32 'Watchdog bans ads Warnie's hair loss treatment company out for a duck', *Hobart Mercury*, 27 November 2009, p. 8.

33 Nick Parker, 'Shane's Warne us Out!; Exclusive: Ace's legover before wicket; Australia cricket legend's maidens; Noisy 2hr romp with 3 women', *The Sun*, 31 August 2019, pp. 6, 7.

34 'Ben Stokes hits fastest England century for 113 years', www.telegraph.co.uk, 24 May 2015.

35 Press Association, 'England's Ben Stokes stuns South Africa with masterful 163-ball double century', www.theguardian.com, 3 January 2016.

36 Ali Martin, 'Ben Stokes experienced his Headingley '81 moment, says Sir Ian Botham', www.theguardian.com, 8 January 2016.

37 'South Africa v England: Ben Stokes could repeat 200 – Bayliss', www.bbc.co.uk, 7 January 2016.

38 Emma Keeling, 'When will Stokes grow up?', *Nelson Mail*, 18 August 2018, p. 21.

39 Mike Selvey, 'Ben Stokes sees his world collapse after Carlos Brathwaite's T20 blast', www.theguardian.com, 3 April 2016.

40 Keeling, 'When will Stokes grow up?'.

41 Rod Minchin and Claire Hayhurst, 'Cricketer Stokes cleared of affray after street fight', *Western Mail*, 15 August 2018, p. 8.

42 Alex West, 'Spoilt Kind: Bouncer's verdict on cleared cricketer: Stokes doesn't care who he hurts', *The Sun*, 19 August 2018, pp. 18, 19.

43 Sports Staff, 'Ben Stokes video: England cricketer filmed mocking Katie Price's disabled son, Harvey', www.independent.co.uk, 28 September 2017.

44 Janet Street-Porter, 'Danny Cipriani and Ben Stokes are the man-children of UK sport – I worry for the men who will copy their behaviour', www.independent.co.uk, 17 August 2018.

45  Barney Ronay, 'Ben Stokes writes his redemption story with World Cup tour de force', www.theguardian.com, 15 July 2019.

46  Ibid.

47  Steve Busfield, 'Ben Stokes: World Cup Glory Gives Redemption For Controversial Cricketer', www.forbes.com, 14 July 2019.

48  Scyld Berry, 'I was there for Ian Botham's 149 and again for Ben Stokes's supreme 135 – both exceeded what we thought was possible', www.telegraph.co.uk, 26 August 2019.

49  'Test cricket isn't boring and Stokesy is Superman', www.espncricinfo.com, 25 August 2019.

50  Ibid.

51  'Cricket's comeback from Covid–19: the state of the game', www.espncricinfo.com, 21 May 2020.

52  Ibid.

53  A. Trevor Tolley, *The Poetry of the Forties* (Manchester, 1985), p. 147.

# SELECT BIBLIOGRAPHY

Agnew, Jonathan, with Nick Constable, *Aggers' Special Delivery* (London, 2005)

Alfred, Luke, *Testing Times: The Story of the Men who Made SA Cricket* (Claremont, South Africa, 2003)

Allen, David Rayvern, ed., *Arlott on Cricket* (London, 1985)

—, *Jim: The Life of E. W. Swanton* (London, 2004)

Arlott, Timothy, *John Arlott: A Memoir* (London, 1994)

Balfour, Sandy, *What I Love about Cricket* (London, 2010)

Batchelor, Denzil, *The Book of Cricket* (London, 1952)

—, ed., *Best Cricket Stories* (London, 1967)

—, ed., *Great Cricketers* (London, 1970)

Bateman, Anthony, *Cricket, Literature and Culture: Symbolising the Nation, Destabilising Empire* (Farnham, 2013)

—, and Jeffrey Hill, eds, *The Cambridge Companion to Cricket* (Cambridge, 2011)

Benaud, Richie, *Anything But . . . an Autobiography* (London, 1998)

Berkmann, Markus, *Rain Men* (London, 1995)

Berry, Scyld, *Cricket: The Game of Life* (London, 2015)

Bird, Dickie, *My Autobiography* (London, 1998)

Booth, Lawrence, *Cricket, Lovely Cricket?: An Addict's Guide to the World's Most Exasperating Game* (London, 2009)

—, ed., *Wisden Cricketers' Almanack* (London, 2015)

Bose, Mihir, *Keith Miller* (Newton Abbot, 1980)

Brookes, Christopher, *His Own Man: The Life of Neville Cardus* (London, 1985)

Brown, Lionel, *Victor Trumper and the 1902 Australians* (London, 1981)

Carby, Hazel, *Race Men* (Cambridge, MA, 2009)

Cardus, Neville, *Good Days* (London, 1937)

Chalke, Stephen, *Summer's Crown: The Story of Cricket's County Championship* (Bath, 2015)

Constantine, Learie, *Colour Bar* (London, 1954)

Cozier, Tony, *The West Indies: Fifty Years of Test Cricket* (Newton Abbot, 1978)

Davidson, Max, *We'll Get 'Em in Sequins: Manliness, Yorkshire Cricket and the Century that Changed Everything* (London, 2012)

Edwards, Alan, *Lionel Tennyson: Regency Buck* (London, 2001)

Evans, Roger, *Cricket Grounds: The Evolution, Maintenance and Construction of National Turf Tables and Outfields* (Bingley, 1991)

Fay, Stephen, and David Kynaston, *Arlott, Swanton and the Soul of English Cricket* (London, 2018)

Foot, David, *Wally Hammond: The Reasons Why* (London, 1998)

Fraser, David, *Cricket and the Law: The Man in White is Always Right* (New York, 2005)

Frindall, Bill, *England Test Cricketers* (London, 1989)

Frith, David, *Bodyline Autopsy* (London, 2003)

—, *England v Australia: The Pictorial History of Test Matches since 1877* (London, 1984)

—, *Silence of the Heart: Cricket Suicides* (Edinburgh, 2001)

Fry, C. B., *Life Worth Living* (London, 1986)

Green, Benny, *The Lord's Companion* (London, 1987)

Green, Stephen, *Lord's: The Cathedral of Cricket* (Stroud, 2003)

Haigh, Gideon, *The Big Ship: Warwick Armstrong and the Making of Modern Cricket* (Sydney, 2012)

—, *Game for Anything: Writings on Cricket* (Melbourne, 2004)

—, *Stroke of Genius: Victor Trumper and the Shot that Changed Cricket* (London, 2016)

Harman, Jo, *Cricketing Allsorts: The Good, the Bad, the Ugly (and the Downright Weird)* (London, 2017)

Hayter, Peter, ed., *Cricket Heroes* (London, 1990)

Hignell, Andrew, *Cricket in Wales: An Illustrated History* (Cardiff, 2008)

Hill, Alan, *Brian Close: Cricket's Lionheart* (London, 2002)

—, *Jim Laker: A Biography* (London, 2002)

Hopps, David, *Great Cricket Quotes* (London, 2006)

Hotten, Jon, *The Meaning of Cricket* (London, 2016)

Howat, Gerald, *Cricket's Second Golden Age* (London, 1989)

Hughes, Simon, *And God Created Cricket* (London, 2010)

—, *Cricket's Greatest Rivalry: Completely Revised and Updated for 2019* (London, 2019)

James, C.L.R., *Beyond a Boundary* (London, 1963)

James, Steve, *The Art of Centuries* (London, 2013)

Knox, Malcolm, *Bradman's War: How the 1948 Invincibles Turned the Cricket Pitch into a Battlefield* (Melbourne, 2015)

Laker, Jim, *Over to Me* (London, 1960)

Lazenby, John, *Edging Towards Darkness: The Story of the Last Timeless Test* (London, 2017)

Lemmon, David, ed., *Wisden Book of Cricket Quotations* (London, 1990)

Levison, Brian, ed., *All In a Day's Cricket* (London, 2012)

Low, Robert, *W. G. Grace: An Intimate Biography* (London, 2010)

Lynch, Steven, ed., *Wisden on the Ashes* (London, 2015)

McCrery, Nigel, *Final Wicket: Test and First Class Cricketers Killed in the Great War* (Barnsley, 2015)

McKinstry, Leo, *Geoff Boycott: A Cricketing Hero* (Glasgow, 2005)

Mailey, Arthur, *10 for 66 and All That* (Crows Nest, NSW, 1958)

Malies, Jeremy, *Great Characters from Cricket's Golden Age* (London, 2000)

Manley, Michael, *History of West Indies Cricket* (Bury St Edmunds, 1988)

Marshall, Michael, *Gentlemen and Players* (London, 1987)

Midwinter, Eric, *The Illustrated History of County Cricket* (London, 1992)

Mortimer, Gavin, *A History of Cricket in 100 Objects* (London, 2013)

Parkinson, Michael, *Parky – My Autobiography: A Full and Funny Life* (London, 2009)

Peebles, Ian, *Spinner's Yarn* (Newton Abbot, 1978)

Perry, Roland, *Keith Miller: The Life of a Great All-rounder* (London, 2007)

Plumptre, George, *The Golden Age of Cricket* (London, 1990)

Pollard, Jack, *Australian Cricket: The Games and the Players* (North Ryde, 1988)

Protz, Roger, *The Beer Lover's Guide to Cricket* (St Albans, 2007)

Raja, Amol, *Twirlymen: The Unlikely History of Cricket's Greatest Spin Bowlers* (London, 2011)

Renshaw, Andrew, *Wisden on the Great War: The Lives of Cricket's Fallen, 1914–1918* (London, 2014)

Rice, Jonathan, and Andrew Renshaw, *The Wisden Collector's Guide* (London, 2011)

Richards, Barry, *The Barry Richards Story* (Newton Abbot, 1978)

Robertson-Glasgow, R. C., *Cricket Prints* (Norwich, 1943)

Root, Fred, *A Cricket Pro's Lot* (London, 1937)

Scott, Les, *Bats, Balls and Bails: The Essential Cricket Book* (London, 2011)

Sen, Satadru, *Migrant Races: Empire, Identity and K. S. Ranjitsinhji* (Manchester, 2004)

Smith, Martin, ed., *The Daily Telegraph Book of Sports Obituaries* (London, 2000)

—, ed., *Not in My Day, Sir: Letters to the Daily Telegraph* (London, 2011)

Steen, Rob, *Floodlights and Touchlines: A History of Spectator Sport* (London, 2016)

Stern, John, ed., *My Favourite Cricketer* (London, 2010)

—, and Marcus Williams, eds, *The Essential Wisden: An Anthology of 150 Years of Wisden Cricketers' Almanack* (London, 2013)

Swanton, E. W., *Cricketers of My Time: Heroes to Remember* (London, 2000)

—, ed., *Barclays World of Cricket* (London, 1980)

Thomson, A. A., *Hirst and Rhodes* (London, 1960)

—, *Cricketers of My Times* (London, 1967)

Trelford, Donald, *W. G. Grace* (Stroud, 1998)

Trueman, Fred, *As It Was: The Memoirs* (London, 2005)

Warner, Sir Pelham, *Lord's, 1787–1945* (London, 1946)

Wilde, Simon, *Ranji: The Strange Genius of Ranjitsinhji* (London, 2005)

Williams, Charles, *Gentlemen and Players: The Death of Amateurism in Cricket* (London 2013)

Winder, Robert, *The Little Wonder* (London, 2011)

Wright, Graeme, ed., *Wisden on Bradman* (South Yarra, 1998)

# ACKNOWLEDGEMENTS

There are many people to thank. Firstly of course, without the incredible game of cricket, there would be no book, but so large are some of the characters you have heard about, many would have emerged somewhere else, doing something different. Next, my thanks to Dave Watkins, Amy Salter and all the good folks at Reaktion Books. Dave's patience, advice and expertise were the key factors in turning it all from an idea to something real, and Amy's care and hard work has been invaluable during the production phase.

I would like to thank my wonderful wife Amanda for standing by my side in this venture, and every other venture. Thanks, too, to my daughters Grace, Amber and Georgia. They all have an ambivalent attitude to cricket, but seem to love me, which is far more important.

Finally, this book is dedicated to my beloved dad, Richard Howard Thomas (1933–2020). I was very happy that he managed to read it in draft form before he died, and that he was able give me his insightful and constructive feedback. He told me about cricket, encouraged me to love it and showed endless patience in trying to make me better at playing it. Useless as I was, he never stopped supporting me and cheering me on. In his day, he'd been a wily slow left-arm bowler, a classic batsman and a shrewd and compassionate captain. Perhaps there will have been better cricketers, but there will have been no kinder, generous or supportive fathers. Thank you, Dad. I miss our chats and you telling me that your favourite cricketer – and the best wicketkeeper anywhere – was Sarah Taylor.

# PHOTO ACKNOWLEDGEMENTS

The author and publishers wish to express their thanks to the below. Every effort has been made to contact copyright holders; should there be any we have been unable to reach or to whom inaccurate acknowledgement has been given, please contact the publishers, and a full adjustment will be made to subsequent printings.

Archives New Zealand: p. 308; *Argus* Newspaper Collection of Photographs, State Library of Victoria: pp. 187, 205; Bahnfrend: p. 341; G. W. Beldham: pp. 32, 39; Ernest Brooks: p. 37; Chris Brown: p. 350; Davis Sporting Collection: p. 164; Alex Davidson/Getty Images: p. 353; Department of Foreign Affairs and Trade: p. 343; Fairfax Corporation: p. 163; E. Hawkins & Co., Brighton: pp. 49, 51, 101; Sam Hood: pp. 83, 160; Ken Kelly/Popperfoto/Getty Images: p. 86; Haywood Magee/Picture Post/Hulton Archive/Getty Images: p. 290; Mdcollins1984: p. 254; Douglas Miller/Keystone/Hulton Archive/Getty Images: p. 217; National Library of Australia: p. 137; Press Association: pp. 282, 317; State Library of South Australia: pp. 116, 144, 169; *Sydney Mail*: p. 157; Whitlock, Birmingham: p. 70.

# INDEX

Page numbers in *italics* refer to illustrations